<u>Bitter Legacy</u>

NewsMax.com Reveals the Untold Story of the Clinton-Gore Years

Edited By Christopher Ruddy and Carl Limbacher Jr.

A NewsMax.com Book

NewsMax.com *Vortex*

Publisher: Christopher Ruddy

Designer: Marketing Solutions Unlimited

Copy Editor: Rita Samols

Chinagate

The Real Bill & Hillary Clinton

Media Bias

American Scene

PART II: NEWSMAX.COM VORTEX ABROAD: THE GROWING RISK OF WAR

Russia

China

INTRODUCTION

"Moral character is of great matter in a leader and will inevitably affect the substance of his performance. Courage, character, and performance cannot be separated."

"In these areas we have found President Clinton and his administration wanting. They have failed in their duty to the national interest. . . . [T]he devastating repercussions of his actions will be felt by Americans for generations to come."

—*Edward Timperlake and William C. Triplett II,*
The Year of the Rat

Alexis deTocqueville has been credited as saying, "America is great because it is good. When America ceases to be good it will cease to be great."

The moral tone of our country is set by its leaders, and no office is more important in setting that tone than "President of the United States." The president is the highest executive official, commander in chief of the armed forces, and leader of his political party. When someone occupying the presidency betrays the trust that has been placed in him, the entire nation suffers.

That was made vividly clear by Bill Clinton after the Monica Lewinsky scandal was made public. Major newspapers across the country called for the president's resignation, arguing that if the president can lie under oath, admit to lying under oath, and suffer no punishment, why should any law be obeyed?

Despite the press spin that the Lewinsky matter was simply "about sex," it was a serious matter. Still, in the growing laundry list of Clinton scandals and abuses of power, the Lewinksy sex scandal may rank as one of the least important.

Yes, the president's character does matter. During the past two years, both editors of *Bitter Legacy* appeared on numerous television and radio programs. Numerous supporters of the president said that people like us were making a mountain out of a mole hill. We were told: "The Europeans are laughing at us. Even Mitterand had a mistress."

One could simply reply that this was about more than sex and an affair with a mistress; it was about sexual harassment, obstruction of justice in the Paula Jones civil law suit, placing of the unqualified Monica Lewinsky into high-level federal jobs to keep her silent — and, of course, the president's own perjury in the case.

But our reply to the "Europeans are laughing at us" argument was even more potent. America is *not* Europe. We are better than Europe. We have always held our leaders to higher standards. Consider that America is the longest, most stable constitutional democracy. No other country beats our record. Consider that France has had 13 forms of government during the same period, wracked by revolutions, war, famines, occupations and the like. During the rise of the American nation, Europe has seen major wars almost every 50 years.

The American president reflects the values of the American people and serves as a beacon to people around the world who wish to be free. Bill Clinton has diminished the standing of America and our president as has no other president in history. As respect for the office of president declines, fewer people will look to the president for leadership.

As badly as Bill Clinton's character, or should we say lack of character, has hurt the image of the United States, it is just one side of the bad coin we have been served during the past eight years.

In truth, Clinton's corruption and betrayals are not merely a matter of "bad character." His low character has affected his decision making and his choices for who helps him run our government.

It is no surprise that Bill Clinton is the same man who proposed that government take total control of our medical care

. . . allowed 86 innocent men, women and children to be incinerated at Waco

. . . turned the Lincoln bedroom of the White House into a bed and breakfast, available to the highest bidder

. . . had his chief of White House security seize over 1,000 private FBI files

. . . took illegal campaign contributions from agents of Communist China

. . . sponsored "know your customer" bank regulations encouraging banks to spy upon every American

. . . unleashed the FBI's Carnivore program to intercept and read our private email

. . . and supported secret trials based upon secret evidence in his "anti-terrorist" bills. This is not the record of a lusty hero, but of a corrupt politician who has betrayed American laws and ideals.

The legacy of the Clinton administration is a seemingly endless list of scandals, corruption and betrayals. This book examines many of them, including:

• How Clinton sexual adventures and drug use led to a massive abuse of power as he tried to cover up his sordid past (Chapter 1)

• The very serious allegations made by Juanita Broaddrick that Clinton raped her, and details of other women claiming they were sexually abused (Chapter 2)

• Chinagate, or how Clinton traded America's defense secrets to China and other avowed enemies of our country — in exchange for campaign cash, then covered it up (Chapter 3)

• The real story about Hillary Clinton, such as assaults on the press by her bodyguards (Chapter 4)

• The mysterious deaths of many of those closest to Clinton, including his friends and agents assigned to protect him (Chapter 5)

• Al Gore's record of complicity, corruption and illegal activity (Chapter 6)

- How the major media have helped further administration corruption by apologizing for it (Chapter 7)
- The steady growth of police power under Clinton (Chapter 8)
- How Clinton's defense cuts have put our country at risk (Chapter 9)
- The shocking (and largely unreported) growth of Russian and Chinese military power during the Clinton years, including growing military cooperation between the U.S. military and our avowed enemies (Chapter 10)
- The growing threat of Chinese military power and how the Clinton administration has facilitated it (Chapter 11)

The Meaning of the Clinton Legacy

At its root, the Clinton legacy will be summed up in one word: lies.

As you read the pages of *Bitter Legacy*, you will be fascinated by the reports as they appeared in NewsMax.com Vortex over the past two years.

Juxtapose these reports with what you have learned from the major media.

No doubt you will feel you have been lied to.

You have been lied to by our president. This we know.

You will awaken to the fact that you have been lied to by the major media, which, almost at every turn, have served as public relations front men for the Clinton-Gore White House.

These Clinton lies have had or will have a significant impact on your lives, freedom and economic well-being.

People today are somewhat ambivalent to the truth, because they are insulated by world peace and great prosperity. They have taken for granted Bill Clinton's massive abuse of power, his crimes, and even such incredible acts as his 'wag the dog' war in Yugoslavia, which was launched for one reason: to bring closure to the Lewinsky and Broaddrick scandals.

In *Bitter Legacy* we demonstrate that the great prosperity the country has witnessed was largely a function of Clinton-Gore administration lies about economic numbers like inflation and the fact that defense spending was cut in half. The "peace dividend" was shifted by Clinton-Gore into the largest social spending splurge ever witnessed by this country. The rise in social spending was bigger than the New Deal of Johnson's Great Society.

Thus America's prosperity was fueled by massive government spending. This works in the short term. But someday taxpayers will have to foot the bill, which will only mount when the next recession hits.

Even worse, because Bill Clinton castrated America's military, the country is vulnerable to great threats from terrorist nations; an unstable, nuclear-armed Russia; and an emerging China.

Bitter Legacy is not a book that will be easily accepted by most Americans. At least for now.

If Al Gore wins the presidency, this book will serve as a road map for the future. The Clinton mafia will morph and thrive in the Gore presidency. If George W. Bush wins, this book also will be important, because it will lay out the problems that need to be fixed so that America's political institutions and national security can be restored.

The editors believe that the future of America rests not in the lies of yesterday, but in the truth of today. The Great Teacher said that "the truth shall set you free." *Bitter Legacy* does not claim to hold "the truth" — but we know that the one-sided presentation of facts we have witnessed over the past eight years will surely not lead us to the truth.

Christopher Ruddy
Carl Limbacher Jr
Editors
NewsMax.com Vortex

PART I:

NewsMax.com Vortex Reports on America at Home

Teamsters Scandal May Reveal More

By Christopher Ruddy

NewsMax.com Vortex, January 2000 — One might think a trial of a major union official, caught in a fraud and embezzlement scheme that has ties to the president's chief fund-raiser, would make Page one headlines in every major newspaper in the country and be a top story on CNN, CBS, NBC, ABC — the works.

Such news did happen recently, but got little press ink. As a result, few know the story.

Here are the facts:

On the Friday before Thanksgiving, a federal jury convicted William H. Hamilton Jr. on six counts, including conspiracy, embezzlement, mail fraud, wire fraud and perjury.

Hamilton, former political director of the nation's second-largest union, the Teamsters, was found guilty of scheming to funnel $885,000 from his union to the campaign treasury of then-Teamsters boss Ron Carey.

In 1996, Carey faced a tough challenge from James Hoffa. He squeaked through to win, but federal union monitors later discovered fraud was involved.

To help fill Carey's coffers, Hamilton and friends engineered a scheme whereby the Teamsters donated nearly $1 million to liberal groups. The groups turned around and gave $200,000 to Carey's campaign chest.

After a three-week trial, the jury took two days to find Hamilton guilty.

The prosecution, led by U.S. Attorney Mary Jo White, demonstrated Hamilton was part of an elaborate scheme that involved several individuals. White's office has indicated more prosecutions may emanate from the case.

Those prosecutions could turn out to be detrimental to the Clinton White House — and to Vice President Al Gore's presidential ambitions.

Carey's Teamsters were big boosters of Bill Clinton's re-election campaign.

The union endorsed Clinton and gave almost $250,000 to the Democrats.

The key figure in Bill Clinton's 1996 fund-raising operation was Terence McAuliffe. A close friend of the Clintons, McAuliffe was even ready to pledge $1.3 million to co-sign the Clintons' mortgage on their new suburban New York home.

McAuliffe is now one of Gore's top fund-raisers.

During the Hamilton trial, Richard Sullivan, former finance director of the Democratic National Committee, testified that McAuliffe had called him frequently requesting that he locate a wealthy Democrat to donate to Carey's campaign.

Sullivan said he was told the Democrat's donations to Carey's campaign would be returned by a large Teamster donation to the DNC.

McAuliffe has not been charged with any crime. His attorney, Richard Ben-Veniste, told the *Washington Post* that McAuliffe engaged in no wrongdoing.

Ben-Veniste said McAuliffe "was never a target of the investigation. . . . He did not raise any money for Mr. Carey, nor did he urge anyone to raise money for Mr. Carey."

Some critics of the Clinton White House aren't so sure the money trail ends with Bill Hamilton.

In Florida, an editorial in the *St. Petersburg Times* referenced McAuliffe as one who "figures prominently" in the Teamsters fund-raising scandal.

The paper, noting McAuliffe's ties to Gore, urged presidential candidate Bill Bradley to remind voters of the Clinton-Gore administration's "egregious abuse of campaign fund-raising laws in 1996."

"The real question on this is who else was involved," U.S. Rep. Peter Hoesktra, a Michigan Republican, told the *Detroit News*. Hoesktra chaired a House subcommittee that probed Teamsters activities.

Despite the obvious national implications of this story, much of the press has taken a hear-no-evil, see-no-evil approach.

An electronic database search of major newspapers across the United States shows that only three stories on the trial appeared in these papers during the days of testimony. Only nine major newspapers reported the conviction.

Compare that coverage to the headline ink and television coverage that the press gave to questions about former House Speaker Newt Gingrich's alleged use of a nonprofit organization for political purposes.

Larry Klayman, chairman of the public-interest law group Judicial Watch, said stories about Carey's Teamsters have "gotten little press coverage" because such coverage would reflect poorly on the Clinton White House and the Democrats.

Klayman has filed a lawsuit on behalf of two Pennsylvania residents against the Teamsters and Philadelphia Mayor Ed Rendell, the current DNC chairman. The residents, Don and Teri Adams, allege they were beaten by Teamsters members while the pair protested Bill Clinton's presence at a Philadelphia event.

Klayman said his suit got little press coverage — even when he held a press conference at the Liberty Bell this past October. "It's like the Hamilton case," Klayman said, "another story that is embarrassing to the Clinton White House that the press won't cover."

FBI Whistleblower Sues White House, FBI

By Carl Limbacher

NewsMax.com Vortex, September 1999 — Dennis Sculimbrene, at one time the most senior FBI agent assigned to the White House, filed suit against the Justice Department, the FBI and the White House for a combined total of more than $10 million.

You may have thought such a lawsuit, filed by Judicial Watch in U.S. District Court for the District of Columbia on July 26, should have received major press attention. The story, in fact, was ignored.

In some ways this former FBI agent's story is typical of so many Clinton-era whistleblowers who found themselves hung out to dry by the very people and organizations that purport to serve the interests of justice, including the press.

Despite the media blackout, Sculimbrene's suit has some startling and important revelations.

Sculimbrene is the one witness whose testimony is backed by unimpeachable documentary evidence, which irrefutably links first lady Hillary Rodham Clinton to the hiring of Filegate's central character, D. Craig Livingstone, once head of White House Security. Her Livingstone connection ties Mrs. Clinton to one of the worst abuses of presidential power in the history of the republic.

In FBI parlance the key evidence is called an "insert," a short memo thought to be of no consequence when Sculimbrene wrote it in March 1993 as part of his background investigation into Mr. Livingstone, then a new White House hire. At the time agent Sculimbrene was so highly trusted that he was the only member of the FBI's White House detail with a special SCI (Secret Compartmentalized Information) security clearance, which allowed him access to highly classifed material.

The highly trusted agent wrote the following, which became part of the then-obscure Livingstone's own FBI background file:

"BERNARD NUSSBAUM, Counsel to the President, advised that he had known the appointee for the period of time that he has been employed in the new administration. He had come highly recommended to him by HILLARY CLINTON, who has known his mother for a longer period of time . . . ."

Just how problematic was this now-six-year-old document detailing the Hillary-Livingstone connection — written at a time when not a single soul had reason to fabricate such a link?

A quick review of the joint White House-FBI campaign to harass, abuse and discredit Sculimbrene sheds a good deal of light on that question.

Before Filegate there was Travelgate, the scandal under examination by the House Government Reform and Oversight Committee in 1996 when it emerged that the White House Counsel's Office had illegally requisitioned Travel Office Chief Billy Dale's FBI file. Within days Dale's single purloined file had metastasized into hundreds and D. Craig Livingstone, the keeper of the confidential dossiers, became a household name overnight.

Sculimbrene knew something was amiss a full two months before Dale and his coworkers were tossed out the door in the Travelgate purge. Top Clinton aides had already begun questioning the FBI agent about the backgrounds and political views of the Travel Office staff. The agent told his superior that it looked to him like the Clinton administration wanted an excuse to fire Dale and the others.

When the Travel Office axe finally fell in May 1993, Sculimbrene witnessed Clinton aides rifling Dale's office, which was left completely unsecured despite the fact that the White House had announced an FBI investigation was under way.

Sculimbrene notified his bosses about what he'd seen. One of his superiors was actually supervising the criminal investigation that would eventually result in Dale's indictment. But despite Sculimbrene's crucial account of White House Travel Office evidence tampering, he would not be interviewed on the subject for another two years.

In January 1994 Sculimbrene suffered a nearly fatal plane accident, which the Clinton administration would later use against him in a number of ways, according to his lawsuit. The accident left him with a severe head wound that forced him to take an extended leave of absence from his White House work.

When Sculimbrene returned to work eight months later, doctors recommended that his schedule be modifed to accommodate his new physical limitations, which meant that he would return to his old White House position but work only during daytime hours and not be assigned any outside field work. Both the administration and the FBI welcomed Sculimbrene back under the new terms.

The arrangement worked well for nearly a year — until Sculimbrene mentioned to the FBI agent then building a case against Dale that he thought the upcoming Travelgate trial would become "a political football." Inexplicably, the senior agent warned Sculimbrene that he was considering filing a complaint against him with the FBI's Office of Professional Responsibility based on the innocuous remark.

After Sculimbrene was subpoenaed to testify at Dale's trial, the heat was gradually turned up. Suddenly, for the first time in his 22-year career, the FBI agent was ordered to take a random drug test. The White House Personnel Office invited him to apply for another job at the Department of Veterans Affairs — then abruptly withdrew the offer after he refused to testify against Dale. And now he was being given work assignments that directly violated the previously agreed-to workplace accommodations his doctors had requested.

Some of the harassment seemed ridiculous, such as the investigation launched by Sculimbrene's FBI bosses into whether he had misused his parking pass. But by April 1996 the once highly trusted agent who consistently received "exceptional" performance evaluations was told that his detail to the White House had been terminated. Two months later Filegate exploded.

In the weeks that followed, agent Sculimbrene would testify to House and Senate committees about Mrs. Clinton's relationship to D. Craig Livingstone, noting that others in the White House Counsel's Office told him they were "stuck" with the former bar bouncer because of his Hillary connection.

Within days of his testimony, Sculimbrene's permanent White House pass was lifted. He says his supervisor explained that his presence "made the first family uncomfortable."

In July 1996 FBI General Counsel Howard Shapiro made the bombshell discovery placing Mrs. Clinton at Filegate ground zero. Combing through Livingstone's own FBI file, Shapiro located Sculimbrene's smoking gun contemporaneous memo.

There it was in black and white, written years before anybody had heard of Filegate: Nussbaum's account to the FBI agent of how Hillary had "highly recommended" the former bar bouncer for a top White House slot. Back then, few doubted Livingstone was acting on orders from some higher-up when he accumulated nearly one thousand government dossiers on potential Clinton enemies.

The next morning Shapiro dispatched two FBI agents to Sculimbrene's home where the agent was grilled like a common criminal. In documents filed with the court, Sculimbrene complains that his interrogators asked him more than thirty times whether he kept other notes on what Nussbaum might have told him about Mrs. Clinton and Livingstone. Plainly the FBI was as concerned as the White House about other evidence emerging that would link the first lady to Filegate.

Shapiro's agents repeatedly warned Sculimbrene that his three-year-old notation was contradicted not only by Nussbaum, but by the first lady and the president as well. Just in case he missed the point, Sculimbrene's supervisor called during the grilling to advise him about an upcoming psychiatric examination that would determine the agent's future fitness to serve the FBI.

If that weren't enough, then–White House counsel Jack Quinn personally wrote to FBI Director Louis Freeh, attempting to link Sculimbrene to another agent who'd been convicted of falsifying background investigations.

Lanny Davis, not yet officially on the White House payroll, popped up on CNN's *Crossfire* and CNBC's *Rivera Live* insisting Sculimbrene's claim that Nussbaum had told him anything linking Livingstone to Mrs. Clinton was "an absolute fabrication."

"I am accusing Sculimbrene of having a political bias and that report is filled with lies," said the future White House damage controller on national television. Ironically, the same kind of hysterical denials greeted the publication of 1996's political book of the year, *Unlimited Access*, written by Sculimbrene's White House partner, former FBI agent Gary Aldrich.

On August 2, 1996, Dennis Sculimbrene resigned from the FBI.

The Clinton administration has successfully stonewalled the independent counsel and Congress for five years on a whole array of serious scandals. Yet private citizen Paula Jones, pursuing justice in civil court, turned Clinton into the only elected American president ever to be impeached.

As with the Jones case, civil court is where Americans will eventually learn the truth about Filegate and the White House's attempts to cover it up, thanks to Dennis Sculimbrene.

Shays Has Little Shame

NewsMax.com Vortex, February 1999 — Quid Pro Quo.

You scratch my back, I'll scratch yours.

The Clinton White House can be nasty with their enemies. They also happen to be very good to their friends.

Witness what just happened to Congressman Chris Shays' wife.

Shays, a Republican who represents the tony suburbs in Connecticut, near to New York, milked his decision on the impeachment for every nauseating publicity minute he could get — even demanding a sitdown with the president.

After playing Hamlet, Shays voted AGAINST impeachment. No one was surprised.

The *Greenwhich Post* now reports that Shays' wife, a school teacher, was recently appointed to head the Peace Corps' World Wide Schools Programs. Shays' press spokesman claimed to the *Post* that the hiring of Mrs. Shays had no bearing on Shays' vote against impeachment, and nothing to do with the president or the White House.

Right. And every day Democratic administrations hire the wives of Republican congressmen for plum political posts. Do they think we were all born yesterday?

The Peace Corps is headed by Mark Gearan, former director of the White House office of communication.

More Than Sex: The Secrets of Bill and Hillary Clinton Revealed by Arkansas State Trooper

By Christopher Ruddy

NewsMax.com Vortex, September 1999 — An Arkansas state trooper who once guarded Bill Clinton has revealed startling new information about Bill and Hillary Rodham Clinton.

Trooper Larry Patterson, a 32-year veteran of the state police, had been assigned for six years as the most senior member of the elite Governor's Security Detail during the period Bill Clinton served as governor.

During that time, Patterson became privy to Bill and Hillary Clinton's most closely guarded secrets.

Patterson told his story exclusively to NewsMax.com. NewsMax.com has published *More Than Sex: The Secrets of Bill and Hillary Clinton Revealed,* a two-hour audiocassette tape of Christopher Ruddy's interview with Trooper Patterson.

In *More than Sex* Patterson makes new, bombshell revelations, some of which have never been disclosed before:

➤ **Womanizing.** Trooper Patterson says Clinton's womanizing was not just "about sex" but an "abuse of power and abuse of people." Patterson admits he and other troopers were "pimps" for Bill Clinton, and Patterson explains how Clinton's sexual appetite, or "obsession," affected his public and private life.

Patterson also makes new revelations in the Gennifer Flowers and Paula Jones cases.

➤ **Violence Against Women.** Trooper Patterson says he believes Bill Clinton is capable of rape. He reveals for the first time his encounter outside the governor's mansion with a women who had been injured.

➤ **Drugs.** Trooper Patterson discusses his experiences with Clinton and why some suspected Clinton may have been a drug user.

➤ **Organized Crime.** The press has ignored reporting of this critical issue, but Patterson says Clinton had a close relationship with the head of the Dixie Mafia—Arkansas' homegrown organized crime family that has grown in recent years through drug trafficking. Patterson said Clinton regularly received gifts from the reputed mob boss.

Patterson also discloses new details of Bill Clinton's relationship with Dan Lasater, a one-time bond dealer who served time in federal prison for cocaine distribution charges.

➤ **Ethnic Slurs About Jews.** Both Hillary and Bill Clinton frequently used slurs during heated arguments with each other, Patterson said. Among the epithets they frequently hurled at each other were anti-Semitic slurs such as "mother f-cking Jew" or "Jew bastard." Patterson said such references were heard frequently during the years he served the Clintons.

Patterson said Clinton loved telling ethnic jokes and frequently told jokes that were anti-Semitic.

➤ **The Use of the "N" Word.** Patterson said Bill Clinton would occasionally use the word "nigger" — the "N" word — when he was angry with African-American opponents. He recalls the use of the word in describing black activist Say McIntosh, who was critical of Clinton. Patterson said Clinton also used the "N" word during the 1992 campaign when referring to Jesse Jackson.

Clinton, according to Patterson, also tolerated use of the "N" word by senior aides and Arkansas business and political figures.

➤ **Hitler and *Mein Kampf*.** Bill Clinton, Patterson said, spoke admiringly of Hitler and was fascinated by his book *Mein Kampf*.

➤ **Vince Foster.** Patterson explains why he believes Vince Foster was murdered.

➤ **Vince Foster and Hillary.** Patterson said he had no doubt Vince Foster and Hillary Clinton had an extramarital affair. Patterson details several occasions upon which he saw Vince and Hillary in compromising situations.

➤ **Helen Dickey's Call.** On the day of Vince Foster's death, Patterson said he learned about the death before the Park Police even found Foster's body and hours before the White House staff said they were informed. Patterson's information, corroborated by another trooper, exposes a cover-up bigger than Watergate.

➤ **Ross Perot.** Ross Perot was a presidential candidate in 1992 and 1996. Patterson reveals that Bill Clinton and Ross Perot were friends and describes contact the two had before the 1992 campaign, as well as a series of phone calls between them during the 1992 campaign.

➤ **Black Child.** It was the plot of the fictional book *Primary Colors* — the story of a Southern governor who had impregnated a young black girl. The story gained credibility when *Star* magazine did DNA testing on a young African-American boy named Danny Williams. Now, Patterson reveals new information suggesting there is more to this story than you ever believed.

In *More Than Sex* Trooper Patterson provides the first reliable insider's account of what Bill and Hillary Clinton are really like. Bill and Hillary Clinton are the two most powerful people in the world. This shocking audiotape explores an abuse of power that major media outlets have ignored.

Trooper Patterson worries that Clinton has plans to stay in office beyond his second term. This unfathomable notion gains credibility, Patterson said, when one considers no one has held the Clintons accountable for their actions.

Analysis:
Janet Reno — the Cornerstone of the Clinton Cover-Ups

By Christopher Ruddy

NewsMax.com Vortex, July 1999 — In the middle of the Chinagate scandal maelstrom sits U.S. Attorney General Janet Reno. Already several top lawmakers have called for her to resign.

Former House Speaker Newt Gingrich said Reno has managed "probably the most disgraceful Justice Department since the Teapot Dome scandal of 1923 when the attorney general had to resign because of corruption."

Reno's efforts to cover up for Chinagate, the Clintons' scandal du jour, are legion. But one fact stands out above all others: Reno refused to authorize a wiretap request in 1997 when the FBI wanted to monitor Los Alamos espionage suspect Wen Ho Lee. According to *Investor's Business Daily,* this was the only wiretap request she denied out of almost 2,700.

Even before the Chinese nuclear espionage allegations shook the political landscape, Reno had been covering for the Clintons' special dealings with China. Despite the FBI director's recommendation and the request of a Justice Department official she appointed, Reno has steadfastly refused to appoint an independent counsel to investigate whether Clinton sold America's most sensitive nuclear and military secrets for campaign cash.

Actually, Janet Reno has been in the middle of every maelstrom involving the Clintons since her appointment as attorney general. From Waco to Travelgate to Vince Foster's death to Whitewater obstruction to China-Lippogate, Reno has done exactly what she was appointed to do. She has held the floodwaters of justice from ever reaching the Clinton White House.

The truth is that Janet Reno was the most important appointment made to the Clinton Cabinet. Bill and Hillary Clinton, professional white-collar criminals, knew that their attorney general would be critical to their hold on the presidency. They also knew their choice for the Cabinet post would come under close scrutiny by Senate Republicans.

Eventually they settled on Reno, a Harvard Law School graduate who had returned to her Miami, Florida, home and become a local prosecutor before being named by Governor Reubin Askew as Dade County state's attorney.

The Clintons' First Choice

The way history records it, Janet Reno was the accidental attorney general, a third choice who luckily got picked because of the unexpected failure of the first two candidates. That history turns out to be falsified one. Janet Reno was no accident.

The real details about Reno's ascendancy were sketched out to me one afternoon by a friend and one-time associate of Janet Reno. We met at a restaurant in the bohemian enclave of Coconut Grove here in Miami — once a stomping ground for Reno.

Reno, her associate told me, was actually the first choice of the Clintons because of her notable track record in Miami: Under Reno's legal stewardship, Miami became a mecca for drug dealers, money launderers, corrupt politicians and other hoodlums. It was during Reno's tenure here that the city earned its well-deserved nickname from the highly rated television show *Miami Vice*.

Last year, Miami became the center of controversy when a state court removed the sitting mayor because of voter fraud. But according to Reno's former associate, voter fraud flourished while Reno served as Miami's chief law enforcement officer.

Investigative reporters James Collier and Ken Collier detailed in the 1992 book *Votescam* how they uncovered pre-printed voter ballots in a warehouse rented by a Miami political candidate. Following the advice of their editor, they seized the evidence and took the illegal ballots to the state's attorney, Janet Reno. Incredibly, Reno had the journalists arrested, rather than investigate how a candidate had pre-printed ballots in his possession.

As Reno's former associate noted, she was a perfect match for the Clintons because she had a near-perfect record of not prosecuting white-collar criminals or politicians. No one ever accused her of taking bribes or conspiring with criminals, but she was frequently criticized by her political opponents for her naivete. She was also alleged to be susceptible to blackmail for personal indiscretions.

It was clear from Reno's tenure as Miami's figurative top cop that she liked holding public office. She focused on safe issues that she cared about, such as preventing child abuse, while drug dealing, money laundering and political corruption were rampant.

It is generally acknowledged that Hillary Clinton, by covering for her husband during the Gennifer Flowers flap, had earned the right to name nominees to a number of Cabinet posts, including the attorney general. Hillary Clinton, whose brother had served as a legal aid attorney representing indigent defendants prosecuted by Reno's office, had firsthand information that Reno was a patsy for the criminal element.

The Dade County state's attorney shaped up as the ideal Clintonian candidate for the post. She was a woman. She was ineffectual in dealing with organized crime and white-collar criminals. She was a yes woman who would not expose political corruption. She did not have the credentials associated with the post of attorney general and would owe the Clintons for the appointment.

Senate Confirmation

According to Reno's former associate, the big problem with Reno was she probably wouldn't pass the FBI background check and the almost certain Senate confirmation process. So the Clintons devised a brilliant plan to get their nominee approved without an FBI inquiry and with no real Senate review.

First, Bill Clinton nominated Zoe Baird, a well-regarded attorney, for the post. She seemed to be sailing through the process when damaging information from her FBI file was leaked that disclosed Baird had hired a housekeeper and had not paid Social Security taxes.

Baird withdrew, and Clinton nominated New York Judge Kimba Wood. Again FBI file details were leaked to the press that Wood, too, had not paid Social Security taxes for her domestic help. She also withdrew.

The Clinton administration, renowned for putting positive spin on damaging information, made no effort to condemn the inappropriate leaks from Baird's and Wood's FBI files. "Baird and Wood were pawns to be sacrificed," my confidential source said.

However, with these nominees thrown overboard, the famed Clinton spin team went into overdrive with the nomination of Janet Reno. It was suggested that she was a tough, Eliot Ness–like prosecutor. After two failed nominations and with the standoff with the David Koresh cult in Waco, Texas, escalating into a hot crisis, the White House press machine urged an immediate confirmation for the vacant attorney general post.

Incredibly, the Clintons pulled it off, getting Janet Reno to head the Justice Department of the United States with virtually no vetting by the FBI, Congress, or the press.

Their control of Justice became complete when Web Hubbell, described as the president's best friend and an intimate of Hillary's from the Rose Law Firm, was named as associate attorney general.

As such, Hubbell became the Clintons' point man and safety check at the Justice Department. Hubbell, a white-collar criminal in the same mold as the Clintons, would later plead guilty to tax and mail fraud charges.

Any pretense of an independent Justice Department disappeared when Reno's top deputy, Philip Heymann, resigned in 1994. He described her performance as attorney general as "amateur hour."

As they were with the Clintons, the press was too willing to overlook horrendous mistakes, such as her decision to have the FBI storm the Koresh compound in Waco, resulting in the deaths of everyone inside, including children. Reno claimed she took the action because of solid evidence that Koresh was abusing children. But, in fact, no written report provided to her during the crisis indicated any children were being abused.

The Clintons have frequently pretended they really dislike Janet Reno, depicting her as a mean, uncompromising "bad cop." Yet she has served continuously throughout both of Clinton's presidential terms, backing him at every critical juncture.

Stopped Smaltz

Perhaps most telling was the experience of independent counsel Donald Smaltz. He was appointed to investigate charges that Clinton-backer Don Tyson had made illegal gifts to Agriculture Secretary Mike Espy.

In the course of his investigation, Smaltz uncovered evidence that Bill Clinton, when governor of Arkansas, had received cash bribes from

Tyson. One of Tyson's airline pilots testified under oath that he had ferried bundles of cash for Governor Clinton to Little Rock Airport, where Clinton's state trooper bodyguards made the pickup.

Smaltz's evidence was strong and included testimony from one or more troopers supporting the pilot's allegations. But Reno opposed his every move to expand his jurisdiction. In 1997, Smaltz described to Peter Boyer of PBS a remarkable showdown he had with Reno and six Justice officials over the Tyson allegations.

Smaltz told Boyer that until that point he had dismissed his wife's fears his life was in jeopardy while investigating the Clintons. But when he saw the control Clinton had over the Justice Department of the United States he said he was truly shaken. His greatest fears, he said, were for the country.

Meanwhile, as she has her entire career, Janet Reno holds an office where she has sworn to see justice done and criminal activity prosecuted — yet she is steadfastly violating that oath by protecting Bill and Hillary Clinton.

Ruddy Analysis: Maybe Saddam Actually Likes Bill

By Christopher Ruddy

NewsMax.com Vortex, January 1999 — As the impeachment of President Richard Nixon loomed, Nixon's chief of staff, Alexander Haig, notified the Joint Chiefs and other key military leaders not to obey the orders of the President.

Haig's directive may not have been constitutional, but it was a smart move and a good safeguard against the possibility that Nixon would use a foreign policy crisis, such as a war, to save his faltering presidency.

Fast-forward to the eve of the impeachment of William Jefferson Clinton.

Literally on the night before the perfunctory debate on the House floor leading to the impeachment vote, Bill Clinton orders American bombers into action over Iraq.

A number of Republicans, including House Majority Whip Tom

DeLay and the Senate Majority Leader Trent Lott, say the president's motives for this action cannot be trusted.

The Clinton action comes as little surprise to those who have seriously studied this administration.

First of all, Bill Clinton has been ruthless in his quest for power, leaving a trail of decimated opponents from his days in rural Arkansas to the halls of power in Washington.

I have related for some time a conversation I had with a Nixon family member. This family member said that the former president always said that he could have saved his presidency by creating a foreign policy crisis.

"This would be easy for a president to do," the family member quoted Nixon. But Nixon "would have never done that, and he would never have risked American lives," the family member explained.

Then the family member added that Nixon said Bill Clinton would not blink an eye to use a foreign policy crisis to save his presidency.

This conversation, now more than two years old, rings today in my ears.

Obviously Nixon grasped who Clinton is. And perhaps congressional Republicans, angered by the latest Clinton attempt to delay his accountability, feel the same way.

Another reason to be disturbed by the latest showdown with Iraq is the larger context of this action. Only this year, Scott Ritter, the head of the U.N. weapons inspection team in Baghdad, resigned. Ritter publicly exposed the Clinton administration for its repeated threats to Saddam Hussein while it duplicitously thwarted him and his team's efforts to conduct thorough inspections in Iraq.

Why would our president do such a thing?

That's a good question. Another one is why Saddam Hussein has consistently taken actions that appear to make Bill Clinton look good.

As Clinton stumbled through his first year as president, he looked rather presidential in June of 1993 when he fired cruise missiles at the headquarters of Iraqi intelligence. Clinton had the missiles fired at night when no one was there. This was done in retaliation for Iraq's plot to assassinate President Bush.

Later, in the fall of 1994, as Clinton's poll numbers looked shaky just before the mid-term congressional election, Saddam Hussein began moving large numbers of his troops to the Kuwaiti border.

At that time Bill Clinton warned, "We will not allow Saddam Hussein to defy the will of the United States and the international community." The chairman of the Joint Chiefs, General John Shalikashvili, said Iraq "will pay the price if he chooses not to withdraw" his troops.

To deal with this menace, commander in chief Bill Clinton ordered nearly 20,000 troops to the region, along with some 500 military aircraft. He put more than 150,000 troops on alert.

Just two weeks before those 1994 congressional elections, Clinton's actions appeared to pay off big-time. Hussein immediately backed down. Clinton looked every bit the hero.

Headlines praised Clinton's resolve. The *Atlanta Constitution Journal*, for example, declared "Fast U.S. Action Averted War with Iraq."

The next major flare-up with Hussein came about in late August 1996. This was a presidential election year, and the official kickoff of the campaign season was just days away with the upcoming Labor Day weekend.

But poor Clinton challenger Bob Dole never got any headlines because Saddam Hussein began moving his troops into the Kurdish "safe haven" of Iraq.

The Kurds constitute a minority group long mistreated by the Iranians, Syrians, Turks and Iraqis—and one that has never received much attention from our government until Saddam Hussein began sending tanks into the "safe haven."

The Clinton administration took swift action, firing some 44 cruise missiles at radar and anti-aircraft batteries in the south of Iraq, far from Hussein's activities against the Kurds in the north of Iraq. The wisdom of using expensive cruise missiles against installations that could be rebuilt in days was questioned ever so briefly, as Saddam quickly removed his troops. Clinton had won another "victory" over Hussein, just two months before the 1996 election.

Though clear and convincing evidence had been available since 1996 that Saddam's programs for developing weapons of mass destruction have been well under way, the issue festered with little Clinton administration action for another two years.

It was not until the Monica Lewinsky scandal broke in January of this year that the Iraqi matter again reached the crisis stage. Clinton again ordered U.S. military assets to the region. As the Lewinsky scandal subsided and it appeared that Clinton would survive, the Iraqi crisis also subsided.

He has taken so many actions to help President Clinton at such critical junctures that it appears Saddam Hussein likes Bill Clinton.

Six years into his presidency, President Clinton has not significantly challenged Hussein, and if Scott Ritter is to be believed, Hussein's weapons programs have prospered.

Meanwhile, Hussein must be aware that Bill Clinton has presided over one of the largest military build-downs in the nation's history, and that surely will be good for Hussein and the enemies of the United States in the long run.

Congressman Graham Talks of Rape, Murder and Mayhem

NewsMax.com Vortex, February 1999 — A NewsMax.com reader, Hap Barko, sent us a fascinating e-mail:

"While listening to the presentation before the Senate, I was struck by words Congressman Lindsey Graham used in discussing 'crimes' that may be impeachable.

"In fact, I was struck so hard by them, I think he understands what's really going on. The similarity between his choice of words and the President's crimes (that are being ignored) are, I believe, not coincidental.

"Could these be inferences to the dead bodies (murder), Jane Doe #5 (rape, mayhem), and bribery/treason (Espionage/Year of the Rat)? See what you think. I've taken a portion of the transcript of Graham's presentation in context; I found it through a link on the (London) Electronic Telegraph:

". . . Senator Mathias, about this idea of public versus private. 'It is my opinion that the impeachment power is not as narrow as Judge Claiborne suggests. There is neither historical nor a logical reason to believe that the framers of the Constitution sought to prohibit the House from impeaching an officer of the United States who had committed treason or bribery or any other high crime or misdemeanor which is a serious offense against the United States and which indicates that the official is unfit to exercise public responsibility, but which is an offense which is technically unrelated to the officer's particular job responsibilities.'

"This hits it head on. Impeachable conduct does not have to occur in the course of the performance of the officer's official duties. Evidence of misconduct, misbehavior, high crimes and misdemeanors can be justified upon one's private dealings as well as one's exercise of public office.

"That, of course, is the situation in this case.

"It would be absurd to conclude that a judge who committed murder, mayhem, rape or perhaps espionage in his private life, could not be removed from office by the U.S. Senate.

"The point you made so well was that we're not buying this. If you're a federal judge and you cheat on your taxes and you lie under oath, it's true that it had nothing to do with your courtroom in a technical sense. But you're going to be judging others and they're going to come before you with their fate in their hands and we don't want somebody like you running our courtroom, because people won't trust the results. . . ."

House Investigators Express Fears

NewsMax.com Vortex, February 1999 — While the mainstream press giggles over "wing nut" concerns about the dozens of Clinton–connected folks who have met mysterious untimely ends, House investigators aren't laughing.

At least not according to Dick Morris, who revealed a chilling tidbit on Fox TV. Matt Drudge asked the former Clinton guru why NBC has suddenly gone wobbly over its blockbuster interview with alleged Clinton rape victim Juanita Broaddrick.

Here's what followed:

DRUDGE: What is the fear factor surrounding [the Broaddrick] case?

MORRIS: When I was called by the House Judiciary Committee [this month] to testify, or to meet with them, I met with three investigators of the committee. They asked me not to use their names and I won't. But they were each 50 years of age or over. They weren't kids.

They had decades of experience working for the IRS, the FBI and all kinds of other investigative organizations. They told me that they were physically afraid of retaliation. They asked me if I would testify . . .

DRUDGE: The ones questioning you were afraid?

MORRIS: Exactly. They asked me if I would testify and I said, yeah. And they said, "Aren't you afraid of retaliation?" And I said, "What, are they going to expose my sex life?" You know, we've done all that already. And I've taken the trouble not to sin since.

And they said, "No, no — don't you know the list of the 25 people who have died under mysterious circumstances in connection with this investigation?"

And I said, "Are you guys out of your minds?"

And they said, "No, no." And one of them said, "I guarantee you that each of us will have an IRS audit when this is over." He said, "I'm saving my receipts. I know I'm going to have an audit."

And I said, "How does that work?" And he said, "Well, the head of the IRS and Hillary are very good friends."

DRUDGE: So, let me get this straight. Those even questioning people at this point are afraid?

MORRIS: And we're not talking here about some right-wing nuts or some people who are really paranoid. We're talking about guys who have spent 20 or 30 years as top-level investigators for the IRS and the FBI, who have retired, and now are on leave and been brought back by the Judiciary Committee. And they specifically asked me not to mention their names on the air.

DRUDGE: Well, we won't.

Morris' answer begs the question: If even House investigators probing Monicagate can be intimidated, then how likely is it that NBC executives are immune from pressure to kill their Broaddrick exposé?

Morris began working for Clinton the year before Broaddrick's friends say she was raped. And though he didn't address the assault charge directly with Drudge, the pollster turned pundit does seem to know something.

"It was date rape if it was anything. I mean, [Clinton] didn't jump out of the bushes with a knife," Dick Morris told Hannity and Colmes last year.

Monica's Mom Afraid for Monica's Life

NewsMax.com Vortex, November 1998 — When the FBI cornered Monica in Room 1012 of the Ritz-Carlton, they hoped to gain her co-operation. Monica didn't cave. She did ask to call her mom. Mom, Marcia Lewis, spoke with the FBI agents by phone. Mom told the FBI that her daughter was "younger than her chronological age." (Then how did this immature woman write the talking points?) Mom also told the FBI that Monica talked about suicide six years ago. Mom also asked the FBI "about Lewinsky's safety if Lewinsky cooperated." Why was Mom so worried about Monica cooperating against the president?

Feared for Her Life?

NewsMax.com Vortex, November 1998 — Prosecutors were curious about statements Monica made to Tripp that she feared for her life. Monica admitted to making the statements, but said she simply exaggerated her fears hoping it would be more reason for Linda to keep quiet in her own deposition. Lewinsky said she told Tripp she feared ending up like Mary Jo Kopechne, Ted Kennedy's girlfriend who was found dead at Chappaquiddick. Monica testified that fear for her life "crossed my mind in some bizarre way," reminding prosecutors of the "Marilyn Monroe theory."

Secret Service Officer Gets Some Threats

NewsMax.com Vortex, November 1998 — Retired Uniformed Secret Service Officer Lewis Fox broke the code of silence. He was the first law enforcement officer to go public, during an interview with a Pittsburgh television station, that he saw Monica and Bill alone, in the Oval Office.

Clinton at first denied the two were ever alone, behind closed doors. (Clinton re-defined "alone," suggesting that he is never alone in his office when Betty Currie sits at her desk, even with his doors closed.)

After Fox went public, he was summoned before Starr's grand jury and into the klieg lights. At the time of Fox's appearance, his attorney told the press that Fox had qualified his previous claims and had testified that Clinton and Monica were never alone.

Odd.

Then comes Starr's report. A footnote in the report states that Fox did, in fact, testify the two were alone, together. Fox's "sworn testimony on this point differs from the public statements of his attorney. . . . "

So, what's going on?

One source familiar with Fox's situation tells us the following: after Fox first went public he received many, many calls of support from Secret Service buddies. He also received a number of calls from Secret Service officers who delivered some not-so-veiled threats.

Firing of Jones' Husband Was 'Retaliation'

By Tim Phares

NewsMax.com Vortex, December 1998 — "It was absolutely retaliation. I have no doubt," said Paula Jones' husband Steve Jones, speaking out for the first time about having been fired from his job.

Jones, who was speaking in an interview with *NewsMax.com*, was sacked by Northwest Airlines from his position as a ticket agent, a job he held for 16 years, just five days after Judge Susan Webber Wright, a former Clinton law student, dismissed his wife's civil rights suit against Bill Clinton.

"They knew that [my job] was the only financial stability for my family," said Jones, the father of two children, ages 2 and 6, speaking bitterly of the loss not only of his income but also of his pension and health benefits.

In another stunning disclosure, Jones told *NewsMax.com* that just after his dismissal from Northwest, Bob Bennett, the president's attorney, called the Jones family's attorney to put "pressure not to appeal" on Paula by suggesting that Paula could have a book or movie deal if she didn't appeal.

"I never saw any book deal," Jones said mockingly of Bennett's suggestion.

Jones intimated that his firing was a reprisal for having pursued the suit, and a move to squeeze the family financially to get Paula to drop the action.

Steve Jones said he always received excellent job performance ratings and that he had never been reprimanded in his 16 years with Northwest. His personnel file includes numerous commendation letters for his work.

Another factor in Jones' firing may have been ties between Northwest and Bill Clinton. The major stockholder in Northwest Airlines and its former chairman is Al Checchi, an active friend and supporter of President Clinton who lost this year's Democratic primary for governor of California despite large financial expenditures.

Jones said that he was fired after his supervisor posted a notice "freezing" his shift — or requiring employees to be held overtime that day. He said that he was never told he was being held over, nor did he see any freeze notice posted.

According to Jones, his shift that day ended at 2:30 p.m. He said that the freeze notice was posted at 2:35 p.m., five minutes after his shift ended. "How can you freeze a shift when the shift is over?" Jones asked.

Jones recounted that at 2:25 he went to the ticket counter to help some last-minute passengers. Then he went to the men's room. He clocked out at 2:40 and went home.

According to Jones, there was no freeze notice on the time clock or anywhere. He saw no one standing nearby or in the hall. Later, the Northwest manager claimed that a supervisor had seen Jones improperly lift up the notice before clocking out, then tape it on the clock again.

Jones asked all of his supervisors which one had made this allegation. They all said that they had not. At a later meeting, he was questioned by his manager. He told her what the supervisors had told him. He then called his union, the International Association of Machinists (IAM). The union, he said, told him not to worry about it. But not one hour later, he was fired.

Steve Kelton, a representative of the IAM, confirmed to *NewsMax.com* that Steve Jones was asked questions in this meeting and presented his side. Kelton is not Jones' union representative, but was called in that day because he was the only union representative on the premises. "Anything Steve Jones tells you would be true," he said.

Three other workers, who clocked out after Jones, told him that they had seen the freeze notice, clocked out anyway, and were not fired, Jones said.

Northwest would not comment on Jones' firing. John Austin, a spokesman for the airline, said that "it's a personnel matter and it's confidential." However, Austin also said that the dismissal "was looked at and reviewed, and it's consistent with our policy."

"I had 16 years of service," Jones said. "My pension was gone, my benefits were gone, I had to liquidate my stock, health benefits, and my 401(k)," he said. "I knew it had to do with Al Checchi."

Jones said that his union has been unable to get his personnel file from Northwest.

As it turns out, IAM has been a strong supporter of President Clinton. Northwest claimed that they had lost his personnel file, Jones said. "They said they can't find it, but it's thick like the telephone book. They finally gave me eight pages of nitpicky stuff," he said.

Jones told *NewsMax.com* that he has repeatedly sent letters to Northwest requesting his file, but the airline continues to say they can't find it. The union has sent out a request letter on Jones' behalf.

"Whatever Mr. Jones is entitled to, I am sure he has received it," Austin said.

The White House has claimed, with wide press attention, that Paula Jones' lawsuit against President Clinton is politically motivated. Yet Steve Jones' allegation of a political firing has received little notice, save a column by media critic Reed Irvine of Accuracy in Media.

Thousands to Die From Arkansas Prison Blood

NewsMax.com Vortex, December 1998 — At least 42,000 Canadians have been infected with hepatitis C, and thousands more with HIV, thanks to poorly screened plasma, some of which has been traced back to the Cummins prison in Arkansas. More than 7,000 Canadians are expected to die as a result of the blood scandal.

The blood was the product of a corrupted blood-for-sale program run in the 1980s during the time that Bill Clinton was governor. According to inmate John Shock, Clinton was a frequent visitor to the prison and was fully cognizant of everything that went on there. Moreover, the lucrative plasma collection contracts were awarded to Clinton campaign finance chairman Leonard Dunn of Health Management Associates and were estimated to have generated millions of dollars in revenue.

Inmates at the Cummins Unit, near Grady, Arkansas, were paid $7 to donate blood. They were able to bypass tests that might have disqualified them because of the presence of HIV or hepatitis C, common among prisoners, by bribing a clerk who was also an inmate.

This potentially tainted blood was then sold to Canada, where it was given to hemophilia victims, many of whom later became infected.

In an average week, inmates lined up by the hundreds to sell their blood. Once the blood was harvested, it was loaded onto trucks and driven to Canada, where it was later fractionated into blood products for hemophiliacs.

Thanks to the program, Arkansas has become synonymous with death for many Canadians who were given tainted blood during the 1980s. It is believed the prisoners' plasma was contaminated with HIV — the virus that causes AIDS — and with hepatitis C.

Canada's *Ottawa Citizen* newspaper questioned why Governor Clinton's administration allowed the prison to collect inmates' blood, even though it was commonly known they carried a greater risk of having AIDS. "Was the prison plasma program operated safely?" the *Citizen* asked. "How did the prison plasma, which U.S. companies refused to buy, make it across the border? Just where were Canada's federal blood regulators?"

A wide-ranging investigation by the *Citizen* disclosed that the prison plasma center experienced serious safety problems in the early 1980s. Among them:

• The U.S. Food and Drug Administration (FDA), following a July 1982 inspection, cited the center for several safety deficiencies. For example, prisoners were "overbled," and there was no "complete record available" to show whether several units of plasma that had tested positive for hepatitis B (a frequent indicator of the presence of HIV) had been destroyed.

• In the summer of 1983, following a recall of hepatitis B–suspected products that had been shipped to Canada and distributed to hemophiliacs, the center was shut down for several months by the FDA. It was discovered during the shutdown that an inmate clerk in the plasma center had been selling the "right to bleed" to fellow inmates who otherwise would have been excluded because they were likely infected.

• In early 1984, the FDA revoked the center's license to operate, citing a litany of problems such as: allowing disqualified donors to bleed; altering records; inadequately storing plasma to prevent contamination; intentionally and willfully disregarding proposed standards; ineffectively supervising plasma center staff; and people in "management positions" at the center attempting to hide from FDA inspectors the fact that they had either "initiated or condoned the destruction or alteration of records concerning these activities."

Within months, after promising to clean up its act, the center was relicensed and back in operation.

The center continued to draw prisoners' plasma for another decade and finally closed its doors in 1994 for a simple reason: It could no longer find a buyer for its controversial product.

Until mid-1985, there were no direct tests to screen out HIV from donated blood. Indeed, the only line of defense was to disallow people considered "high risk" from giving blood, and by testing all donated units for hepatitis B.

As well, a direct test for hepatitis C was not available until 1990. Until then, again, the only defense was "donor screening" and hepatitis B tests.

According to Mike Galster, an expert in building and fitting prosthetics who worked in the prison in the early 1980s, the plasma center was essentially run by the inmates themselves and the medical histories taken on potential donors were infrequent and incomplete.

Galster who interviewed many prisoners who donated blood, said, "If they were asked anything, they were asked: 'Are you sick? Have you had homosexual sex? Have you had hepatitis?' Now, here's an inmate sitting there knowing he's only going to get his $7 if he answers no. . . . When they're asked these questions, what are they going to answer?"

Prison officials insist they did everything they could to prevent infections.

John Byus, medical director of the Arkansas Department of Corrections, told the *Citizen*: "We had a decent program. We tried to operate it as long as we could, and we did. I don't think we were wrong. Unfortunately, there were some cases that got out. And I sure hope to the blue devil that there is not any direct travel [of contaminated plasma] back to these inmates."

He acknowledged it was unfortunate that potentially infected donors got through the screening process by paying off the inmate clerk.

"We conducted an internal review, because that's traffic and trading as far as we're concerned. We removed the clerk, we fired some staff that allowed it to occur, and we disciplined those that we needed to, to the extent that we could."

Byus admitted that prisoners are more likely to have AIDS and hepatitis C than the general public.

Dr. Francis (Bud) Henderson, who was medical director of Health Management Associates, the private firm the state hired to run the plasma program, says studies have found that 40 percent of prisoners carry hepatitis C, the sometimes fatal blood-borne virus that causes liver damage.

A November 1984 "information bulletin" prepared by the American Correctional Association for its members warned prison officials about the pitfalls inherent in prison plasma programs.

The bulletin, obtained by the *Citizen*, listed the benefits and drawbacks of prison plasma centers. It was prepared after consulting officials in various states — including Byus, who is listed in the acknowledgments.

Under the section headed "Ethical and Moral Issues," the bulletin noted that research indicated a higher percentage of prisoners were "illicit drug abusers before their incarceration" and that many tested positive for hepatitis B. Also, it pointed to research indicating that "because of the close living conditions of large groups of inmates, a high incidence of homosexual activity is found."

Clinton: It's Not a Lie Unless I Say It Is

NewsMax.com Vortex, June 2000 — The man who said the meaning of the word "is" is open to question now insists that a lie is only a lie if he says it is. In his up-to-now secret plea to an Arkansas Supreme Court committee in which he sought to avoid disbarment for giving false testimony, President Clinton makes the astonishing claim that his testimony was "not false as he defines the term."

Clinton's apparent assumption of ultimate lexicographic authority giving him the right to define the meanings of words at his sole discretion came in a document submitted by his attorneys to the Arkansas Supreme Court Committee on Professional Conduct and kept secret until the Southeastern Legal Foundation made its response to Clinton's 80-page filing public, thereby revealing the gist of Clinton's pleading.

Foundation President Matthew J. Glavin, during a press conference, characterized the president's 85-page plea, submitted on April 21, as "a pathetic attempt to defend the indefensible."

"[The president] acknowledged in his response that he misled the nation, his family, his friends and indeed the court. The president then spent 50 pages in his response . . . trying to argue that he did not commit a crime," Glavin said.

According to Glavin, Clinton's filing disputes the need for disbarment and "suggests that a sanction no harsher and perhaps more lenient than a letter of reprimand would be appropriate."

By asking for nothing more than "a mere reprimand," Clinton "ignores the plain language of the . . . most obvious, analogous case of presidential misconduct, that of Richard Nixon," who, the Foundation notes, was disbarred in New York despite the absence of criminal conviction or impeachment conviction. Nixon resigned before the Senate could hold an impeachment trial, thereby avoiding being convicted. In being pardoned by President Ford, he also avoided the possibility of a criminal conviction.

In its rebuttal, the Foundation argued that Clinton's admissions during his impeachment provided enough evidence that he misled courts in the Lewinsky matter to warrant revocation of his law license.

"The president is no ordinary Arkansas lawyer. Rather, he is the president of the United States of America and, as such, is held to the model rules requiring the higher ethical standard for attorneys who hold public office, even those who may become litigants or defendants," the Foundation's response said.

Citing the fact that U.S. District Judge Susan Webber Wright had fined the president for contempt for giving false testimony about his relationship with Monica Lewinsky in the Paula Jones case, the Foundation used the judge's 1999 findings when she mentioned 10 alleged lies by the president that "no reasonable person would seriously dispute," as well as Clinton's own admission he misled people during the Lewinsky affair.

"First, the president frankly admits the conduct at issue. Second, the allegations are findings of fact by a federal judge in a fully and fairly contested litigation as well as by the Congress in impeachment proceedings," the Foundation's response said.

Describing Clinton's filing as a document in which "President Clinton spends the bulk of his 80-page brief attempting to show that his testimony was not 'false' as he defines that term," the Foundation said that the American Bar Association rules for professional conduct "proscribe misleading conduct" as the standard and do not even use the words "false testimony."

"While it is true, as the president asserts in his response, that 'charges of false testimony under oath with possibly penal consequences are a serious matter,' the matter before this committee does not deal with perjury by litigants as that term is used in criminal law but rather misconduct within the applicable standards for lawyers," the group argued.

The Foundation response also cited the president's legal filings from the impeachment trial as evidence he has already admitted to misleading Congress.

"What the president did was wrong. . . . The simple moral truth [is] that his behavior in this matter was wrong. . . . He misled his wife, his friends, and our nation about the nature of his relationship with Ms. Lewinsky," the response said, quoting one of the president's impeachment filings.

In revealing to the American people how Clinton defends his conduct, Clinton's lawyer David Kendall said the Foundation is just picking on the president.

The Foundation sparked the Arkansas Supreme Court committee's investigation by filing a complaint in September 1998 demanding that the president be disbarred from practicing law for lying under oath and obstructing justice about his relationship with Monica Lewinsky during the Paula Jones suit.

Judge Susan Webber Wright charged the president with two counts of civil contempt and fined him $90,000 but left open the possibility that the president could face criminal charges filed by the independent counsel's office after he leaves office.

Kendall issued a statement criticizing the Foundation, saying it "isn't interested in issues relating to Arkansas lawyers and legal services, it's just interested in attacking the president in any way it can. . . . Releasing its papers to the public is just another part of the long-running partisan mudslinging campaign against the president."

Starr: FBI Believed Story of Clinton Rape

NewsMax.com Vortex, January 2000 — Former independent counsel Kenneth Starr says that FBI agents who interviewed Juanita Broaddrick believed she was telling the truth when she claimed President Clinton raped her 21 years ago.

"The investigators found her entirely credible," Starr told a gathering of reporters. Only Cox News Service's Julia Malone reported the former independent counsel's comments on the rape charge, breaking ranks with her Washington press corps colleagues, who ignored the development.

Starr did not personally meet with the Clinton accuser.

On Jan. 20, 1999, the 55-year-old Arkansas nursing home operator told NBC's Lisa Myers that Clinton had brutally raped her when he was the state's attorney general. But the network held Broaddrick's story for more than a month as the clock ran out on Clinton's impeachment trial.

Calling Broaddrick's story "sobering to the point of devastating," Starr's remarks bolster arguments of critics who say that NBC deliberately sat on its exclusive report to save the Clinton presidency. Network spokespersons had insisted that the delay was necessary because NBC needed more time to check out Broaddrick's account. But six days after she sat for an eight-hour interview with Myers, Broaddrick told NewsMax.com that the NBC star reporter had just informed her: "The good news is, you're credible. The bad news is, you're very, very credible."

Three weeks later, the alleged Clinton rape victim gave the *Wall Street Journal* an identical account of Myers' comment. NBC finally ran its Broaddrick exclusive on Feb. 24, 1999.

Starr's positive assessment of Broaddrick's credibility blatantly contradicts reports that appeared in the *Washington Post* and the *New York Daily News* in December 1998, when House impeachment managers were weighing whether to call Broaddrick as a trial witness. Both newspapers printed erroneous assertions that Broaddrick's FBI interrogators found her account "inconclusive."

Sources close to the investigation have confirmed to NewsMax.com that it was Broaddrick's account, and not Clinton's attempted cover-up of consensual sex in the Oval Office, that convinced up to 40 wavering House members to impeach the president.

Transcripts of Broaddrick's FBI interview, her tape-recorded comments to Paula Jones investigators Rick and Beverly Lambert and evidence of other similar misconduct by Clinton remain under seal in Washington, D.C.'s Gerald Ford Building.

In August 1999, House Republican Bob Barr, an impeachment trial manager, told NewsMax.com that the House Judiciary Committee had no plans to make that evidence public.

Juanita Broaddrick Sues White House for Using Files to Smear Her Reputation

NewsMax.com Vortex, January 2000 — An Arkansas woman who says that President Clinton brutally raped her while he was the state's attorney general has filed suit against the White House.

Juanita Broaddrick's suit accuses the president and Attorney General Janet Reno's Justice Department of seeking to "smear and destroy her reputation" by keeping a file on her in violation of federal privacy laws.

In her lawsuit, she is asking that a court order force the White House and Justice Department to produce all records involving her and to cease "unlawfully disseminating information" from her FBI files and any others maintained by the government.

In an exclusive interview with NewsMax.com, Broaddrick said that she decided to take legal action after watching former Clinton scandal spokesperson Lanny Davis on FoxNews Channel on December 16, 1999.

Based on several of Davis' statements during his appearance on *Hannity & Colmes*, the Clinton accuser believes the administration may have illegally obtained her FBI file.

"I just want my FBI file," she told NewsMax.com. "You know, the White House has refused to turn it over, and I want to know what's in it. I want to know what information they have on me."

The suit was filed on her behalf in federal court December 20 by Judicial Watch. The Washington-based legal watchdog group has pledged to hold President Clinton accountable for what chairman Larry Klayman says are gross violations of law.

Judicial Watch currently has more than 40 legal actions pending against the Clinton administration, including a $90 million class action suit on behalf of the victims of Filegate.

Broaddrick first asked the administration for her FBI file months ago.

"They've just refused to turn anything over," she told NewsMax.com.

Following up after the NewsMax.com interview with Broaddrick, CNN Cable News Channel reported that Klayman said, "We want to find out what information they have on her in violation of the Privacy Act and how she's been damaged by that information.

"We know based on the Filegate lawsuit that the White House keeps files of perceived adversaries and critics."

Klayman was referring to an earlier disclosure that the White House once improperly possessed some 700 FBI background files, including those on numerous prominent Republicans.

Broaddrick's lawsuit contends that after she wrote to the White House on October 12, requesting the documents related to her, Associate White House Counsel Meredith E. Cabe replied that federal disclosure laws "apply only to records maintained by 'agencies' within the Executive Branch.

"The president's immediate personal staff and units in the Executive Office of the President whose sole function is to advise and assist the president are not included with the term 'agency' under the FOIA and Privacy Act."

Thus, Cabe concluded, Broaddrick does not have a statutory right to the files, "if such records exist."

The Clinton administration has agreed in the past it is subject to federal laws, Klayman said, and a recent ruling by U.S. District Judge Royce C. Lamberth in the FBI files matter supports Broaddrick's position.

Broaddrick told NewsMax.com it was Davis' claim that she lied to the FBI about the Clinton rape allegation that hardened her suspicions the White House may be using her FBI file against her.

"When Lanny Davis alluded to some information that he was privy to, it just made me feel like, well, there's something he's seen," Broaddrick said.

"He kept referring to my lying to the FBI. I never lied to the FBI."

Broaddrick admitted she was less than candid with laywers for Paula Jones, who subpoenaed her in 1998 as part of Jones' own lawsuit against Clinton, because, she said, "I didn't want to get dragged into it." But the Clinton accuser said she was interviewed just once by the FBI and was completely honest during that interrogation.

"When the FBI and [independent counsel Kenneth] Starr got involved, I told the absolute truth," Broaddrick emphasized to NewsMax.com.

In a Washington press conference earlier in December, Starr revealed that FBI agents who grilled Broaddrick found her "entirely credible."

Broaddrick's legal action is sure to pose a problem for network news editors, most of whom have ignored the Broaddrick story, as well as the Clinton White House.

The president himself has never directly refuted Broaddrick's charge, but instead had David Kendall, his lawyer, make a denial in his name.

Now that the most damaging allegation yet leveled against Clinton is attached to a court filing, he could be forced to address the charge through a subpoena.

Broaddrick told NewsMax.com that she still hadn't decided whether to respond to Vice President Al Gore's characterization of Clinton's alleged sexual assault as a "personal mistake."

Did the Senate Duck Phone-Sex Blackmail?

NewsMax.com Vortex, April 1999 — Less than three weeks after Sen. Trent Lott and his timid crew made a mad dash for the impeachment exits, the *New York Post* reports a charge which, if accurate, suggests that Monicagate was, after all, about crimes that threatened U.S. national security. That's the kind of allegation for which even President Clinton's defenders said they would consider giving him the boot.

In his upcoming book *Gideon's Spies*, Gordon Thomas claims that the Israeli spy agency Mossad secretly taped 30 hours of Clinton-Lewinsky phone sex, then blackmailed the president to shut down an FBI investigation into a Mossad mole, dubbed MEGA, installed inside the White House. If true, Clinton's termination of a duly authorized FBI investigation to cover up his own wrongdoing would mirror Nixon's smoking gun order to torpedo the FBI's probe into Watergate. Only this time, what was being covered up was a good deal more serious than a third-rate burglary.

More troubling still, just before they shut down Clinton's trial, GOP senators had clues that pointed toward MEGA-gate. Author Thomas says that FBI counterintelligence was also taping the White House hot-sex line. This part of his story appears to be corroborated by earlier reports. Here's what the *Wall Street Journal* revealed on its editorial page on February 12, the day the Clinton trial closed: " . . . U.S. intelligence agencies taped White House phone calls central to the Lewinsky investigation, and the Senate has passed the tip from bureaucratic insiders along to independent counsel Kenneth Starr."

Sen. John Kyl, according to the *Arizona Republic* a day earlier, "compared the allegations of the tapes' existence to the 'smoking gun' evidence in the Watergate scandal." On February 10, *Newsday* covered the tape tip, reporting that impeachment trial boss Trent Lott nixed any further investigation, indicating "he had no interest in having the Senate delay the trial to pursue the matter."

If the allegations in the Thomas book are true, Lott may have lots to answer for. And Clinton? He may go from being the second impeached president to the first president impeached a second time.

Flowers Stands By Clinton Coke, Sex Charges on National TV

NewsMax.com Vortex, September 1999 — During a national TV broadcast, Gennifer Flowers refused to back away from her explosive new charges that President Clinton once offered her cocaine and had also revealed secrets about his wife's sex life.

Flowers even added more fuel to the fire, dangling the possibility that a fresh sex scandal may hit the White House before the Clintons leave Washington. Also, the one-time Clinton lover could provide some context to new White House-inspired rumors about George W. Bush and what is now being described as "the abortion question."

While the mainstream press whipped itself into a feeding frenzy over completely unsubstantiated, unsourced rumors that Bush may have used cocaine, Flowers told Fox News Channel's Sean Hannity and Alan Colmes that Clinton made no attempt to hide his drug use from her.

HANNITY: When you were around the president, did he ever use drugs?

FLOWERS: Yes, he did. He smoked marijuana around me.

HANNITY: As the governor, though?

FLOWERS: Well, he was the attorney general [of Arkansas]. And then as governor.

HANNITY: In front of you?

FLOWERS: In front of me, yes.

HANNITY: Any other drugs?

FLOWERS: He made it very clear that if I ever wanted to do cocaine that he could provide that. And he also told me that there were times that he did so much cocaine at parties that his head would itch. And that he would be standing there trying to talk to people and he would feel like a fool because all he wanted to do was this [imitates Clinton scratching his head]. So I clearly knew that Bill did cocaine.

HANNITY: This is the chief law enforcement officer . . .

FLOWERS: Yeah, I'd like to know why some of the reporters are so concerned with George W., while they don't ask Bill that question.

Dallas Morning News reports that Bush now flatly denies he ever used cocaine during the last seven years, the time period covered by a standard FBI background check. That means any theoretical drug use by Bush took place while he was a private citizen, since the Texas governor didn't enter public service until 1994.

Clinton, on the other hand, used drugs while he held the two top law enforcement jobs in his state, according to Flowers and a number of other witnesses.

Flowers also stood by charges that Clinton had discussed with her his wife's sexual proclivities, a claim she made to Clinton scandal expert Larry Nichols during an appearance on his radio show.

HANNITY: [Hillary] is now running, it appears, to be senator from the state of New York. Let me ask you, what would you want the people of New York to know about her? . . . Any shockers?

FLOWERS: You need to go down to Arkansas. I mean, there have been some things going on down there that would shock a lot of people.

COLMES: Did Bill confide anything to you about Hillary that you think the public should know?

FLOWERS: Let me see if I can figure out what you're really asking here. No, what Bill told me about Hillary he never planned for the public to know. Clearly he knew that she was bisexual. That didn't matter to him.

COLMES: Clearly he knew that?

FLOWERS: He knew that. He told me that. That's been knowledge in Arkansas for a number of years. I'm very surprised that that hasn't come to light in a more definite manner.

In her 1995 book, *Passion and Betrayal*, Flowers notes that Bill Clinton once told her Hillary has had oral sex with more women than he has.

Flowers also alluded to a new sex charge that could hit the White House before Clinton's term is up.

FLOWERS: I have some information about a couple of people that [Clinton] has had some involvement with . . .

HANNITY: Stories that may be breaking?

FLOWERS: That might come forward.

HANNITY: Because we hear these rumors all the time in the media but we haven't heard any confirmation. Have you spoken to any woman that's saying that, that may go public?

FLOWERS: I have not personally spoken to her.

HANNITY: But somebody you know has?

FLOWERS: Yes, someone who has spoken to somebody.

And what about the mainstream press's latest wild goose chase? The *New York Observer*'s Joe Conason told an MSNBC audience, "A question should be asked about George Bush and these candidates: 'Have you ever caused an abortion to happen?' "

Matt Drudge reports, "Conason has been talking to White House friends who have been telling tabloid reporters who — surprise — have already been put on the 'abortion hunt' by their editors."

Have these editors lost their journalistic marbles? Or is *Inside Cover* the only press outlet that remembers Gennifer Flowers' account, long ignored by Conason and the rest, of how Bill Clinton paid her $200 cash to abort his baby.

NOW Chief: Broaddrick a Waste of Time

NewsMax.com Vortex, April 1999 — Numero uno feminist Patricia Ireland is irked at Cynthia Alksne, the cable TV legal-beagle who spent months defending Bill Clinton on Monicagate charges. Why? Apparently because Alksne is one of the few high-profile feminists to break ranks over Juanita Broaddrick's allegation that Clinton had raped her.

In a March 5 *Wall Street Journal* op-ed piece entitled "Clinton Insults All Rape Victims," Alksne explained that, in her own experience as a sex crimes prosecutor, men have been sent to the jug based solely on credible victim accounts like Broaddrick's, which, she added, certainly deserved more than Clinton's pass-the-buck response: See my lawyer.

Back when Broaddrick's charges were front-page news, Ireland had at least given sympathetic lip service to her ordeal. But now that the coast is clear, those days are over. Now Ireland writes, "If [Alksne] or others care about women's rights, they should stop wasting time on unprovable charges and start working to improve the lives of women."

Ireland did not explain why she and her cohorts wasted so much of their own time touting unprovable charges against Clarence Thomas and Bob Packwood.

Clinton Harassment Continued After 'Rape'

NewsMax.com Vortex, April 1999 — Bill Clinton personally tried to contact Juanita Broaddrick within a year of an April 25, 1978, encounter where, she says, he brutally raped her at Little Rock's Camelot Motel. The stunning revelation was offered by Broaddrick herself in a message she asked to have posted on the Free Republic (www.freerepublic.com) Web site.

"Freepers" have been following her case closely ever since NBC refused to air an exclusive interview with the alleged Clinton rape victim in January. Broaddrick had previously acknowledged only two instances where she and Clinton had personal contact: the month of her alleged rape and again in 1991, when she was summoned out of a meeting to hear Clinton's apology.

In her latest communique, she mentions a third contact from Clinton: ". . . once on the telephone in '78 or '79 when I told him to stop calling me." Broaddrick did not indicate how many times Clinton tried to contact her before she demanded that he "stop calling me."

Broaddrick wrote Daniel Stidham, founder of the Web site "Boycott NBC!" to deny that she was the "Juanita" alluded to in taped conversations between Monica Lewinsky and Linda Tripp. The two women had referenced a two-hour-plus conversation between Clinton and a "Juanita," whom many presumed to be Juanita Broaddrick. "Please be assured that the 158-minute [phone call with] Juanita is not me and that I have nothing to hide regarding Starr, Clinton or anyone," Broaddrick explained to Stidham, who posted her message to Free Republic.

Broaddrick's son Kevin Hickey denied that Broaddrick was the "Juanita" in question. Linda Tripp, who knows the identity of the mystery "Juanita," backed Hickey's denial on ABC's *This Week with Sam and Cokie.*

A White House Juanita?

NewsMax.com Vortex, March 1999 — As America digests Juanita Broaddrick's televised accusation that its president is a rapist, Lucianne Goldberg appears ready to move on — to the next Jane Doe.

In an interview with Canada's *National Post*, Goldberg hinted that not all allegations of forcible sexual assault by Bill Clinton are 20 years old.

Here's how the *National Post* covered Goldberg's revelation:

Lucianne explains, for instance, that she is unsurprised by the failure of the latest "cold bastard" allegations of "rape" against Clinton involving Jane Doe 5. So far, this charge has failed to get much beyond the *Drudge Report*, the tabloid *New York Post* and the *Wall Street Journal*. That is why she is now promising yet another tale, a Jane Doe 6.

"It's assault, not rape, because there was no sexual entry," she says. "It occurred since he became president, and comes from someone who cannot be faulted."

Bill's Biting Ways

NewsMax.com Vortex, March 1999 — One of the more shocking aspects of Juanita Broaddrick's rape allegation against President Clinton is the way she says he forced her to submit.

After pushing her down on a hotel-room bed, Broaddrick says Clinton bit her lips until they bled. Broaddrick's nurse-friend Norma Rogers told Paula Jones' investigators Rick and Beverly Lambert, who were recently interviewed for an upcoming NewsMax.com report, that the wounds were so bad that one lip was nearly torn in two.

What accounts for such rabid brutality?

According to a former rape investigator with the New Orleans Police Department, who contacted NewsMax.com confidentially, lip biting is a common M.O. for rapists. She told *Inside Cover:*

"The reason rapists bite is because, even with the full weight of her attacker on top of her, the woman is often able to resist the parting of her legs by locking her ankles. The rapist's arms are busy keeping her pinned down. The only weapon the rapist has left is his teeth, which he uses to bite while demanding she open her legs.

The lips are very sensitive. Biting them is so painful it distracts thae victim, allowing a rapist to overcome her resistance. The victim can only hold out for so long as the blood flows into her mouth. Some women are stronger than others and I've seen their lips half-torn from their faces before they give up.'"

White House Spin on Juanita

NewsMax.com Vortex, March 1999 — Alan Dershowitz was on the *Today* show calling the Broaddrick allegations nothing more than "gossip" that didn't fit journalistic "standards" for publication.

Oh, really!

What does Dershowitz know about journalistic standards? What paper has he ever reported for?

The Broaddrick allegations are serious and credible. They come from an upstanding member of the community, a business owner and former Clinton supporter.

Gossip — an unfounded rumor — is not what we have here, despite Dershowitz's claims.

Was it just gossip that led to the judicial inquisition of Clarence Thomas when a young woman, Anita Hill, came forward to make a number of allegations against her former friend and superior?

Where was Dershowitz then? Citing journalistic ethics and standards? Hardly.

Hill, like Broaddrick, came forward years after the alleged incidents. Like Hill, Broaddrick had friendly contact with the man she accused after the incident.

Unlike Hill, Broaddrick has much more contemporaneous corroboration, including the statement of a medical nurse.

And unlike Hill, Broaddrick's allegations have nothing to do with sexual harassment. Broaddrick is alleging the president committed a capital crime, rape, against her.

Yet the press was ever so eager to report the Hill story. More than that, Hill was molded into a national heroine as the press relentlessly advocated her case for years.

Where was Dershowitz when the Hill case broke? On national television lashing out at gossip?

Clinton Rape Victim Watch

NewsMax.com Vortex, April 1999 — A highly placed source who served with the now-defunct House impeachment investigation tells *Inside Cover* that congressional probers had uncovered other Juanita Broaddrick-like allegations against President Clinton.

"We had information that there were other rapes," said the tipster, speaking only on background information. "But we didn't get to investigate them in any fine detail. I can't honestly say that we had developed evidence of other rapes. But we had indications."

Were those "indications" gleaned from the files of Paula Jones investigators Rick and Beverly Lambert, which were turned over to Ken Starr and then forwarded to House probers? "No," our source replied. "I'm talking about independent stuff that we were picking up."

Inside Cover then mentioned the name of one woman whom the Lamberts said had been raped by Clinton at a cocaine party when she was just 14 years old, according to an intermediary who revealed her account to them.

"[Woman's name]? Now, where did I hear that name before?" Without elaborating, our source said of the allegation about the 14-year-old, "I'll tell you, it fits."

Rick Lambert traced the woman, now in her late 20s, to California but was unable to locate her before the Paula Jones case was dismissed.

Inside Cover was given the name of a former Clinton intimate who may have additional information. "She knows where the bodies are buried," our source said. "It's just that nobody has ever asked her about this before." Stay tuned.

Dick Morris: More Rapegate Victims to Come

NewsMax.com Vortex, March 1999 — As he was finishing up his stint with Fox News Channel's *Hannity & Colmes* Feb. 25, longtime Clinton confidant Dick Morris wanted to address a question that hadn't come up during that evening's debate on the Juanita Broaddrick case.

Out of the blue, Morris interjected: "[Juanita Broaddrick] is Jane Doe No. 5. They ought to do this in Roman numerals, because there will be a six, a seven, an eight, a nine. When you do this, you just don't do it once."

Morris has known and worked closely with the president since 1977, the year before Broaddrick says she was attacked. The pollster-turned-pundit said that the Clinton he knows would not be capable of rape.

But, Morris added, the Clinton *he* knows would not have been capable of the assaults alleged by Paula Jones and Kathleen Willey, whom Morris now says he believes.

Last September, Morris responded to reports of Juanita Broaddrick's alleged attack with a curious denial: "It was date rape if it was anything. [Clinton] didn't jump out of the bushes with a knife."

David Kendall, call your office.

Senator Who Says Rapegate 'A Private Matter' Stung by Grassroots Journalism

NewsMax.com Vortex, March 1999 — Vermont's Jim Jeffords, the first Republican senator to announce he would vote to acquit President Clinton on impeachment charges, finally weighed in on Rapegate a full week after the story broke — calling it "a private matter."

Appearing on the Mark Johnson radio show, heard on WKDR Burlington, Jeffords was asked if he believed Juanita Broaddrick's charge that Clinton had raped her two decades ago.

Jeffords immediately veered off course into some pretty deep water. The exchange went like this: [excerpt]

JEFFORDS: . . . I think things like that are supposedly a private affair that should stay that way unless they get into the public domain by the abuse of the use of the office of the president, as he did in carrying on in the White House. . . . but other than that, I'm not interested in what people did 21 years ago.

JOHNSON: How would that be a private matter?

JEFFORDS: Well, I don't know why it wouldn't be a private matter. I can ask you [to look at this] the other way around. If something had happened 21 years ago with a woman who invited, at least under her story, the president up to her hotel room and she was not happy with what happened, I don't know why that's not a private matter.

JOHNSON: OK. Rape usually isn't done in public.

JEFFORDS: Well, no — she claims she was raped. Whether she was or not, then why did she wait that long and all that? I'm not going to make judgment on the veracity of those things. And I think we could all spend the whole day trying to figure that one out. But if you wait 21 years or whatever to reveal something, you have to question what her reasons are. [end of excerpt]

Jeffords must have wondered how his gaffe on Rapegate traveled from a small-market Burlington radio station to New York's 50,000-watt blowtorch, WABC — only to wind up in the *Washington Post* the next day.

It's simple — citizen journalism.

NewsMax.com reader Margaret Booth had taped Jeffords' remarks and the recording was copied by NewsMax.com's *Inside Cover* two hours later.

Inside Cover shared the recording with WABC's afternoon drivetime host Sean Hannity, who had his producer, Eric Stanger, copy the tape from the listener's original before airtime.

Hannity opened his show saying, "We're going to make a little news here today," then played the Vermont senator's own words for his audience. The talk host revisited Jeffords' "private matter" characterization of the presidential rape charge throughout the show, prompting a call from Jeffords' press office.

Stanger took the call and later told Hannity's audience that Jeffords' press office complained that WABC misinterpreted the quote — only to back down when informed it was on tape. Hannity then aired Jeffords' written apology, which withdrew his earlier remarks. "Rape is wrong," read the Jeffords correction, "no matter when, where or how it takes place."

That night, the Associated Press picked up Jeffords' retraction, covering his earlier gaffe in its report. The next day, the *Washington Post* carried the AP story.

And that's how one citizen armed with a tape recorder alerted a nation to the first substantive congressional response to Juanita Broaddrick's presidential rape charge.

For the GOP, the Jeffords imbroglio demonstrated the perils of trying to minimize the most serious allegation ever to face a sitting president.

'Titans of 'Tude'
Meet in TV Rapegate Roundtable

NewsMax.com Vortex, March 1999 — Cyber-sleuth Matt Drudge and NewsMax.com executive editor Christopher Ruddy debated Juanita Broaddrick's presidential rape allegations February 27, on Drudge's own Fox News Channel television show. It was the first time the two had appeared together publicly since *Newsweek* dubbed them "Titans of 'Tude," along with a handful of other "Stars of the New News."

Drudge and NewsMax.com had led the way on the explosive Broaddrick story months before it hit the mainstream press — a fact acknowledged by a recent *Wall Street Journal* editorial crediting the role played by "Internet start-ups" in bringing the scandal to light.

The "Drudge" discussion focused on parallel reports authored by Ruddy and Drudge revealing the "civil war" that raged at both ABC and NBC News over whether to report Broaddrick's allegations.

Drudge first revealed that NBC's Lisa Myers had an on-camera interview with Broaddrick just days after her January 20 interview, raising questions about the network's news judgment as it sat on the story for weeks.

A month earlier, Ruddy had reported that an internal ABC News memo updating Broaddrick's allegation was circulating through that network's news division. The memo argued, "the potential that a rape charge could be leveled at the president makes the story one that can't be totally ignored."

Drudge revealed on air that night that reporters are now in hot pursuit of another Jane Doe with a story similar to Broaddrick's. *Inside Cover* can confirm that the search is on, and we were pumped for information by a major network on other assault charges against Clinton.

The segment closed with the cyber-scribe noting that Ruddy "early on, detected [independent counsel Ken] Starr probably didn't have the guts to go all the way with indictments of everybody."

The comment prompted a stunning prediction from the NewsMax chief:

"If we depended on Starr, hell would freeze over before anything happened with Bill Clinton. But I do think, now that this allegation has come forward on Broaddrick, that Clinton will not finish out his term. . . . You cannot have a sitting president with a rape allegation hanging over his head."

Poll Rigged Against Juanita?

NewsMax.com Vortex, March 1999 — A *USA Today*/CNN/Gallup poll showing that 54 percent of Americans surveyed do not believe Juanita Broaddrick's claim that Bill Clinton raped her heavily loaded its sample with people who were hearing the charge for the first time. The survey was taken a week after the allegations surfaced and was reported in *USA Today*.

The poll, receiving wide attention as media spinmeisters sought excuses to drop the story, reported that 44 percent of those surveyed had not even watched Broaddrick's gripping account aired on *Dateline NBC* February 24, and in fact had never even heard of the Clinton rape allegation before.

For those unfamiliar with Broaddrick's account, the only basis to judge her credibility came from these questions:

"A woman in Arkansas named Juanita Broaddrick has recently stated that Clinton raped her in 1978. Clinton has denied the allegation. Have you heard about this allegation? Do you think that Broaddrick's allegation is true?"

Of those surveyed, including those previously in the dark about Broaddrick's story, only 34 percent said it was "probably or definitely true." But among those who had heard of the allegation, the verdict was split, with 44 percent finding Broaddrick believable and 48 percent doubting her.

The Gallup poll made no distinction between those who had merely heard of Broaddrick's charge and those who actually watched her first-hand account on *Dateline*. A spokesman for *USA Today* could not say what percentage of those familiar with her story had seen her *Dateline* interview.

An unscientific survey conducted on MSNBC immediately after the NBC broadcast found that 83 percent of those who watched Broaddrick believed her.

Just days before, the *New York Post* had reported that a Fox News Dynamics poll yielded nearly the exact opposite result of the Gallup survey, with those polled believing Broaddrick by a margin of more than 2 to 1 (54 percent to 23 percent). The numbers suggest that those questioned had seen Broaddrick on *Dateline*, though no one at the *Post* was available to confirm that.

Clinton Administration to 'Combat Violence Against Women'

NewsMax.com Vortex, March 1999 — Just days after Juanita Broaddrick charged on national television that Bill Clinton brutally raped her 21 years ago, Vice President Al Gore announced a new White House initiative to combat violence against women.

One particularly poignant passage of Gore's speech went like this:

"What the true experts in this field have taught all of us is that these crimes trigger the beginning of patterns that cascade down through many generations. How tragic and ironic it is to realize that so many of the perpetrators of abuse were themselves victims of abuse or close witnesses to abuse of their mothers, often when they were children."

Rewind to 1995, when author David Maraniss described the physical abuse Clinton's stepfather heaped upon Clinton's mother, Virginia, often in young Clinton's presence, in his best-selling Clinton biography, *First in His Class:*

"In seeking to end the marriage [between herself and Clinton's stepfather Roger], Virginia testified in April 1962 that Roger's drinking, a problem since the start of their marriage, had worsened in recent years. She said there had been two violent eruptions three years earlier when he became drunk and kicked her and struck her, then at home, on March 27, 1959, when 'he threw me to the floor and began to stomp me, pulled my shoe off and hit me on the head several times.' "

"In Bill [Clinton's] affidavit, he recounted more fights. 'On one occasion last month I had to call my mother's attorney because of the defendant's conduct causing physical abuse to my mother, and the police again had to be summoned to the house. . . . The last occasion in which I went to my mother's aid when he was abusing my mother, he threatened to mash my face in if I took her part.' "

In an eerie echo of the generational scenario outlined by the vice president, the young witness to domestic violence became sexually violent himself, according to Juanita Broaddrick:

"Then he tries to kiss me again. And the second time he tries to kiss me he starts biting on my lip. He starts to bite on my top lip. I tried to pull away from him. Then he forces me down on the bed. And I just was very frightened. I tried to get away from him and I told him no, but he wouldn't listen to me. . . . I told him, please don't.

"He was such a different person at that moment. He was just a vicious, awful person. . . . It was a real panicky, panicky situation, and I was even to the point where I was getting very noisy, yelling to please stop. And that's when he would press down on my right shoulder and bite on my lip. "

ABC Memo Details Clinton Rape Charges

By Christopher Ruddy

NewsMax.com Vortex, January 1999 — A civil war is brewing in the newsroom of ABC's *World News Tonight* over allegations that in 1979 Bill Clinton may have raped Juanita Broaddrick, an Arkansas woman, when he served as the state's Attorney general.

NewsMax.com has obtained an internal ABC News memo that was e-mailed to the top news producers earlier today about the controversy.

Chris Isham, a top ABC News producer, distributed the memo, which lays out out the scintillating facts surrounding the alleged incident and the interest sparked in the subject by Republican congressmen who were permitted to review the Starr documentation of the case.

Independent counsel Kenneth Starr had turned over additional documents and FBI statements with new details about the president's sexual activities. The ABC memo reports that about two dozen Republicans reviewed the new material the Thursday and Friday before the historic impeachment vote. Some may have been swayed to vote for impeachment based on the material.

The memo states that Arizona Republican congressman J.D. Hayworth told ABC News — off the record — that the material makes Clinton out to be "a sexual predator."

The Broaddrick incident may be cited in a Senate trial of the president, Isham suggests.

NewsMax.com has learned that Isham's memo comes as a result of a feud between *World News Tonight* Executive Producer Paul Freidman and network anchor Peter Jennings. Jennings — reputed to have an eye for the ladies much like the president's — has vehemently objected to ABC News reporting on the subject.

The memo, in an apparent shot at Jennings, states, " . . . the potential that a rape charge could be leveled at the president makes the story one that can't be totally ignored."

Verbatim ABC News memo follows:

From: Isham, Chris
Sent: Tuesday, December 22, 1998 12:45 PM
To: Friedman, Paul E.;
          Dunlavey, Dennis;
          Murphy, Bob
Subject: Broaddrick
Forwarding a memo by Josh Fine which is a good summary of the Juanita Broaddrick (Jane Doe No. 5.) Her case MAY have tipped some moderate Republicans to vote yes on impeachment and MAY be introduced in the Senate proceedings.

Juanita Broaddrick was subpoenaed in the Paula Jones case. She filed an affidavit that said "These allegations (that Clinton had made unwelcome advances towards her) are untrue." The allegations are that she met Clinton in 1979 when he was attorney general and that he raped or assaulted her. She owned nursing homes in Northwest Arkansas and was in Little Rock for a convention. Clinton met her in the afternoon and they made plans to meet later that night. He said the best place to meet was in her room (at the Camelot Hotel) since that way no one would see them (he was, after all, married).

They then went up to her hotel room in Little Rock and evidently had sex. It is unclear if he raped or assaulted her but that is the allegation made by Phillip Yoakum. Yoakum is a Fayetteville man who says Broaddrick told him in 1992 that she was raped by Clinton in the late 70's. I interviewed Yoakum in March and found him entirely uncredible. He had facts wrong, was a total Clinton-hater, and his claims to being friends with Broaddrick are untrue. The other person who supposedly knows about what took place is Norma Rogers-Kelsay, a friend of Broaddrick's who went to the convention with her in Little Rock and drove back with her to Van Buren where they live). Tamara Lipper spoke with Rogers on the phone in March. Rogers said that Yoakum was telling the truth. She was with Broaddrick before and after the incident and said that she was in "quite bad shape after."

In 1991 Broaddrick was at a nursing home convention in Little Rock and a man pulled her out of a meeting (this is all according to Rogers-Kelsay). The man took her to Bill Clinton and he apologized for hurting her and asked if there was anything he could do. She didn't understand at the time why he had taken that step but soon realized the real reason after he announced his candidacy for President a few months later. In the 1992 campaign these rumors began to circulate and Sheffield Nelson, a longtime Arkansas Clinton-hater, tried to get her to come forward. She did not. Yoakum evidently was at a meeting with Rogers and Broaddrick where they discussed the incident and whether or not Broaddrick should talk publicly about it. Evidently Broaddrick was worried no one would believe her (similar to what happened with Gennifer Flowers).

That was the last anyone heard of her until she was subpoenaed in the Jones case. Apparently Lisa Myers went to Van Buren and spoke with Broaddrick about her giving an interview. I also spoke with Broaddrick. She made it abundantly clear that she had no interest in her name getting out and didn't want to talk about it. She also made it clear that she was not denying that something had happened.

Last month the Schippers group sent two investigators to talk to her. One of them was Diana Woznicki, a Chicago police sergeant who is on loan to the investigation. We're not sure who the second person was. The conversation took place at the office of Broaddrick's attorney, Bill Walters, in Greenwood, AR. Walters says that the ground rules for the interview was that there would be no discussion of the underlying incident. The only topic that could be discussed was the possibility of obstruction. According to Walters, there is no obstruction despite the claims in the Yoakum letter. The Yoakum letter claims that Broaddrick's husband Dave said he was going to get a few favors from Clinton for keeping his wife silent.

Late last week Republicans began to stream over to the Ford building to look at the materials. According to a source of mine there were about two dozen members who went to look at the material on Thursday and Friday. Many Republicans were talking up the new material as evidence that could come up at trial because it would show a pattern and practice of behavior (paying off or influencing women to keep quiet). According to Rep. Inglis under federal rule of evidence 441(B) something showing a pattern or practice can be admissible in a trial. But it is unclear if Rehnquist would rule this admissible since it isn't a typical trial.

There is some question whether there is actually new evidence from the Woznicki interview or members are just seeing the Yoakum/Rogers evidence for the first time and consider it new. The big question is what does Broaddrick say. If she won't talk about the incident then there is only Yoakum and Rogers to show that she was raped/assaulted. If she won't say she was obstructed it would be hard to prove that. Still, the potential that a rape charge could be leveled at the President makes the story one that can't be totally ignored.

I'm told by two senior Republican members of Congress that Stephen Buyer (IN), Jim Ramstad (MN), and Steve Chabot (OH) were encouraging their colleagues to look at the materials. I'm also told George Radanovich (CA) took a special interest in the Broaddrick interview. Rep. Hayworth told me on background that the materials make Clinton out to be a "sexual predator."

There were rumblings from some Democrats (none of whom have seen the materials) that there was pressure put on undecided Republicans to vote for an article of impeachment based on the new materials. But two of the members rumored to be swayed, John Porter of Illinois and Jay Dickey of Arkansas told Ariane and I that they never went to view the materials.

Call me if any of this isn't clear. I've put down some links to a couple helpful documents:

Broaddrick's affidavit

Yoakum's Letter

[End of Isham Memo]

Phone Sex

NewsMax.com Vortex, November 1998 — Monica said that on the night Admiral Boorda died Clinton called her. He rebuffed Monica's request for phone sex. On the day of Boorda's funeral Clinton called Lewinsky and they did have phone sex. Typically, Monica remembers, Clinton called when Hillary was out of town. On one occasion Clinton called her at 6:30 a.m. for phone sex. Monica's FBI statement reads: "Clinton exclaimed 'good morning!' . . . after having orgasm."

Unzipped

NewsMax.com Vortex, November 1998 — Monica said in one deposition that her oral sex encounters were quickies. Clinton simply unzipped his pants and did not disrobe. She said on one occasion, as she performed oral sex in a hallway, someone came into the Oval Office and Clinton "zipped up really quickly and went out and came back in. . . ." She added, "I just remember laughing because he had walked out there and he was visibly aroused, and I just thought it was funny . . . It wouldn't necessarily be noticeable . . . but it was just funny to me."

These Footnotes Are Unbelievable

NewsMax.com Vortex, November 1998 — Chris Matthews, the always-on-the-edge host of CNBC's *Hardball*, told his viewers to read the footnotes of the Starr report.

We did just that.

If you thought the Starr report was lurid. . . .

Part 1, Footnote 443: Lewinsky claims she didn't save the semen-stained dress as a souvenir. In fact, she wasn't really sure Clinton's semen was on it. She explained that she thought the stain "could be spinach dip or something."

Part 1, Footnote 837: Lewinsky defined her "phone sex" with Clinton this way: "He's taking care of business on one end, and I'm taking care of business on another."

Part 2, Footnotes 25 and 31: Lewinsky observes Clinton masturbating, including one time in aide Nancy Hernreich's office.

Part 2, Footnotes 28 and 35: Lewinsky alleges Clinton engaged in oral-anal contact with her.

No Denial in Clinton Sex Assault Charge

NewsMax.com Vortex, November 1998 — The allegations may have appeared in a supermarket tabloid, but they certainly deserved some due diligence.

Recently, *Star* magazine reported that OUR president, William Jefferson Clinton, groped and verbally harassed a waitress at the exclusive Robert Trent Jones Golf Club near Washington, D.C. *Star* claimed this happened ONLY two months ago — when we thought our president was in sackcloth and ash making up for his singular lapse with Monica (oops, not to mention Kathleen Willey, Paula Jones, Gennifer Flowers, etc.).

The tabloid quoted anonymous sources, one of whom described how "[Clinton] seems to do it almost without even knowing he does it," and reported that the golf club did not return its phone calls asking for comment.

Club manager Rick Gorman told NewsMax, "I've been told by the board of the club not to comment on this issue — or any issue to do with members." Then the manager's statement got more interesting: "That's the idea of a private club; you can come through the gates and you've reached a safe area. . . . So as long as I'm employed at this club, I have no comment. . . . see me when I've left the club."

Call me when I've left the club!?!

Why is everyone afraid of telling the truth about our president? The alleged incident is especially signifigant because *Star* reports that Vernon Jordan, a member of the club under whose auspices the president was playing golf that day, was overheard asking for the home telephone number of the waitress, who was said to be visibly shaken by the president's advances.

As for Jordan, the world knows it was Jordan who helped Monica Lewinsky get a lawyer and a job interview. We also heard — from a source very close to Ron Brown — that Brown was aghast about just how close Clinton and Jordan were in sharing their girlfriends!

Clinton and Women: Up to Seven May Have Been Assaulted

By Carl Limbacher

NewsMax.com Vortex, November 1998 — The dark underside of the current sex scandal engulfing the Clinton administration has yet to receive much media attention.

White House spinmeisters complain that the president is being persecuted for an inappropriate — but nonetheless consensual — sexual relationship with a woman not his wife. But before the entire Paula Jones-Monica Lewinsky saga plays out, that perception could radically change.

That's because a review of accounts by numerous women linked to Clinton reveals no less than seven allegations of sexual abuse — and in several cases even rape.

Kathleen Willey's now-famous claim that Clinton groped her against her will the day she came to plead for a paying White House job was finessed by feminists who concocted the "he took no for an answer" defense. But that rationale crumbles in the face of new revelations buried in the documents released by Congress recently.

It turns out Willey's story is far more harrowing than the one she told *60 Minutes* last March — at least according to Linda Tripp, to whom Willey confided just moments after her close encounter of the Clinton kind.

As NewsMax.com reported exclusively, Tripp said Willey told her that Clinton's sexual approach "came out of nowhere and was forceful, almost to the point of an attack. . . . The president had his hands on her breasts and all over her body. The president put Willey's hand on his penis. . . .

"Willey said that the president was so out of control that his face was purple, and the veins were showing on his neck and forehead. The meeting ended when someone entered the adjacent office." (FBI Statement of Linda Tripp; House Document 105-316; Part 3; Page 3998)

That last line is key, since it reveals that Clinton's assault stopped only when discovery seemed likely — and not because Willey said "no." What might have happened if the president hadn't been interrupted? Perhaps what Juanita Broaddrick says happened to her some 20 years ago.

At the time, Broaddrick was a Clinton campaign worker. And according to a friend who says she confided in him, Clinton, who was then the Arkansas state attorney general, visited Broaddrick's room in Little Rock's Camelot Motel on the pretext of discussing business. Once there, he pounced.

That friend, Phillip Yoakum, reminded Broaddrick of her nightmare in a letter he wrote hoping to convince her to go public in 1992:

"I was particularly distraught when you told me of your brutal rape by Bill Clinton. . . [how] he started trying to kiss you and ran his hands all over your body until he ripped your clothes off, and how he bit your lip until you gave into his forcing sex upon you." (ABCNews.com, March 28, 1998)

Yoakum's version of Broaddrick's story is corroborated by a nurse who treated her after the assault. Norma Rogers told NBC News last March that Juanita Broaddrick was "distraught, her lips were swollen at least double in size. . . . She told me they had intercourse against her will."

Norma Rogers not only backs up Phillip Yoakum on the rape charge here, but her observation about Broaddrick's swollen lips seems to confirm Yoakum's report that Clinton bit Broaddrick's lip until she submitted to unwanted sex. That's a curious detail for two witnesses to simply make up.

Broaddrick herself first denied the rape story in an affidavit submitted to Paula Jones' lawyers, only to retract her denial when questioned under oath by independent counsel Ken Starr's investigators.

The House Judiciary Committee has thus far decided to keep all of Starr's material on Broaddrick under seal — including a reported audiotape recorded by Jones' investigators where Broaddrick discusses the impact her traumatic encounter with Clinton had on her life.

Biting figures in yet another allegation of sexual assault by Bill Clinton, this one from a Little Rock lawyer who told Clinton biographer Roger Morris about an attack she suffered the same year Clinton allegedly raped Broaddrick. In his best-selling book *Partners in power*, Morris reports:

"A young woman lawyer in Little Rock claimed that she was accosted by Clinton while he was attorney general and that when she recoiled he forced himself on her, biting and bruising her. Deeply affected by the assault, the woman decided to keep it all quiet for the sake of her own hard-won career and that of her husband. When the husband later saw Clinton at the 1980 Democratic convention, he delivered a warning. 'If you ever approach her,' he told the governor, 'I'll kill you.' Not even seeing fit to deny the incident, Bill Clinton sheepishly apologized and duly promised never to bother her again." (page 238)

This anonymous woman's story sounds similar enough to Juanita Broaddrick's that some believe they are one and the same. But Broaddrick wasn't a lawyer and she wasn't quite so young. At 35, she was actually three years older than Clinton at the time.

In a November 1997 interview about this explosive paragraph, author Morris told me that he had interviewed both the victim and her husband several times in late 1993 and early 1994. He refused to divulge their names but did say that the couple was more socially prominent than the Clintons were at the time of the attack, which was not true of Juanita Broaddrick and her husband.

Not every accusation of sexual abuse by Clinton is quite so frightening. Still, Christine Zercher's encounter with then-candidate Clinton was scary enough to her. In 1992, Zercher was a stewardess aboard Clinton's campaign plane, Longhorn One. By all accounts, a party atmosphere prevailed as Clinton continually flirted with the all-blonde flight attendant cadre.

A recently broadcast ABC News video showed Clinton snuggled next to Zercher's co-worker, Debra Schiff, as the two exchanged affectionate touches. Of course, when Mrs. Clinton was aboard, all such shenanigans were put on hold.

But while flight attendant Schiff may have been receptive to Clinton's advances, Zercher recounted an episode to *Star* magazine last March that left her paralyzed with fear.

For forty minutes late one airborne night, Zercher sat frozen after Clinton awoke, plunked himself down next to her, and casually began caressing her breasts — as Mrs. Clinton slept all the while just feet away.

For a time, it seemed that Elizabeth Ward Gracen, Miss America of 1982, might have suffered a fate similar to Juanita Broaddrick's, the woman whose rape allegation against Bill Clinton we have detailed here.

Gracen friend Judy Stokes told Paula Jones' lawyers that Gracen had recounted her experience with then–Governor Clinton in a way that suggested their one-time liaison may have been forced.

Stokes said her friend was in tears when she described Clinton's approach in the back seat of a limo and revealed that the sex they had was something Gracen "did not want to happen." On the run from a subpoena from Jones' attorneys, Gracen's silence only fueled the speculation.

Then finally, last April, Gracen came forward to the *New York Daily News* to acknowledge that she and Clinton did indeed have sex, something she denied when Clinton first ran for president. But, Gracen stressed, the sex was strictly consensual — though the encounter was something she said she regretted almost immediately afterward.

That should have cleared the matter up. But then the Clinton White House did something very unusual. Clinton spinmeisters did nothing to challenge Gracen's acknowledgment of a consensual liaison, as if the fact that yet another woman claiming to have sex with the president was almost a relief, as long as the rape allegation was off the table.

Recall, this was the same Bill Clinton who had his operatives trash Gennifer Flowers mercilessly for going public the way Gracen just had. He himself would not confess to a consensual relationship with Flowers till he was put under oath.

And Gracen's more recent accounts only complicate the story. She told the *Toronto Sun* in September that she believed White House investigators had kept her under surveillance and that even her family had been staked out. She said that at one point she even feared for her life and described the president as a very "dangerous and manipulative" man.

Then Gracen told the *New York Post* she felt compelled to hire her own private investigators to investigate the White House gumshoes who dogged her as she traveled from country to country. Once her hotel room was broken into in what she believes was an attempt to gather evidence of her relationship with the president before it fell into the hands of Jones' attorneys.

Gracen's ordeal begs the question: If the White House was so worried that she would finger Clinton in a consensual relationship, taking the extraordinary measure of surveiling her every move — then why the nonchalant reaction when Gracen finally did spill the beans?

Or did Casa Clinton have reason to worry that Gracen's account might have turned out to be more damaging than a story about a now-regretted one-night stand?

There's more. Even Paula Jones, whose lawsuit opened up Clinton's Pandora's boxer shorts, may have a legitimate complaint of assault.

Reporters have focused on her claim that Clinton exposed himself to her and merely asked for oral sex. But most Americans don't realize that Jones alleges she was subject to unwanted groping and momentary imprisonment as part of her ordeal.

In her amended complaint, Jones says that before Clinton coaxed her to "kiss it," he stroked her hair and complimented her on her "curves." She retreated to the couch, whereupon Clinton followed, says Jones, placed his hand on her thigh, and began sliding it toward her "pubic area."

After Clinton exposed himself, she made a break for the door. Clinton interrupted her escape and held the door briefly while he warned, "You're smart. Dave Harrington [Jones' boss] is a friend of mine. Let's keep this between ourselves."

In a detail reminiscent of what Kathleen Willey told Linda Tripp about Clinton's demeanor during her own assault, Jones said Clinton's face turned "beet red" as he became fully aroused.

And finally there's Monica Lewinsky herself. No one disputes the fact that she consented to — and even instigated — a sexual relationship with Bill Clinton. But just as relations with a wife or even a prostitute can become rape the moment the sex turns nonconsensual, there may have been instances when Clinton's behavior went beyond anything Lewinsky had in mind.

The *New York Post* reported that Linda Tripp, sourcing Monica herself, told the grand jury that Clinton sometimes enjoyed "rough sex" with Lewinsky.

"I don't mean abusive," said Tripp, "I mean very over the top, out of control, physically powerful, where he would repeatedly say to Monica, 'I'm not hurting you, am I?' And essentially he was, but she didn't say he was."

A fiftyish boss engaging in sadomasochistic sex with a 22-year-old underling? And six other women who may have been abused or even raped? Could all these people with no known connection to one another simply be making these accusations up?

Patricia Ireland — call your office.

James Woods: Remove Clinton

NewsMax.com Vortex, January 1999 — Actor James Woods, one of Hollywood's most outspoken liberals, is glad to see that Bill Clinton has been impeached.

Woods, whose own experience with impeachment may come from his stellar performance as H. R. Haldeman in Oliver Stone's *Nixon,* told the *Washington Post* he is ashamed of Bill Clinton.

"He's a certified liar, a card-carrying liar, and lying is the cancer at the base of the spine of every crime ever committed," the actor told the *Post.*

Woods then declared Clinton a "sociopath" who, he predicted, would be removed from office by the Senate.

Woods told the *Post* he was outraged by Clinton's sellout to the Chinese of national secrets and suggests the Lewinsky scandal is like "getting Al Capone for income tax evasion."

Barbra Streisand, cross Woods off your Christmas card list, permanently!

Did Bill Clinton Overdose on Cocaine?

NewsMax.com Vortex, September 1999 — Now that the press has raised the "coke" question in their dogged pursuit of George W. Bush, questions about Bill Clinton's drug past are also fair game.

One area of inquiry for the newshounds at, let's say, the *Washington*

Post, might be an incident that supposedly took place in the early 1980s when Bill Clinton was governor of Arkansas.

Dr. Sam Houston, a respected Little Rock physician and once a doctor for Hillary's cantankerous father, Hugh Rodham, says it is well known in Little Rock medical circles that Clinton was brought to a Little Rock hospital for emergency treatment for an apparent cocaine overdose.

According to Houston, who told us he spoke to someone intimately familiar with the details of what happened that night, Clinton arrived at the hospital with the aid of a state trooper. Hillary Clinton had been notified by phone and had instructed the hospital staff that Clinton's personal physician would be arriving soon.

When Mrs. Clinton arrived, she told both of the resident physicians on duty that night that they would never again practice medicine in the United States if word leaked out about Clinton's drug problem. Reportedly, she pinned one of the doctors up against the wall, both hands pressed against his shoulders, as she gave her dire warning.

Like most tales that reflect poorly on Bill Clinton, the press has ignored any inquiry into this one. In 1996, however, columnist R. Emmett Tyrrell located and telephoned one of the nurses who had been on duty the night Bill Clinton was brought into the emergency room. According to Tyrrell, the nurse didn't deny the story, but said she couldn't talk about it because she could lose her job. Welcome to Arkansas!

Kenneth Starr — The Clintons' Accomplice

By Christopher Ruddy

NewsMax.com Vortex, August 1999—The independent counsel law has lapsed. And independent counsel Kenneth Starr said the law should not be re-authorized.

Obviously, Starr believes that, because his own investigation was a waste of tens of millions of dollars, the independent counsel law should be trashed.

The truth is that the independent counsel law is a good law. When corruption has been rooted out in places like France and Italy, it has usually been the result of an independent magistrate — their version of our independent counsel.

We also know that when independent counsels like Donald Smaltz and Daniel Pearson did their jobs, the Clintons were in a high state of panic and used every possible means to stop them. We know that Bill Clinton has been fearful of another independent counsel being assigned to investigate Chinagate, allegations that he took Chinese campaign cash and gave away nuclear secrets.

The law should stay. It's Ken Starr who must go. A weak, pathetic character, he has more responsibility than any other man in America for the woe the Clintons have wreaked, and will wreak, on this country.

The Hubbell Deal

Just how pitiful Starr's "prosecution" has been was demonstrated recently when Webster Hubbell admitted to committing a felony by misleading federal investigators and a misdemeanor by failing to pay taxes.

Any normal citizen would have been jailed and fined for such crimes. Not Webster Hubbell. Under Starr's plea agreement, Hubbell will be on parole and serve no jail time. He won't even pay any fine or restitution.

Worse, Webb Hubbell still doesn't have to cooperate with Starr in his investigation of the Clintons. Hubbell continues to insist, ". . . I have no knowledge of any wrongdoing on behalf of the president or Mrs. Clinton."

Starr's failure to seek Hubbell's cooperation — a basic condition of granting a plea agreement — violates the most fundamental procedures followed by federal prosecutors. But flouting procedure is nothing new for Starr.

In December 1994, when Hubbell admitted to having bilked his clients at the Rose Law Firm and evading taxes, Starr purposefully botched the plea agreement by not demanding Hubbell's cooperation. Starr's actions so infuriated Starr's own trial attorney, Russell Hardin, that Hardin resigned.

Hardin was incensed that Starr planned on signing a plea agreement without debriefing Hubbell as to what he knew and how he would cooperate — a mandatory procedure for any plea bargain.

This time around, Starr simply made no pretense that he would seek Hubbell's cooperation.

Recently, the *New York Times* reported that Kenneth Starr had decided not to seek indictments against Bill and Hillary Clinton for crimes they had committed related to Whitewater or related scandals. It's hard to get indictments if no one will talk. It's nearly impossible to get people to talk if the prosecutor doesn't pressure them.

As any honest prosecutor on Starr's staff will admit, Starr long ago decided not to indict the Clintons — or, for that matter, any White House official. Some believe Starr actually cut a deal with the Clintons soon after coming aboard.

Pet Worm

Ken Starr is Bill Clinton's pet worm. Starr has played out a role in the greatest Mutt and Jeff, Good Cop/Bad Cop routine ever perpetrated on the American public.

Even good folks, who realize how bad the Clintons are, have fallen victim to Starr's charade, taken in by the propaganda that Starr is the "tough, mean prosecutor" out to get the president, just like James Carville says.

That's simply a mirage, cooked up by the White House spin machine.

What Nolanda Hill Told Me

Is it really possible that Bible-toting Ken Starr — arch Republican, shirt-sleeve Christian and Monica prosecutor — is on the Clintons' side?

Let me answer by relating this story:

As the longtime lover and business partner of Clinton confidant Ron Brown, Nolanda Hill had intimate knowledge of the inner workings of the Clinton White House.

As a result of congressional complaints, Janet Reno was forced to appoint an independent counsel to investigate Brown, his business dealings with Nolanda Hill, Brown's son Michael, and several other people.

The independent counsel in this case was Daniel Pearson from Miami. Unlike Starr, Pearson and his deputy were no one's patsies. Instead of using Starr's delaying tactics, Pearson had, within months, built a strong case against Brown, Brown's son, and Hill. Nolanda Hill told me they were going to be indicted.

Then Brown made a desperate bid to save himself. Just weeks before his death on April 6, 1996, Brown met with Clinton at the White

House and made it clear he was not going to take the fall for an administration rampant with corruption. Brown wanted Clinton to handle Pearson the same way the White House had handled Starr.

Handled Starr?

Hill explained. Starr was appointed independent counsel in August of 1994, after the three-judge panel decided not to appoint Robert Fiske. The Clinton White House publicly expressed outrage that Starr, a "partisan" Republican, had been selected as independent counsel.

That's the way the Clintons wanted the world to see it.

In fact, Hill told me, "when Starr was appointed, they were opening champagne bottles in the White House, they were celebrating." According to Hill, Starr had actually been on Janet Reno's short list for the post of special counsel at the time she picked Robert Fiske.

"They would never have put him on the short list if they were worried about him," she said.

In his meeting with Clinton, Brown knew that Starr was under the White House's thumb. He pleaded with Clinton to do the same with Pearson by having Reno interfere in Pearson's probe and by ordering Justice Department attorneys on Pearson's staff to back off.

Brown also asked Clinton to have the FBI obstruct the Pearson probe by withholding critical information. Brown, Hill said, was well aware that FBI agents were not working for Ken Starr in his Whitewater probe but for Reno and the White House, giving the Clinton administration *de facto* control over the Starr investigations

According to Hill, Clinton told Brown not to worry. "I'll take care of it," Clinton said.

Just weeks later, Brown's plane mysteriously crashed into the side of a mountain in Yugoslavia and the Pearson probe was closed.

Starr Betrayed the Country

Starr's inquiry has continued. This August will mark Starr's fifth anniversary as independent counsel. During his five years on the job, the public has received more than enough information to evaluate his performance.

There are dozens of examples of how Starr has betrayed the American people and his oath as an independent counsel. To cite a few:

• During the time Starr was investigating the Clintons, he was working for a company wholly owned by China's Peoples Liberation Army and notorious arms dealer Wang Jun.

• Starr hired Mark Tuohey as his Washington deputy. Tuohey is a liberal Democrat close to the Clinton White House who even threw a party at his home for Janet Reno. (It came as no surprise that when Tuohey left Starr's office, he joined Vinson & Elkins, the law firm representing the Rose Law Firm before Starr's office.)

• Starr trashed a fundamental principle of American jurisprudence: equality before the law. He created a new and bizarre standard for deciding when to issue indictments. Under Starr's new formulation, ordinary citizens and lower-level officials needed little evidence of wrongdoing to warrant an indictment. But Starr raised the bar absurdly high for White House officials. Thus, Starr's office could indict a banker in Arkansas, but Hillary Clinton would not be indicted for the exact same offenses. This is nothing less than a grant of titles and nobility for government officials, which is expressly prohibited by the Constitution and a major reason why we fought the Revolutionary War.

• Miquel Rodriguez, Starr's lead prosecutor in the case of Vincent Foster, resigned rather than be part of a cover-up. Starr's out-and-out cover-up of Vince Foster's death began with his wholehearted acceptance of the report issued by Robert Fiske. Key witnesses, such as several Arkansas troopers who said they knew of Foster's death hours before the White House claims it did, were never put before a grand jury.

• Starr's prosecution of the Lewinsky case was a wild goose chase. He had no original jurisdiction to investigate this matter and only did so at Janet Reno's request. Starr waited nearly eight months to sign a plea agreement with Monica. In essence, she never really cooperated against the Clintons at all, claiming to this day that Clinton "never told me to lie; no one offered me a job. . . ."

Still, some Starr fanatics argue that Starr did pursue the Lewinsky matter and seek Clinton's impeachment. I ask: So what?

When the Lewinsky scandal broke, I accurately illustrated, in the *Pittsburgh Tribune-Review*, what would happen. Starr would delay his scathing report on Lewinsky, which would be so damaging to Clinton that it might even call for his impeachment.

And Starr's report was delayed and issued at the end of the year, pushing the impeachment vote until after the elections and saving Clinton again. Throughout the Lewinsky matter it became clear that Starr was creating a diversion for Clinton's real crimes; Clinton would never be removed from office over a sex scandal.

Most egregious of all was Starr's mishandling of key Whitewater witnesses David Hale and Jim McDougal. Hale spent some 18 months in prison and was punished with huge restitution demands — even though he was the chief cooperating witness.

McDougal, who also cooperated, was sent to federal prison and was apparently murdered when prison officials purposefully withheld life-sustaining medications.

But convicted criminals like Webb Hubbell and former Arkansas governor Jim Guy Tucker, who both stubbornly refused to cooperate, got off easy. Tucker never served one day in prison.

If the guilty and unrepentant get off easy, what type of prosecution is this? It's not time to blame the independent counsel law; blame the prosecutor who wouldn't do his job. Because of Kenneth W. Starr's complicity, the most corrupt administration in the history of the country continues with no end in sight. God save us all.

The Hubbell Deal: Blackmail or Incompetence?

NewsMax.com Vortex, August 1999 — Has Ken Starr been blackmailed by the Clinton Justice Department into short-circuiting his prosecution of Webster Hubbell?

That's the inference one might draw from what Judicial Watch Chairman Larry Klayman said:

"With the recent offer of Janet Reno to drop all ethics probes of Starr's office if he and his prosecutors would end their investigations, as published a few weeks ago by Robert Suro in the *Washington Post*, it is clear the independent counsel is bailing out. It is sad to say that Starr's latest retreat coincides with the death of the independent counsel law this Wednesday."

In fact, news that Starr has let Hubbell off the hook with a deal that involves no jail time and apparently no cooperation is more than sad. It's downright eerie, given the way circumstances around the Hubbell plea bargain resemble the blackmail scheme hinted at in that June 6 *Washington Post* report:

"The Justice Department has put its misconduct investigation of independent counsel Kenneth W. Starr on hold while waiting to see whether Starr resigns or significantly curtails his activities after the independent counsel law expires on June 30, according to sources familiar with the deliberations."

Hmmmm. It sure looks like Starr has "significantly curtailed his activities," what with no further prosecutions expected after Hubbell accepted his plea deal on June 30, the exact target date mentioned in the article.

This is especially good news for the first lady, whose name popped up recently on a list of witnesses who could have been called at Hubbell's trial — and who was referenced in Hubbell's indictment more than 30 times.

But surely (as the mainstream press will no doubt contend) Hillary's hand-picked Justice Department lawyers wouldn't really do anything so heavy-handed as to put the screws to Starr on the eve of her U.S. Senate bid. Or would they?

The June 6 *Post* report continued:

"If Starr were no longer serving as an active prosecutor, the Justice Department could simply forgo the inquiry into Starr's handling of the Monica S. Lewinsky matter. Some senior department officials would welcome that outcome as a chance to avoid a potentially contentious and politicized proceeding, the sources said."

That's the ticket. It's a win-win deal all around. Well, except for the American people and the cause of justice. But hey, you can't have everything.

In truth, Starr has never been the Clinton nemesis the White House claimed he was. But the image of Captain Ahab-Starr obsessed with getting the great Whitewater whale was parroted by the Washington press corps, which dutifully demonized any reporter who saw through the act and had the nerve to say so.

The first and perhaps only American journalist to do so was none other than NewsMax.com's executive editor, Christopher Ruddy. As

early as 1995, while William Safire, Robert Novak and the *Wall Street Journal* editorial page were breathlessly reporting about how Starr was "closing in" on the Clintons, Ruddy saw the handwriting on the wall, particularly in the Hubbell case:
In "Which Hubbell Was Telling the Truth?" (*Pittsburgh Tribune-Review*, July 23, 1995), Ruddy documented how Hubbell had completely buffaloed investigators with two contradictory accounts about whether Vince Foster was depressed the weekend before he was found shot to death.

While others found Starr's 1996 convictions of the McDougals and Jim Guy Tucker very impressive, Ruddy sounded a note of caution, noting that Starr's main cooperating Whitewater witness, David Hale, received 25 percent more jail time than the stonewalling Hubbell — even though Hale's cooperation made Starr's case:
"The importance of the stiff sentence handed down to Hale, and the way Hubbell essentially got off the hook, cannot be underestimated. The success of this prosecution, as is true with complex legal cases, depends on a prosecutor's ability to get key witnesses to cooperate," explained Ruddy in a May 1996 *Chicago Sun-Times* report.

Starr's reluctance to play hardball with potential witnesses against Clinton would haunt even the case that ended in the president's impeachment. Monica Lewinsky would toy with his office for seven crucial months while the White House spin machine neutralized the impact of Starr's final report to Congress.

In the end, Starr got the blue dress — but key evidence of witness tampering, like the talking-points memo and the smoking-gun Tripp-Lewinsky tapes themselves, were ignored in order to win Monica's so-called cooperation.

If anything, Lewinsky ended up as a witness for the defense—offering little on Clinton that couldn't be spun as "lies about sex," finishing her grand jury testimony with the words, "I hate Linda Tripp." Key witness Tripp, like Hale before her, is now being hounded by Clinton-friendly state prosecutors as Starr watches from the sidelines.

Two days after the Monicagate story broke in the mainstream press, Ruddy wondered in print, "Is Starr up to the job? He's blown the big cases in the past."

Now we know the answer.

Kenneth Starr's China Connection

By Jeremy Reynalds

NewsMax.com Vortex, February 1999 — A Miami lawyer is seeking the removal of Kenneth Starr as independent counsel because Starr, at the same time he was investigating the Clintons, worked for a company wholly owned by the Chinese government.

"This is one of the most egregious examples of conflict of interest and ethics violations I have seen," lawyer Jack Thompson said, explaining his motion seeking Starr's ouster. The motion was filed February 4 with Attorney General Janet Reno, a federal ethics official, and the three-judge panel that appointed Starr.

In his motion, Thompson claims that Starr violated the conflict of interest provisions of the independent counsel law.

According to the 1994 independent counsel statute, only the attorney general can remove a court-appointed independent counsel.

Thompson said he also filed the motion with the three judge panel that appointed Starr "because there is nothing in the law prohibiting them from finding Starr violated conflict of interest rules."

Thompson also has requested the panel use its power to order his motion appended to all reports Starr has filed or will file with the court.

Specifically, Thompson notes that at the same time Starr was independent counsel he served as a paid legal counsel to CitiSteel, a Delaware steel company wholly owned by CITIC. CITIC — the Chinese International Trust and Investment Company — is considered the financial arm of China's People's Liberation Army (PLA) and is chaired by Wang Jun.

According to court records, Starr represented CitiSteel in a case before a federal appellate court. Starr argued that the new Chinese owners were lawful when, after they bought the company, CITIC refused to recognize the company's union. The court agreed with Starr and the Chinese owners in a ruling issued in 1995.

Wang Jun is a shadowy, high-level communist official who also is chairman of Poly Group, another enterprise controlled by China's PLA. Poly Group was mired in controversy in 1996 when it was revealed that Wang Jun had met Bill Clinton at the White House. Days after the meeting, the administration moved to waive customs restrictions and allowed the company to import semiautomatic rifles into the United States.

Thompson said the Chinese connection raises so many questions about Starr's "independence" that Starr should be removed from office.

In his motion to Reno, Thompson wrote, "You should treat as a red flag the fact that Ken Starr, a man reputed to be highly sensitive to any appearance of improprieties by the OIC [Office of independent counsel], did not even alert you to this Chinese connection. This is very troubling."

Thompson, a conservative Republican who once opposed Reno in an election for the post of Miami-Dade's prosecutor, reminded Reno that the independent counsel statute prohibits Starr from representing "in any matter any person involved in any investigation or prosecution under this chapter."

"It has been widely publicized that Wang Jun attended a White House fund-raising 'coffee' for Clinton, that the Chinese government made efforts to help the Clinton-Gore '96 campaign. And it is also clear that Starr was on Wang Jun's payroll at the same time he was supposed to be prosecuting the Clintons," Thompson told NewsMax.com.

Press reports have indicated widespread attempts by the Chinese government to influence the American electoral process. The *Washington Post* has reported that the FBI concluded the Chinese funneled millions of dollars to Democratic National Committee coffers during the 1996 election.

The Year of the Rat, a 1998 book authored by two former House investigators who examined campaign finance abuses, details close ties between the Chinese and Bill Clinton — ties dating back to his days as governor of Arkansas.

Thompson's motion also notes that Starr's China connection raises another conflict in the person of Webster Hubbell.

"There is a Starr indictment pending against your former No. 3 person at Justice, Mr. Webster Hubbell, for alleged receipt of $600,000 in hush money and failure to pay federal income taxes thereon. It is alleged that much of this hush money to Mr. Hubbell was paid by the Indonesian Riady family. The Riadys have direct ties to the . . . People's Liberation Army arms merchant, Wang Jun."

Thompson said that, while Starr may be willing to "inconvenience" Clinton by pushing the Lewinsky case, there's an even more important issue to consider. With an obvious conflict of interest, is he willing to "inconvenience" his client, Wang Jun?

"To be more direct, if the money trail leads from Hubbell to the Riadys to Wang Jun, the American people deserve, and the statute specifically mandates, an independent counsel unfettered and not compromised by loyalties to clients in following that money trail," Thompson wrote to Reno.

A spokesperson for the Office of the independent counsel said that Starr had no comment on Thompson's actions.

Thompson agrees that Starr has made a serious effort to prosecute the president on the Lewinsky matter, but added that the independent counsel's performance has been less than stellar.

"You have to remember, Starr never really received Monica's cooperation against the president. So his case that Clinton obstructed justice is a weak one. If the Senate doesn't convict, Starr may have put us on a wild, sexual goose chase.

"Starr has had many areas to investigate, from the death of Vincent Foster, the Whitewater matter, the Travelgate scandal, witness tampering, and the outrageous FBI Filegate case, and Starr claims he found no evidence of wrongdoing by the Clintons in any of these matters.

"It's time he be removed and a new independent counsel be appointed to properly finish the job," Thompson said.

If Monica Made Love to Webster Hubbell . . .

By Christopher Ruddy

NewsMax.com Vortex, December 1998 — If only Monica Lewinsky had made love to Webster Hubbell, the scandal known as "Whitewater" may have long been settled.

Independent counsel Kenneth Starr recently indicted Webster Hubbell for the third time on charges of 15 felonies, alleging that he was a key player in efforts to defraud a federally insured savings and loan.

Still, Hubbell has yet to spill the beans on his First Friends, Bill and Hillary Rodham Clinton.

Starr made the announcement of the Hubbell indictment on a Friday. Friday is the best day to make sure a story is buried in Saturday's newspapers and old news by Monday. Presumably, Starr wanted to make little fanfare of his prosecution of Hubbell and the Whitewater scandal.

Compare Starr's inquiry of the Whitewater/Hubbell matters and the Lewinsky scandal.

Starr was advised of the Linda Tripp tapes of Monica Lewinsky in mid-January. Within days he was hauling key figures in the case before his grand jury.

By September, the ninth month of his investigation, Starr issued a voluminous and scathing report, and thousands of pages of ancillary documents to Congress, detailing a sordid sexual relationship between Clinton and the intern, and an abuse of power so serious it warranted impeachment proceedings.

The sex-related scandal investigation was signed, sealed and delivered to Congress in nine months.

Starr took over the investigation of Webster Hubbell when he was appointed independent counsel in August 1994.

Hubbell, the former law partner of Hillary Rodham Clinton and deputy White House counsel Vincent Foster, had served as associate attorney general before he resigned under a cloud in 1994.

Starr had inherited a surefire case of fraud by Hubbell, who had been double-billing clients and pocketing money at the Rose Law Firm.

As part of the Clinton's Arkansas inner circle, Hubbell was in a unique position to connect the dots for Whitewater prosecutors. Hubbell not only knew about Whitewater matters from Clinton's days as governor of Arkansas, he could link these events to administration efforts to obstruct justice after Clinton became president.

For instance, Hubbell, who spent the weekend with Vincent Foster before his untimely death in 1993, could have shed new light on administration efforts to interfere with investigations into Foster's death, as well as the efforts by the administration to impede the RTC (Resolution Trust Corporation) inquiry into Madison Guaranty bank.

Hubbell's cooperation with prosecutors could have deciphered the rosetta stone for most of the Clinton scandals, Vince Foster's death.

A cooperating Hubbell could have explained why, on the night of Foster's death, he indicated to another Rose Law Firm partner, Philip Carroll, that Foster had been murdered and his death was not a suicide. Hubbell might also have buttressed claims by Linda Tripp. Tripp testified before the Lewinsky grand jury that she "had reason to believe the Vince Foster tragedy was not depicted accurately under oath by members of the administration."

Starr missed the golden opportunity Hubbell offered. Instead of "hammering" Hubbell into telling all, Starr foolishly agreed in December 1994 to a plea agreement with Hubbell on mail fraud and tax evasion charges before Hubbell delivered the goods on the Clintons.

Hubbell reneged on his agreement. Starr has acknowledged that. In 1995 Hubbell received a relatively light sentence of 19 months in federal prison, while Starr's cooperating witnesses, David Hale and Jim McDougal, were sentenced to much harsher terms.

Though Starr violated Justice Department practice in not debriefing Hale before signing the plea agreement, his mistake was further compounded by a failure to immediately reindict Hubbell on new charges, legal experts familiar with the case have stated.

Starr eventually did reindict Hubbell this past spring, almost three and a half years later. This indictment on tax evasion charges was quickly dismissed by a federal judge.

Today, almost four years after Hubbell promised to assist Starr, he has yet to open his mouth and Starr has yet to force Hubbell to do so. Starr's Hubbell prosecution has been lackadaisical, and the delays have only benefited the Clinton administration.

With Starr dawdling, Clinton and his wife sailed through a first term and have comfortably ensconced themselves in a second one, unshaken by the sex-related allegations Starr dished out after a record-setting time for the procrastinating prosecutor.

Secret Service Officer Pape Tells All

NewsMax.com Vortex, November 1998 — Included in the 4000 pages of Starr documents are the FBI interviews and grand jury testimony of Secret Service agents and uniformed Officers who work at the White House.

Most of these interviews are filled with monotonous details: where officers were stationed in hallways, etc. Most of the officers were mum about what they really saw. See no evil, hear no evil, speak no evil. Take Larry Cockrell, the head of the president's Secret Service detail, who said he was completely unaware of Clinton's relationship with Monica.

A very candid account, however, was given by Uniformed Secret Service Officer Steven Philip Pape.

Pape told the FBI and the grand jury that he had heard many rumors about the president's relationship with Lewinsky. He referred to her as the president's "mistress."

At one point he told the FBI he didn't inspect a package Monica had for the president "[B]ecause Lewinsky was the president's mistress, [Pape] did not want to treat her poorly or make her wait any more than was necessary, since it could come back on him."

Pape then told the FBI — rather interestingly — that whatever was in the box would not be used to harm the president. "If Lewinsky wanted to hurt the president, she would do what Lorena Bobbitt did." Presumably, Pape was referring to Bobbitt's knife and the fact that he cleared Monica's packages through an X-ray machine.

Pape said other Secret Service officers were more concerned and thought Monica was a physical danger to the president. It was suggested she be added to their "watch list." Officer Greg Ladow was one officer who told Pape that "he thought Lewinsky was a threat and Ladow wanted to put Lewinski on a 'do not admit' list."

Pape continued that the "do not admit list" is used to protect the president's physical safety, and the list includes Billy Dale, the former head of the White House Travel Office and Gary Harlowe, a former FBI agent who was closely associated with Hillary Clinton.

Lewinsky's visits were the source of some merriment, though. Pape said he gambled with agents on her activities. Pape explained that as soon as Lewinsky arrived at the White House, Pape would bet another agent that Clinton "would move to the Oval Office within ten minutes." Pape won the bet when the president moved to the Oval Office "approximately nine minutes and fifty seconds after Lewinsky arrived."

China's Penetration of the United States

By Colonel Stanislav Lunev

Colonel Lunev Joins *Vortex* and NewsMax.com

Colonel Stanislav Lunev has joined Vortex *and NewsMax.com as a regular columnist on issues relating to national security, foreign affairs and intelligence. Colonel Lunev is the highest-ranking military officer ever to defect from Russia to the United States. He defected in 1992, after Boris Yeltsin came to power.*

As a GRU Russian military intelligence agent, Lunev was considered one of Russia's premier spies and was assigned to the countries most important to Russia: China and the United States.

Lunev's information to the CIA, DIA, FBI and other national security agencies was deemed so vital, he was placed in the FBI's Witness Protection Program.

As one of Russia's top spies in America, Lunev was involved in making Russian war plans against America, as well as ferreting out American military secrets.

Some of Lunev's information was revealed in the 1997 best seller Through the Eyes of the Enemy *(Regnery). Among many revelations, Lunev reported that Russia is preparing a surprise nuclear attack against America.*

NewsMax.com Vortex, July 1999 — Published recently by the United States Congress, the Cox Report on Chinese intelligence activity in the United States is an eye-opener for the American public. Of course, this report couldn't disclose all the facts about Communist Chinese intelligence penetration inside American society, which began a long time ago and has become a full-scale spy attack against the most important institutions of the U.S.

It is well known to specialists that Red China's intelligence services have been operating abroad very actively and carefully for a very long time and that they also have been extremely successful worldwide.

Drawing upon an ancient tradition of strategic espionage that goes back to Sun Tsu's famous book, *The Art of War*, the leadership of the Chinese Communist Party (CCP) has given this kind of activity the very highest priority.

With thousands of years of tradition, Chinese intelligence has been operating in the U.S. for about four decades. Inheriting old China's intelligence experience, Red China modernized its spy machine with help from the well-known Soviet KGB and the little-known Soviet GRU in the 1940s and 1950s and developed its own operations against America since the formation of Communist China.

During the Cold War, the intelligence agencies of the East and West were busy with their own spy games and didn't pay enough attention to what the Chinese were doing. This gave Beijing plenty of time to maneuver between the superpowers. Even now, with the Cold War "officially" over, Western nations still are dealing with China without careful examination of its cultural, historical and military traditions.

Espionage is extremely important to China, not only for traditional military and political purposes but also for economic development, particularly development of defense and industrial manufacturing and trading organizations.

There are two main Chinese intelligence services: political intelligence/foreign counterintelligence from the Ministry of State Security and military intelligence, directed from the Second Directorate of the People's Liberation Army (PLA) General Staff.

The chief intelligence officer, General Ji Shengde, is well known in America because of his direct involvement in illegal money transactions during the last presidential election campaign, in August 1996.

These services are under the tight control of the general secretary of the Central Committee of the Communist Party (CCCP), through his deputies in the ministries of National Defense and State Security. Thus the main policies, directions and targets for intelligence collection are established by secret decisions of the Politburo, which lays out primary strategy, keeps the intelligence community working in the necessary directions, and concentrates efforts against the most important targets.

Most practical issues are handled directly in the Central Military Commission (CMC) of the CCP, in charge of supervising the entire

Chinese military machine, including military-industrial institutions and organizations. This commission collects, analyzes and summarizes the needs of Chinese industry for foreign technologies, foreign production and proprietary information. It receives requests from Chinese industry and directs the intelligence community to act upon those requests. Chinese communist leaders are very practical people. They cannot afford to maintain an extremely expensive intelligence bureaucracy unless it can pay for itself by boosting economic development. Of course, their intelligence operatives at the same time are collecting hard information on military and political secrets of other countries, but their main mission is to provide practical support to develop the defense-industrial complex.

The CMC is supervised by General Liu Huaqing, father of Liu Chaoying, a Chinese aerospace executive and lieutenant colonel in the PLA, who was directly involved in the U.S. fund-raising scandal. The CMC provides annually a top-secret "tasking list," delivered to all intelligence units in the field on a regular basis. The list includes information about foreign leaders who might influence current affairs and state policy. This list also includes specifications for particular items, and quantities, needed for military production.

This unified command enables Chinese leadership to organize effective cooperation among different intelligence services in order to fulfill strategic operations, the most important concerned with the development of weapons of mass destruction.

It was well known before the Cox Report that the Chinese nuclear and missile industries were created with assistance from the Soviet Union. The Cox Report exposed the fact, known previously only to specialists, that the Chinese missile arsenal was created by native Chinese specialists trained in the U.S. who took part in American missile programs. The information was transferred by Chinese intelligence to the People's Republic of China (PRC).

Dozens of these native Chinese specialists were delivered by Chinese intelligence agencies from the U.S. to the PRC in the 1950s and 1960s, and Chinese nuclear and missile programs were based on American technology and Soviet machinery and equipment. In the 1980s and 1990s the basis shifted fully toward the United States as China used American technology, machinery and equipment, received by China legally or illegally from the U.S. and other Western countries.

With a small but robust nuclear arsenal, Communist China isn't interested in just Asia anymore. It is seeking development and recognition as a world power. The Chinese intelligence community will play a much more important role, maybe even the decisive role, in Red China as it finds its future geostrategic situation in the world. Unfortunately, America remains a primary and successful target for the Chinese intelligence machine.

Colonel Stanislav Lunev is the highest-ranking Soviet military spy ever to defect to the United States. He is a regular contributor to NewsMax.com and Vortex.

Chinagate: The Third-Way Scandal

By Richard Poe

NewsMax.com Vortex, July 1999 — Chinagate is fast going the way of every other Clinton scandal. It is being minimized, rationalized, covered up and forgotten. The only question is why.

Conservatives pin the blame on a vast left-wing conspiracy. They see liberal journalists shielding their favorite president, and lily-livered Republicans cringing before Clinton's poll ratings.

If only it were as innocent as all that. Sadly, the evidence suggests that more sinister forces may be at work.

Chinagate is a new kind of scandal. It arises from the Big Business-Big Government partnership that Bill Clinton calls the "Third Way."

Under this new style of governance, Democrats, Republicans, defense contractors, mass media and intelligence agencies all share a common interest in covering up Clinton's misdeeds.

"I'm grateful that the Third Way seems to be taking hold around the world," said Clinton in a September 21, 1998, speech at New York University. And well he should be. Without press or fanfare, world leaders from British Prime Minister Tony Blair to German Chancellor Gerhard Schroeder are quietly joining Clinton's crusade for a new economic order that is neither capitalist nor communist, but something in between.

"Socialism and communism have passed away, yet they remain to haunt us," writes Anthony Giddens in his book *The Third Way*. A left-wing British economist, Giddens is widely known as Tony Blair's guru. "We cannot just put aside the values and ideals that drove them," Giddens continues, "for some remain intrinsic to the good life that it is the point of social and economic development to create."

The trick, Giddens explains, is to find a way to promote the good qualities of Marxism (whatever he imagines those to be) in a world that no longer trusts socialism.

Benito Mussolini faced a comparable dilemma 80 years ago. He resolved it in a way very similar to Giddens' and Bill Clinton's.

Originally a hardline communist, Mussolini recognized that he would gain more followers if he toned down his Marxist rhetoric. So, in 1919, he announced that he had found a "third way" between capitalism and communism. Mussolini called it fascism.

Under this system, Big Government would run the economy, while Big Business owned it. Adolf Hitler followed the same model in 1933, offering full employment to the masses and corporate welfare to the industrialists.

Now it is Clinton's turn. Like Hitler and Mussolini, Clinton calls for a partnership between business and government. And, as with his jack-booted predecessors, Clinton's Third Way has fostered corruption and favoritism beyond measure.

Consider the role of the CIA in the Chinagate cover-up.

When the Cold War ended, the CIA took on a new job — helping U.S. corporations compete in the global marketplace.

Time magazine worried that CIA meddling might corrupt private business. On September 23, 1991, it wrote: "And how should [intelligence] agencies make information available without favoring one company over another — a prospect that opens the way to the possibility of corporations bribing American agents to get access to information that would give them an advantage over other American companies."

Time was right to be worried. But who could have imagined, in 1991, that the bribery would go all the way to the top?

According to *The Year of the Rat* by Edward Timperlake and William C. Triplett, the top contributors to the 1992 Clinton campaign were Chinese agents. In 1996, the leading Clinton donors were U.S. defense contractors doing business with Chinese missile manufacturers.

Where was the CIA in all this? Right in the thick of it. According to the Cox Report, congressional investigators sought the CIA's help in probing Hughes Electronics for leaking missile technology to the Chinese.

But instead of helping, the CIA tipped off Hughes about the probe. It revealed the names of employees slated to be interviewed and told the company what questions they would likely be asked.

On another occasion, a CIA scientist named Ronald Pandolfi raised the alarm that Hughes might be leaking missile secrets. The CIA killed his report, according to the *New York Times* (December 7, 1998).

Chalk it up to the Third Way. Hughes Electronics — a division of General Motors Corporation — supplies the CIA with satellites and communications equipment. The mutual back-scratching that went on between these two organizations perfectly fulfills Clinton's vision of public-private cooperation.

As for the Republicans, don't expect much action from them. Defense contractors donate big bucks to the GOP too.

And don't bother asking why the O.J. Simpson trial or the Littleton massacre merited nonstop media coverage while Chinagate doesn't. The corporations that control the mass media — such as defense contractor and NBC owner General Electric — are no doubt just as eager to cash in on the Third Way as anyone else.

When business and government join hands, no power in the world can stop them. They can do what they like with impunity, be it selling missile secrets to China or building Volkswagens with slave labor.

The Third Way worked admirably for Hitler and Mussolini. God help us, it is working for Clinton too.

Richard Poe is a freelance journalist and a New York Times *best-selling author. His latest book is* Black Spark, White Fire *(Prima, 1998).*

Hazel O'Leary Gave Reporter Secret Nuke Plans

NewsMax.com Vortex, September 1999 — Bill Clinton's one-time keeper of nuclear secrets, former Energy Secretary Hazel O'Leary, literally gave away plans for our top-secret W-87 atomic warhead, over the objections of her aides, according to Pennsylvania Republican Representative Curt Weldon.

Worse still, the beneficiary of O'Leary's generosity was a reporter whose publication wasted no time spreading the classified information around the globe.

Writing in the August 23 issue of *Insight* magazine, Weldon describes a 1995 meeting between O'Leary and the journalist, who worked for *U.S. News & World Report:*

"O'Leary opened up a ledger of classified documents sitting on her desk and proceeded to show the reporter a diagram of the W-87 warhead to prove a point. She then handed the classified diagram of the nuclear warhead to the reporter. Her staff attempted to protest, pointing out that the document was classified. O'Leary hesitated a moment, took the document back from the reporter, crossed out the word 'classified' and promptly gave it back to the *U.S. News* staffer."

The diagram was promptly published by *U.S. News* in its July 31, 1995, edition. Thanks to O'Leary, one of America's most sensitive defense secrets ended up on every magazine rack in the world.

"Any competent nuclear scientist could use [the W-87 diagram] to work back to the actual design," defense expert Sam Cohen told *Insight.*

According to Weldon, the Energy Department conducted an investigation into the episode, which was terminated after probers determined that O'Leary herself was the culprit.

Hazel O'Leary's Rocky Flats Horror Show

NewsMax.com Vortex, July 1999 — In a hair-raising Nukegate report that was largely overlooked, William J. Broad wrote in the *New York Times:*

"For more than half a decade, the Clinton administration was shoveling atomic secrets out the door as fast as it could, literally by the ton. Millions of previously classified ideas and documents relating to nuclear arms were released to all comers, including China's bomb makers."

The *Times* quoted then-Energy Secretary Hazel O'Leary (1993–

1997), who proudly proclaimed at the beginning of her tenure: "The United States must stand as a leader. We are declassifying the largest amount of information in the history of the department."

Now the *American Spectator*'s Kenneth Timmerman adds another dimension to O'Leary's "openness initiative," in a report that zeroes in on the new policy's impact at nuclear storage sites like Rocky Flats, Colorado.

The Rocky Flats security scandal may be the most damaging yet, since the cover-up is apparently still ongoing. Current Energy Secretary Bill Richardson, who just gave department whistleblower Notra Trulock a $10,000 reward for exposing security breaches at Los Alamos, is desperately trying to keep what O'Leary did at the Colorado site under wraps.

According to Timmerman, "Richardson is now attempting to prevent a top DOE [Department of Energy] official in charge of safeguards and security from testifying before Congress. Why? Because that official, Edward J. McCallum, had made clear his intention to warn Congress and the public of devastating gaps in security procedures at nuclear storage sites such as Rocky Flats."

Richardson already knows what McCallum has to say, since McCallum privately warned the Clinton administration last January about trouble at Rocky Flats. The consequences of the cover-up could be dramatic. "Terrorists could easily penetrate the facility and steal weapons grade plutonium, or construct and detonate a nuclear bomb on the site without DOE security teams being able to prevent it," reports the *Spectator*, based on what McCallum told Timmerman.

It gets worse. McCallum was fired from his DOE post, or rather, "placed on adminstrative leave without pay" just last month. Bill Richardson personally gave the order to axe the whistleblower because he was "pissed off" at McCallum's attempts to inform Congress, according to what sources have told the *Spectator*.

White House flaks may have a tough time spinning the Rocky Flats scandal for other reasons. Not only has the administration "repeatedly and obstinately" refused to correct the problem, but Mrs. O'Leary may be vulnerable to conflict-of-interest charges. Timmerman writes:

"Under O'Leary's stewardship, Rocky Flats cut its security force by 40 percent, allowing prime contractor Kaiser-Hill LLC to improve its profit margin despite an overall reduction in the funds it received from DOE. Indeed, Kaiser-Hill actually earned performance bonuses from DOE, because its cleanup operations were going ahead on schedule."

Kaiser-Hill was apparently grateful for Mrs. O'Leary's indulgence, since she wound up on the board of ICF Kaiser, its parent company, upon her retirement from DOE. She remains on Kaiser's board today, while her husband does consulting work for the company.

O'Leary's Rocky Flats horror show only adds to the former Energy secretary's Nukegate woes. In 1997 probers discovered that she accepted $25,000 from Chinese businessman Johnny Chung in the name of her favorite charity, Africare.

Chung testified last month that the chief of Red Chinese intelligence gave him $300,000 to help get Bill Clinton re-elected in 1996.

Poll Indicates Most Americans Favor New Impeachment Inquiry

By Christopher Ruddy

NewsMax.com Vortex, January 2000 — A NewsMax.com/Zogby International poll finds that two-thirds of Americans want Congress to consider a second round of impeachment proceedings against Bill Clinton for possibly swapping United States military secrets to China in exchange for campaign cash.

Americans overwhelmingly indicated they are seriously concerned that President Clinton may have authorized the sale and transfer of nuclear and ballistic missile technology to China. The national survey of 1,005 registered voters was conducted by NewsMax.com/Zogby.

The poll comes on the heels of a CNN/*USA Today*/Gallup Poll released earlier in December 1999 that found that 50 percent of Americans now approve of Congress' impeachment of Clinton in December 1998 after the Monica Lewinsky scandal.

Americans apparently take the China allegations more seriously.

Since 1996, federal law enforcement and congressional sources have claimed that large amounts of money — some estimates place the amount as high as $10 million — were funneled from Chinese government sources to help the Democratic National Committee (DNC) fund Bill Clinton's re-election campaign in 1996.

Nearly 10 percent of Americans surveyed said the allegations were serious enough that Congress should immediately convene impeachment hearings against the president.

Another 56 percent said Congress should begin a preliminary investigation to decide if impeachment is warranted.

In 1998, the House of Representatives impeached the president. He avoided removal from office when the Senate decided not to convict him after a brief trial in 1999.

Support for a fresh look at a possible Chinagate impeachment inquiry, however, enjoys broad support from Democrats, Republicans and Independent voters. African-American voters, considered among the president's staunchest supporters, also backed the popular impeachment examination by 63 percent.

Concerns about the president's treatment of China and military transfers to the communist country have simmered for several years.

In 1996, the *New York Times* reported that U.S. defense contractors Hughes Electronics and Loral Space & Communications assisted China in developing and improving the launch capabilities of their ballistic missiles. After a grand-jury investigation was convened to investigate Loral's transfer of classified technology to China, President Clinton moved to authorize the transfer of such technology.

Since 1993, the chairman of Loral, Bernard Schwartz, donated more than $1 million to the DNC, making Schwartz the committee's largest donor.

The Clinton administration has also moved to issue more than 350 waivers, largely beginning in 1996, to transfer American supercomputers to China. Previous to Clinton's authorizations, China had received few clearances, because the computers could be used to develop advanced nuclear weaponry.

Recently, ABC News reported the Clinton administration authorized the sale of an ultra-high-speed IBM computer that the network claimed would enable China to develop its nuclear-carrying ballistic missiles.

President Clinton has made technology transfers of previously classified technology a priority. Early in Clinton's first term, administration officials changed the screening process for technology transfers, moving the approval process away from the State and Defense departments to the Commerce Department. The move was said to have increased the flow of technology transfers to China.

Chinagate figure John Huang, who had been a major Clinton fundraiser, also served in the Commerce Department. Congressional investigators believed Huang served as an agent of China, using ties through his previous employer, the Riady family of Indonesia.

Chi-Com* Clinton: Donor Behind Threat to Nuke L.A.

NewsMax.com Vortex, July 1999 — Three years ago, reports emerged of a then-unidentified Chinese official who warned that Los Angeles would be nuked if the United States interfered with China's plans to "reunify" with Taiwan. Two months later, China lobbed an unarmed nuclear-capable M-9 missile over Taiwan's capital, Taipei.

Big-time Democrat donor Johnny Chung told congressional investigators that General Ji Shengde, head of Chinese military intelligence, had given him $300,000 to donate to President Clinton's re-election campaign. Ji told Chung, "We like your president."

Now Jennifer Hickey, reporting in *Insight* magazine, has noticed a startling connection between the two events after combing through Chung's testimony before the House Government Reform and Oversight Committee. The generous General Ji, who likes our president, was the very same Chinese official who threatened Los Angelos with nuclear incineration in 1996.

In 1998, the *Washington Post* interviewed the person to whom China's nuke threat was delivered. Chas. W. Freeman Jr. was a China specialist who served as President Nixon's interpreter for his breakthrough 1972 China trip. More recently Freeman was assistant secretary of defense.

In January 1995, Freeman informed then-National Security Adviser Anthony Lake about a heated discussion he had with Chinese officials in Beijing that had taken a decidedly ugly turn:

"I said you'll get a military reaction from the United States" if China attacks Taiwan, Freeman recalled.

* *Chinese Communist*

"And they said: 'No, you won't. We've watched you in Somalia, Haiti and Bosnia, and you don't have the will.' "

Then, according to Freeman, one senior Chinese officer added: "In the 1950s, you three times threatened nuclear strikes on China, and you could do that because we couldn't hit back. Now we can. So you are not going to threaten us again because, in the end, you care a lot more about Los Angeles than Taipei." (*Washington Post* — June 21, 1998)

Freeman would not give the Post the identity of the Chinese officer who made the nuclear threat three years ago. But earlier this month, in sworn congressional testimony, Johnny Chung fingered General Ji Shengde.

Chung says he met Ji at a Hong Kong eatery, where Chung was introduced as "a good friend of President Clinton" by Liu Chaoying, vice president of China Aerospace Corporation.

Chung said Ji told him: "We like your president. I will give you 300,000 U.S. dollars. You can give it to the president and the Democratic Party. We hope he will be re-elected."

While Ji was busy placing his bets on Clinton, U.S. security officials took up Freeman's report about Ji's nuclear threat with Liu Huaqing, a senior Chinese national security official. "[Nuclear blackmail] is not our policy," Liu responded.

But comments from other Chinese officials are not always so reassuring:

The same year Ji threatened Los Angelos, the vice commandant of Beijing's Academy of Military Sciences offered this ominous assessment of Sino-U.S. relations:

"For a relatively long time, it will be absolutely necessary that we quietly nurse our sense of vengeance. . . . We must conceal our abilities and bide our time." (*New York Post*, April 5, 1997)

In September 1997, a Pentagon study of Chinese military writings was disclosed to the Senate Intelligence Committee. Defense Department China expert Michael Pillsbury told senators that Chinese military planning had a common theme:

"America is proclaimed to be a declining power with but two or three decades of primacy left. U.S. military forces, while dangerous at present, are vulnerable, even deeply flawed, and can be defeated with the right strategy." (Associated Press — September 19, 1997)

One senior U.S official, speaking to the *Washington Post* on condition of anonymity, described the uncomfortable months of early 1996 after Ji's January threat to nuke Los Angeles was followed in March by missile volleys over Taiwan:

"It was very tense. We were up all night for weeks. We prepared the war plans, the options. It was horrible."

The *Post* added: "At camp H.M. Smith in Honolulu, Admiral Joseph Prueher ordered his U.S. Pacific Command to form a 'crisis action team' to coordinate air-and-sea operations around the clock. Chinese public rhetoric became as warlike as any heard in decades, including vows to 'bury' the Americans if it came to a fight."

Bury America? In 1961, Soviet Prime Minister Nikita Khrushchev banged his shoe on a U.N. podium while bellowing a similar threat. Imagine if one of his generals was caught greasing the palms of a White House fund raiser with hundreds of thousands of dollars while uttering the words: "We like your president. We hope he will be re-elected"?

Cox Report Media Myths

NewsMax.com Vortex, July 1999 — Fresh from their success spinning Monicagate as "just about sex" (as opposed to more weighty matters like witness intimidation and obstruction of justice), our friends in the mainstream press are up to their old tricks again. This time their target is the Cox Report.

One of *Inside Cover*'s favorite media whoppers about America's newfound national security hemorrhage is this: Most of the secret information the Chinese now have access to disappeared over the transom during the Reagan and Bush administrations.

Not according to the actual chronology available in the Cox Report.

Turns out, of the 11 most serious episodes of nuke-related tech transfers noted by the bi-partisan panel, eight took place during the Clinton years. Except for data on the neutron bomb, which China obtained during the Carter administration, not a single serious breach of nuclear security came to light before 1993.

But doesn't that bolster the arguments of Clinton spinmeisters that it was this administration, and not prior Republican presidents, who ferreted out Chinese spying?

Not exactly. Except for a "walk-in," an unidentified Chinese agent who popped up out of the blue in a Far East CIA office in 1995, Clinton national security officials — along with the rest of us — might still be in the dark about the most serious spy case of the nuclear age. To the astonishment of U.S. intelligence, the Chinese tipster revealed that his Beijing bosses had the plans for America's deadly W-88 Trident D-5 nuclear warhead.

And what about the ever-popular claim that there's no evidence the Chinese have actually implemented the high tech they got from us?

Tell it to the Taiwanese.

Even a cursory reading of the Cox Report (e.g., the "Overview") reveals that the Chinese stole guidance technology from advanced aircraft like the F-14, F-16 and even the F-117 Stealth fighter — Which, the report states, "is directly applicable to medium and short-range PLA missiles, such as the CSS-6 (also known as the M-9)."

The Cox Report continues: "CSS-6 missiles were, for example, fired in the Taiwan Strait over Taiwan's main ports in the 1996 crisis and confrontation with the United States."

What's worth noting here is that the CSS-6 (M-9) is nuclear capable, a fact which made U.S. defense experts extremely nervous when they saw that particular missile soaring over a Pacific Island that we have a treaty obligation to defend.

What's also worth noting is that China launched its CSS-6 over Taiwan just three months after Chinese Military Intelligence Chief General Ji Shengde threatened U.S. Assistant Secretary of Defense Freeman with the prospect that Los Angeles might be vaporized if we attempted to honor our treaty commitment to Taiwan:

"In the 1950s, you three times threatened nuclear strikes on China," General Ji told Freeman, "and you could do that because we couldn't hit back. Now we can. So you are not going to threaten us again because, in the end, you care a lot more about Los Angeles than Taipei."

China's Theft of Nuclear Secrets

By Senator James M. Inhofe

NewsMax.com Vortex, April 1999
Senate Floor Statement
March 15, 1999

Mr. President, I want you to listen. I am going to tell you a story of espionage, conspiracy, deception and cover-up — a story with life and death implications for millions of Americans — a story about national security and a president and an administration that deliberately chose to put national security at risk, while telling the people everything was fine.

If it was written in a book, it wouldn't sell, because no one would believe it. If it was fictionalized in a novel, few could conceive it. But it is true.

Now for the sake of my statement today, I am stating that the president withheld information and covered up the Chinese theft of our technology. But I'm realistic enough to know that a person with the history of deception this president has will have provided himself with some cover in case he gets caught. So I'm sure there is a paper trail that he can allege. The way the president probably covered himself was to include tidbits about this theft buried in briefings on 40 or 50 other items, so the significance of it would not be noticed. But a paper trail would be established.

Anticipating that, I talked to the chairman of the House Intelligence Committee, Representative Porter Goss, and the Chairman of the Senate Intelligence Committee at the time of the discovery of this information, Senator Arlen Specter. Neither chairman was notified of the W-88 nuclear warhead technology theft. And these would have been the first to be notified. There can be no doubt that President Clinton engaged in a cover-up scheme.

Let me read three paragraphs from last week's op-ed article by Michael Kelly in the *Washington Post*, entitled "Lies About China."

"In April 1996, Energy Department officials informed Samuel Berger, then Clinton's deputy national security advisor, that Notra Trulock, the department's chief of intelligence, had uncovered evidence that showed China had learned how to miniaturize nuclear bombs, allowing for smaller, more lethal warheads. . . ."

"The *Times* reports that the House Intelligence Committee asked Trulock for a briefing in July 1998. Trulock asked for permission from Elizabeth Moler, then acting energy secretary. According to Trulock, Moler told him not to brief the committee because the information might be used against Clinton's China policy. . . ."

"The White House's secret would have remained secret had it not been for a select investigative committee headed by Republican Christopher Cox. . . ."

But even using the president's fictitious paper trail, the earliest either chairman could have known about it would have been late spring of 1997, years after the Clinton administration learned of it and, of course, after the 1996 elections.

I start, Mr. President, by listing a few things which we now know to be true, factual, incontrovertible . . . and not classified.

For years, the Clinton administration covered up China's theft of top secret U.S. nuclear weapons data. They never informed the Congress or American people about what had happened or its significance to our national security.

Let me tell you what President Clinton did during this period of time:

• During this period of time, the president misled the American people on numerous occasions about the threat posed by strategic nuclear missiles in the post-Cold War era.

• During this period of time, President Clinton made statements on over 130 separate occasions, such as the following: "For the first time since the dawn of the nuclear age, there is not a single solitary nuclear missile pointed at an American child tonight. Not one. Not a single one."

• During this period of time, he knew that China was targeting up to 18 intercontinental ballistic missiles at American children.

• During this period of time, President Clinton signed export control waivers which allowed his top campaign fund-raisers' aerospace company to transfer sensitive U.S. missile guidance technology to China.

• During this period of time, he shifted the prime satellite export responsibility from the State Department to the Commerce Department, making it easier for China and others to get sensitive military-related U.S. technology.

• During this period of time, President Clinton hosted over 100 White House fund raisers as part of a larger aggressive scheme to raise campaign contributions, many from illegal foreign sources, primarily including sources in China. Among guests permitted to attend these White House fund raisers were a convicted felon and a Chinese arms dealer.

• During this period of time, John Huang, Charlie Trie, Johnny Chung, James Riady and others with strong ties to China were deeply involved, with the president's knowledge, in raising Chinese-tainted campaign cash for the Clinton campaign.

• During this period of time, John Huang, who had been given a security clearance without a background check, was permitted to receive numerous classified CIA briefings, both during and after his stay at the Commerce Department.

• And during this period of time, President Clinton was successfully stopping the deployment of a national missile defense system, exposing every American life to a missile attack, leaving us with no defense against an intercontinental ballistic missile.

Mr. President, China's theft of secret data on the so-called W-88 nuclear warhead may be one of the most serious breaches of national security in our lifetimes. . . . More serious than Aldrich Ames. Perhaps more serious than the Rosenbergs.

The public needs to understand that this story is true. This is not about partisanship. This is not about some ancient history of some long-gone Cold War.

This is about the real world here and now. This is about national security in its most important aspects. This is about protecting our freedom and our existence as a nation. This is ultimately a matter which concerns the life and death of every citizen.

The W-88 is the most advanced nuclear warhead in the U.S. arsenal and is carried on top of Trident SLBMs (submarine-launched ballistic missiles).

This is the cornerstone weapon of our nation's nuclear deterrent. As many as eight of them can fit atop our submarine-launched missiles. As many as 10 can be put atop our largest land-based missiles . . . or on China's land-based missiles.

We are talking about a miniaturized warhead — much smaller in size than the Hiroshima atom bomb but 10 times more powerful.

As you can see from the chart, which appeared in the *New York Times* March 6, 1999, the Hiroshima bomb was huge and unwieldy. It was 10 and a half feet long and weighed over 4 tons — 8,900 pounds.

By contrast, the modern W-88 warhead is compact. It is only two and a half feet long and weighs only 300 pounds, but is at least 10 times more powerful.

The technology on which it is built is super top secret and represents billions of dollars and years, if not decades, of investment on the part of dedicated scientists and engineers working in the supreme American national interest.

Some might ask, why does America have this weapon? Because it is part of our responsibility as a world superpower to have the most advanced, efficient and credible nuclear deterrent, not only to protect our own freedom, but that of our allies as well.

It is part of our policy of "peace through strength." While we do not intend to ever use nuclear weapons, it is a fact of life in a dangerous world that we must be prepared to deter any potential adversary and any potential weapon any adversary may have.

The W-88 allows for multiple warheads to be placed on one missile. With this technology, China will now be able to put up to 10 warheads on a single long-range missile. Each warhead targeted at a different city. Each city subject to an explosion 10 times as great as that which destroyed Hiroshima at the end of World War II.

You know, Mr. President, I'm from Oklahoma. In 1995, a 4,800-pound truck bomb exploded outside the Murrah Federal Office Building in Oklahoma City. The building was destroyed, 168 people were killed, and 674 were wounded. This was a horrible event, the worst act of terrorism ever on American soil. That bomb had a force of 1,000 pounds (one-half of one ton) of TNT.

By way of contrast, the Hiroshima atom bomb had an explosive force of 15 kilotons (or 30,000 times as large as the Oklahoma City bomb). The W-88, while smaller in physical size, has a force of 150 kilotons (or 300,000 times as large as the Oklahoma City bomb). And by carrying 10 of these on one missile, 3 million times the force of the Oklahoma City bomb.

The more compact W-88 warhead makes possible what is called MIRV (multiple independent re-entry vehicle) technology, something China was thought to be many, many years away from developing on its own. And they stole this technology and President Clinton covered it up.

We also used to think North Korea was many years away from building long-range multiple-stage rockets.

Listen, Mr. President: On August 24 last year, the chairman of the Joint Chiefs of Staff, General Henry Shelton, wrote me a letter saying he was confident we would have three years' warning of any new long-range missile threat. Seven days later, on August 31, North Korea launched a three-stage Taepo Dong 1 missile that scattered a small payload off the coast of Alaska.

All of this only confirms what the Rumsfeld Report explained to us last year. We remember the Rumsfeld Commission which was chaired by former Secretary of Defense Donald Rumsfeld. This bipartisan commission, appointed jointly by Republicans and Democrats, included nine of the nation's most distinguished, qualified and informed experts in the field of assessing foreign missile threats. They concluded unanimously that when it comes to advanced missiles and weapons, with countries willing to buy, sell and steal technology, "we live in an environment of little or no warning." Which means we must immediately be prepared.

Last year, you may remember how it was revealed that the Clinton administration had changed the approval process for high-technology satellite transfers — and how waivers were granted for American companies so they could launch satellites in China. This ultimately resulted in China acquiring advanced U.S. missile guidance technology, making their missiles more accurate and more reliable. President Clinton personally signed the waiver allowing China to acquire this missile technology. Let me repeat, President Clinton personally signed the waiver allowing China to acquire this missile technology.

Executives of these two corporations that benefitted — Loral and Hughes — were among the largest financial contributors to President Clinton's campaign effort. But this is not important, Mr. President, because the motive for aiding and abetting our adversaries could be money, or it could be some kind of perverted allegiance to these countries, or it could be a total indifference to the security of the lives of Americans. The motive is not important. The fact is President Clinton did it and he knew exactly what he was doing.

Now coupling the transferred missile guidance technology with the stolen nuclear weapon technology, China can threaten U.S. cities with accurate, reliable and horribly destructive multiple warhead nuclear missiles.

This is not science fiction fantasy, Mr. President. Two years ago, a high-ranking Chinese official actually said that China was prepared to hit Los Angeles if the U.S. would take steps to defend Taiwan. No American should assume these are idle or impossible threats.

Now, by helping China develop their long range missile program, President Clinton was also helping North Korea and other rogue nations with theirs. Let me read three paragraphs from last week's *Washington Times* article entitled "China Assists North Korea Space Launches."

"China is sharing space technology with North Korea, a move that could boost Pyongyang's long range missile program, White House and Pentagon officials told the *Washington Times*. . . ."

"Another Pentagon report on a 1996 Chinese booster that failed to launch a U.S. satellite concluded that 'U.S. national security was harmed' by the improper sharing of technology with China by Hughes and another satellite maker, Loral Space & Communications Ltd . . . ."

Keep in mind, President Clinton signed the waiver to give the Chinese this technology. The article concludes:

"In 1994, the Pentagon's Defense Intelligence Agency reported that it believed China had helped design the Taepo Dong 2 missile (this is the North Korean missile) because its first-stage diameter is very close in size to China's CSS-2 intermediate range missiles."

So it is factual to say that President Clinton knew he was giving our missile technology to North Korea as well as China.

I take this moment to remind my colleagues once again that America today has no defense whatsoever against such a threat. The Clinton administration today — despite its rhetoric — opposes the deployment of any national missile defense system.

It was 16 years ago, on March 23, 1983, that President Reagan announced his intention to develop a national missile defense system to protect America. We have come a long way since then. Our technology has improved, we know what to do to meet this challenge.

Had we kept steadily on the course that President Reagan set, we would have a missile defense system deployed right now. Instead, we have an administration which killed the Reagan-Bush Strategic Defense Initiative program, which vetoed missile defense bills passed by Congress and which is wedded to the outdated ABM Treaty, which Henry Kissinger, the architect of the treaty, says has outlived its usefulness.

Clinton today is obsessed with maintaining the philosophy of the old ABM Treaty at all costs. He is locked into the mentality of a world with two lone superpowers — the United States and the Soviet Union.

The theory is that if both sides keep their populations defenseless, then neither side would dare attack out of fear of a devastating retaliation. This is what they call mutual assured destruction (MAD). It is a theory that Dr. Kissinger believes makes no sense in the modern world where many countries are getting their hands on long-range missiles and weapons of mass destruction.

President Clinton is solely responsible for the fact that we are totally defenseless against an incoming ICBM from China or anywhere else.

From news reports, this is some of what we know about China's theft of our nuclear secrets:

Apparently a spy at the Energy Department's Los Alamos weapons lab succeeded in transferring data on this highly classified W-88 warhead technology to China in the mid-1980s.

But our government did not find out about it until April 1995. (This is a critical date. We did not know about the theft until April 1995.) Detection came when experts analyzed data from then-recent Chinese underground nuclear tests and saw remarkable similarities to the W-88 U.S. warhead. Later in 1995, secret Chinese government documents confirmed that there had been a security breach at Los Alamos.

Deputy National Security Adviser Sandy Berger was first briefed about it in 1996. President Clinton did not respond then because he was obviously a little preoccupied with what he considered more important matters at that time.

After all, there were White House fund raisers to host, foreign campaign contributions, satellite transfers to approve, high-technology trade with China to promote, and — of course — an election to be won . . . at all costs. Mr. Berger was well aware of all this. We know he sat in on all the key campaign strategy meetings in 1996.

This was also the time when President Clinton was running around the country telling audiences that "for the first time since the dawn of the nuclear age, there is not a single, solitary nuclear missile pointed at an American child tonight. Not one. Not a single one."

Of course, everyone cheered, believing it to be true.

Of all the lies this president has told, this is the most egregious of all.

Scientist: Clinton Administration Gave China Top Nuclear Secrets

By Christopher Ruddy

NewsMax.com Vortex, March 1999 — A scientist at Lawrence Livermore National Laboratory has provided information that seriously contradicts Clinton administration claims that nuclear secrets obtained by China were solely the result of espionage during the late 1980s.

In the wake of allegations that the Clinton administration has been slow to investigate the theft of nuclear secrets by China, Vice President Al Gore has sought to deflect criticism onto the Reagan and Bush administrations.

"This happened in the previous administration, and the law enforcement agencies have pressed it and pursued it aggressively with our full support," Gore told CNN.

A nuclear weapons scientist, who has sought anonymity "to keep my position and keep supporting my family," has informed NewsMax.com that the Clinton administration has, in fact, aggressively sought to provide China with some of the nation's most closely guarded nuclear weapons technology.

"It seems like every day there are more and more Chinese at Livermore," he stated. The scientist said the administration had facilitated the transfer of laser technology employed in the process of making nuclear weapons-grade plutonium.

"Early in the 1980s a process was developed at Lawrence Livermore for producing weapons-grade plutonium," the scientist explained, revealing for the first time details of a U.S. government project then considered the government's most important.

Plutonium is a critical ingredient in a nuclear warhead, but for military applications, plutonium must be processed to change the isotope to weapons-grade. Weapons-grade plutonium is critical for developing nuclear weapons that are both highly reliable and produce a predictable yield when exploded.

The *New York Times* reported recently that U.S. intelligence officials had evidence China had made significant advances in it's nuclear weapons program. Specifically, China had designed and tested miniaturized nuclear warheads. Federal authorities have suspected the technology for the specialized weapons was the result of espionage at Los Alamos National Laboratory, the sister facility to Lawrence Livermore.

Chinese success in developing such nuclear weapons, as well as large strategic warheads, while increasing their stockpile of approximately 500 warheads, has been dependent on China's ability to process plutonium.

For decades, creating weapons-grade plutonium was an expensive and time-consuming process. A huge plutonium processing plant at Hanford, Washington, completed this task for U.S. defense needs.

According to the Livermore source, in the 1980s, at the height of the Cold War, the U.S. government had a "prime interest" to create a more efficient process to "separate or enrich fissile materials to enriched weapons-grade" plutonium.

The development of this plutonium process paralleled Livermore's development of a laser technology to process uranium, needed for civilian nuclear power plants. This technology to process uranium, called AVLIS, or the Atomic Vapor Laser Isotope Separation, was turned over in 1995 to the United States Enrichment Corporation, a private company that uses the technology for the benefit of nuclear power plants.

The plutonium project was, however, at the heart of Livermore's mission to develop America's strategic arsenal.

"This was the highest-funded project and the most secret project the government had, said the Livermore scientist. So secret, in fact, a special security compound known as the 'super block' was created within the processing area, simply known as Building 332."

The "super block" — a series of buildings housing nuclear weapons design and development programs — is one of the nation's most highly guarded complexes, with rings of barbed wire fence and a complement of specially trained federal guards who have access to automatic weapons and an armored personnel carrier on the premises. Deadly force is authorized against intruders.

The Livermore scientist states that within the secure compound, a special building was constructed for the development of this "new highly secret process" for plutonium.

During the Reagan and Bush administrations, the compound's already intense security was beefed up because of the "global implications if this technology ever leaked out."

Such technology could not only allow Third World countries like Iraq and Iran to overcome the significant obstacles in processing plutonium, it would allow existing nuclear club members like China to cheaply and quickly build a large nuclear stockpile.

Ominously, the scientist stated that all persons who worked on the project "were warned of the worldwide political instability that would occur if a foreign power was to get this secret."

This concern for security for the weapons-enriching laser process, however, quickly faded during the Clinton administration. During the Clinton administration's first year, China began making overtures to gain access to Livermore's weapons-grade enriching process.

For years the work at Livermore had been a prime target for Chinese espionage. In 1988, the FBI's chief of counterintelligence, Harry Godfrey III, told the *Los Angeles Times* that China was "the most active foreign power" seeking America's military secrets. Godfrey said Livermore National Laboratory was among China's main targets.

Concerns about China's intentions diminished after Clinton's inauguration, and China began more formal steps to gain access to Livermore.

China's efforts culminated with a delegation of Chinese scientists who visited Livermore in the winter of 1994, and another visit by Department of Energy Secretary Hazel O'Leary at about the same time.

The Department of Energy and the University of California jointly administer Livermore, with the DOE in charge of ensuring control over nuclear secrets.

"O'Leary's meeting was held in the California Room in Building

111. She arrived very late that day because of the flu or suspected food poisoning while in Silicon Valley that morning."

After the meeting, the scientist recalled, several Livermore scientists were in a heated debate over whether "this type of information [relating to weapons-enriching laser process] should be considered for technology transfer" to China.

The deal with China for the technology transfer was consummated, the scientist said, sometime later that year after O'Leary's visit, when top DOE officials, Department of Commerce officials representing Ron Brown, White House representatives and Chinese government officials met in a guarded room at the Pleasanton Hilton near Livermore.

O'Leary, now in private business, did not respond to a call for comment.

Lawrence Livermore officials voiced skepticism about the scientist's claims.

Jeff Garberson, senior manager for external relations for Livermore, said that to the best of his knowledge he was unaware of any process developed at the laboratory using lasers in the plutonium process or, for that matter, any transfer of nuclear secrets to the Chinese.

He said Chinese contact at Livermore has been "small." In recent years, he said, the lab had stepped up non-proliferation programs with Russian scientists, and Chinese scientists had expressed interest in joining that program.

He had no information about a secret meeting at the Pleasanton Hilton relating to these matters.

Garberson said that the rules at Livermore "remain by law: no transfer of classified technology to Russia and China" is permitted, and said he was familiar enough with programs there to know that no technologies had been reclassified to allow for Commerce Department officials to sell the technology abroad.

The Clinton administration had reset long-standing policies relating to technology transfers. By March 1994, the administration had abolished the COCOM system that had safeguarded technology transfers from Western countries to East Bloc or communist nations.

Later the White House took the key decision-making powers over technology transfers from the State and Defense departments and gave them to the Commerce Department.

These changes greatly expedited sales of U.S. technology, including supercomputers once prohibited for sale to communist countries and useful in developing nuclear weapons.

Another oft-cited example of the administration's method of reclassifying military secrets surfaced in a 1998 *New York Times* report by Jeff Gerth. Gerth revealed that in 1996, Loral, an American aerospace company, had, without a license, provided China with ballistic missile technology that enabled China to improve its rocket guidance systems.

When the Justice Department began a grand jury probe of this apparent illegal transfer, President Clinton quickly reclassified the technology and approved its transfer, effectively undermining the Justice Department's case against Loral.

Edward Teller, former director of Lawrence Livermore laboratory, told NewsMax.com that while he regards the allegations surrounding technology transfers to China as serious, he was less concerned about espionage and more concerned with the Clinton administration's failure to fund new weapons development programs during the past six years.

First Lady for President?
Possible, Poll Says

NewsMax.com Vortex, January 2000 — Hillary Clinton is a viable presidential candidate, new poll results show.

A NewsMax.com/Zogby International poll reveals that if presidential elections were held today, first lady Hillary Rodham Clinton would garner nearly 25 percent of the vote in a hypothetical three-way race with Republican George W. Bush and Reform Party convert Pat Buchanan.

Political pundits have said that any candidate who can poll 25 percent of the national vote has reached a serious threshold, and is capable of winning the presidency.

The NewsMax.com/Zogby nationwide survey of 1,005 likely voters found that 24.4 percent of those polled said they would vote for Hillary Clinton.

Bush failed to gain a majority, taking 47 percent of the vote.

Buchanan came in third, mustering a paltry 6 percent.

Another 22 percent of those polled said they weren't sure for whom they would vote.

These poll numbers are certain to be encouraging news to Hillary Clinton.

Some Hillary watchers believe her true intention all along has been to run for president, not be simply a junior senator from New York.

Dick Morris, one-time Bill Clinton campaign guru, believes Hillary will decide to opt out of the Senate race from New York later in 2000 and apply her campaign funds in 2004 to either the Senate race in Illinois or a presidential run. Federal Election Commission rules would allow her to do this.

These latest poll results, however, indicate she would be a viable candidate even four years sooner, in the 2000 presidential race, in a three-way race against Bush and Buchanan.

Were Hillary to go that route, she would have to beat out both Vice

President Al Gore and former New Jersey Senator Bill Bradley for the Democratic nomination.

There have already been signs of friction between the first lady and the Tennessean who has twice been her husband's running mate.

Author Barbara Olson, in her new Hillary biography *Hell to Pay*, agrees with Morris that Hillary's real ambition has been the presidency.

The first lady's poll numbers today compare favorably with those for Ross Perot when he first ran for the presidency in 1992. Poll numbers show that Hillary has a strong base of support in the Democratic Party.

The NewsMax.com/Zogby poll queried likely Democratic voters about Hillary's chances should she enter the Democratic primaries today — not four years from now.

In a three-way primary field of Bradley, Hillary and Gore, the vice president came out on top, with 36 percent, and Bradley second, with 31 percent.

The first lady received 19 percent — a respectable chunk of the vote for someone not even considered in the running at this point. Her number zooms higher were Gore not in the race for the nomination.

In a two-way contest today between Bradley and Hillary, Bradley would take 45 percent of the vote — but she would be nipping at his heels with 38 percent of the vote, with 17 percent of Democratic voters still undecided.

The NewsMax.com/Zogby poll indicates Hillary's prospects for future elections may improve markedly.

She racks up high support from young voters between ages 18 and 24. Among those voters in a presidential election, Hillary would outpoll both Bush and Buchanan by a comfortable margin.

Running in Democratic primaries, Hillary could also expect to win big with young voters. Among those between 18 and 34, she would beat Gore and Bradley by at least 20 points.

The survey does reveal some cracks.

Jewish voters, a large voting bloc in New York City and vital for any Senate run in that state, apparently have grave reservations about a Hillary presidential candidacy.

In a run for the White House, Bush would outpoll her by two to one among Jewish voters, with almost 50 percent undecided.

In a Democratic primary race among Gore, Hillary and Bradley,

Hillary would get a mere 7 percent of the Jewish vote — against Bradley, some better, but still only 12 percent.

Jewish voters may be responding to concerns that Hillary has not been a keen supporter of Israel, and did not distance herself from anti-Israel comments made by Yasser Arafat's wife during a recent speech.

Larry Sabato, an election analyst and professor of government and foreign affairs at the University of Virginia, believes these poll results suggest the first lady does have a chance to win the presidency, but she first must prove she can win an election to a lesser office.

Dick Morris Shocker: Hillary 'Exploded' with Anti-Semitic Slur

NewsMax.com Vortex, December 1999 — One-time White House political guru Dick Morris alleged that first lady Hillary Rodham Clinton once insulted him by suggesting that, as a Jew, he was obsessed with money.

"That's all you people care about is money!" Mrs. Clinton shouted, after Morris requested a pay raise during a meeting while Bill Clinton was governor of Arkansas. Morris, who is Jewish by birth, told Fox News Channel's *Hannity & Colmes* that Hillary's anti-Semitic outburst came as she "exploded in anger" over his request.

Morris says his account of Hillary's anti-Jewish insult will be included in Gail Sheehy's upcoming biography of the first lady, *Hillary's Choice*.

The former Clinton confidant detailed two separate examples to Fox News Channel illustrating Mrs. Clinton's apparent personal discomfort with Jews. Jewish voters comprise a significant portion of the electorate in New York, a state the first lady hopes to represent in the U.S. Senate.

Hours before his appearance on Fox, NewsMax.com questioned Morris on Sean Hannity's WABC radio show. When asked about the account of former Clinton bodyguard Larry Patterson, who alleged in September that fights between Bill and Hillary would often degenerate into shouting matches laced with anti-Semitic vulgarities, Morris, a Fox consultant, promised he would address the issue on *Hannity & Colmes*.

The mainstream press has completely ignored Patterson's charge that both Clintons privately indulged in bigoted and hateful language.

But now, with Patterson's claims bolstered by Morris' twin anecdotes, questions about Mrs. Clinton's true feelings toward Jews may be more difficult to dismiss.

Morris' account appears here verbatim for the first time in print:

HANNITY: Let's talk about this new book that's coming out about the Clintons by Gail Sheehy. You were interviewed for it and the questions about charges of anti-Semitism by the Clintons. What did you tell her?

MORRIS: Well, I'm not going to draw conclusions — it concerned Hillary, not Bill. And I'm not prepared to draw a conclusion as to whether she's anti-Semitic or not. I will just present you with the facts that I gave Gail Sheehy.

HANNITY: OK.

MORRIS: I'm Jewish. And I would often go to the governor's mansion and I would often have dinner with them. And it was kind of a joke. Every time before dinner, Hillary would take me aside and say, "Dick, I'm sorry. We're having pork. I just wasn't thinking about it." And I would say, "It's OK, Hillary, I don't mind pork.' And the third and the fourth time, I finally said, "You've asked me this four times. I eat pork. I like pork." So we joked about it, we kidded about it.

Then about a year later, I was having a meeting in the breakfast room in the governor's mansion with Betsy [Wright, Clinton's then–chief of staff], Hillary, Bill and me. And Bill and I were fighting about my fee. I was pushing for more money.

HANNITY: That's something a good consultant would do.

MORRIS: And Hillary was upset because of the limited income they had to live with and that I was making so much money from their campaign. And she was getting really annoyed at me for the battle. And she exploded in anger and I'll just quote her. She said:

"That's all you people care about is money!"

And I backed up. And I said, "Hillary, I assume by 'you people,' you mean political consultants."

And she said, "Yeah, yeah, that's what I meant, political consultants."

And I said, "I'm glad to hear that."

Hillary and the Jews

NewsMax.com Vortex, December 1999 — When NewsMax.com reported Dick Morris' charge that Mrs. Clinton once insulted him with an anti-Semitic comment, the story had no takers in the mainstream press.

"That's all you people care about is money!" Morris claims the first lady shouted at him after he asked for a pay raise during her husband's 1990 race for governor. (See previous story, Dick Morris Shocker: Hillary 'Exploded' with Anti-Semitic Slur.")

Though Morris' bombshell was nationally telecast on the Fox News Channel, it took two days for even fellow News Corporation property, the *New York Post,* to mention it — and only then under a headline that gave no indication of Morris' incendiary accusation. Mum's the word on this incident in the rest of the media.

Now Hillary is in trouble again for sitting idly by during a West Bank address by Mrs. Yasser Arafat, who accused the Israelis of gassing Palestinian women and children on a regular basis. Journalists are "shocked, shocked" at Hillary's stone-faced reaction and failure to condemn Arafat's remarks even after she left the scene.

Despite the outrageous charges, Mrs. Clinton's meeting with Mrs. Arafat ended the way it began, with a warm embrace and a kiss on the cheek.

In fact, the first lady has a long history of insensitivity toward Jews — one which the elite media seldom deigns to comment upon.

Arkansas State Trooper Larry Patterson, who guarded the first family for six years before they moved to the White House, told NewsMax.com in September that Mrs. Clinton repeatedly engaged in anti-Semitic invective during arguments with her husband.

During the height of the Monica Lewinsky scandal, Hillary caused an international brouhaha when she blithely called for the establishment of a Palestinian state. The official U.S. policy endorses no such thing. But the comment won Hillary effusive praise from the same Palestinian officials who charged Israel with using poison gas on them.

During the late 1980s, Hillary served as chairwoman for the New World Foundation, which bankrolled an assortment of radical left causes, including Grassroots International — an unabashedly anti-Israel outfit that funded two PLO groups on the West Bank.

At the White House, Hillary has entertained extremist Muslim groups with known connections to Hamas, the most notorious anti-Israel terrorist operation in the Middle East.

And then there's this curious tidbit regarding her brother Hugh's 1994 U.S. Senate bid in Florida, courtesy of old Arkansas hand Wesley Pruden:

"Hugh Rodham, for whom sister Hillary Rodham Clinton campaigned over the weekend, has descended into the most toxic slime of all. Hugh Rodham's opponent in the Democratic runoff primary is, as it happens, Jewish. But he has a name that is not readily identifiable as Jewish, so the Rodham campaign dispatched Ellis Rubin of Miami, a Jew who ran third in the first primary, to Florida's rural panhandle to make sure the Klansmen they imagine populate the territory will understand why they must vote for Mr. Rodham, like him or not, lest they unwittingly vote for a Jew." (*Washington Times* — October 4, 1994)

FAA to Controllers: Treat Hillary's Plane Like the President's

NewsMax.com Vortex, December 1999 — The Federal Aviation Administration has ordered air traffic controllers nationwide to handle first lady Hillary Clinton's government jet as if the president of the United States were on board, a top Republican Party official charged.

Republican National Committee chief Jim Nicholson confirmed the story to WOR radio's Bob Grant, saying he had just learned of the development. Unofficial reports of Hillary's new airborne status began circulating earlier in the day on the Free Republic Web site.

"The FAA has issued an edict to all its controllers that her campaign plane, which is a United States Air Force plane, by the way, is supposed to be treated exactly the same as Air Force One," Nicholson told Grant.

The top Republican said the advisory from the FAA to air traffic controllers warns that the first lady's special treatment will cause "much delay up and down the Eastern Seaboard from Washington to Boston."

The Free Republic report revealed that Hillary's plane, codenamed

"Fox Trot," will now take precedence over all other aircraft landing or taking off.

Nicholson also complained about Mrs. Clinton's use of Air Force jets for her campaign trips to New York. "It's this imperial arrogance that she has to be on an Air Force plane. And now her Air Force campaign plane has to be treated like Air Force One."

Police Video Exposes Bigotry in Clinton Clan

NewsMax.com Vortex, September 1999 — If an American president used the "N" word and it was captured on tape, undoubtedly the news media would be all over the story. But what about a presidential brother?

A controversial videotape depicts first brother Roger Clinton repeatedly and enthusiastically using that most offensive of all racial epithets while he was under investigation for suspected drug dealing during the 1980s.

Here's an excerpt of Roger's clearly audible comments in a June 27, 1984, police surveillance video, as he was using cocaine and discussing a recent encounter his dealer had with a local African-American teenager:

"Some junior high n——r kicked Steve's ass while he was trying to help his brothers out; junior high or sophomore in high school. Whatever it was, Steve had the n——r down. However it was, it was Steve's fault. He had the n——r down, he let him up. The n——r blindsided him."

The clip appears in the blockbuster 1996 documentary, *The Mena Cover-Up: Drugs, Deception and the Making of a President*, distributed by Citizens for Honest Government. Another Citizens for Honest Government video, *Obstruction of Justice: The Mena Connection*, is currently the subject of a defamation trial in Little Rock, Arkansas.

While debate rages about the central question of *The Mena Cover-Up* — was Bill Clinton a kingpin in a Latin American drug smuggling operation? — the video of Clinton's brother casually using the "N" word is smoking-gun proof that at least one member of the first family has a problem in the racial tolerance department. But is Roger's attitude on race unique among the Clintons?

The White House line from Day One has been that the president's grandfather, Eldridge Cassidy, taught him to respect the black customers. Cassidy served as a grocer in the poor section of Hope, Arkansas. Cassidy's racial mentoring was even cited at Clinton's impeachment trial as proof that the president didn't mean to violate Paula Jones' civil rights.

But didn't Roger Clinton have the same grandfather? Yup. So how did little brother manage to miss out on all that racial sensitivity training? Or has some carefully crafted public relations obscured the entire Clinton clan's redneck sensibilities?

And how come Roger's tape-recorded hate speech never found its way into the mainstream press?

Is it because a story about slurs hurled by someone very close to the president isn't news? Tell that to Newt Gingrich's mom, who used the "B" word on videotape to describe the first lady in a 1994 interview with Connie Chung. Her faux pas was recycled for days on end just as Gingrich was about to assume the speakership.

Would the media have given Nixon or Reagan such a break had a brother of theirs been caught using the "N" word on tape? Don't bet on it.

Some say President Clinton is America's "first black president." *Inside Cover* suspects that the first black president's brother is underwhelmed by the honor.

Flowers Says Bill Told Her About Hillary

NewsMax.com Vortex, September 1999 — In a freewheeling one-hour radio interview, Gennifer Flowers revealed new details about Bill's and Hillary's personal lives.

Other revelations included news that the former Clinton girlfriend began monitoring her health with regular AIDS tests after learning that the Arkansas governor had sex with dozens of different women during the years she shared an intimate relationship with him.

Flowers was interviewed by freelance investigator and longtime Clinton critic Larry Nichols on Nichols' own Genesis Communications Network program.

The conversation between Nichols and Flowers was somewhat historic. The interview marked the first time the two had talked since Nichols introduced Flowers' name to the world in a 1990 lawsuit alleging that then-Governor Clinton was using state funds to underwrite his womanizing. The rest, as they say, is history.

Flowers let slip perhaps the biggest news of the broadcast when Nichols broached the topic of the first lady's bid to become U.S. senator from New York.

NICHOLS: What is one of the most juicy things that Bill told you about Hillary that would have some impact, that the people of New York need to know?

FLOWERS: The things that Bill told me about Hillary, I think a lot of this has already been out there. You know, he called her "Hilla the Hun." And he told me that she was bisexual. But everybody knows that . . .

NICHOLS: Whoa, Whoa. Now wait a minute . . .

FLOWERS: I'd like to make a point. Now, we'll get back to that . . . .

Flowers' point was that the Clintons' recent search for high-priced digs in New York's tonier precincts belies their supposed concern about the millions of dollars in legal bills they face. But the one-time Clinton paramour never did return to Clinton's characterization of his wife's sexuality.

The interview ended before Nichols could get Flowers to explain whether she believed Clinton's claim was true or merely the posturing of an unfaithful husband.

Flowers said that Clinton's own sexual recklessness had caused her a great deal of worry about her own health:

"When I found out about all of the other women, I was angry, not necessarily because he had represented our relationship as something different, but because I felt that he had literally put my life in danger. Because he was having sex with all these people — and I assume not protected sex — and we've all heard of AIDS. And I said, 'Oh my God, he's exposed me to this.' I went and had an AIDS test, and I continually now thereafter have myself tested. I'm OK so far, but he clearly put my life in danger in that situation."

On another matter, Flowers said that a reported upcoming gathering in Dallas featuring women linked to the president was news to her. "I don't know much about that meeting at this point, to tell you the truth. I did read the press releases and heard some things through the media. I don't know any more than what I've read in reference to that."

Flowers said she would consider joining a lawsuit brought on behalf of women abused by Clinton and his damage controllers. "I possibly could do it. It's my impression that the ladies involved in this cannot file a class-action lawsuit. But that certainly there would be an opportunity to pursue something legally as a group."

Flowers added, "I have at times been very tempted to file a defamation suit against Bill Clinton — certainly after he lied about our relationship in his deposition and committed perjury."

As the interview drew to a close, Nichols mused at the irony of both he and Flowers winding up as "a sidebar in Clinton's legacy." Nichols then apologized to the former Clinton girlfriend for the years of grief his 1990 lawsuit had caused her.

"Now Larry, I have told you that I accept your apology and I have realized since I've gone though my situation that we all had to do what we felt we needed to do," replied Flowers. "And I clearly feel that you filing that lawsuit and its becoming public knowledge saved my life. So you don't owe me an apology anymore."

Imelda Rodham Clinton?

NewsMax.com Vortex, August 1999 — She's come a long way, baby.

A long way from those Arkansas days when she used to itemize her tax deductions right down to the last pair of her husband's used BVDs. (Back then, Bill Clinton's underwear wasn't considered evidence.)

But those days are long gone. Now it's time for Hillary Rodham to start livin' large. Imelda Marcos-style, if you will. As in, eighteen pairs of Bruno Magli shoes on a single Euro shopping spree — according to recent reports.

In fact, even *Paris Match* took notice when Imelda Rodham availed herself of the local finery during a pit stop en route to the Clintons' Kosovo victory party. According to one English translation that popped over our cyber-transom, Mrs. Clinton sounds like a regular chug-a-lug shopaholic:

"23,190 francs ($3500.00 U.S.) for Hillary's one-hour whirlwind

Paris shopping spree. At the Italian shoe designer Tod's, Hillary bought the same leather sac, L'Bag, in the large and medium sizes for 4,900 and 4,400 francs each ($1408.00 U.S. total) and a pair of loafers for 1,490 francs ($225.00 U.S.). By the French designer Apostrophe, the blouse that she wore the same evening to the restaurant, L'Ami Louis, with Chirac and his wife, for 1,200 francs ($181.00 U.S.), a pantsuit for 5,000 francs ($757.00 U.S.), a silk scarf in khaki for 1,200 ($181.00 U.S.), a black coat for 3,900 francs ($590.00 U.S.), and a turquoise blouse for 1,100 francs ($166.00 U.S.)."

Not too shabby for someone who just parted with $850,000 to settle her hubby's sex harassment suit. Not to mention that $10 million in legal bills the Clintons are facing.

Then there's the new real estate Mrs. Clinton is reportedly looking over in her brand-new favorite state, New York. She skipped out on her mister's Broadway fund raiser to examine a $3.8 million waterfront spread featuring 5 bedrooms and 6.5 baths — in Westchester's tony North Salem.

No wonder Hillary & Company have us taxpayers picking up the tab for her frequent New York junkets. Some habits, like writing off old underwear, die hard.

Plastic Surgery for Hillary?

NewsMax.com Vortex, February 1999 — *Inside Cover* reported last September that Tipper Gore had gone plastic, but what about Hillary?

Rumors have abounded in Washington for years that the first lady has had one or more "makeovers."

Now eyebrows are being raised all over New York. In the January 18 edition of *New York* magazine, an advertisement for a "cosmetic surgery consultant" named Denise Thomas features a glowing picture of Hillary.

Thomas' ad says she can serve as "your personal shopper, answer your questions and recommend the Best Certified Plastic Surgeons to meet your needs and your budget."

Hillary is depicted smiling as she shakes Thomas' hand, as in, "Job well done, girl."

Inside Cover called Denise Thomas. She wasn't in, but her secretary said Hillary has "never, absoltutely never" had plastic surgery.

The secretary said Hillary is simply a friend of Denise Thomas. She said the White House is "thrilled" by the ad and she had just gotten off the phone with Hillary's secretary when we called.

Chelsea's Graduation Gift: Plastic Surgery

NewsMax.com Vortex, March 1999 — So many folks in Washington are going "plastic," it's becoming difficult to keep track.

Last year, NewsMax.com's *Inside Cover* revealed that second lady Tipper Gore had gone under the knife, getting a minor tuck and eyelift. The operation, we heard, took place in a posh New York hotel suite as Secret Service agents stood guard.

Then eyebrows were raised — no pun intended — when the January 18 edition of *New York* magazine hit the stands. An advertisement in the back of the magazine for a "cosmetic surgery consultant" named Denise Thomas appeared. The ad featured a glowing picture of Hillary Rodham Clinton shaking Denise's hand.

Thomas' ad claimed that as part of her consultancy she can serve as "your personal shopper, answer your questions and recommend the Best Certified Plastic Surgeons to meet your needs and your budget."

The ad once again raised talk about Hillary's own purported makeovers.

But a source familiar with the New York plastic surgery scene tells *Inside Cover* that Hillary may have been smiling more for her daughter than for any cosmetic surgery she has had.

The source reports that sometime before Chelsea arrived at Stanford she had plastic surgery.

"It was a rather massive reconstruction of her lower jaw and lower lip," the source said, reminding *Inside Cover* that any photo showing Chelsea a few years ago will show "a horribly recessive chin" and "an uneven lower lip."

The work was deemed remarkable, and Chelsea, said to be the nicest person in the Clinton household, looks fine.

Clinton Cracks Jewish Jokes

NewsMax.com Vortex, November 1998 — When Ronald Reagan cracked an off-color joke about Poles and Italians during his 1980 presidential campaign, it became a top news story. Some in the press said he should drop out of the race. Fast-forward to the Clinton presidency.

According to edited transcripts, Clinton enjoyed making anti-Jewish jokes with Lewinsky, herself a Jew.

According to one transcript of a phone call between Lewinsky and Tripp, Lewinsky recounts how she told Clinton a joke her father had been telling.

"Why do Jewish men like to watch pornos [films] backward?" Lewinsky asked Tripp.

"So they can watch the prostitute give back the money," Lewinsky answered.

Lewinsky told Tripp that when she told Clinton the joke, he laughed and quickly responded with his own joke. Clinton's joke was apparently so obscene it was redacted by censors.

Lewinsky responded to Clinton's blacked-out joke by saying, "A bad joke still sucks after 20 years."

Clinton then retorted, "Oh, did I tell you the Jewish American Princess and apple one—?"

Tripp interrupted Lewinsky's account by suggesting that Clinton and Bruce Lindsey "tell raunchy jokes."

The U.N. — No Place for a Jewish Girl!!

At another point in the same conversation, Lewinsky explained to Tripp why she was not taking a job at the U.N. Lewinksy stated her mother opposed the idea.

"My mom refuses to let me take [the U.N. job.]," Lewinsky told Tripp.

Tripp found this curious. "What do you mean?" she asked Lewinsky.

"Because she absolutely refuses for me to work at the U.N."

Tripp: "Really?"

Lewinsky: "Mm-hmm."

Tripp: "Tell me why."

Lewinsky: "Because she went there, and she hates the building.

She says it's going to be just like the Pentagon, and she just—she thinks it's no place for a Jewish girl."

Tripp: "Really? Did she—now, did she just look in the lobby or what?"

Later, Lewinsky explained that she was also turned off to the U.N. job because she was not impressed by U.N. Ambassador Bill Richardson because she really had no idea who he was.

She explained to Tripp—in Valley Girl fashion—that she let Richardson know "I have a mental block on who you really are. . . . I'm like, 'That's why I don't get nervous [around you], you know.'"

The Other FBI Book: Is Clinton a KGB Spy?

NewsMax.com Vortex, November 1998 — So Gary Aldrich wrote a best-selling book, *Unlimited Access*, detailing a myriad of scandals and security lapses at the Clinton White House.

He was not the only FBI agent to write a book.

Inside Cover has learned that Dennis Sculimbrene, Aldrich's long-time partner and the most senior FBI agent then at the White House, also wrote a book. It has never been published.

Source tells *Inside Cover* it is a fictional, thinly veiled account of Sculimbrene's days at the White House and the arrival of William Jefferson Clinton.

Source says the "novel" was written before Aldrich's book was published.

The book's plot: the story of how a KGB mole becomes president.

Source says Sculimbrene has no evidence Clinton was, or is, a spy. Sculimbrene simply believes, we hear, that had anyone else with Clinton's background and activities undergone an FBI background check, the person would have been rejected as too great a security risk.

Sculimbrene resigned the FBI in July of 1996, shortly after Aldrich resigned. His complaints about improper drug use at the White House got him on the Clintons' hit list. A decorated veteran of the FBI, Sculimbrene was sent for his own drug test and then told to report to Chicago for psychological re-evaluations. Sounds like Romania before the fall of the Berlin Wall.

Sculimbene also became disgusted by the Clinton-friendly FBI agents who the Clintons were bringing to the White House. Sculimbrene proudly had a photo on his desk of him and Newt Gingrich. One of the Clinton FBI agents would regularly pass Sculimbrene's desk and knock the photograph to the ground.

More St. Pat's Day Intimidation by Hillary's Bodyguards

NewsMax.com Vortex, May 2000 — Reports of intimidation by Mrs. Clinton's bodyguards as she marched in New York's St. Patrick's Day parade continue to surface in the alternative press, despite the establishment media's refusal to cover the story.

A woman who marched in the parade told Bob Grant's WOR audience that Mrs. Clinton's bodyguards harassed and intimidated her family because they heckled the first lady from the sidewalk while holding signs supporting her Senate rival, New York Mayor Rudy Giuliani.

Grant's caller, "Maureen," said that, after her family joined the crowd in jeering Mrs. Clinton, "they were surrounded by men in trench coats with radios" who told them that "they do not have the right, that she is the first lady and [they] did not have the right" to heckle. "They told them, 'We think you should stop this now.'

"My relatives weren't using any obscene words or anything of that nature. They were telling her to go back to Arkansas," Maureen said.

"My niece met me later when I was finished marching. She was very upset. She said, 'I was so frightened.' She told me she shut up because she figured she was going to be arrested."

Grant's caller, apparently unfamiliar with Metro Network newsman Glenn Schuck's account, told the talk host that she hadn't heard anyone else report the abusive behavior by Mrs. Clinton's security detail.

"They just lost their minds. . . . Agents literally were pushing press to the ground. I mean, they just started pushing and shoving; female camera people five feet tall were getting thrown to the ground, cameras flying," Schuck told WABC after the parade.

"Myself, I was grabbed by the shoulder, I was thrown back over. I think somebody from Channel 11 landed on my back," said Schuck, who claimed he was one of at least six reporters who were assaulted by Mrs. Clinton's guards, who resorted to similar violence at several different stops along the parade route.

That night, local CBS-TV reporter Marsha Kramer showed video shots at the parade showing Clinton's bodyguards trying to stop a CBS cameraman from filming the booing crowd. Other than that, though, no mainstream news outlet has covered the harassment and intimidation by the first lady's security detail.

Hillary and the 'Brutal' New York Press

NewsMax.com Vortex, July 1999 — A recent *New York Times Magazine* cover story asks the burning question: "Is Hillary willing to put herself on the line?"

It sounds like an allusion to the allegedly "brutal" New York press corps, which media wags promise will put the first lady through the wringer after she announces her lurch for Pat Moynihan's soon-to-be-available New York Senate seat.

We'll see how tough these press pussycats become, after years of orgasmic coverage every time the First Mr. and Mrs. deign to clog Manhattan streets in hot pursuit of a DNC dollar.

For instance, have any of the New York pressies — or their D.C. counterparts, for that matter — wondered aloud lately whether the $50,000 Johnny Chung donated to offset expenses for Hillary's 1995 White House Christmas party came from Chinese military intelligence?

It was, after all, Chung himself who testifed just weeks ago that Chinese Military intelligence chief General Ji Shengde told him, "We like your president" (and presumably his Mrs.), after promising Chung $300,000 to get the Clintons re-elected.

In 1997, Chung told reporters he had assurances from Mrs. Clinton's chief of staff that Hillary herself knew it was he who underwrote the first family's Yuletide hoedown.

Or will those hardbitten New York scribes ask Hillary if she knew where the $25,000 that flowed into her Whitewater public relations fund, a.k.a. "The Back to Business Group," came from? Chung again claims credit for that generosity, though we still don't know if General Ji was the ultimate moneyman behind the pro-Hillary PR.

And while the oh-so-tough Empire State media is at it — Yes, Hillary, that's what New York calls itself — why not find out whether what the late Ron Brown's girlfriend, Nolanda Hill, says is true? Was it really you, Miss Hillary — as Hill told ABC News two years ago — who insisted that Chinagate's main man John Huang be inserted into the Commerce Department over Secretary Brown's objections?

And what about L.D. Brown? Darn it, Miss Hillary, we hate to bother you again with all that sex stuff, but he recently went public with the claim that you hit on him — out-and-out propositioned the man — not once, but twice while he was in your hubby's employ as an Arkansas state trooper and gubernatorial bodyguard. And he claims you got physical, not just with him, but with the late Vince Foster.

Inside Cover can't wait for New York's media big boys to get curious about Hillary's role in Chinagate. But we're not holding our breath.

Brown Case Witness May Have Been Slain

NewsMax.com Vortex, February 2000 — Oklahoma's chief medical examiner is exploring the possibility that a key government witness in the independent counsel's investigation into the death of Commerce Secretary Ron Brown may have been murdered.

In 1997, Oklahoma businessman Ron Miller provided the government key evidence — including audiotapes — against Eugene and Nora Lum, two fund-raisers with close ties to Brown and the Clinton White House.

For more than two years Miller's death has been officially classified as "natural." Now, legal consultant Stephen Dresch has persuaded the Oklahoma state medical examiner to reclassify Miller's cause of death as "unknown," saying that the available medical evidence was also "consistent with homicide."

Dresch is involved in a lawsuit stemming from the 1996 plane crash death of Commerce Secretary Ron Brown.

Evidence Miller provided to the independent counsel then probing Secretary Brown's business dealings helped prosecutors build a case against the Lums. They had given Brown's son Michael gifts of stock in their company, Dynamic Energy Resources, made him a board member and lavished him with six-figure consulting fees.

The Lums' daughter Trisha won a slot in the Commerce Department and even accompanied Brown on his 1994 trade mission to China. Suspicions that the Lums used Michael Brown to funnel money to his father were never proven.

Nora Lum made at least 13 visits to the Clinton White House between 1993 and 1995.

Miller had owned Gage Corporation, which was sold in 1993 to Dynamic Energy. Miller also audiotaped his telephone conversations with the Lums and provided federal probers with 165 cassette recordings believed to be crucial to their prosecution.

Dresch told NewsMax.com that Miller had taken elaborate steps to document his dealing with the Lums, bugging his own office and even his briefcase.

"He realized he was in the middle of something big," Dresch said. Anticipating the Lums' indictment in May 1997, Miller was elated that his evidence-gathering had resulted in the first real prosecution of the 1996 campaign finance scandal.

"I'm really glad to see it," the Oklahoma businessman told American Lawyer News Service. "It needs to be exposed to the light of day. It could focus light on a portion of the Lums' activities, and that would expand to shed light on the rest."

However, the Clinton Justice Department, which had taken over independent counsel Daniel Pearson's probe of Commerce Secretary Brown's activities after Brown's April 1996 death, brought no action against the Lums related to their ties to Brown, his son or the Commerce Department.

The Oklahoma couple was instead charged only with making illegal campaign contributions to Senator Edward Kennedy and an Oklahoma Democratic House candidate.

Less than four months after the Lums pleaded guilty, Ron Miller was rushed to a Norman, Oklahoma, hospital after becoming ill at home. Doctors were never able to determine the cause of his affliction. Miller died days later.

"He went from being healthy to dying in a week," J. Dell Gordon told the Associated Press at the time, adding that Miller had just turned over "boxes of material" to congressional investigators.

Integris Baptist Medical Center, where Miller died in early October 1997, turned the case over to the state medical examiner because hospital officials said the witness's death "was not fully explainable."

Dr. James Marvel, a local physician who has studied the evidence in Miller's death, told NewsMax.com he suspected the Oklahoma businessman may have been poisoned.

After examining Miller's autopsy report, Marvel noted that several of his vital organs, particularly his lungs, were much heavier than normal. "It tells me that he sustained serious physical insult to his lungs," he said.

Marvel suggested such an injury would be consistent with someone gradually overcome by an airborne toxin. "Whatever it was that killed

Ron Miller entered through his lungs," he said.

Dresch said Miller had received death threats in the months before he died. NewsMax.com has obtained a copy of a Norman police report that backs up this claim. Dated January 14, 1997, the "Offense Report" reads in part:

"Suspect told Miller, 'You haven't been shot at yet.' Mr. Miller said that the subjects he is dealing with have made a number of references to certain people wanting Mr. Miller dead. Mr. Miller said he recorded this telephone conversation."

The police report names Dallas businessman Donald Sweatman as the source of the most recent threats.

Though Dresch said local police took Miller's complaint seriously at the time, a criminal investigation was never opened.

The Miller tapes, still in the possession of the FBI, could have far-reaching consequences. It is believed that on one recording, Sweatman even implicates first lady Hillary Clinton in the Lums' financial scheme.

"Apparently the assertion that Sweatman made on tape was that Hillary had been instrumental in arranging a $4.5 million loan to Dynamic Energy back in 1993, so the Lums could purchase Miller's Gage Corporation," Dresch told NewsMax.com.

Norman police are reviewing the case with an eye toward opening a new investigation.

Starr Deputies Doubt Foster Was 'Suicide'

NewsMax.com Vortex, January 2000 — The establishment press wasn't particularly curious when deputy White House counsel Vince Foster turned up dead six years ago in a Virginia park — from what the Park Police said was a self-inflicted gunshot wound.

And despite the dozens of unanswered questions, anomalies and flat-out contradictions that have emerged from the Foster case file in the intervening years, independent counsel Ken Starr enjoyed a rare burst of positive press when he seconded the Park Police findings in 1997.

Starr's report on the matter even went so far as to describe the suicide conclusion as "a 100 percent medical certainty."

However, it emerged recently that fewer than 100 percent of the investigators who probed the Foster case for Starr actually felt that way.

Fox News Channel's Bill O'Reilly did some investigating of his own before he grilled the former independent counsel about his Foster probe on Dec. 20, 1999. So far, the rest of the press has ignored their revealing exchange:

O'REILLY: Now, some of your investigators have told us off the record that they believe Vince Foster did not commit suicide and that your office was not aggressive enough in investigating the Vince Foster situation. How do you reply?

STARR: Bill, you didn't get that from my investigators. I don't know who you got it from.

O'REILLY: I did.

STARR: Oh, I . . .

O'REILLY: I did.

STARR: They — they did not think that . . .

O'REILLY: I got it from one of your investigators, I have to tell you. I would never say an untruth on this program.

STARR: All right. OK. All right. Let me just say this.

O'REILLY: Go ahead.

STARR: We looked at every aspect of that invest — of that death, and we came unanimously — those of us involved in it, so I will look forward to finding out who this person was . . .

O'REILLY: You'll never get it from me because, you know, just like you, I keep confidences. But, look, this person said — and it was backed up by another — that there were unanswered questions about Vince Foster's suicide. Are you 100 percent sure that Vince Foster committed suicide?

STARR: Absolutely.

O'REILLY: You're a hundred percent positive.

STARR: One hundred percent that he committed suicide, that it was done at the very point where his body was found.

O'REILLY: OK. Now let me ask you a second question.

STARR: Not a shadow of a doubt.

O'REILLY: All right. Fine. You're on the record there.

Gennifer Flowers: 'Clinton Is a Murderer'

NewsMax.com Vortex, September 1999 — Gennifer Flowers broke one of the most powerful of all media taboos when she unequivocally called her former lover, the president of the United States, a murderer.

The most famous of all pre-presidential Clinton paramours also insisted that had she not protected herself by going public with her story of a 12-year affair with the then–Arkansas governor, she would have been killed.

Appearing on CNBC's *Hardball* to discuss Hillary Clinton's bombshell *Talk* magazine interview about her husband's philandering, Flowers was asked by host Chris Matthews if she thought Mrs. Clinton's renewed victim status would help her win the New York U.S. Senate race.

FLOWERS: Well, in the first place, I hope that she does not succeed at becoming a United States senator from New York. I think that would be a travesty. We've had enough of these people — these criminals, these liars, these murderers. We need to get them out of political office, please.

MATTHEWS: Murderers?

FLOWERS: Well, there is a Clinton death list. If anyone would like to go to my Web site and take a look at it . . .

MATTHEWS: Well, we have your Web site here — www.genniferflowers. com. But what will they find if they go there in terms of murder? I didn't know that one.

FLOWERS: Well, there are a number of deaths associated with Bill Clinton and his administration and his operatives. I would just suggest that they go on and take a look at it.

MATTHEWS: Do you believe that the president ordered the killing of anyone?

FLOWERS: I believe that he did. And I believe that I wouldn't be sitting here talking with you today had I not become high profile as I did. Even though I didn't do it on purpose, it saved my life.

Matthews challenged Flowers to cite "one hard case" of Clinton ordering a murder. Flowers named Luther "Jerry" Parks, the one-time chief of campaign security in 1992 who was gunned down execution-style eigth months after Clinton entered the White House.

Parks' wife Jane and son Gary claim that he was building a dossier on Clinton's private life, which was stolen shortly before his murder. Gary Parks has told reporters, "I believe my father was killed to protect Bill Clinton's political career."

Matthews continued to press Flowers for evidence:

MATTHEWS: But you don't know if there's any connection [to Bill Clinton].

FLOWERS: I didn't hear Bill Clinton get on the phone and call and place the order to have this man killed.

MATTHEWS: But, you know — you sort of need evidence like that to accuse even this guy, a guy you don't like perhaps, of murder, don't you?

FLOWERS: Well, I think if it looks like a chicken and walks like a chicken — perhaps it's a chicken. I mean, come on. All of these things are just not a coincidence.

MATTHEWS: Perhaps.

The Clinton Curse: Another Presidential Helicopter Pilot Dies — The Body Count Rises

NewsMax.com Vortex, September 1999 — Lt. Colonel Mark Cwick, a Marine Corps helicopter pilot who served President Bill Clinton, died recently in what appears to have been a car accident.

Cwick, 41, was pronounced dead at Mary Washington Hospital in Fredericksburg, Virginia.

Colonel Cwick suffered fatal injuries when driving to his home.

Police told the Associated Press that "a car [Cwick] was trying to pass moved in front of him, and to avoid it, he swerved off the road into an embankment and hit some trees."

Colonel Cwick was no ordinary person. As a member of the elite Marine Corps HMX-1 Unit, he was responsible for ferrying the President and other high-ranking officials around the Washington area.

Apparently, Colonel Cwick has also fallen victim to the Clinton Curse.

It has become undeniable that an unusually high number of people close to Bill Clinton have died in accidental, violent and often suspicious deaths.

Within Cwick's own elite HMX-1 Unit, two other strange deaths are known to have occurred.

This past April, Major Marc Hohle, who had been a pilot for Bill Clinton during the first year of Clinton's first term, died in a helicopter crash in Okinawa. Three others also died in the crash.

In March of this year, just a month before Hohle's untimely death, another member of HMX-1 Unit died.

Marine Corporal Eric S. Fox, a helicopter crewman, was found dead with a gunshot wound to his head. Police authorities said Fox's body was found near a schoolyard in West Virginia.

Fox was on leave and driving along Interstate 68 to his native Indiana "when he ran off the road, hit a guard rail and damaged the front and rear ends of his black, 1994 Nissan 300ZX before going to the school."

Police ruled Fox's death a suicide but gave no explanation as to why, after the accident, Fox decided to take his life.

No doubt, the deaths of Cwick, Hohle and Fox will join the growing list of names Linda Tripp referred to as the Clinton "body count."

Tripp told a federal grand jury one of the reasons she began taping Monica Lewinsky was that she feared for her own life, especially after Lewinsky left a detailed list of people close to Clinton who had been murdered or had died unusual deaths.

Clinton critics and conspiracy buffs have already listed and identified as many as 100 people who comprise the "body count."

The "body count" includes such notable names as former deputy White House counsel Vince Foster (died by gunshot wound to head, July 1993) and former Commerce Secretary Ron Brown (died in plane accident and by possible gunshot wound to head, April 1996), and lesser-known figures such as former Clinton bodyguard Jerry Luther Parks. Parks, one-time head of the Clinton-Gore 1992 security team, was gunned down in September 1993 while driving his car in Little Rock.

The Kennedy Cycle

NewsMax.com Vortex, August 1999 — As news was breaking about the disappearance of JFK Jr.'s Piper Saratoga off the chilly waters of Martha's Vineyard, CBS was fortunate to have Mike Wallace on the scene.

The elderly Wallace — who usually can be found with the limousine liberal horde — has been a fixture on Martha's Vineyard for decades.

Not missing an opportunity, Dan Rather interviewed Wallace via phone during CBS's broadcast on the Kennedy crash.

Wallace, without any prompting from Rather, remarked that everyone on Martha's Vineyard was talking about the remarkable coincidence that the weekend marked the 30 anniversary of the infamous Teddy Kennedy "accident" at Chappaquiddick Bridge.

Rather seemed stunned by Wallace's reminder to the public of this highly embarrassing, and possibly criminal, incident involving Ted Kennedy.

"We have to go now," was Rather's only rejoinder to the Old Narrator of CBS News as he jettisoned him from the live broadcast. Rather hadn't forgotten, as Wallace apparently had, the old rule of American journalism: "Thou Shalt Never Speak Ill of a Kennedy."

Inside Cover has to remind its readers that during the 1970s, Kennedy's involvement in the death of Mary Jo Kopechne was under blanket censorship from the American press for almost a decade. The veil was cut only when, in 1979, the *Reader's Digest* published a blockbuster expose of the cover-up and unanswered questions involving Senator Ted in the death of his campaign aide.

The *Digest* article became one of the most widely reprinted articles in the magazine's history, thanks to the 1980 Carter campaign, which used the Chappaquiddick scandal to quietly and successfully torpedo Uncle Ted's primary challenge.

Of course, the death of JFK Jr. is no scandal but a true tragedy. The son of a beloved president, Junior carried himself with a quiet dignity and decency befitting his parents.

No doubt this tragedy will become part of the Kennedy cycle. As we have seen repeatedly, tragedy begets sympathy.

Ted Kennedy, for instance, has for years played the "assassination card" — the public sympathy his family has received after the slayings of his brothers John and Robert — to explain away personal scandals like Chappaquiddick, not to mention other womanizing and booze problems that would have sent any other politician packing for early retirement.

As recently as 1994 Kennedy was still invoking "Jack and Bobby" in his Senate campaign when challenger Mitch Romney mounted the most serious challenge Kennedy had ever had. Tragedy dies hard.

He Was No JFK Jr.

NewsMax.com Vortex, August 1999 — The Clinton administration has pulled out all the stops to get to the bottom of the Kennedy plane crash mystery.

But six years ago another untimely, high-profile death received far less investigative attention — both from the press and from agencies then under the president's control.

The victim was said to be a personal friend of Clinton's who worked closely with the first lady for years back in Arkansas. He also happened to be the highest-ranking White House official to die violently since JFK Jr.'s father was felled by an assassin's bullet more than a generation ago.

Yet no federal agencies were put on alert and no Cabinet officials were rousted from bed, as was the case with news of JFK Jr.'s disappearance. Likewise, there was no high-tech equipment hastily dispatched to the park where his body was found.

The case was handed, not to the FBI or any other federal agency with the stature of those now looking for answers in the Kennedy crash, but to the U.S. Park Police. For the detective in charge, it would be his very first homicide investigation.

At the White House, where some believe this close presidential friend really died, his office was combed for damaging evidence by Clinton aides who simultaneously kept investigators at bay. Papers were removed and hidden in the White House residence.

Vince Foster's gunshot death was ruled a straightforward suicide by special prosecutor Robert Fiske on June 30, 1994. At the time Fiske said his investigation into what went on in Foster's office the night he died would be complete around the middle of July. July 1994, that is.

Five years later, neither Fiske nor his successor, independent counsel Ken Starr, have made public their conclusions about the Foster office fiasco. That's a long time to wait for answers.

But then again, even federal investigators must prioritize. Vince Foster, after all, was no JFK Jr.

JFK Crash *Déjà Vu* for Ron Brown's Son

NewsMax.com Vortex, August 1999 — Because he knew John F. Kennedy Jr. relatively well, Michael Brown, son of late Commerce Secretary Ron Brown, has been in demand on the talk show circuit lately. And until now, the questions have focused largely on Brown and JFK Jr.'s mutual experience: the challenges posed by growing up in the shadow of politically powerful fathers.

But at one point during the JFK coverage the discussion turned uncomfortable for young Brown, as he was invited to comment on a topic that most broadcasters consider taboo. How did Michael Brown feel about his father's own 1996 plane crash death — and the questions that arose 20 months later when three senior Army pathologists and a highly experienced forensic photographer went public with evidence suggesting that Brown Sr. may have been shot?

Appearing on FOX News Channel's *Hannity & Colmes*, Brown looked stunned when the subject was broached and quickly tried to return the conversation to the Kennedy tragedy. But co-host Sean Hannity persisted:

HANNITY: Michael, it is amazing to me that whenever you talk about the Kennedys you always get conspiracy theories. And already, if you can believe it, these types of things are springing up all over the place about the Kennedys, about the tragedy. And I want to ask you because you've lived through this, in a sense. You had your dad's business partner, Nolanda Hill, question whether or not this was an accident. Your sister Tracey, for example, questioning the integrity of the accident (investigation). Other leaders in the black community saying that they wanted an investigation, that there should have been an autopsy. Does that make it that much harder for you, hearing these types of statements? And we're now seeing it happen to the Kennedy family. Is that fair? What are your thoughts on that?

BROWN: Well, Sean, if you don't mind — let me go back to the piece you guys just did on Senator Kennedy. I think history will show that possibly Senator Kennedy may come down in history as possibly the strongest Kennedy ever. He has had to endure things that no one else has had to, [as] when he steps out in front of the microphone to give eulogies. Coincidentally, he gave a eulogy at one of my father's memorial services that frankly, I heard today, which shook me a little bit. He ended the same way he ended John's today, which was something really special. He said, "John, we love you, we miss you, and we always will." And that's what he said at my father's and it touched me today.

HANNITY: Well, there's no doubt that he has suffered greatly in his life and he's dealt with a lot of trauma. But I just want to go back to that question if I can. You hear all these things. Does that make it harder on the family?

BROWN: Well, I think it's part of, I think, what we talked about in the first segment. About when you grow up in a fishbowl, so to speak. You're going to have those kinds of issues. But again, as the family rallies around and friends rally around, you have to be able to move on and put those kinds of things in their proper perspective. I don't think people really spend too much time on it; I think you guys spend more time on it than anybody else.

HANNITY: You know how horrible we are in the media. I might agree with you at points.

BROWN: But when you get to closure and you understand what kind of life, that you have to live in a fishbowl and things like that, in politics that kind of stuff comes with the territory and it doesn't bother anybody.

Though Michael Brown's comments on questions surrounding his father's death were short on substance, his sister Tracey was far more forthcoming last year. In April 1998 Ron Brown's daughter told a New York talk radio audience that she believed that the Air Force investigation into her father's plane crash was slipshod and inadequate.

Tracey Brown also revealed that the family had hired its own private pathologist to evaluate photographic evidence that her father was shot in the head. Because there was no record, photographic or otherwise, of an exit wound, Brown said she was not bothered that her father had been denied an autopsy.

Then–chief of forensic photography for the Armed Forces Institute of Pathology Kathleen Janoski, who was the first to notice Brown's unusual head wound the day his body arrived at Dover Air Force Base, has subsequently revealed that doctors attending Brown's body failed to look for an exit wound.

The Death of Commerce Secretary Ron Brown

By Professor James E. Starrs

NewsMax.com Vortex, December 1998

Reprinted with permission of *The Journal of Scientific Sleuthing*

A Failure to Autopsy Perpetuates a Homicide Theory

A fate worse than death! Can there be such a thing? Is the death of Commerce Secretary Ron Brown on April 3, 1996, while on a trade mission to Croatia illustrative of his having avoided a fate worse than death?

Brown Was Under Investigation

At the time of Secretary Brown's death while a passenger in an Air Force Boeing 737 which crashed into a mountainside while attempting to land at Croatia's Dubrovnik airport he was under intense investigation by independent counsel Daniel Pearson. Brown had been targeted by the probe on evidence that he had taken money improperly or even illegally just before he took the post of secretary of Commerce.

There was also more than a suggestion that DNC fund raising had wormed its way into the decision-making at the Commerce Department, courtesy of Secretary Brown. Subpoenas were flying in the probe, with the names of Brown and his son Michael listed among those scheduled to receive such subpoenas, even as Brown's plane soared toward Croatia.

With Death Came a Termination

But Brown's death brought a close to the investigation of any financial finagling or perfidy by him. Indeed just six hours after Brown's death Pearson, without ado or fanfare, terminated his probe of Brown.

Out of this rich and fertile pasturage, suggestive of things more foul than fair, have burst Brobdingnagian rumblings on the death of Secretary Brown.

Might the results of the aborted Pearson probe and that of Judicial Watch, a private conservative group, into Brown's alleged insider-trading shenanigans have caused Brown a fate worse than his death? Did his death save him and the others with or for whom he trafficked in fundraising affairs from the public obloquy that might have been theirs if all that could be told of his financial dealings was told?

Could the potential of such public and professional scorn have been a motive for him to commit suicide for fear of a fate worse than death? Or could it even have moved others to assassinate him to insure that their fate would not be worse than Brown's death?

More Grist for the Conspiracy Mill

Other circumstances can be read as indicative of foul play in the death of Brown. Why was it initially reported that "the worst storm in a decade was raging" when Brown's plane sought to land when, in fact, an Air Force investigation concluded "the weather was not a substantially contributing factor to this mishap"? In the minutes before Brown's plane crashed, five other planes landed without difficulty at the same airport. Brown's plane was piloted by seasoned pilots with many hours of flying time in such an aircraft.

Could it be that the Brown plane was misled by ground navigational aids? If so, we may never know, for the airport maintenance chief at the Croatian airport died from gunshot wounds just three days later. Officials have said his death was a suicide.

The Air Force's investigative report reveals that a backup portable navigation beacon at the airport had been stolen before the crash and never recovered. Could the Brown plane have been "spoofed" — which is aviation vernacular for using a spurious navigational aid to trick a pilot to change course?

These are the sinister intimations, some might say the maunderings, of those who view the death of Secretary Brown as being sufficiently suspicious to warrant a thorough investigation of its cause, particularly in light of the nettlesome scientific evidence.

A Melee of Scientific Intrigue

The scientific investigation began on the gurney at Dover Air Force Base where Secretary Brown's body lay some four days after his death in Croatia. As Chief Petty Officer Kathleen Janoski, then a photographer for the Armed Forces Institute of Pathology, and a member of the United States Navy for 22 years, tells it, she looked at Ron Brown's skull and exclaimed, "Look at the hole in Ron Brown's head! It looks like a gunshot wound." Janoski's off-hand assertion caused all heads to turn to Brown's body.

Among those who hastened to view the wound was United States Army Lt. Colonel David Hause, a deputy medical examiner with the A.F.I.P. Hause agreed with Janoski that the head wound appeared to be a gunshot wound and added that it "looked like a punched-out .45-caliber entrance hole." But the A.F.I.P.'s Colonel William Gormley, the pathologist who was examining Brown's body, did not concur with the Janoski-Hause evaluation.

Gormley did not see the wound as having penetrated the skull. For that and other reasons it could not be a wound from a bullet, in his estimation. As a consequence, Gormley did not perform an autopsy on Brown's body, save for an external examination of it, which was not informative on the possibility of a bullet wound to Brown's skull. Gormley's decision has caused the manner of Brown's death to hit the conspiracy fan in such a way that sparks are spurting in all directions.

Hause's gurney-side opinion has been seconded by Air Force Lt. Colonel Steve Cogswell, who reviewed the records as well as the photographs and X-rays of Brown's body. It was his opinion that "Brown had a .45-inch inwardly beveling circular hole in the top of his head, which is the description of a .45-caliber gunshot wound."

Colonel Gormley, however, has remained convinced and adamant that Brown's head wound was accidentally inflicted and not by a bullet. He reviewed the skull X-rays and saw no evidence of an exit wound or a bullet or fragments from a bullet. Gormley emphasized that, in his view, the circular hole "didn't go all the way through the skull." The "punched-out" bone plug had simply been depressed into the skull, and was evident, to Gormley for one, as covering the brain. To Gormley, the skull hole was most likely to have been caused by a rivet or other fastener in the downed plane and not a bullet.

Joining A.F.I.P.'s Hause and Cogswell in dissent from Gormley's opinion was Air Force Major Thomas Parsons, another A.F.I.P. pathologist. But in January 1998 the Justice Department and Attorney General Reno announced that they found no "credible evidence" of homicide in Brown's death. That affirmation, however, has not made the issue disappear.

All those who have espoused the possibility of homicide in Brown's demise have been silenced by the military in one way or another. Chief Petty Officer Janoski, the prime whistleblower, has further fueled a conspiracy flame by pointing to the fact that the X-rays of Brown's skull have vanished. Other body X-rays are still in existence, but the whereabouts of the skull X-rays as they were displayed (for the last time?) in the light box at Dover Air Force Base are not known.

As sure as shooting, the death of Secretary Brown will continue to fester in the minds of both those who demand answers and those to whom answers will never be satisfactory. Declaring a brownout on those at the A.F.I.P. whose opinions are deemed insubordinate will only propel the matter to a more frenzied height of conspiratorial complexity. The forced closing of mouths has a nasty propensity to foment legitimate skepticism among those who are informed of it. It may also be a fate worse than death in a democratic society.

The Body Count — Add One More:
William Colby's Death Mystery

By Christopher Ruddy

NewsMax.com Vortex, December 1998 — It was March of 1996. My cell phone rang. My literary agent was on the line.

"Cross Colby off the list. He's dead."

"Colby is dead," I said with some shock.

"Yes, I just heard on the radio he died in a car crash," my agent said.

I did not know former CIA Director Bill Colby, nor did my agent. But we both knew James Dale Davidson, editor of the investment newsletter *Strategic Investment*. Davidson was not only an associate of Colby's, but Colby had worked for Davidson as a contributing editor for his newsletter.

At the time of my agent's call, he was attempting to find a publisher for my book on the Vince Foster case. We still had no publisher, and my agent had floated the idea of William Colby writing the proposed book's foreword. This would serve several purposes. Colby, as a former CIA chief, would give the book some credibility with a publisher.

Colby had been a key figure in the Watergate scandal after he refused to allow the CIA to block the FBI probe on the Watergate burglary. Colby could not be accused of being part of a right-wing conspiracy. After leaving the CIA, he argued for unilateral disarmament and became a fixture at the left-wing Institute for Policy Studies.

My agent thought Colby might be open to the idea. After all, he worked for Davidson and Davidson openly claimed Foster was murdered, pointing the finger at the Clinton White House.

But now the idea of a Colby foreword seemed lost.

I called Davidson and asked him if he had heard the news about Colby. His voice became strained. He sounded stunned when I told him.

But, of course, Colby had not died that March. He died a month later. My agent was wrong. To this day, he swears he heard something, and to this day, we laugh about the Jungian wrinkle in time. Davidson was peeved at me for the false report, as he well should have been.

On April 29, 1996, the wires flashed with hot news: Former CIA Director William Colby had disappeared from his country home on the Wicomico River in Maryland. Authorities suspected he died in a canoeing accident, as his waterlogged canoe was found on the shore near his home.

A week later, his body surfaced in the marsh near his home. After a perfunctory autopsy, local police authorities closed the case as an accident.

Still, there were many reasons to suspect foul play.

These suspicions began as soon as the initial press reports came out. As expected, the Associated Press ran the first wire story. Colby "was missing and presumed drowned" the AP reported. The wire story said he died as the result of "an apparent boating accident."

Quoting a source close to Mrs. Colby, who was in Texas at the time her husband disappeared, the AP stated Colby had spoken via phone with his wife on the day he disappeared. He told her he was not feeling well, "but was going canoeing anyway."

This would be an important clue pointing to an accidental death, had it been true. But someone fabricated this story out of whole cloth. A week later, Colby's wife rebutted the AP report, telling the *Washington Times* her husband was well and made no mention of canoeing.

This initial, false report that relieved obvious suspicion was, for me, a red flag of a cover-up.

Interesting, too, were the obituaries being written. All detailed Colby's fabled career in the World War II-era OSS, the James Bond-like spy who parachuted behind Nazi lines and became a stellar CIA agent. After heading up the Company's Phoenix program in Vietnam, Colby was tapped by President Nixon for the position of DCI — Director of Central Intelligence. These obituaries detailed a formidable list of Colby's associations after he left the CIA.

Yet, nowhere did any media report Colby's most significant occupation at the time of his death — contributing editor for Davidson's *Strategic Investment*.

Odd that Colby's major affiliation at the same time of his death deserved no notice.

Strategic Investment is a prestigious financial newsletter with more than 100,000 readers each month. It is co-edited by James Dale Davidson, a national figure, as well as William Lord Rees-Mogg, former editor of the *Times* of London.

This curious omission takes on great importance when one understands one of *Strategic Investment*'s key aspects. It has been one of the leading, real opposition publications to Bill and Hillary Clinton in the United States.

Davidson and Rees-Mogg have never pulled any punches about the Clintons. Each month, the newsletter detailed the Clintons' sordid drug, mob, and murder connections. Davidson had been a friend of Bill Clinton and had frequented Little Rock. He even had donated the maximum amount allowable to Clinton's 1992 presidential campaign.

In 1993, Davidson had an awakening about Clinton. My reporting on Foster, investigative reports by British reporter Ambrose Evans-

Pritchard, and columns by *Strategic Investment's* Washington insider Jack Wheeler had convinced Davidson that Clinton was linked to organized crime, had subverted the U.S. law enforcement agencies, and was a danger to America's institutions and financial well-being.

As an editor for Davidson's newsletter, Colby never wrote about the Clintons or touched upon these matters. He did, however, lend his name to Davidson's enterprise. The newsletter's reach was multiplied by the effect of the millions of direct-mail pieces Davidson's organization sent to homes across the country seeking new subscribers.

I was shocked by one such direct-mail booklet. The cover headlined the Clintons' connection with murder and drugs. I opened the first page, and the first picture I saw was William Colby's. Another headline blazed that *Strategic Investment* was "An Investor's CIA." Colby was prominently displayed, as was his endorsement. This was brilliant marketing on behalf of *Strategic*, but when I saw it, I thought Colby was swimming in dangerous waters.

This turned out to be literally true when he was found floating on the Wicomico. Like the Foster death, the circumstances of Colby's passing made little sense.

When police entered his country home, they found both his radio and computer left on. "Investigators found dinner dishes on a table and clam shells in the kitchen sink." Friends say this was unusual for Colby, a meticulous man.

The canoe was found conveniently waterlogged near the waterfront part of his home. Considering the swift current of the Wicomico, that made sense only if he died very close to the shoreline near his property. Yet authorities using sCuba divers and sophisticated radar couldn't find his body there.

And a canoe is an extremely seaworthy boat. How did it become lodged and waterlogged on the riverbank? Had Colby been stricken by a heart attack and fallen off, as has been speculated, the canoe should have completely capsized or safely righted itself, not become waterlogged and moved by the current to the Colby waterfront.

Then there were other telling problems. Colby was found with no life jacket. He always wore one when on the water. The scrupulous search for him should have turned up the floating life jacket or the buoyant paddle. Neither was found.

An autopsy by a Maryland coroner found that Colby had died of drowning. The autopsy also claimed that the drowning was precipitated — get this — by a heart attack or stroke. Take your pick. But the coroner found no evidence of either!

Police homicide investigators always treat drowning deaths with great suspicion. Trained killers know that someone killed by drowning is "buried" in deep water, a target of predatory sea life. After days there, the body is mutilated by sea life to such a degree that any signs of a struggle are difficult to identify.

In the days after Colby's demise, I was disturbed by the many parallels with the Foster death: the circumstances that just didn't add up, the outrageously phony initial press reports, the quick official rush to judgment by investigative agencies, the questionable autopsy.

My feathers were ruffled more when I received a call from Peter Birkett, an investigative reporter from Britain's *Daily Express*. Peter had been rushed over to the United States, he said, because the paper's intelligence sources in MI5 had claimed Colby was assassinated by U.S. government operatives. Peter's job was to ferret out the facts.

The *Express* is a credible paper, and Peter seemed genuinely interested in the truth. He had heard about my Vince Foster reporting and was told by contacts in Britain that I could offer him some insight. I told him my concerns, notably the unreported Colby connection to Davidson's newsletter.

Peter began his own investigation and gave me progress reports as things unfolded. He spoke to the local police, some of whom, he claimed, didn't buy the boating story accident. For one thing, one of the investigators told Peter that Colby's body was found fully clothed. His socks were on, but his shoes were missing. Colby always wore shoes when canoeing, particularly on a blustery April day.

Peter told me that the cop asked incredulously: "How did his shoes come off? In the middle of a heart attack or stroke, he began untying his shoes after his canoe capsized?"

Peter left for England with few answers and more doubts.

In the weeks after the death, I bumped into a former very high intelligence official who served in the Reagan administration. He was quite agitated about Colby's death. He believed that the Clinton White House must have gone ballistic when they saw Colby's endorsement of

Davidson's newsletter. This former official had little doubt the hit was ordered at the highest levels.

He drew for me a diagram of the main players at *Strategic Investment* organization and explained that Colby was at risk because he "gave the whole thing credibility."

I have no idea whether Colby was murdered. His unusual death, added to the many others with some Whitewater connection, was not something that could be ignored.

The Body Count

As the impeachment deliberations continue here in Washington, and the press continues to downplay their significance, undercurrents of the real danger posed by the Clintons are well known.

Inside the Beltway, even the most ardent impeachment supporters — such as Bob Barr or Dan Burton — won't utter the "M" word. M for murder.

Bob Barr, appearing on a recent edition of Geraldo, suggested that Linda Tripp had every reason to tape herself, because she had legitimate "fears."

But even the intrepid Bob Barr wouldn't explain clearly to the American public what those fears were. Of course, NewsMax.com laid it out in black and white: Linda was afraid of being murdered. She was afraid of Monica being murdered.

Tripp said so, under oath, before the Starr grand jury. So here the key government witness to ignite the whole Lewinsky matter testifies that she knows top government officials perjured themselves about the circumstances of Vincent Foster's 1993 death. And the press ignores the story.

Linda is not without credibility, as she was right there as a secretary in the counsel's office when Foster died. Tripp said she knew of a flurry of unusual activities at the White House after Foster's death.

Tripp also testified about murder in the first degree of Jerry Luther Parks, the former security chief at the Clinton-Gore 1992 campaign headquarters.

Trying desperately to explain to a bewildered, pro-Clinton grand jury why she began tape-recording her young friend, Monica Lewinsky, Linda told of a Clinton "body count" — a list of many people associated with Bill Clinton who had died under mysterious circumstances, such as plane crashes, mysterious illnesses, "suicides," and even outright murder. Linda said the list she saw had 40 names on it, including Foster's and Parks'.

This dramatic testimony by Tripp got no mention in the major press. The establishment press has made any talk of murder in relation to the Clintons absolutely taboo. Bob Barr won't mention it. Dan Burton, who dared to raise questions about Foster's death by gunshot in 1995, was quickly skewered by the press and is on the permanent target list of the White House.

The only discussion of the murder issue was raised by Hillary Clinton herself, when, in the aftermath of the Lewinsky matter, she told NBC's Matt Lauer that the people behind the vast right-wing conspiracy had even accused her and her husband of murder.

According to press reports, Hillary's strategy was dreamed up by none other than Sid Blumenthal, a key adviser to both Bill and Hillary. Sid has been obsessed with this idea of murder. In the 1970s he edited a book entitled *Government by Gunplay*. Ironically, Blumenthal's book argued that the U.S. government had regularly and systematically used murder to advance its agenda, killing the likes of JFK, Dr. King, the Black Panthers and others.

It would be interesting to know if Blumenthal believes the left, once in power, has a right to knock off right-wing opponents.

The idea that right-wingers murder their left-wing opponents has had currency with the left for some time. During Watergate, Katherine Graham's *Washington Post* invested its resources in investigating the 1972 assassination attempt on presidential candidate George Wallace. As detailed in Woodward and Bernstein's *All the President's Men*, the *Post* editors were suspicious because Nixon had too much to gain by eliminating Wallace from the presidential race.

Today, the press, heavily dominated by the left and Clinton allies, scoffs at any notion of murder linked to governmental authorities.

Yet discussion of the high number of deaths associated with Bill Clinton has received wide interest from the public. Via the Internet, various e-mails circulate constantly about the Clinton "body count."

Within the highest levels of our government, the fear of murder is talked about openly, but in closed circles.

For instance, a California Republican congressman who took a keen interest in the Foster case in 1996 and had pressed for a review of the Park Police handling of the case, abruptly dropped the matter. He told an associate of mine that he consulted with four other members of his committee. All agreed Foster was murdered and that they were scared to death to proceed.

Others use the lame excuse that "the country just can't handle the truth." For instance, Free Congress Foundation Chairman Paul Weyrich wrote in his newsletter that Republican Senator Don Nickles explained to him why the Senate would not probe Foster's death.

"If Foster didn't die the way Fiske said he did, then it is likely the president is somehow involved, and if he is, the democratic process simply can't survive such a disclosure," Weyrich quoted Nickles as saying.

Similarly, Accuracy in Media chief Reed Irvine was skeptical at first about the notion that Vince Foster might have been murdered. When Irvine asked a top aide to Sen. Jesse Helms why this matter was not being looked into, the aide told him bluntly that since the Clinton White House was capable of resorting to murder, people were afraid to mount a challenge.

Another case in point: Earlier this year, I gave a speech about my reporting on the Clinton scandals. I won't disclose where. But I will reveal that the wife of one of the federal judges that sits on the three-judge panel that oversees Starr's independent counsel probe showed up. The judge's wife asked me a pointed question about the credibility of one of the witnesses in the Foster case, and seemed disturbed by the whole matter.

After my talk, a prominent businessman said he was close to the judge's family and said the judge had told his family that some "82 people have been murdered since Clinton became president."

Perhaps the most important disclosure of this year was made by Donald Smaltz, the independent counsel investigating former Agriculture Secretary Mike Espy and possible payoffs made to Espy by Clinton backer Don Tyson.

Appearing on PBS' *Frontline* with Peter Boyer, Smaltz detailed how the Janet Reno Justice Department blocked his inquiry at every turn. When Smaltz discovered significant evidence that Tyson had made cash bribes to Bill Clinton when Clinton served as governor of Arkansas, he wanted to investigate.

Smaltz admitted on PBS that his wife 'has always been concerned my life was in physical danger.'"

Smaltz shrugged off such suggestions of danger, he recounted, until he had a "High Noon" confrontation with Reno and the six highest officials in the Justice Department. Reno and gang told Smaltz that he wouldn't be allowed to investigate the evidence of wrongdoing.

After this meeting Smaltz told his wife, "You know, Lo, for the first time since I've been back here, I'm afraid." Smaltz quickly added that he was also afraid for the country.

Smaltz is right. Rather than preserving "democracy," as Nickles suggested to Weyrich, the whole country has been put at risk by the failure of the nation's legal institutions and the major press to confront the Clintons' takeover of the nation's law enforcement agencies.

Their politicization of the administration of justice is demonstrated by the failure of the government to conduct adequate death investigations. Instead, when one questions the deaths of Vince Foster, Ron Brown and Jerry Parks, asking why the most basic death investigations have yet to be conducted, the establishment media brands the skeptic a "conspiracy theorist" or "Clinton hater." Other establishmentarians exclaim, "How dare you accuse the Clintons of murder!"

Obviously, many elites inside Washington's Beltway believe that Foster's death was anything but a suicide. And the Clinton body count is taken quite seriously in many circles.

The high number of unusual deaths is a prism by which to understand what has happened to America during the past six years. Contrary to Senator Nickles' claims, America won't collapse if we learn the truth about Foster, Brown, and the others.

The truth would be ugly, but America would be stronger. The danger is when the cancer is not exposed and eliminated. This is the real danger for America.

If a group of people become legally unaccountable, as we have seen with the Clinton administration, then the nation risks a dictatorship. This could take many forms, the least likely a bunch of brownshirts marching down the street.

The Mexican model is more likely, where leaders are "tapped" by the ruling elite and the baton passes from one to another under the guise of "democracy."

I recall Huey Long was once asked if he thought America would ever become fascist. He responded, "Of course it will, but we'll call it anti-fascism."

Jim McDougal, Whistleblower

NewsMax.com Vortex, December 1998 — The feisty, left-wing newsletter *CounterPunch* reports that "Jim McDougal's death in a federal prison, apparently caused by medical negligence, is having a sinister sequel."

According to *CounterPunch* — among the first to report the suspicious circumstances of Jim's March 6, 1998, death — the man who told them about the murky events surrounding McDougal's death has now been targeted by federal prison officials.

CounterPunch names that man as inmate T. J. Lowe. Lowe had been in a holding cell at Fort Worth Medical Center near McDougal on the day of his death.

He told *CounterPunch* that McDougal had been taken to solitary confinement, where officials denied McDougal life-saving medications. As McDougal's condition worsened, his cries for help were ignored by prison officials. McDougal later died of cardiac arrest.

CounterPunch says that last month prison officials conducted a raid on Lowe's cell and "seized all of his correspondence on the preposterous claims that it posed a fire hazard."

Officials also took medications Lowe needed for a serious medical condition.

Lowe, who has been put in solitary confinement, is serving the last year of a six-year term for having grown marijuana. A friend tells *CounterPunch* he might not make it through.

Though McDougal was a key cooperating witness for independent counsel Kenneth Starr on the Whitewater matter, Starr has yet to investigate McDougal's death. McDougal was said to have implicated Hillary Clinton in efforts to defraud Madison Guaranty bank.

Inside Cover notes that McDougal died on March 6, six years to the day that Jeff Gerth of the *New York Times* first broke the Whitewater story linking the Clintons to the land development scam.

Arkansas' Murderous Ways

By Christopher Ruddy

NewsMax.com Vortex, November 1998 — Bill Clinton doesn't come out of a vacuum.

He is the product of an Arkansas political machine that has long been corrupt and tied to organized crime.

Writer L. J. Davis once explained our president to me this way: "All you need to know about Bill Clinton is that he was governor of Arkansas."

That one sentence, spoken to me four years ago, has resonated.

Davis' explanation became more meaningful after a conversation I had with a member of the Rockefeller family. I'll identify him only as "Rock."

Rock was very impressed by my work and even asked me to speak on the subject of Vincent Foster's death to an organization he headed.

One can't get more establishment than the Rockefeller family. So I was surprised by the enthusiasm. Then Rock explained to me that members of the Rockefeller family could believe the worst about Bill Clinton.

I asked Rock why.

He responded that the family understood the political milieu from which Clinton came. Rock reminded me that Winthrop Rockefeller — Rock called him "Uncle Win" — was governor of Arkansas.

Win, who has passed away, was the first Republican to win the governorship since Reconstruction, and he did so by spending his wealth and running against the one-party machine that later elected Bill Clinton.

It was a dangerous machine, Rock said with some passion — one that almost killed Uncle Win. Rock said that, while governor, Winthrop had survived no fewer than three assassination attempts.

All were attempts made by sabotage on his private jet, he said.

Winthrop was an outsider and a reformer, which earned him the enmity of the cozy club of the Little Rock elite. What really ruffled feathers with the club was Win's decision to eliminate illegal gambling in Hot Springs, Arkansas.

Illegal gambling there was controlled by a loosely knit organized crime group Rock called the "redneck mafia." Law enforcement agencies call the group the Dixie Mafia.

Gambling in Bill Clinton's hometown had flourished openly for decades because of the corruption of the local political establishment and the complicity of the state police. Winthrop thought his job would be easy. It wasn't.

Rock said his uncle hired, then fired, several state police commanders to crack down on the vice. His police chiefs were all either bribed, threatened, or blackmailed into ignoring Governor Rockefeller's orders.

Finally Rock found a young, clean-cut FBI agent named Lynn Davis and named him state police commander. Davis was Arkansas' version of Eliot Ness. He did wipe out the illicit Hot Spring's gambling nests — at times literally using bulldozers.

His accomplishment was achieved at some risk. Rock detailed the sacrifice he, his uncle, and Davis almost had to make.

As Rock told the story, Winthrop owned a private jet. Rock had joined his uncle on a jet trip he was taking to Memphis along with Davis and two troopers.

The short, peaceful trip from Little Rock was interrupted by the pilot, who came into the passenger cabin with an ominous report. "Governor, it looks like the landing gear won't stay down," he said. "We are going to have to make a controlled crash."

Rockefeller and the other passengers were shaken. They knew what the pilot's action meant: probable combustion of the plane and death for them.

One of the troopers came up with the bright idea of using the plane's fire ax to break through the floor to examine the landing gear.

Circling above Memphis, the troopers cut a wide hole in the jet's floor. They discovered the plane had been sabotaged. Metal rods had been placed in the landing mechanism, so when the gear had retracted upon takeoff, the metal braces needed to keep the tires down had broken. Without the tires locked into place, the plane would immediately skid on its belly. Disaster would surely follow.

Rock said his uncle was livid. After two previous attempts to sabotage the plane, he had lavished money on round-the-clock security at the Little Rock hangar where the plane was kept.

Plane crashes were a favorite method of assassination with the Dixie Mafia, Rock said. He added that it was the "perfect cover for murder" because most of the evidence is destroyed or mutilated in a crash. Also, many people have an inability to accept the notion murderers would kill so many innocent passengers to get one target. So the death of the target appears purely accidental.

The plane crash was a good strategy for still another reason. Had a gunman simply shot Uncle Win to death, Rock continued, this would have drawn all sorts of attention and sparked an FBI investigation. The mob doesn't want the feds on their backs.

Fortunately, the plane did not crash. One of the troopers came up with an ingenious idea: Break up some of the passenger seats and jam the metal pieces into the landing gear to keep the tires stable as they landed. It worked.

Rock's harrowing tale is not without corroboration. Lynn Davis, now a lawyer in Little Rock, confirmed the incident.

Still, the threat of assassination always loomed for Winthrop. Rockefeller ordered the staff at the governor's mansion to keep the curtains always closed, day and night, lest a shooter decide to kill him. He frequently had a bodyguard with him as he walked from room to room in the mansion.

Rockefeller's experience was not an isolated one. Gene Wirges, a veteran Arkansas journalist and a Rockefeller ally, wrote in his book *Conflicts of Interest* about the diabolical nature of the Dixie Mafia. Wirges himself suffered several assassination attempts, including a phony car crash. Wirges' life-threatening work has been cited by many journals, including the *Wall Street Journal* and the *Saturday Evening Post*.

To be sure, Bill Clinton was a relatively young man at the time Rockefeller was taking on the mob in Hot Springs. But the time period is not so far removed from him, either. Winthrop left the governorship in 1971; Clinton was elected attorney general, the state's chief law enforcement officer just five years later, in 1976.

There is no evidence that Clinton, as the Democratic machine candidate, was the subject of an assassination attempt or ordered the assassination of anyone.

Interesting, though, were the many ties Clinton himself made with various organized crime figures. One was a gentleman who was the reputed head of the Dixie Mafia. Trooper Larry Patterson told me this man would send a case of fine whisky to the governor's mansion for Clinton every Christmas.

Another sordid character Clinton associated with was Dan Lasater, who was convicted on cocaine distribution charges. Though drug trafficking has made the Dixie Mafia very powerful in the past two decades, there is no evidence Lasater is a member of the Dixie Mafia or any organized crime group. Still, this highly dubious man was such a close friend of Clinton's, Trooper Patterson told me, that Lasater had free access to the governor's mansion at any time. He usually entered through the back door, the portal for close friends and family.

Arkansas State Police files also show that one of Clinton's longtime financial backers was the subject of a police inquiry involving allegations of drug dealing and murder for hire. No indictments were ever brought against the man. And the police investigator who handled the case was forced into early retirement after pressing for indictments.

Understanding Bill Clinton and the regime he and his wife brought to Washington is as easy as connecting the dots.

Tripp Testifies on Foster Death Cover-Up, Murder of Jerry Parks and Clinton's Body Count

NewsMax.com Vortex, November 1998 — Linda Tripp told Starr's grand jury this summer that she had significant reasons to question official claims about former deputy White House counsel Vincent Foster's July 1993 "suicide."

Tripp, one of the White House counsel's office secretaries, and among the last people known to have seen Foster alive, told the grand jury she knows that top White House officials committed perjury in their accounts of Foster's death.

Tripp indicated to the grand jury that Foster's death was only one reason she feared for her life as she gained knowledge of Monica Lewinsky's affair with President Clinton.

Tripp also detailed, cryptically, to the grand jury her heightened concern after the murder of Jerry Luther Parks, the former head of security at the Clinton-Gore 1992 Little Rock headquarters. Parks was murdered just two months after Foster's death, in September of 1993 while driving through a Little Rock intersection. His car was intercepted and stopped, and a lone assassin fired seven shots at Parks. At least three bullets were believed to be fatal.

Parks was found reaching for his gun. His wife and son have both stated that Parks feared for his life in the aftermath of Foster's death. They claim Parks said Foster had been murdered. Other sources have confirmed that Foster and Parks knew each other on a personal and business level. Independent counsel Kenneth Starr investigated Foster's death and ruled it a suicide. Starr rebuffed attempts by the Parks family to investigate Parks' death and a possible connection with Foster's. The Little Rock police have never solved the case.

The following is the verbatim grand jury testimony of Linda Tripp from her July 28 appearance before the grand jury:

Juror: To save your job, you went public and that in turn would probably cause you not to continue in the career that you had?

Tripp: It was far more than that. . . . It was for me really far more than that. It was a question of I am afraid of this administration. I have what I consider to be well-founded fears of what they are capable of. I believe that I have had a far more informed perspective than most people in observing what they are capable of and I made a decision based on what I felt I knew to be the possibilities that could befall me.

Juror: Could you give some examples of what's happened in the past to make you feel as if your life might be threatened?

Tripp: There was always a sense in this White House from the beginning that you were either with them or you were against them. The notion that you could just be a civil servant supporting the institution just was not an option. I had reasons to believe the Vince Foster tragedy was not depicted accurately under oath by members of the administration. I had reason to believe that — and these are, remember, instances of national significance that included testimony by — to my knowledge also Mrs. Clinton, also in Travelgate. It became very important for them for their version of events to be the accepted version of events. I knew based on personal knowledge, personal observations, that they were lying under oath. So it became very fearful to me that I had information even back then that was dangerous.

Juror: But do you have any examples of violence being done by the administration to people who were a threat to them that allowed you to come to the conclusion that that would happen to you as well?

Tripp: I can go — if you want a specific, a personal specific, the behavior in the West Wing with senior staff to the president during the time the Jerry Parks came over the fax frightened me.

Juror: Excuse me, Jerry Parks?

Tripp: He was one of the — if not the head of his [Clinton's] campaign security detail in Arkansas, then somewhere in the hierarchy of the security arrangements in Arkansas during the '92 campaign. And based on the flurry of activity and the flurry of phone calls and the secrecy, I felt this was somewhat alarming.

Juror: I don't understand.

Tripp: I don't know what else to say.

Juror: Meaning that you were alarmed at his death or at what people [in the White House] said? Or did you have knowledge that he had been killed or —

Tripp: He had been killed. I didn't even at this point remember how but it was the reaction at the White House that caused me concern, as did Vince Foster's suicide. None of the behavior following Vince Foster's suicide computed to just people mourning Mr. Foster. It was far more ominous than that and it was extremely questionable behavior on the parts of those who were immediately involved in the aftermath of his death. So — I mean I don't know how much more I can be specific except to say I am telling you under oath today that I felt endangered and I was angry and I resented it and I still do.

Juror: [Questions about her current job.]

Tripp: I am still being paid at the GS-15 level. I was demoted from my position and assigned administrative tasks which are now under discussion with the Pentagon. Quite beyond that, Mike Isikoff made a very good point early on [to Tripp] which was you will protect yourself and your job far better if your name does surface because once you're out there as a known source of information they will be less inclined to have something happen to you. . . .

Juror: I'm sorry. We were talking about the incident that happened and how the people were acting at the White House and you said they were acting strange. Can you give us some examples of what you saw to draw that conclusion? What are some of the examples? You said they were not acting as if someone had just passed or whatever, something was strange. What were the strange things?

Tripp: It replicated [referring to the Parks murder, apparently] in my mind some of the behavior following the death of Vince Foster. A fax came across the fax machine in the counsel's office from someone within the White House, and I think it was from Skip Rutherford, who was working in the Chief of Staff's office at the time [September 1993]. At the same time the fax was coming, phone calls were coming up to Bernie Nussbaum which precipitated back and forth meetings behind closed doors, all with — you know, we have to have copies of this fax and it was — an article, it came over the wire, I think, I can't remember now, but I think we actually have that somewhere, of this death, this murder or whatever it was [referring to the Parks death]. And it created a stir, shall we say, in the counsel's office which brought up some senior staff from the Chief of Staff's office up to the counsel's office where they, from all appearances, went into a meeting to discuss this. It was something that they chose not to speak about. One of our staff assistants asked what is going on and it was never addressed. Which was primarily the same way that the Vince Foster death — in the aftermath of the Vince Foster death things proceeded as well. So, for people not in law enforcement, for people just government workers it was — it was behavior that was considered questionable, cause for concern.

Juror: Just because they were having meetings behind closed doors?

Tripp: Because of the flurry of activity, because it was hush-hush, and that a fax could cause that level of activity. The White House is a very busy place, it's generally short-staffed, but there is pretty much a constant flow. It starts in the morning, it never really ends, you go home, you sleep, you come back. There are times as I am sure you can imagine during the Vince Foster thing that the pace changed somewhat and this was another such time. Maybe you had to be there. I know. I left and I will say under oath with the same sense that this was something they wanted to get out in front of. There was talk that this would be another body to add to the list of 40 bodies or something that were associated with the Clinton administration. At that time, I didn't know what that meant. I have since come to see such a list.

Vince Foster's Role

NewsMax.com Vortex, November 1998 — Clifford Bernath was Linda Tripp's supervisor at the Pentagon. He served as deputy assistant Secretary of Defense for Public Affairs.

During grand jury questioning, Starr's prosecutor focused on the White House's sudden "need to create a job for Linda Tripp" at the Pentagon.

Bernath said the White House made this decision to move Tripp to the Pentagon. He had received a call from the White House liaison, who told Bernath he had to make room for a "priority placement, [Tripp] is going to go to Public Affairs, create a job for her."

Bernath said he was "never given any reasons why [Tripp] was assigned to the Pentagon" from the White House.

Tripp, however, made certain "allusions" as to why she had been sent to the Pentagon.

Asked what those allusions were, Bernath said under oath, "It must have been her first day, [Tripp] said, you know, I'm involved in the Vince Foster affair and I'm involved in a lot of things and I know a lot of things and this is why I need privacy and this is why I should be treated differently."

Previous to her Pentagon job, Tripp had worked at the White House. At the time of deputy White House counsel Vincent Foster's death, Tripp worked as a secretary in the counsel's office. She was among the last people to see Foster alive. Tripp received her transfer to the Pentagon approximately two weeks after Starr was appointed Independent counsel.

Parks' Son Demands Murder Inquiry

By Christopher Ruddy

NewsMax.com Vortex, November 1998 — Gary Parks, the son of a murder victim referenced by Linda Tripp during her grand jury testimony, is livid that independent counsel Kenneth Starr has not investigated his father's murder. Parks told NewsMax.com that he was not shocked by recent revelations about Tripp's testimony.

Tripp explained to Starr's Washington grand jury probing the Lewinsky matter that she had reason to fear for her life because of the suspicious way top White House officials behaved in the aftermath of the murder of Parks' father, Jerry Luther Parks.

In September 1993, Jerry Parks, former head of security for the Clinton-Gore 1992 campaign headquarters, was shot repeatedly while driving to his home on the outskirts of Little Rock, Arkansas. Local police have never solved the murder case, nor identified possible suspects.

Parks' death came on the heels of deputy White House counsel Vincent Foster's sudden death in July of 1993. Young Parks, and his mother, have alleged that the two deaths were connected and that Parks feared for his life when he learned of Foster's death.

Tripp had served as a secretary to Foster. Asked why she taped Lewinsky, Tripp said she was frightened and cited Foster's death. She told the grand jury she believed senior White House officials lied under oath about the circumstances of Foster's death.

She added that Parks' murder sparked a flurry of activity among senior officials in the counsel's office.

Gary Parks said he knew his father was in contact with Foster in the days before Foster's death. Parks said his family has phone records showing at least twelve calls made by Parks to the White House in the months before Foster's death, at least four of which went directly to the counsel's office.

Gary said he suspects Tripp knows more about Parks' contacts with the counsel's office. He said his father had been calling the White House to demand payment for services rendered during the campaign.

"It's obvious to anyone with a brain that Starr's job has been to make sure Clinton is not indicted and finishes out his second term," a frustrated Parks said. He said Starr's office has not been helpful.

Undeterred, Parks said he plans to drive some two hours from his Memphis area home to Starr's Little Rock office.

"I'm going to ask them what they are going to do about this," he said, referring to Tripp's testimony. "Why hasn't this been investigated?"

Parks, 27, said he recently married. His mother, Jane Parks, recently remarried and resigned herself to the fact that an official cover-up prevents any justice in her husband's death, he said.

The Colombian Connection:
Al Gore and Big Oil

NewsMax.com Vortex, June 2000 — It's a major scandal waiting to break, the story of a Colombian tribe of Indians, a major oil company and the vice president of the United States. In a startling exposé in a recent issue of *The Nation*, writer Ken Silverstein uncovers the shocking tale of Gore's historical super-close connection to the giant Occidental Petroleum company, its ongoing attempts to despoil the U'wa tribal ancestral homeland, and the shady role the Clinton administration is playing behind the scenes.

And the exposé is given more weight in view of the fact that it appears in an ultra-left-wing publication one would expect to be backing ultra-liberal Al Gore's presidential bid to the hilt.

Briefly, the dispute — which turned violent when Colombian security forces used tear gas against members of the tribe demonstrating against Occidental's drilling plans, resulting in the subsequent deaths of three children, who drowned when fleeing the melee — involves the company's plan to drill on U'wa tribal land, which the company believes holds 1.4 billion barrels of oil worth about $35 billion in today's prices.

Interestingly, in view of Gore's pretensions to be a dedicated environmentalist, one of the principal objections to Occidental's drilling is its record of disastrous oil spills from its Caño Limon pipeline, just north of U'wa land and repeatedly bombed by guerrillas. The spills, Silverstein reports, have badly polluted rivers and lakes.

"The Colombian Oil Workers' Union published a report in 1997 saying that Caño Limon is 'the best example that petroleum exploitation should not be permitted [on the U'wa reservation] at any price,' " he wrote.

Silverstein says the U'wa opposition to Occidental's plans represents something of a last stand. "A 1998 report by Terry Freitas — one of three U'wa supporters from the United States killed by leftist guerrillas while visiting the tribe's territory last year — says that the

Colombian government stripped the tribe of 85 percent of its land between 1940 and 1970," he explains.

He quotes Roberto Perez, president of the Traditional Authority of the U'wa People, as saying: "The key issue for indigenous groups is defending our territory. . . . The Occidental project is an affront to our livelihood, our lives and our culture."

Gore has repeatedly refused pleas from fellow Democrats to meet with Perez.

Rep. Cynthia McKinney of Georgia, for example, told Silverstein she wrote to Gore and asked him to meet with U'wa leader Perez and to support an immediate suspension of the Occidental project.

"I am concerned that the operations of oil companies, and in particular Occidental Petroleum, are exacerbating an already explosive situation, with disastrous consequences for the local indigenous people," she wrote. "I am contacting you because you have remained silent on this issue despite your strong financial interests and family ties with Occidental."

She wrote to Gore again on March 30 to complain about his failure to answer her previous letter. Finally Gore sent her a note saying he simply didn't have the time to meet with Perez.

Most fascinating is the historical connection between the Gore family and Occidental Petroleum, in which Gore holds about a quarter of a million dollars' worth of stock in trust for his mother. The connection goes back to Gore's father's close relationship with the late Armand Hammer, Occidental's founder and the son of Julius Hammer, the man who founded the U.S. Communist Party. For all of his life, Armand Hammer remained close to the murderous Joseph Stalin, his successors and the entire Soviet leadership during the Cold War.

He also remained close to Albert Gore Sr., and later to Al Jr., bestowing his largesse lavishly on both.

Hammer, Silverstein notes, liked to brag that he had Gore Sr. "in my back pocket."

When Gore Sr. retired from the Senate in 1970, he got a $500,000-a-year job at a subsidiary of Occidental, as well as a company directorship. When the elder Gore died, his estate included hundreds of thousands of dollars' worth of Occidental stock.

In the 1960s, Silverstein reports, the Gores discovered zinc ore near land they owned in Tennessee. "Through a company subsidiary Hammer bought the land for $160,000 — twice the amount offered by the only other bidder. He swiftly sold the land back to Al Gore Sr. and agreed to pay him $20,000 a year for mining rights." Gore Sr. then sold the property for $140,000 to Al Jr., who has gotten a $20,000 check just about every year since, although Occidental has never mined an ounce of zinc or anything else on the property.

In 1985, Al Jr. leased the property to Union Zinc, a competitor of Occidental.

In his book *Witness to History*, Neil Lyndon, an employee on Hammer's personal staff and the ghost writer of his memoirs, revealed that whenever Hammer came to Washington he met with Al Gore for lunch or dinner.

"They would often eat together in the company of Occidental's Washington lobbyists and fixers who, on Hammer's behest, hosed tens of millions of dollars in bribes and favors into the political world," Lyndon revealed.

The ties between Gore and Occidental outlived Hammer. In 1992 the company lent the Presidential Inauguration Committee $100,000. In 1996, the company gave $50,000 in soft money to the Democrats in response to a phone call from Gore.

"All told, Occidental has donated nearly half a million dollars in soft money to Democratic committees and causes since Gore joined the ticket in 1992," Silverstein writes. In the current presidential campaign Occidental is his No. 2 oil industry donor, with company executives and their wives kicking in $10,000 to Gore's campaign.

It's paid off handsomely. In 1997 Gore, the fanatical opponent of vehicles powered by fossil fuels such as oil, supported the $3.65 billion sale to the company of the government's interest in the Elk Hills oilfield in Bakersfield, California, the largest privatization of federal property in U.S. history.

"On the very day the deal was sealed Gore gave a speech lamenting the growing threat of global warming," Silverstein reports.

Al Gore's Skeletons:
The Hammer Connection

By Reed Irvine

NewsMax.com Vortex, May 2000 — In January 1997, Bob Zelnick, a veteran ABC News correspondent, obtained permission from ABC to write a biography of Vice President Al Gore Jr.

In September 1997, after he had spent eight months researching it, and only weeks before his contract was up for renewal, ABC News told him that if he wanted his contract renewed, he would have to give up writing the book and return the advance he had received from the publisher.

Zelnick says he was told that it was a conflict of interest for him to write a book about someone he might be covering in the presidential contest a few years down the road. Zelnick commented, "This is a standard that has never been applied by any network or any other news organization to any journalist. You should be happy when there are journalists who know enough to author a book on the subject."

Zelnick refused to comply with the ABC demand, and *Gore, A Political Life* as published by Regnery last year. He is now teaching journalism at Boston University. His book is not one that the Gore campaign will be recommending to voters.

It would be out of character for the Clinton White House not to let ABC News know that it would prefer that Bob Zelnick not write a biography of Al Gore, and that is the most reasonable explanation for ABC's sudden withdrawal of its approval of the project. The TV networks have shown that they like to do favors for the Clinton White House.

Early on in the project, Zelnick says he was informed by the vice president's office that Gore had decided against cooperating with him.

Zelnick says Gore's office told him that Gore would "personally resent attempts to contact his family, particularly his aged parents." This is understandable.

The Gore family has a closet full of skeletons, and when you aspire to the presidency of the United States you don't want a nosy reporter opening up closet doors.

Zelnick has a good reputation as a reporter. During his more than two decades in the media, he covered Capitol Hill, the Middle East, Russia and the Pentagon. He won numerous journalism awards, including two American Bar Association Gavel Awards and two Emmys.

Hammer Ties "Extremely Sensitive"

Roy Neel, a former top Gore aide, told Zelnick that Gore was "extremely sensitive" about his father's connection with the late Armand Hammer, the head of Occidental Petroleum, who was notorious for his close ties to the Soviet Union.

When Gore Sr. was first elected to Congress in 1938, he was a poor schoolteacher. But by the time he was elected to the Senate in 1952, he had become rich enough to live in a plush hotel on Washington's embassy row and send Al Jr. to the expensive St. Albans School in Washington.

Armand Hammer had helped make Al Gore Sr. a wealthy man. Zelnick's book and a new book just released in January, *The Buying of the President 2000* by Charles Lewis and published by his organization, the Center for Public Integrity, tell how Armand Hammer bought the services of Al Gore Sr. and helped Al Jr. launch his political career.

Hammer's father, Julius, had linked up with Lenin in 1907 and had agreed to become part of Lenin's underground cadre dedicated to the proletariat revolution. After Lenin seized power in Russia in 1917, Julius used his company, Allied Drug and Chemical, to ship goods to the Soviet Union, and used money from the sale of diamonds smuggled to the United States to finance the Communist Labor Party. That name was later changed to the Communist Party, USA.

Lenin granted young Armand Hammer a monopoly on the manufacture of pencils in the Soviet Union. He used him to raise money in the United States through the sale of confiscated Czarist art and jewelry.

FBI director J. Edgar Hoover wanted to prosecute Hammer for his activities on behalf of the Soviet government, but Charles Lewis says that "Hammer had friends in Congress who, Hoover believed, would attempt to protect him from prosecution." Hammer had bragged that he had Sen. Albert Gore Sr. "in my back pocket."

Hammer helped Gore Sr. get started raising Black Angus cattle, giving him sperm from his own prize stock.

Zelnick says residents in the area where the Gore farm was located claim that Gore was able to sell his cattle at much higher prices than anyone else in the area.

They say that "lobbyists and others with an interest in Gore's work" would come to Carthage and "bid outrageously high prices for Gore's stock." One of them was Joe DiMaggio, who in 1958 bought 10 calves from Gore "on behalf of clients whose identities he refused to disclose."

Zelnick says the prices paid cannot be documented, but newspaper records show that "many distinguished folks" came to buy the Gores' cattle. He quotes former Governor Ned McWherter, a staunch ally of Al Gore Jr., as saying, "I've sold some Angus in my time too, but I never got the kind of prices for my cattle that the Gores got for theirs."

Zelnick also claims that in 1969, when Hammer bought the Hooker Chemical Company (of Love Canal fame), he sold Gore Sr. 1,000 shares of Hooker stock for $150 a share, far less than the stock was worth. House majority leader Hale Boggs accused Hammer of having violated insider trading rules in buying Hooker, but "a Securities Exchange Commission investigation proved inconclusive."

When Gore Sr. was defeated for re-election in 1970, Hammer made him president of Occidental's coal division, paying him $500,000 a year, which was extremely generous compensation at that time.

Reed Irvine is chairman of Accuracy in Media at http://www.aim.org.

Al Gore Jr.'s Debt to Armand Hammer

By Reed Irvine

NewsMax.com Vortex, May 2000 — *The Buying of the President 2000* tells about a suspicious land deal between Armand Hammer and Gore Sr. that appears to have been a way of putting Gore Jr. on the Hammer payroll.

After Gore Sr. informed Hammer that zinc ore had been discovered near the Gore farm in Smith County, Tennessee, Occidental Minerals

Corporation, a subsidiary of Hammer's Occidental Petroleum, bought 80 acres in 1972 for $160,000, double the only other offer.

A year after he bought the acreage, Hammer sold the land and the mineral rights to Gore Sr. and his wife for the same price he paid for it, but he also paid them $20,000, ostensibly to cover royalties for the coming year even though no zinc had as yet been mined. The same day, the Gores transferred the property to their son and their daughter for $140,000.

Lewis says, "Perhaps even more astounding than Hammer's decision to sell the land and pay royalties is that Occidental never actually mined the land. In 1985, Gore began leasing the land to Union Zinc Inc., a competitor of Occidental Minerals Corporation Gore still receives $20,000 a year in royalties.

In all, the Hammer-engineered sweetheart deal has put hundreds of thousands of dollars in profits in Gore's pocket." Gore refers to this land as his "farm," supporting the false claim that he is a farmer.

Zelnick says that Hammer helped finance Gore Jr.'s runs for the House and Senate, met frequently for lunch or dinner with Gore during Hammer's visits to Washington, and put his private jet at the disposal of the Gores. This relationship continued throughout the 1980s.

He discloses that Hammer was involved in Gore's 1988 quest for the presidency. He called Senator Paul Simon of Illinois, who was also seeking the Democratic nomination. Hammer told Simon that if he would drop out of the race and endorse Gore, he could have his choice of Cabinet positions.

Repaying The Debt

What did Gore do for Hammer and Occidental in return? Zelnick reports, "Hammer was Gore's guest at the 1981 Reagan inauguration and used the Tennessee senator to obtain a favored place at the 1989 inauguration of George Bush."

With the election of Clinton and Gore, things changed. After the collapse of the Soviet Union, Occidental sought to develop Russian oil and gained access to important Russian officials through the late Commerce Secretary Ron Brown's trade missions.

Occidental chairman Ray Irani accompanied Brown on a trade mission to Russia in March and April of 1994. Occidental gave $161,014 to the Democratic Party in the 1993-94 election cycle, including a $25,000 contribution on March 29, 1994, a day when Irani was in Russia with Brown. In the fall, he was one of 130 guests at Clinton's second official state dinner for Russian President Boris Yeltsin.

David R. Martin, president of Occidental Oil & Gas Corporation, accompanied Brown on the trade mission to the Middle East in January 1994.

Today, Occidental is lobbying the administration for permission to return to oil fields it once managed in Libya. However, Libya must be dropped from the State Department list of state sponsors of terrorism, and United States economic sanctions on the regime of Moammar Gadhafi have to be dropped and diplomatic relations restored. The upcoming trial of two Libyans for their role in the 1988 Pan Am 103 bombing case is another hurdle this pro-Libya policy must overcome.

It is believed that the Clinton-Gore administration, in order to facilitate the resumption of diplomatic relations with Libya, has agreed not to charge Gadhafi in the case.

With the help of the administration, Occidental has also tripled its U.S. oil reserves. The Energy Department in October 1997 sold the 47,000-acre Elk Hills oil reserve in California to Occidental. This had been held in reserve since 1912.

Both Nixon and Reagan had tried to open it up to development but were blocked by Congress. Vice President Gore, despite his reputation as an environmentalist, recommended that the president give oil companies access to this land. Although the Energy Department was supposed to review the environmental impact of the sale, it did not do so.

It turned the job over to a private company whose board of directors included Tony Coelho, who is now the general chairman of Gore's presidential campaign.

The acquisition of this land tripled Occidental's domestic oil reserves. Al Gore Sr. owned over half a million dollars of Occidental stock. He died in 1998, and Al Jr. became the executor of his estate.

If he played any role in the decision to sell the land to Occidental, he could be accused of feathering his own nest. Occidental is said to have been the highest bidder, but if the handling of the environmental impact statement was irregular, who is to say the bidding was not flawed as well?

According to *The Buying of the President 2000*, Occidental "loaned $100,000 to the Presidential Inaugural Committee to help pay for the ceremony and the celebrations surrounding it.

"And Gore used his connections to bring in money from Occidental for the Clinton-Gore re-election campaign. According to a memo from White House Deputy Chief of Staff Harold Ickes, Occidental gave $50,000 in response to one of Gore's 'no-controlling-legal authority' telephone calls from his White House office.

"Since Gore got the vice presidential nomination in 1992, Occidental has given more than $470,000 in soft money to various Democratic committees and causes." The book also reports that Occidental provided $100,000 to the Democratic National Committee two days after its chairman, Ray Irani, slept in the Lincoln Bedroom.

Credibility-Enhancing Deceptions

Zelnick's book is critical of Gore, but it is not nearly as damaging as it might have been. It tells how Gore agonized before voting to support the resolution approving the Gulf War in 1991.

Zelnick says this vote "deserves to be recognized as an act of conscience and moral courage. . . . If military action failed, the Democratic Party would likely discard him for higher office. Had he voted the other way, following the party line, he could have safely hidden behind the caution of expert opinion."

Senator Alan Simpson, the Senate Republican whip in 1991, tells a different story.

He recently said on MSNBC's *Hardball* that the day before the vote, Gore asked him and Bob Dole, the minority leader, how much time they would give him to speak in the floor debate if he supported the resolution. He told them that the Democratic leadership had offered him seven minutes. Dole offered him 15 minutes, and Simpson said he thought he could raise that to 20.

Gore said he wanted to think about it overnight. They later sweetened their offer, sending word that they would schedule his remarks during the news cycle.

Gore accepted it and was the only Democratic senator with presidential aspirations to break with his party. It appeared to be "an act of conscience and moral courage," as Zelnick said, but if Senator

Simpson's recollection is accurate, Gore really sold his vote for 20 minutes of time in front of the Senate's television cameras.

Pot-Smoking Denials

Zelnick's book has only this one sentence about Gore and drugs: "Marijuana was abundant [in Vietnam] and Gore smoked his share." He did not mention, much less dispute, Gore's claim that his use of marijuana was "rare and infrequent."

At the time, this was hailed as an indication of Gore's honesty because he volunteered the statement without being asked. Thanks to Bill Turque, a *Newsweek* reporter who has written the book *Inventing Al Gore: A Biography*, we now know his claim was a lie.

In November 1987, Judge Douglas Ginsburg withdrew his name as a Supreme Court nominee when it was reported that he had used marijuana while he was teaching at Harvard Law School. Reporters then began asking potential presidential candidates if they had smoked pot.

Turque says in his book that Gore had a meeting with some of his campaign staff and his father to discuss what he should do. He decided to make a public statement, saying that he had smoked marijuana only occasionally and not since 1972.

He assured his father, who was angry when he learned that his son had smoked marijuana, that the statement he planned to make was the truth.

Turque says: "Supporters hailed Gore for breaking new ground with his candor about drugs. 'Al Gore is the first real political leader of his generation . . . to come clean on the '60s,' said the late media adviser Bob Squier. 'It's an indication of his honesty.' "

Turque had interviewed three of Gore's friends who had smoked pot with him after he returned from Vietnam. One was John Warnecke, who had been a close friend of Gore's since 1970 and had worked with him when they were both reporters for the *Nashville Tennessean*.

Warnecke, the son of a famous architect, claims he smoked pot with Gore hundreds of times, often on a daily basis, over a six-year period. He says he supplied, free of charge, the high-quality marijuana they smoked and that Gore "loved it." This went on until 1976, when Gore ran for Congress.

Bill Turque confirmed Gore's frequent use of marijuana in that period with two other Gore friends, Andrew Schlesinger, the son of Arthur Schlesinger Jr., and another who didn't want his name used.

Warnecke says Gore personally telephoned him in 1987 and demanded that he tell reporters nothing about his use of marijuana. Warnecke said Gore wanted him to stonewall the press, but he did not want to do that.

When asked, he told reporters that Gore smoked pot a couple of times but he didn't like it. He says his conscience has bothered him ever since because he had lied.

Gore was angry because he had said anything, and they haven't spoken since 1987. Warnecke says he still intends to vote for Gore, but he feels betrayed by him.

He favors decriminalizing marijuana and thinks that Gore is a hypocrite, having spent years smoking the stuff and now being part of an administration that is carrying out a war against it. He admits that he abused both drugs and alcohol, but he says he has been "clean" for 21 years. He is being treated for depression, and a former Gore aide has tried to discredit him by calling him "a schizophrenic who hears voices."

The 'Old News' Gambit Works

Just before *Newsweek*'s January 24 issue went to press, Richard M. Smith, the chairman and editor in chief, canceled plans to include the excerpt from Turque's book that covered Warnecke's charges.

At the same time it was announced that Houghton Mifflin was delaying publication of the book until March.

Angered, Warnecke gave his story to a pro-drug-legalization Web site, with greater detail and minor differences from Turque's account. This was picked up by Matt Drudge and *Salon*, an Internet magazine, on the weekend of January 15-16.

It was downplayed or ignored by the establishment media. The Associated Press put out a 144-word story that gave Gore's denial that he had smoked pot on a daily basis after returning from Vietnam. "No," he said, "When I came back from Vietnam, yes, but not to that extent. . . . This is something I dealt with a long time ago. It's old news."

The 1987 lie that had elicited praise for his candor now helped Gore divert the media from reporting the truth. It was successfully dismissed as "old news."

When the excerpt from Turque's book was finally published in the February 14 issue of *Newsweek*, it was treated as old news squared. It was posted on MSNBC's Web site, but we saw no stories about reporters challenging the truth of Gore's claim that his use of marijuana was rare.

No one reported Turque's claim that Andrew Schlesinger, a friend who had joined the Gores in New Hampshire to celebrate the primary victory, had said that "in 1971, he had smoked with him 'at least a dozen times' at the Warneckes'."

Useful Lies Versus Harmful Truths

Bill Clinton has been called a pathological liar. To hide serious misdeeds and crimes he tells big lies, such as "I never had sex with that woman," with no shame and with such conviction that millions of people believe them.

Al Gore is a frequent liar, but he is not as good at it as Clinton. From force of habit, he tells little lies designed to make himself look better than he is. These are almost always quickly exposed as false, making him look worse.

But he also tells big lies to cover up his wrongdoing or damage his opponents. Lying to cover up a harmful truth is more serious than exaggerating one's achievements, but both reflect badly on one's veracity.

Gore's denial of his heavy use of marijuana from 1970 to 1976 was a lie told to conceal a harmful truth. In 1987, when it was first told, the truth would have been enough to derail his presidential campaign, as it did Judge Douglas Ginsburg's nomination for the Supreme Court.

In 1992, it would have kept him from being the running mate of "I didn't inhale" Bill Clinton. In these more decadent days, many more voters appear willing to overlook marijuana use by the baby boomers, but those who are sick of Clinton's lies may prove to be equally sick of a candidate who denies claims by his friends that he was a heavy smoker of pot.

There are other serious lies that call Gore's veracity into question — the denial that he knew the event at the Buddhist temple was a fund raiser, his denial that he knew that fund-raising calls he made from his office were illegal, because there was "no controlling legal authority," his claim that he has always been pro-choice, and his claim in a televised debate with Bill Bradley on January 26 that he has never said anything during the campaign that he knew to be untrue are all efforts to replace a harmful truth with a useful lie.

Two days after that debate, the *Boston Globe* published an article on Gore's veracity record. The writers unearthed two memos written to Gore during his run for the 1988 presidential nomination, one by Mike Kopp, his press secretary, and the other by Arlie Schardt, his communications director.

The Kopp memo of September 1987 warned him that his image "may continue to suffer if you continue to go out on a limb with remarks that may be impossible to back up." Six months later, this was still a problem. Schardt wrote, "Your main pitfall is exaggeration."

In a *New York Times* op-ed column on February 16, Schardt argues that Gore's exaggerating is being exaggerated. Listed below are 17 Gore lies.

Al Gore's Lies

1) His use of marijuana was "rare and infrequent."

2) He didn't know the Buddhist temple event was a fund raiser.

3) He didn't know that fund-raising calls from his office were illegal.

4) He has always been pro-choice.

5) He has never said anything in the campaign that he knew to be untrue.

6) He was co-sponsor of the McCain/Feingold campaign finance reform bill in the Senate.

7) He took the initiative in creating the Internet.

8) He and Tipper were models for "Love Story."

9) He uncovered the pollution at Love Canal.

10) His reporting for the *Nashville Tennessean* "got a bunch of people indicted and sent to jail."

11) His views on the Vietnam War were written into Hubert Humphrey's speech to the 1968 Democratic National Convention by a journalist who had interviewed him.

12) He claimed that as an army reporter in Vietnam "I pulled my turn on the perimeter at night and walked through the elephant grass and was fired upon."

13) One reason he enlisted and went to Vietnam was to spare some other family the agony of sending a son.

14) He had been a small-business man and a homebuilder, helping develop a subdivision on his father's land in 1969.

15) He is responsible for the "one-click-away" tool that helps parents block, filter or monitor Internet content to protect their children.

16) He was taught how to clean out hog waste, how to clear land with a double-bladed ax and how to plow steep hillsides with a team of mules.

17) He claimed at the *Des Moines Register* offices in January that he bought his own farm when he came back from Vietnam and that he has owned and operated it for 26 years. (This is the 80 acres Hammer sold to his father on which he has collected $20,000 a year in mining royalties since 1974.)

Reed Irvine is chairman of Accuracy in Media at http://www.aim.org.

'Stay Away From Clinton,' Gore's Mom Warned

NewsMax.com Vortex, May 2000 — Vice President Al Gore's mother Pauline was a sexual harassment victim who once warned her son to avoid Bill Clinton because she believed he was "not a nice person" and would get him into political trouble, a new Gore biography reveals.

Pauline Gore was known to be the political brains of the family, reports Bill Turque in *Inventing Al Gore: A Biography*.

"She was also a woman of strong instinctive opinions about whom Al Gore could trust in politics and who should be avoided. Falling squarely in the latter category, years before her son became his vice president, was Bill Clinton. 'She thought he had bad moral character,' said James Fleming, a Nashville physician and longtime family friend."

Fleming recalls overhearing an exchange between Pauline Gore and Albert Jr. one day in the mid-1980s, just after Clinton had come to town and met the family for the first time. "She looked at [her son] and said, 'Bill Clinton is not a nice person. Don't associate with him too closely.'"

What accounted for Pauline's sixth sense about Clinton? Her parents hailed from Arkansas and Turque speculates that she may have heard scuttlebutt on the governor from home-state relatives.

Another likely reason: She'd encountered Clinton's type before, when she began her own legal career in the office of Texarkana attorney Bert Larey. The experience was "a disaster," reports Turque, and after a year Gore's mother abruptly returned to Nashville.

"She said that she planned to wed Albert [Sr.] and help him with his political career. But there was another reason, one she did not discuss for many years: Larey sexually harassed her."

"Maybe her own experience in the workplace had left her with a gut feeling about men who were trouble," surmises Turque about Pauline Gore's eerily accurate first impression of Bill Clinton.

Bill Turque is a Washington correspondent for Newsweek *magazine.*

Gore Won't Rule Out Pardon for Clinton

NewsMax.com Vortex, February 2000 — Vice President Al Gore has refused to say whether, if elected president, he would pardon Bill Clinton if Clinton is criminally charged in the Monica Lewinsky scandal after he leaves office.

The pardon issue came up during a wide-ranging interview with the *Los Angeles Times.*

Calling the question "completely hypothetical," Gore complained, "I don't think it's responsible to . . . I don't think it's a responsible way to deal with an issue like that, in the political context."

Times writer Edwin Chen described Gore as "taken aback by the question."

The pardon issue could be a real one for Gore. As the Lewinsky debate raged, more than a few Senate Democrats argued that Clinton's offenses did not rise to the level of impeachment, but suggested instead that Clinton could be prosecuted after he completed his term.

"Whether any of his conduct constitutes a criminal offense such as perjury or obstruction of justice is not for me to decide," insisted Senator Joseph I. Lieberman, D-Conn., who then added, "That, appropriately, should and must be left to the criminal justice system."

"Rejecting these articles of impeachment does not place this president above the law," echoed Clinton in-law Senator Barbara Boxer, D-California. "As the Constitution clearly says, he remains subject to the laws of the land just like any other citizen of the United States."

The pardon issue may turn out to be just as explosive for Gore as it was for President Gerald Ford, who pardoned Richard Nixon for his Watergate crimes after succeeding Nixon to the White House.

Without a clear denial by Gore, suspicions about a pardon deal may dog him just as they did Ford, contributing to Ford's re-election defeat.

Most-Decorated Veteran Calls Gore 'War Hero Wannabe'

NewsMax.com Vortex, December 1999 — Colonel David Hackworth, the most-decorated U.S. battle veteran since World War II, described Vice President Al Gore as a "war hero wannabe," as new questions emerged about Gore's military service in Vietnam.

NewsMax.com rekindled interest in Gore's Vietnam record after an October 15 *Los Angeles Times* report claimed that several of his wartime colleagues were ordered to serve as his VIP bodyguards. Gore's father was a U.S senator at the time.

Since then, new details have come to light, including the vice president's controversial characterization of the U.S. Army as "fascist and totalitarian" in a 1969 letter to his father. And at least two reports also contend that Gore considered fleeing to Canada to avoid Vietnam.

The vice president, who was an Army reporter during the war, has also exaggerated his battlefield exploits along the campaign trail, according to some who served with him in the 20th Engineering Brigade.

Appearing on Fox News Channel's *Hannity & Colmes*, Hackworth questioned Gore's truthfulness about his wartime past:

COLMES: Colonel Hackworth, we don't know what Gore says specifically. We don't know that he was trying to avoid the military, running to Canada — that's speculation. The fact is we do know he enlisted. We do know he went and he served in Vietnam, which is a lot more

than can be said for lots of other candidates and lots of other kids . . . .
HACKWORTH: [Sarcastically] Gore is bad. He's a Cong killer. He
walks, he talks, he crawls on his belly like a reptile. This man is not only
bad, he invented the Internet.
COLMES: All right, you want to bring up all that dirty laundry?
HACKWORTH: What we have here is a classic wannabe. And I've
seen so many of these types that wannabe a war hero. But he wasn't
there. . . .
COLMES: He served. He went to Vietnam.
HACKWORTH: But people who served with him [like] Mike
O'Hara, the *Detroit News*, [who] wouldn't make up fairy tales, he said,
"I was with him. There was never any incoming fire. We were never
under any danger." The guy at the *L.A. Times* says, "Hey, I was his
bodyguard." Which tells me that for an enlisted man in Vietnam he
was the only guy with a bodyguard. So he was connected.

Hackworth's allusion to "the guy at the *L.A. Times*" is a reference to
Henry Alan Leo, who told *Times* reporter Richard Serrano that he was
assigned to be Gore's bodyguard to "keep him out of trouble."

NewsMax.com reached Mike O'Hara, described in press reports as
Gore's best buddy in Vietnam. O'Hara remembered Leo as the brigade's
photographer.

When asked about Leo's bodyguard allegation, O'Hara would neither confirm nor deny the story, telling NewsMax.com emphatically
that he had nothing to say about Leo's account.

Gore Got VIP Treatment in 'Nam, Army Buddy Tells NewsMax.com

NewsMax.com Vortex, December 1999 — Al Gore's Vietnam tour of
duty was cut in half because he was the son of a powerful U.S. senator,
according to a Vietnam veteran who served with him.

In an exclusive interview with NewsMax.com, Henry Alan Leo also
claimed that he acted as Gore's "security escort" on the battlefield, but
took issue with a *Los Angeles Times* characterization of him as Gore's
Vietnam "bodyguard."

Still, even with that clarification, Gore's one-time Army buddy left little doubt that the Washington VIP's son received special treatment while "in country" and challenged assertions that Gore was sent home early merely because his unit had been deactivated.

Gore served in Vietnam as a reporter with the 20th Engineers Brigade from January 8 to May 24, 1971, when he was honorably discharged. His unit, headquartered in Bien Hoa some 20 miles northeast of Saigon, was deactivated in April 1971, a development Vice President Gore's defenders have cited to justify his early departure. The normal Army tour of duty in Vietnam was 12 months.

Henry Alan Leo was attached to the 20th Engineers as a photographer and, having been in country since October 1969, was one of the more senior members of the brigade when Gore arrived. When asked to explain how Gore got out more than six months early, Leo told NewsMax.com, "If your dad is a senator, you can do anything."

What about Gore's unit being deactivated?

"He could have come right back down and gone to Engineer Command Headquarters, which was the next command up," Leo said. "That's what the rest of us in the 20th Engineers did.

"He got out because of his dad," the Vietnam veteran repeated without equivocation. Al Gore Sr. was U.S. Senator from Tennessee at the time.

Leo said he was dismayed by the special handling Gore received in Vietnam, treatment that included a general's request that he look after Gore because he was the son of a powerful politician.

"I was shocked that someone would get that kind of treatment over in a combat zone. I thought we were all, you know, under the same flag. In my opinion, I thought nobody should be getting that kind of treatment."

Leo said that he was never specifically assigned to be Gore's "bodyguard," as the *Los Angeles Times* had reported on October 15.

"I was never ordered to be a bodyguard. As far as I know, Gore never had any bodyguards," Leo told NewsMax.com. "I was asked to be, more or less, a security escort because I had a lot more time in country and I already had multiple tours over there."

The *Times* reported that at least one other soldier besides Leo was warned that a senator's son, whose safety would be a priority, was joining the 20th Engineers. NewsMax.com asked Michael O'Hara, described in press accounts as Gore's best friend in the unit, about reports that Gore had bodyguards while in Vietnam. O'Hara refused to confirm or deny the allegation.

Leo told NewsMax.com that O'Hara and Gore were fast friends but wasn't sure whether he was the other brigade member who was told to watch out for the senator's son.

Brig. General Kenneth B. Cooper personally requested that Leo take precautions to see that no harm came to Gore, during a one-on-one meeting.

"It was natural for General Cooper to make the request — once again, it was never a direct order — for me to keep an eye out for Al Gore just to make sure that he did not get into any situations that we might have difficulty extracting ourselves from."

Leo took pains to not to exaggerate his role. "I wasn't like a bodyguard where I was going to take a bullet for the guy. I wouldn't do that for anybody. But it was just a matter of not letting Gore get caught out there in a situation where something might happen."

General Cooper's request that he protect Gore was an honor, in Leo's view:

"Wow, I thought, here the general thinks I have a good reputation. I lived on the edge. I liked being out in the field, but I used a lot of common sense. And I learned a lot while I was out there. So I was a natural survivor. And I believe that to be the real reason for my being asked to keep an eye out on Gore."

Leo said he was also the natural choice to be Gore's security escort because, as the unit photographer, he would have accompanied Gore on field interviews anyway. As it happened, they never found themselves in any close-call situations. "I'd say that most of the areas we went into were relatively secure already," Leo told NewsMax.com.

For Leo, Gore's special treatment was merely another example of Washington business as usual. "As a general rule the military jumps when Congress requires it to do so. So it doesn't surprise me that a senator had enough power to pull strings to ease his son's way anywhere."

Still, the Vietnam veteran bears Gore no ill will today. Leo said that after he got to know him, the future vice president seemed like "just one of the guys." After a while it became "second nature" for him to see that Gore was kept in "an OK situation."

Should the revelation that Gore got kid-glove care in Vietnam while others had to take their chances be an issue in the upcoming presidential campaign? Leo doesn't think so.

"Yes, I think it was unfair that he got special treatment. But it wasn't like I was told to guard this guy with my life. It was a simple matter of wanting us to take special caution to make sure that Gore didn't get into situations that may require a combat effort."

Now, Henry Alan Leo looks back on the enitre episode with a jaundiced view. "That was thirty years ago. It's not important to me now. I'm a native Washingtonian. Politics has always been a dirty word to me regardless of who the politicians are."

Unlike Gore, Roosevelt's Son Didn't Get Battlefield Bodyguards

NewsMax.com Vortex, December 1999 — Al Gore may have been assigned bodyguards to protect him during his military service in Vietnam, as several of his friends now allege. But such special privilege wasn't always the norm for the politically well-connected.

During World War II, for instance, President Roosevelt's son served in the U.S. Navy. One of John Roosevelt's shipmates contacted NewsMax.com after reading our Gore Bodyguard-gate exposé:

"In 1944 & 1945 I served aboard the USS Wasp, CV-18, in the Pacific Theatre," wrote the navy vet. "A supply officer on our ship was Lt. John Roosevelt, son of the president. Mr. Roosevelt's general quarters station was topside on a gun mount!!! I know and remember it well — mine was beside him!! He was not protected."

The vice president has yet to comment on Bodyguard-gate, as well as new allegations about the rest of his military record. Multiple reports now contend that Gore exaggerated his battlefield experience for political gain and considered fleeing to Canada before joining the Army to try to save his father's U.S. Senate seat.

Gore Letter Attacked Military as 'Fascist, Totalitarian'

NewsMax.com Vortex, December 1999 — Vice President Al Gore once wrote that the U.S. military was a "fascist, totalitarian" institution, reports former ABC News correspondent and Gore biographer Bob Zelnick in a recent issue of *National Review*.

Gore offered his scathing appraisal of America's Army in a letter he sent to his father after enlisting during the height of the Vietnam War. Gore "despised" U.S. involvement in Vietnam but decided to join up, Zelnick says, for one reason and one reason only: to save his father's U.S. Senate seat.

Zelnick confirms that Gore toyed with the idea of fleeing the country to avoid service — with his mother offering to accompany him if he decided to bolt. But finally politics took precedence, and Gore, to help his father, joined up just one jump ahead of his Tennessee draft board.

"Canada was, of course, farfetched; there were plenty of other ways to avoid military service," Zelnick writes. "But in the end, Gore decided to join the Army in an unsuccessful effort to save his father's seat."

Zelnick said that neither he nor one-time Gore profiler David Halberstam could find any contemporaneous evidence that Gore joined to spare others the risks of Vietnam, as the vice president would later claim to reporters.

Gore's 1969 attack on the Army as fascistic and totalitarian is sure to remind many of the letter his boss, Bill Clinton, wrote the same year, in which he thanked Arkansas ROTC Colonel Eugene Holmes for "saving me from the draft" and confessed that he sympathized with those who "loathed the military."

Zelnick spoke to many of the vice president's Vietnam-era friends and could find no evidence to back reports that Gore had used political pull to win his relatively safe job as a military reporter.

But the former ABC newsman evidently did not interview H. Alan Leo, one of several of the vice president's Vietnam colleagues, who told the *Los Angeles Times* that they were assigned to keep Gore from getting hurt during his five-month tour in Southeast Asia.

Gore Considered Fleeing to Canada to Avoid Vietnam

NewsMax.com Vortex, December 1999 — Before he enlisted in the Army in 1969, Vice President Al Gore considered dodging the draft and fleeing his country.

According to a 1992 wire report reviewed by NewsMax.com:

"Gore had just graduated from Harvard and shared an opposition to the war with much of his generation. According to many accounts, Gore carefully weighed his options, and even briefly considered fleeing to Canada, as many did to avoid the draft." (Associated Press — July 29, 1992)

Rumors that Gore considered the Canada option swirled when a C-SPAN caller who identified himself only as a former Gore aide claimed to know the behind-the-scenes story of why the vice president changed his mind and decided to enlist.

According to the caller's account, Gore's father advised him that seeking asylum in Canada would destroy his political viability and promised that if he enlisted no harm would come to him.

Before President Carter granted amnesty to Vietnam draft-dodgers in 1978, those who fled the country were not allowed to return.

In a report that lends some credibility to another aspect of the caller's account, several of Gore's Vietnam colleagues told the *Los Angeles Times* that they were assigned to act as his "bodyguards." If true, the vice president's physical risk while in Vietnam was indeed minimized, just as his father had allegedly promised.

"It blew me away," H. Alan Leo told the *Times*. "I was to make sure he didn't get into a situation he could not get out of. They didn't want him to get into trouble. So we went into the field after the fact [after combat actions], and that limited his exposure to any hazards. [See: Al Gore Had Bodyguards Protecting Him in Vietnam]

Vietnam had an impact on political viability for both father and son.

At the time of Gore's enlistment, his father was in the fight of his political life. Senator Gore had opposed the war early on, which had made him increasingly unpopular in conservative Tennessee. In an apparent attempt to compensate for his own anti-war position, the senator had his son appear in campaign ads wearing military fatigues after young Gore had enlisted.

His family has always insisted that Gore's decision to volunteer for the Army had nothing to do with political considerations. Still, young Albert was scheduled to ship out by Election Day, which couldn't hurt with voters who viewed Vietnam service as the ultimate patriotic act.

But Gore's orders were delayed. In a 1988 *Washington Post* interview, Gore family members said they suspected that President Nixon had delayed a 1969 Vietnam call-up solely to deny Gore's father any benefit at the polls from having a son at the battlefront.

Gore himself told the *Post*, "All I know is I was not allowed to go until the first departure date after the November election."

Gore's father lost the election.

Al Gore Had Bodyguards Protecting Him in Vietnam

NewsMax.com Vortex, December 1999 — "I could have done that," Vice President Al Gore told *USA Today*. "I thought about that, and because a lot of those decisions were made with political influence, I could have done that, but it did not feel right."

The "that" to which Gore referred was an opportunity to join his home state's National Guard. Instead, Gore was shipped to Vietnam after he volunteered for the Army in 1969, a decision he hopes will contrast favorably with George W. Bush's service record as a pilot in the Texas Air National Guard.

But the vice president best tread lightly as he uses his Vietnam experience to play the egalitarian card. Because, according to a recent *Los Angeles Times* report that the rest of the press pretended not to notice, Gore's Vietnam tour of duty was notable mainly for the special treatment he received, a "handle with care" order that required bodyguards to keep the senator's son from getting hurt.

"Several of his [Vietnam] colleagues remember they were assigned to make sure this son of a prominent politician was never injured in the war," reported *Times* correspondent Richard Serrano, in a lengthy piece headlined "Struggle with Conscience Was Gore's Biggest Vietnam Battle."

"Other soldiers with long experience in Vietnam said that Gore was treated differently from his fellow enlistees," Serrano noted. "Two of them recalled that before Gore arrived Brig. General Kenneth B. Cooper advised them that a senator's son would be joining the outfit.

"H. Alan Leo said soldiers were ordered to serve as Gore's bodyguards, to keep him out of harm's way. 'It blew me away,' Leo said. 'I was to make sure he didn't get into a situation he could not get out of. They didn't want him to get into trouble. So we went into the field after the fact [after combat actions], and that limited his exposure to any hazards.'" (*Los Angeles Times* — October 15, 1999)

During his first run for the White House in 1988, Gore didn't hesitate to remind reporters about his service in Vietnam, which he tended to mischaracterize as combat-oriented. "I was shot at. I spent most of my time in the field," he told the *Washington Post* 11 years ago.

"I carried an M-16 . . . I pulled my turn on the perimeter at night and walked through the elephant grass and I was fired upon," Gore told the *Baltimore Sun* during the same period. To *Vanity Fair* he revealed, "Something would move, we'd fire first and ask questions later."

But eight Vietnam vets who served with the vice president told the *Los Angeles Times* that Gore was never in the middle of a battle. These days, Gore admits his wartime service was primarily as a reporter.

But Gore has yet to respond to allegations that bodyguards kept him out of harm's way in Vietnam, a charge that — except for the *Los Angeles Times* — has gone largely unreported by the press.

Tipper's Facelift

NewsMax.com Vortex, November 1998 — When Paula Jones recently came to Manhattan to visit a Park Avenue plastic surgeon for a nose job, word quickly leaked out. Headlines everywhere.

Celebrities come to New York for plastic surgery all the time. Rarely does it make print.

Earlier this year, after the Lewinsky scandal broke, Al Gore's attractive wife Tipper slipped into town for a little tuck and eyelift, *Inside Cover* has learned.

Like most stars, Tipper didn't go anywhere near a doctor's office. A suite at a posh New York hotel was reserved. The operation took place right there. Recovery took about a week. Al was nowhere to be seen. But a bevy of Secret Service agents guarded the second lady as she lay in hiding.

A source close to the Gores tells *Inside Cover* that there are cracks in the Clinton-Gore relationship. During his long years of public service, Gore had an impeccably clean record. Now he has to carry Bill's baggage into 2000.

Huey Long and Media Manipulations

By Christopher Ruddy

NewsMax.com Vortex, June 2000 — Populist Huey Long was once asked during the Great Depression if he thought the United States could succumb to fascism.

Long, known for his wit, gave a revealing response: "Yes, but in America we'll call it anti-fascism."

Thankfully, fascism did not take root in America.

But Long grasped something about Americans. If you label something with a good name — even if it's bad — many people will gullibly accept the idea as good.

It's frightening to think how gullible so many Americans have become in believing the major media – even when they engage in obvious manipulations to turn bad into good, lies into truth.

This has really been brought home to me watching over the past few months the major media coverage of the Elian Gonzalez story.

Here are just some of the manipulations of the media:

• Polls consistently say Elian should be returned to his father.

Every decent person wants a boy with his father and mother. But the truth is the boy is being returned not "to his father" but to Fidel Castro. A fair poll question would ask if Elian should be returned "to communist Cuba" or "to Fidel Castro."

By framing the question, the media got the response they wanted. The polls have a strong effect on people (nobody likes to think they are the oddball) and certainly the polls lead the politicians.

• The Miami Cubans are crazy and out of control.

That was the spin out of the press that covered the Elian story in Miami.

Forget about the fact they are a hardworking ethnic group who pay their taxes, serve in the military, and have made a success for themselves in the United States.

For weeks Cuban-Americans engaged in peaceful demonstrations, obeying all police requests. But the major press painted a picture of a mob capable of violence.

• Mayor Carollo is out of control for firing his city manager.

The major press, like CNN, have been savagely attacking Miami Mayor Joseph Carollo for firing his city manager for allowing the police chief to OK the federal raid without informing the mayor.

Excuse me, but when in America does the federal government dictate orders to the local police? We don't have a national police. The U.S. Constitution clearly lays out a separation of powers. The local police chief answers to the local mayor, who answers to the local electorate. That's how the system is supposed to work. Carollo was absolutely justified in his anger over this federal intrusion into his municipality.

• Images of a happy Elian demonstrate he wants to be with his father.

When the world saw Elian smiling outside his Miami home, frolicking with friends, the Justice Department had a medical doctor — without examining the child — conclude the boy was really being abused and needed to be "rescued."

The media seemed to accept that assessment.

When the world saw the horrifying scene of a SWAT-suited INS agent seizing Elian at gunpoint, the picture was breathtaking — not only for capturing a dramatic news event, but also for revealing the naked abuse of power.

Incredibly, publications like the *New York Times, Newsweek, USA Today* and others did not publish this photo on their covers. Most media outlets were much happier publishing propaganda photos put out by Greg Craig [lawyer for Elian's father].

And where were the "experts" the media had been trotting out before to talk about abuse?

The media know that images are usually more powerful than words, hence the steady diet of Elian-with-his-dad photos. Meanwhile, the storm-trooper-in-the-bedroom photo has almost fallen off the radar screen.

These are just some of the ways the major media have manipulated the truth — and ultimately public opinion. In my career in journalism, I have been amazed at how the media bias has become more and more blatant — and how the people recognize it less and less.

There was a belief that with the explosion of cable TV, a multitude of TV news programs, the rise of talk radio and even the Internet, the media influence of the really powerful outlets like the major networks would decline and there would be a greater diversity of views.

But the opposite has happened. With so many outlets, the media propaganda has become much more effective. With so many programs reporting the same story with the same spin, the brainwashing effect is much more powerful.

Perhaps Huey Long was right. We could have fascism here in America after all. We'll just say the brownshirts here don't have their fingers on the trigger — and they don't point their guns at you.

Bryant Gumbel Ridicules Catholics As Ratings Slide

NewsMax.com Vortex, May 2000 — The press made a big stink about George W. Bush's alleged anti-Catholicism for having spoken at Bob Jones University. That was well and good, because the press were pulling for McCain — and so, overnight, many major media figures became, well, more Catholic than the pope.

Not Bryant Gumbel, though. He has been quite virulent against Catholics for some time. His animosity also extends to conservative Republicans.

After NBC tossed him, he ended up at CBS and, as ratings for his specials proved disastrous, he was stuck back in the basement program.

Apparently Gumbel has yet to figure out why viewers don't like him.

CBS's *The Early Show* recently featured another attack on Catholicism, his third outburst in less than two months, according to the Catholic League.

Joining Gumbel in this attack was his co-host Jane Clayson, anchor Julie Chen and meteorologist Mark McEwen. Here is a sample of their extended discussion:

McEwen: Do you go to church?

Gumbel: No.

McEwen: Then why do you give up stuff for Lent?

Gumbel: Because I think there is a great deal of Catholic guilt that remains.

McEwen: That's what — that's what drives the Catholic Church, is guilt.

Gumbel: I mean, so if you even — if you even think about Betty Sue in the backseat, forget about doing it. Save your effort. You already sinned.

Chen: I haven't thought of Betty Sue in the backseat.

McEwen: . . . if you do go to the backseat, you can go say you're sorry.

Gumbel: That's right.

McEwen: It's called confession.

Gumbel: . . . were, like no matter what you did, if you had a double murder, he'd give you, like, a Hail Mary.

McEwen: That's right.

Gumbel: Say a Hail Mary and go home. And the other one, if you, like, ate meat on Friday, he'd make you take a trip to Lourdes. Seriously. I mean, no, the penance was different . . .

Catholic League president William Donohue commented on Gumbel's remarks: "I mean, like, hey man, like, when will Bryant grow up?"

Never, Bill, never. Just say a Hail Mary for him.

Mike Wallace Targets Farm Bureau Using Radical Group

By Stephan Archer

NewsMax.com Vortex, May 2000 — The nation's largest and most respected organization of farmers came under harsh criticism from Mike Wallace and CBS' *60 Minutes* last Sunday — apparently because the group's conservative political views don't sit well with the liberal-leaning television program.

If you were one of the 30 million Americans who tuned into *60 Minutes*, you would have come away believing that the nonprofit American Farm Bureau Federation cares less about its 5 million members than it does about making big profits for its executives and directors.

Despite *60 Minutes* claims, there is no evidence that the Farm Bureau has engaged in any wrongdoing or improprieties.

Wallace and *60 Minutes* made it appear that the group had done something wrong. But not once during the 20-minute segment did Wallace bother to disclose to the show's viewers the critical fact that the *60 Minutes* segment had been researched and organized by a radical environmentalist group.

The group, Defenders of Wildlife, is fighting to protect wolves and other predatory animals considered dangerous to humans.

In the past few years the Defenders have targeted the Farm Bureau, upset that the Bureau has sought to remove dangerous wolves from Yellowstone National Park and has argued in Congress for private property rights.

A review of the Defenders Web site indicates the extremist group has focused its efforts on the Farm Bureau.

In another indication that the group's efforts had been coordinated by *60 Minutes*, the Defenders released a special white paper on the Farm Bureau on April 10, the day after *60 Minutes* aired its critical "Voice of the Farmer" feature.

The special white paper offers almost identical criticism of the Farm Bureau that Wallace made on his show.

The Defenders and *60 Minutes* faulted the Farm Bureau for ties to large agribusiness, for investing in start-up businesses, offering services like insurance to non-farmers, and advancing a conservative political agenda. The Bureau opposes gun control and has called for the abolition of the Department of Education and the Department of Energy.

Again, Wallace never disclosed the basis of the criticism of the Bureau, nor did he disclose that almost all of the dissident farmers he interviewed were either members of the Defenders or were referred to *60 Minutes* by the group.

Farm Bureau president Bob Stallman defended his organization, saying that it "has been the target of malicious propaganda" and that the CBS *60 Minutes* report was "one-sided and a gross distortion of many facts."

Wallace portrayed the Farm Bureau as an elitist organization that had done little to serve the interests of the struggling family farmer.

"We found that people at the top of the Farm Bureau have been building a financial empire worth billions, some of it invested in the very agribusiness giants that many family farmers say are running them out of business," Wallace reported.

One of these "agribusiness giants" Wallace referred to is FBL Financial Group, a company that has investments on Wall Street through companies such as ConAgra.

ConAgra is one of the large agribusinesses said to be squeezing out the small family farmer. Another AFBF investment is Access Air, a start-up airline in Des Moines in which the farm organization and two of its affiliated companies had invested at least $1 million, according to Wallace.

"I don't understand why we're being criticized for success," said Joe Fields, director of public relations at the Farm Bureau.

Fields explained that many of the affiliated companies of the Farm Bureau were developed in the thirties to help the small farmer to acquire such needed services as medical and car insurance.

These services were and still are difficult for many farmers to get. Other non-insurance investments, Fields explained, are also used to help finance the farmers' needs.

"America's farm and ranch families decide what Farm Bureau supports and they know the organization represents their interests," said Stallman.

"Just as Farm Bureau's farmer members renew their memberships on an annual basis, they also review the policies they set to guide us — the world's most influential organization."

But CBS didn't just accuse the Bureau of mishandling funds.

The news organization also attacked the Farm Bureau for wanting to repeal the Voting Rights Act of 1965.

"[The manual] does call for the repeal of the Voting Act of 1965, [and] the reason it does is because that act, we felt, was an infringement on states' rights because it gave the federal government the power to come in and manage all elections, every detail of local, county and statewide elections," explained Fields.

"Farm Bureau supports civil rights and voting rights," Stallman stated. "We do, however, oppose federal election regulations that impose mandates on state governments — in particular those mandates that have led to a decrease in political representation in rural America. That sentiment is in our policy book."

Fields and the Bureau were angry that Wallace didn't give a balanced presentation of the facts and failed to disclose to his viewers the involvement of the Defenders of Wildlife.

"We believe in good stewardship of the land and wildlife, but we feel that we need to also honor personal property rights," Fields said, explaining the real reason his organization had been targeted by Defenders.

Fields said Defenders had been making postings on the Internet seeking disgruntled members of the Bureau.

"And they surface, of course, especially during bad economic times, so they surfaced these people and those are the ones on *60 Minutes*," Fields said.

Contacted by NewsMax.com, a spokesman for Defenders took credit for the *60 Minutes* segment and expressed disappointment that his organization wasn't credited for the story.

As it turned out, Defenders of Wildlife was briefly mentioned when the owner of a bread store in Chicago was interviewed by Wallace.

Wallace briefly noted that Linda Shutt, the owner of the store, had collected petitions for Defenders of Wildlife in an attempt to stop the Farm Bureau's campaign to remove wolves from Yellowstone National Park.

Shutt told Wallace she had delivered the petitions to the Farm Bureau and believed that to be the end of it until the Federal Bureau of Investigation came into her store.

"We had FBI agents come to our bread store and investigating us as though we were a threat to the Farm Bureau," Shutt said.

Though *60 Minutes* and Wallace clearly implied the Farm Bureau was behind the FBI visit, Wallace didn't air the Farm Bureau's denial that it asked the FBI to investigate the Shutt store.

Fields said the FBI visit may have been sparked by an article in the *Chicago Sun-Times* around the same time about the Farm Bureau receiving bomb threats from radical animal rights activists.

Wallace's duplicity was evident again when he interviewed Sally

Ann Garner, a vice president for a Chicago bank who, according to Wallace, was surprised that she had become a Farm Bureau member when she bought Farm Bureau car insurance in 1991.

Wallace asked her if she was aware of the Farm Bureau's position on the Voting Rights Act or that the group wants to eliminate the departments of Education and Energy and opposes gun control. To all the questions, Garner appeared surprised by Wallace's questions and answered that she had not been aware that she was a Bureau member or that the group held such positions.

However, in the fall of 1998, *Defenders* magazine, a publication of Defenders of Wildlife, reported that Garner knew that her car insurance purchase would give her an automatic membership with the DuPage County, Illinois, Farm Bureau.

According to the article, Garner has been angered by the Farm Bureau's efforts to remove wolves from Yellowstone. Wallace made no mention of Garner's involvement with the Defenders.

Wallace's segments inluded nothing on how the Farm Bureau had improved the conditions of farmers, opened economic opportunities or advocated and protected farmers before Congress.

Wallace's handling of the Farm Bureau is not an isolated case of journalistic malpractice. Wallace has had a long, checkered career of questionable professional ability and ethics.

In one incident Wallace was caught on video, but off-air, saying that blacks and Hispanics would have difficulty filling out bank loan applications because they were "too busy eating watermelons and tacos."

During the famous controversy over tobacco insider Jeffrey Wigand, Wallace claimed on the Charlie Rose program that *60 Minutes* had not paid Wigand. In fact, Wigand had been paid by *60 Minutes* and Wallace later admitted he had lied.

Wallace once told the *Washington Post* he has lied and feels it's acceptable for a journalist to do so. Half-truths, distortions and outright lies have been hallmarks of Wallace's reporting for years. It's no secret that other *60 Minutes* professionals like Ed Bradley, Morley Safer and Leslie Stahl have distanced themselves from their often cantankerous and bitter colleague.

Farm Bureau chief Stallman is unfazed by the smear of Wallace and *60 Minutes*.

"Our success representing American agriculture makes us a target of those opposed to our mission," Stallman said, adding, "We answer to our members, farm and ranch families who know Farm Bureau is supported and controlled by farmers. Farm Bureau will continue to work toward its two main goals — to enhance net farm income and to improve the quality of rural life."

Stephan Archer is a staff writer for NewsMax.com.

Harry Hopkins: Soviet Traitor, Not an American Hero

By Reed Irvine

NewsMax.com Vortex, February 2000 — Each of the panelists on CNN's *Capital Gang* has to come up with an "Outrage of the Week" at the end of the program. One of those panelists, Al Hunt, a liberal columnist for the *Wall Street Journal,* recently committed the outrage of the century in his final column for 1999.

In that column, Hunt listed his choices for the 20th century's best American government officials and included Harry L. Hopkins, President Franklin D. Roosevelt's closest adviser, as one of the best presidential aides of the century.

In selecting Hopkins, Hunt revealed his ignorance of what has been learned about Soviet espionage in recent years.

Someday, historians will have to acknowledge that Harry Hopkins was the greatest traitor in American history, overshadowing Benedict Arnold by far. Arnold, at least, was open in his betrayal, and his potential for damaging the American cause was small by comparison.

Hopkins was a Soviet agent who pretended to put America's interests first while secretly advancing the interests of Stalin.

In his 1990 book *KGB: The Inside Story,* Oleg Gordievsky, a high-level KGB defector, reported damning information about Hopkins he heard from Iskhak Akhmerov, an undercover spymaster who controlled the KGB's "illegal" agents in the United States during World War II.

He said that Akhmerov had described Harry Hopkins as "the most important of all Soviet wartime agents in the United States." He said that other KGB officers in the directorate in charge of illegals and the

U.S. experts in the KGB's code section "all agreed that Hopkins had been an agent of major significance."

Gordievsky's co-author, Christopher Andrew, was not comfortable in publishing this charge. He said Gordievsky had gradually come to believe that Hopkins was an "unconscious" agent, meaning that Hopkins did not realize that Akhmerov was a Soviet spymaster.

Akhmerov, who served as a liaison between Hopkins and Stalin, had no open connection with the Soviet Embassy or any official Soviet organization in the U.S. His cover is believed to have been running a clothing store in New York. He used at least three different aliases in dealing with the agents under his control.

Hopkins was not so naive as to think that a small businessman who could deliver and receive messages from Stalin was anything other than a high-ranking Soviet intelligence agent. Hopkins never told anyone about this strange little man who was in close touch with the Soviet dictator. He didn't ask the FBI to investigate him because he knew he was dealing with a Soviet spy.

Further confirmation of Hopkins' conscious collaboration with the KGB came with the 1999 publication of *The Sword and the Shield: the Mitrokhin Archive*. This was based on copies of KGB files spirited out of Russia by retired KGB officer Vasili Mitrokhin.

One of the files disclosed that Hopkins had informed the Soviet Embassy that the FBI had bugged a secret meeting between Steve Nelson, a member of the U.S. Communist underground, and a Soviet Embassy official.

The official had gone to California to give Nelson money to finance his espionage operations. FBI Director J. Edgar Hoover informed Hopkins in writing that the FBI had planted bugs in both Nelson's home and in the Communist Party headquarters in New York City.

In passing this information to the Soviet Embassy, Hopkins proved that he put the interests of the Union of Soviet Socialist Republics above those of the United States.

Further confirming Hopkins' treachery, Akhmerov said that an agent identified as "19" reported a conversation between Roosevelt and Churchill. An endnote in the Mitrokhin book says that "it is probable almost to the point of certainty that Hopkins was '19.' "

Over strong opposition, Hopkins persuaded the ailing Roosevelt to go to Yalta, where the fate of Poland and other countries under Soviet occupation was sealed.

Hopkins said the Russians had been "reasonable and farseeing." Robert Sherwood, a Roosevelt speechwriter, called Yalta "a monstrous fraud."

Hopkins had been instrumental in our supplying, with no conditions, the arms that enabled Stalin to defeat the Germans. He helped seal their control of Eastern Europe, and he is suspected of having authorized shipments of uranium that helped them develop their A-bomb.

No wonder Akhmerov considered Hopkins his most important agent. According to Gordievsky, the KGB believed he helped it triumph "over American imperialism."

Hero of the Soviet Union? Yes. American hero? No way!date

Reed Irvine is chairman of Accuracy in Media at http://www.aim.org.

Reporters Pouncing on Bush's Intellect Never Questioned Clinton's

NewsMax.com Vortex, December 1999 — Thanks to a nosy group of Yale students who ferreted out his academic records, we now know that George W. Bush squeaked through his four years at the august institution with a C average.

After Bush was able to name only one of four obscure foreign leaders in an interview with a Boston TV reporter, the Gore campaign wasted no time trying to capitalize on the gaffe, specifically citing the Texas governor's lackluster Yale grades.

"I guess we know that C at Yale was a gentleman's C," taunted Gore spokesman Chris Lehane.

Since Al Gore's gang finds the subject of college grades of such interest, perhaps they could help shed some light on one of the more enduring mysteries of the Clinton era: President Clinton's own academic record.

To this day, America doesn't know whether Clinton got by during his own time at Yale Law with a gentleman's C or better. And his reason for leaving Oxford University after only one full year remains completely shrouded in mystery. In fact, Clinton's college grade secrets have been as closely guarded as his never fully released medical records. The same reporters now having a field day with questions about Bush's intellectual qualifications have by and large turned a blind eye to the question of Clinton's grades. But here's how former FBI agent Gary Aldrich dealt with the subject in his 1996 blockbuster book, *Unlimited Access.*

On Clinton's undergraduate record at Georgetown University:

"Mr. Clinton has refused to allow a review of any disciplinary records at Georgetown and has also refused to supply any records related to his attendance or performance as a student while attending classes there. . . . There were no grades available for review to prove or disprove claims regarding Clinton's achievement, since the university will not release such records absent the candidate's authority."

On Clinton's stint as a Rhodes Scholar at Oxford:

"[Clinton] will neither sign a release form nor will he provide documentation related to his attendance and performance at Oxford. . . . There have been claims that Mr. Clinton is 'highly intelligent' or 'brilliant,' but no testing data have been made available to substantiate these claims."

On Clinton's Yale years:

"Mr. Clinton attended Yale Law School from 1970 to 1973, at which time it is reported that he graduated with a degree in law. Again, no records are available to confirm or deny his performance at the Law School."

Aldrich summarized:

"[Clinton] has attended prestigious institutions, though investigation has revealed that Mr. Clinton had important political sponsors who may have helped sway admissions boards. . . . Absent any objective criteria being made available, measures of Mr. Clinton's academic achievements are speculative."

U.S. Media Spike July Fourth Clinton Embarrassment

NewsMax.com Vortex, August 1999 — A picture is worth a thousand words, or so the saying goes. But when it comes to President Clinton, there are some pictures that the American media would rather you didn't see.

One such amazing moment, undoubtedly captured on film by all the major networks, took place as America's president and America's symbol, a bald eagle named Challenger, stood side by side on the White House lawn.

The ceremony was meant to celebrate the removal of Challenger and his brethren from the endangered species list. But the moment soon turned embarrassing when Challenger, whom Clinton had just described as "the living symbol of our democracy," reached out and bit the president on his left hand.

This on the eve of the July Fourth weekend, the most patriotic of all American holiday celebrations.

So what happened to the press coverage of this most symbolic of all Clinton moments? Photos of the president smiling at the bird before the bite appeared in papers. But when Challenger loosed his noble beak upon the impeached president, media photographers must have been reloading.

In fact, but for the foreign press — specifically the *London Telegraph* — American news readers might have no idea that this amazing incident had even taken place. More questions for George W.

Now that the mainstream press has browbeaten the truth out of George W. Bush (he's been cocaine-clean for at least 25 years), that's no reason for reporters to let up. There's blood in the water — and who knows what other evil lurks in the heart of this seemingly mild-mannered Texan.

Inside Cover suggests that our intrepid fourth estate continue to press Bush on all relevant questions. Here are just a few he has thus far failed to address:

1) Has your wife ever had an affair with your lawyer, after which he ended up shot to death in some out-of-the-way park?

2) Has a Texas state trooper ever brought to your hotel room a woman who later claimed you exposed yourself and asked her to "kiss it"?

3) Did you ever rape a nursing home operator who had volunteered to help elect you governor?

4) Has your wife ever fired the entire Texas state travel office and then had its employees maliciously prosecuted on bogus embezzlement charges?

5) Did you ever instruct the Texas Air National Guard to attack Oklahoma on the same day your ex-girlfriend was scheduled to testify before a grand jury?

6) How many of your close friends and associates have been indicted or have died prematurely in suspicious accidents or suicides?

7) Have you ever called Mario Cuomo a mafiosi on tape?

8) Did you ever travel to Moscow at the height of the Cold War after protesting against America on foreign soil?

9) Did you ever lie to an ROTC colonel after getting your third Vietnam draft notice?

10) Do you have any brothers who say you have a nose like a vacuum cleaner and repeatedly use the "N" word on police surveillance videotape?

11) Does your wife think your mother and grandmother abused you?

12) Do you do anything with cigars besides smoke them?

Michael Reagan Corrects Liz Smith: Reagan Kids Did Not Abandon Father

NewsMax.com Vortex, November 1999 — Liz Smith, whose syndicated gossip column appears in the *New York Post* and hundreds of papers across the country, blasted Ronald Reagan's children.

"Heroic Nancy Reagan" headlined Smith's column. Smith reported that Nancy Reagan "cares for the former president with virtually no family support."

Smith adds that none of Ronald Reagan's children had visited him in the past seven months. "Maureen, Patti and Ron Jr. visited last March," Smith writes.

Not true, responds son Michael Reagan.

Reagan, who hosts a nationally syndicated radio talk show from Los Angeles, told NewsMax.com he regularly visits his ailing dad at his Bel Air home. In fact, he was there twice in the past month, once with sister Patti and another time with his daughter.

Reagan called Smith today and explained why her report was inaccurate and misleading.

"It's being written to sound like the kids are not going to see Dad," Reagan said he told Smith. He said some of the family can't visit regularly because they do not live in the area and have work commitments. Ron Jr. and Maureen don't live near their father's Los Angeles home, Reagan said. Ron Jr. lives in Seattle and hosts a syndicated show called "TV.com." Maureen lives in Sacramento. Michael Reagan said Maureen calls her father's home every day to check on him. "She works very hard speaking out about Alzheimer's and helping a foundation in Ronald Reagan's name raise funds."

In recent months, similar inaccurate reports about the Reagan children have been circulating in the press. Smith cited "family friends" of the Reagans for her report. "I'm questioning why 'family friends' would be saying such lies," Michael Reagan said.

Mike Wallace Talks of 'Penis Envy'

NewsMax.com Vortex, November 1999 — Mike Wallace is said to be bracing for next week's release of the movie about tobacco whistleblower Jeffrey Wigand, *The Insider*.

Wallace is reportedly furious that the film depicts him as a foppish prima donna — nothing like the hard-as-nails journalist he's portrayed as by *60 Minutes*.

Wallace is also angry because Lowell Bergman (portrayed by Al Pacino in the film), his former producer for the Wigand story, comes off as one of the heroes.

Newsweek quotes Wallace as saying that Bergman is suffering from "penis envy."

Bergman told the magazine Wallace can't stand the fact that producers for *60 Minutes*, rather than the celebrity hosts, are getting some of the credit.

It has been well known at CBS for years that Wallace does little, if any, investigative reporting. Wallace has been known to arrive at a shoot for a *60 Minutes* feature fresh from Martha's Vineyard with his most significant preparation — a tan — completed.

The Wigand tobacco story also reveals Wallace's underside.

No one can forget Wallace's appearance on the *Charlie Rose* program during the controversy, when Wallace emphatically said Wigand had not been paid by the network. He also had told Morley Safer, his CBS colleague, the same thing.

Later it was revealed that Wallace had lied. Wigand had been paid $13,000 as a consultant to *60 Minutes*.

Despite the obnoxious lie, Wallace skated, as he has during several previous fumbles. *Inside Cover* remembers when Wallace was caught off-air, on film, saying that blacks and Hispanics might have a hard time filling out bank applications because they "were too busy eating watermelons and tacos."

Media Mum on Clinton Cocaine Witness List

NewsMax.com Vortex, September 1999 — Is it just *Inside Cover*, or has anybody else noticed that reporters have suddenly cooled on their favorite pursuit, hounding George W. Bush on the cocaine question?

Maybe it's the recent surveys showing Americans don't care if Bush used the drug a generation ago. But more probably it's the fact that the press's own double standard has become so blatantly apparent that even they now worry about seeming unfair.

Reporters have been slammed lately for not going after President Clinton on the same question — and the entire U.S. media knows it risks a credibility crisis should the Bush bashing continue.

Thanks to Gennifer Flowers' August 6 allegation — first reported here — where she claimed Clinton used a "substantial amount" of cocaine, news editors have been faced with a stark choice: Find an allegation against Bush as credible and damaging as Flowers' account — or let the coke rumors about him die a natural death.

Otherwise America's information gatekeepers might be forced to cover the list of witnesses who have gone public about what they say was our president's own nasty habit.

Besides Flowers, those witnesses could include:

SHARLINE WILSON, the former Little Rock drug dealer who told a federal grand jury in 1990 that she watched as Bill Clinton used cocaine in her presence. Her testimony is sealed. But she recounted the Clinton coke shocker, which she witnessed at Little Rock's LeBistro restaurant, for the *London Telegraph*'s Ambrose Evans-Pritchard in 1994.

" 'Roger the Dodger' [Clinton's brother] came back to the bar and said he needed two grams of cocaine right away. They carried out the deal near the ladies room. The Dodger then borrowed her 'tooter,' her 'one hitter' as she called it, and handed it to the governor.

" 'I watched Bill Clinton lean up against a brick wall . . . he casually stuck my tooter up his nose. He was so messed up that night, he slid down the wall into a garbage can and just sat there like a complete idiot.' " (*The Secret Life of Bill Clinton*, by Ambrose Evans-Pritchard)

Wilson also claimed to have seen then-Governor Clinton use the drug at Little Rock's Coachman's Inn. She is currently serving a 31-year jail sentence that she believes is retribution for her candor.

SALLY PERDUE, the former Arkansas beauty queen who claims she had a four-month affair with the president in 1983, has told reporters that Clinton used cocaine in her presence and that he seemed quite familiar with how the drug is used:

"He had all the equipment laid out, like a real pro," said Perdue.

Perdue says she was threatened with violence if she didn't stay silent about the details of her Clinton affair. She currently resides in China.

L. D. BROWN, the former Clinton bodyguard and one-time head of the Arkansas Police Association, recounts his own suspicions about Clinton's cocaine use in his book, *Crossfire: Witness in the Clinton Investigation*.

Brown says he was guarding Clinton at a Boca Raton hotel when the then-governor suddenly disappeared from sight:

"Bill stepped out for a few minutes, long enough for me to become concerned. . . . I first checked the bathroom. I called his name but got no answer. Just as I was about to leave I saw his number 13's [shoes] protruding from under one of the stalls. 'Bill, are you okay?' I asked, knowing that there couldn't be another foot that big in Boca Raton. 'Yeah, yeah, L. D., these damn sinuses are killing me.' As I retreated to the bar I realized what was going on. . . . Bill knew that with my prior experience in drug enforcement, I didn't tolerate illicit drug use — particularly 'nose candy.' "

JANE PARKS, Roger Clinton's one-time landlady, has said that during the mid-1980s Bill Clinton was a "frequent visitor" to his little brother's expensive Vantage Point apartment, which shared a wall with Parks' office. According to the account Parks has given reporters, the Clinton brothers enjoyed partying with girls who appeared to be high school age.

"There was drug use at these gatherings . . . and [Parks] could clearly distinguish Bill's voice as he chatted with his brother about the quality of the marijuana they were smoking. She said she could also hear them talking about the cocaine as they passed it back and forth." (*Partners in power*, by Roger Morris)

ROGER CLINTON, the president's own half-brother, is said to have offered one of the most damning accounts of his sibling's cocaine use. A 1984 police surveillance videotape reportedly shows Roger telling one of his coke connections, "Got to get some for my brother. He's got a nose like a vacuum cleaner."

Roger himself would do time for distributing coke, as would one of his older brother's biggest campaign contributors, Danny Ray Lasater. According to L. D. Brown, then-Governor Clinton casually dismissed the cocaine smuggling Brown had witnessed at Mena airport, saying, "That's Lasater's deal."

TERRY DON CAMP, an Arkansas prisoner who testified on behalf of fellow inmate Perry Steve Risinger in Risinger's 1996 jail break trial, put Clinton in the company of Mena cocaine smuggler Barry Seal on at least one occasion.

Camp told the court that he "saw Seal get off an airplane with Clinton and two apparent plainclothes police officers at the Magnolia Airport in the early 1980s." Risinger, a one-time drug dealer himself, told the court that he feared for his life while in jail "because of his knowledge of convicted drug smuggler Barry Seal's ties to President Clinton and other powerful people in Arkansas and Louisiana." (*Arkansas Democrat-Gazette* — March 19, 1996)

DR. SUSAN SANTA CRUZ claims no direct knowledge of Clinton's involvement with cocaine. But in 1992, instead of releasing the then-candidate's medical records, Santa Cruz and other doctors who had treated Clinton were called upon to verbally detail Clinton's medical history for the press.

"Her listing of Mr. Clinton's history included allergies, a strained ligament in his left knee from unspecified causes and rectal bleeding from hemorrhoids in 1984. His surgical history includes a procedure to open up his sinuses in 1979 and a tonsillectomy in 1952." (*Washington Times* — March 12, 1996)

Medical experts say that heavy cocaine usage often leads to sinus damage.

When asked to respond to the Clinton coke question, Dick Morris told Fox News that his client had a "perpetually runny nose" while Morris worked for him in Arkansas. Morris goes back with Clinton to 1977. Sharline Wilson alleges that she witnessed Clinton using cocaine in 1979 and 1980.

MONICA LEWINSKY, the sex-crazed White House intern who nearly destroyed a presidency, told Linda Tripp that Clinton sometimes seemed to "zone out" on her. When Tripp asked for an explanation, Monica replied, "I think he's on drugs." (*New York Post* — October 3, 1998)

Can You Trust Bob Woodward?

By Reed Irvine

NewsMax.com Vortex, August 1999 — Bob Woodward's new book, *Shadow: Five Presidents and the Legacy of Watergate*, contains material that has given rise to new charges that revive old memories of how "Mortuary Bob" has relied on lies, fabricated stories and other ethical violations to produce the best sellers that have made him rich. Mr. Woodward is famous for his ability to come up with what he presents as verbatim accounts of confidential one-on-one conversations. *Shadow* contains many of these.

When Mr. Woodward appeared on *Meet the Press* on June 20, Tim Russert asked him how it was possible to find out what President Clinton and his attorney, Bob Bennett, said when they were talking one on one. For example, Woodward describes them strolling on the White House grounds, discussing the rumors "connecting Clinton sexually with various women." He writes: " 'If you're caught . . . in the White House,' Bennett said, 'I'm not good enough to help you.' 'This is a prison,' Clinton responded. 'I purposefully have no drapes on the windows.' As for women, 'I'm retired,' the president declared, repeating himself emphatically, 'I'm retired.' "

Here is Mr. Woodward's answer: "There are all kinds of avenues and sources where you can get information, documents, notes and figure out — and significantly no one has challenged any of those conversations." Figure out what? It appears that he started to say, "figure out what was said." That would have been an admission that he makes up the dialogue and puts quotation marks around it, but he caught himself and abruptly changed course. Larry King pressed him on the same issue and got essentially the same answer, minus the revealing slip.

Mr. Woodward told Larry King, "The only thing I'm interested in is no one has questioned any of the information. They're discussing, like you are, who, what, where? I think the significance is that the information is exhaustively reported. It's not challenged."

But that is not true. Many of the conversations Mr. Woodward included in earlier books have been challenged. Victor Lasky, veteran journalist and author, found 36 statements in an earlier book, *The Final Days*, that were denied by the attributed sources or declared false by those in the best position to know. In his 1987 book, *Veil*, Mr. Woodward quoted 19 words that he said William J. Casey, the CIA director, had spoken in an interview with him not long after Mr. Casey had undergone brain surgery. This was a complete fabrication. Bill Casey could never speak intelligibly after his operation, and Bob Woodward never entered his carefully guarded hospital room. Mrs. Casey accused Woodward of lying, a charge he never challenged.

Jane Sherburne, a former assistant counsel in the Clinton White House, in a deposition taken by Larry Klayman of Judicial Watch on June 21, testified that Mr. Woodward had put words in her mouth in *Shadow* about a conversation she had with Hillary Clinton concerning a *Newsweek* article. She testified that the "dialogue does not resemble what I recall of the conversation."

She also testified that the interview was entirely off the record. She said Mr. Woodward called to tell her that when she saw the excerpts from his book that were to be published in the *Washington Post* she might think he had broken this agreement. He claimed there was no violation because he had heard of Hillary's reaction to the *Newsweek* article from many other people, and so he decided to put the words in her mouth.

Ms. Sherburne said that she had not expected to see anything she told Mr. Woodward in quotes because of their agreement and the fact that she had rejected a subsequent request that he be allowed to put some of it on the record. She testified that she sent a written apology to Mrs. Clinton, saying that "as she well knew, the dialogue was made up" by Mr. Woodward and that "to believe in Woodward's professionalism" was not good judgment.

Journalists have been fired for fabricating stories, lying and violating their commitments to keep material off the record. Bob Woodward's publishers and peers take no notice of his sins.

Reed Irvine is chairman of Accuracy in Media at http://www.aim.org.

Navy Hired Director Who Urged Heston's Shooting

NewsMax.com Vortex, July 1999 — It all started when controversial film director Spike Lee shared his thoughts about violence in America with the *New York Post*: "We've got to dismantle the NRA," said Lee, whose film credits include *Do the Right Thing* and *Malcolm X.*

What about NRA president Charlton Heston? "Shoot him — with a .44-caliber Bulldog [magnum pistol]," Lee urged with a laugh.

The moviemaker's comment outraged talk jockey Steve Malzberg, who devoted hours to the topic on his Saturday night WABC New York radio show.

Malzberg, the only professional talker to make an issue of Lee's anti-Heston jibe, managed to strike a nerve with his rant. The *Washing-*

ton Times picked up Lee's "Shoot him" remark from Malzberg's show — and that's how it came to the attention of House majority Leader Dick Armey.

Armey and Malzberg commiserated on the air over the director's politically incorrect hate speech, with the top Republican urging Lee to apologize to Heston immediately.

Recently, a new wrinkle emerged. It seems that prior to Lee's anti-Heston outburst, the U.S. Navy had hired him to put together six ads to boost sagging recruitment, which fell 7,000 sailors short of its goal last year.

"We needed to do something outside the box," Navy spokeswoman Lt. Commander Karen Jefferies told *USA Today*. But with the anti-establishment Spike "Shoot Him" Lee, the Navy may have pushed the envelope too far.

When the offices of Armey and fellow NRA supporter Representative Bob Barr were apprised of Lee's Navy deal Thursday, *Inside Cover* could hear the jaws drop to the table over the phone. At the NRA, one stunned staffer wondered about handing over military public relations to somebody with such rabidly anti-gun views, adding, "After all, the Navy has guns too."

Armey, Barr and Heston were unavailable for comment.

Inside Cover wonders whether Heston allies in Congress will, upon their return, tell the Navy to "Do the Right Thing" and dump Spike "Shoot Him" Lee before somebody takes him seriously.

Reagan Navy Chief Urges Response to Spike Lee's Comment

NewsMax.com Vortex, August 1999 — Former Navy chief James Webb told *Inside Cover* that his Clinton-era counterpart, Navy Secretary Richard Danzig, has a responsibility to address controversial comments made by Spike Lee — in light of the Navy's multimillion-dollar advertising contract with the outspoken film director.

Webb, a one-time assistant secretary of defense and former Navy secretary under Ronald Reagan, urged Danzig not to duck the issue:

"The secretary of the Navy has an obligation to make public his views about the nature of [Spike Lee's] comments," Webb told *Inside Cover* in an exclusive interview.

The provocative moviemaker was quoted recently in the *New York Post* urging that National Rifle Association president Charlton Heston should be shot. "Shoot him — with a .44-caliber Bulldog," said Lee, when asked what he would do to solve the problem of violence in America.

A week earlier, Navy spokeswoman Lt. Commander Karen Jefferies had announced that Lee had been awarded a $2.5 million contract to film six recruiting ads.

Within days of the *Post* report, House Majority Leader Dick Armey complained about Lee's outburst during radio and TV interviews. On June 3, Georgia congressman Bob Barr wrote to Secretary Danzig requesting that the Navy sever all further ties to Lee. Barr summed up his objections during a television debate the next week, saying, "It sends a very bad message when we say that $2 million of taxpayer money is going to go to this man for Navy recruiting films."

Lieutenant Dora Staggs at the Navy News Desk told *Inside Cover* that Secretary Danzig would respond to Barr privately. But that was weeks ago. Barr has yet to receive Danzig's reply, according to his press office.

So where's Danzig's promised response? It's hard to say, since neither Lieutenant Staggs nor Lt. Commander Jefferies have returned repeated calls to their offices.

Spike Lee's Navy Filming Continued Despite Uproar in Congress

NewsMax.com Vortex, August 1999 — *Inside Cover* has learned that production on Spike Lee's U.S. Navy recruitment ads continued until last month, weeks after the *New York Post* revealed that the controversial film director said of National Rifle Association president Charlton Heston: "Shoot him — with a .44-caliber Bulldog."

Lt. Commander Karen Jefferies, spokeswoman for the Navy Recruiting Command, explained that the first of Lee's six spots has appeared in approximately 10,000 movie theaters already this summer.

The other five ads are still being edited and have not yet been approved by the Navy for release.

Filming for the last commercial was wrapped up in Hawaii last month, weeks after Georgia Representative Bob Barr formally requested that the Navy sever its ties with the outspoken moviemaker because of his Heston remark — and more than two months after House Majority Leader Dick Armey's complaints catapulted the issue to national attention.

Jefferies confirmed that the Navy paid $2.5 million for the Spike Lee spots but stressed that the money went to the Navy's New York ad agency, Batton, Barton, Durstein and Osborne, which actually hired Lee. BBD&O determined how much Lee would be paid — a figure *Inside Cover* could not learn by press time.

Jefferies was reluctant herself to comment on Spike Lee's "shoot him" remark, which she said she learned about in late May. But she did deem the comment "inappropriate."

Navy Brass Backs Spike Lee

NewsMax.com Vortex, August 1999 — Rear Admiral B. E. McGann, chief of the U.S. Navy's Recruiting Command, has sided with Spike Lee in response to congressional protests over a multimillion-dollar contract that had the controversial director producing six Navy commercials.

In a June 25 letter, shared exclusively with *Inside Cover*, McGann praised the film director for his documentary style but made no mention of the May incident that has drawn fire from two prominent GOP congressmen.

At the Cannes Film Festival weeks ago, Lee suggested that NRA president Charlton Heston should be shot "with a .44-caliber Bulldog." The comment prompted House Majority Leader Dick Armey to condemn the moviemaker's remark in TV and radio interviews as well as in a press release issued from his office.

The *Summer of Sam* director claimed he was merely joking. But few saw the humor in such a blatant call for gun violence just a month after the Columbine High School massacre.

When the Navy's $2.5 million ad deal with Lee came to light, Georgia Congressman Bob Barr wrote to Navy Secretary Richard Danzig to complain that the director was "a divisive hatemonger" whose call for Heston's shooting was "beyond the pale of any acceptable human conduct." Barr requested that the Navy sever its ties to Lee "immediately." But Admiral McGann had only compliments for Spike Lee. Responding to Barr's letter on behalf of Secretary Danzig, McGann explained:

"The documentary style of filmmaking we deemed most likely to help us achieve our recruiting goals is one for which Mr. Lee is both well known and for which he has received critical acclaim in feature films and advertising."

McGann added, "Mr. Lee has completed his work on the commercials and they are receiving an extremely favorable response thus far. With the completion of the commercials, Mr. Lee is no longer under contract with the Navy."

The admiral said nothing about Lee's incendiary remark, a fact that did not escape Representative Barr's notice.

In his June 30 response to McGann, the Georgia Republican chided the admiral, pointing out "your letter really did not address the issue I raised."

Barr continued: "The issue I presented for answer focused on the propriety of the United States Navy paying millions of dollars of taxpayer money to a filmmaker who promotes racial division and publicly calls for the murder of public figures such as Charlton Heston."

Representative Barr seemed irked by the Navy's attempt to sidestep Lee's inflammatory rhetoric, adding, "I would appreciate a direct response to my letter, not simply a chronology concluding that the matter is moot; it is not moot."

In fact, when Barr first wrote Secretary Danzig about the Navy's Spike Lee contract on June 3, the director's ad project was still ongoing. Navy Recruiting Command spokeswoman Lt. Commander Karen Jefferies told *Inside Cover* that filming continued through the third week in June, when the last of six ads was finished in Hawaii.

Just two days before Admiral McGann told Barr that Lee's work was done, Jefferies explained to *Inside Cover* that five of his six ads were still being edited and had not yet been approved by the Navy for release.

Lee's defense by Navy brass may be part of the new Clinton-era political correctness that animates so much military policy these days. In June, for instance, Secretary Danzig raised eyebrows by criticizing the Navy's submarine service for operating "a white-male preserve." That will change beginning this summer. Danzig has authorized co-ed overnight cruises for the first time in Navy submarine history, a move defense experts say could devastate crew morale and combat readiness.

Sources Contradict NBC's Rapegate Alibi

NewsMax.com Vortex, February 1999 — According to the insider political tipsheet *Hotline,* NBC sources claimed that Lisa Myers and her *Dateline* team are still working to corroborate serious allegations, believed to involve rape, leveled by Juanita Broaddrick against President Clinton. Reportedly, the network wants the story to be "rock solid" before airing it.

The Drudge Report blames White House pressure for the apparent media cover-up, which NBC, not suprisingly, denies.

But *Inside Cover*'s exclusive on-the-scene source revealed that Broaddrick's claims had been corroborated in NBC interviews by multiple witnesses close to the victim.

"They are still stalling," our source revealed. "NBC's investigators have gone through everything." Broaddrick's husband and four of her friends were interviewed, people in whom Broaddrick had confided within days of her alleged Clinton attack.

In the Paula Jones case, the strongest evidence that she was telling the truth came from six contemporaneous witnesses who backed her claims.

NBC appears to have interviewed at least five similarly strong corroborating witnesses, including nurse Norma Rogers — who treated Broaddrick's bruises on a bus ride home from the scene of the crime.

One source close to Broaddrick describes her as exasperated and bewildered: "After keeping this secret for 21 years, going public was the hardest decision she's ever made in her life. Why did they send a crew down here for if they didn't want to run the story?"

Broaddrick is said to have described NBC's on-again, off-again waffling as "unreal." She wonders if "Clinton people" at NBC are pressuring *Dateline* to back off.

One source who spoke to her recently said, "Juanita's been raped twice. First by Clinton, now by NBC."

'Shecky' Clinton?

NewsMax.com Vortex, April 1999 — The Beltway press corps was rolling in the aisles as President Clinton road-tested his latest material for 2,000-plus guests at the Radio and Television Correspondents' Dinner.

There were jokes about Chinese nuclear espionage, the House managers who tried him for perjury and obstruction, and even a little ethnic humor — the kind for which the reporters on hand regularly beat up Republicans.

None of that bothered the assembled journalists, however, who were doing their best to show why the 1992 Roper poll revealing that 89 percent of them voted for Clinton was, if anything, a low estimate.

Still, not everybody was laughing. Larry Klayman's Judicial Watch put out a press release the next day under the headline: "There's Nothing Funny About Bill Clinton," which zeroed in on some of "Shecky" Clinton's most offensive shtick — the line insinuating that House trial manager Bob Barr is a racist: "This is a pretty tough time for the right wing. The president of the Council of Conservative Citizens had to resign because of his alleged ties to Bob Barr."

Mike Wallace Used Fake Memo

NewsMax.com Vortex, September 2000 — CBS's Mike Wallace got caught again — this time fooling his *60 Minutes* audience with a phony document that made it look like a U.S. Customs official was trying to help Mexican drug smugglers.

On April 20, 1997, Wallace hosted a *60 Minutes* segment that claimed Customs officials were allowing trucks with drugs to cross easily into the United States.

As proof of his allegations Wallace cited what he claimed was a U.S. Customs memo written by Rudy Camacho, then the San Diego Customs district director.

Last week, Michael Horner, a Customs Department whistleblower who had anonymously provided Wallace and *60 Minutes* with the memo, admitted he had fabricated the document.

Horner, 47, pleaded guilty to two felony counts last week.

The bogus memo *60 Minutes* said was written by Camacho provided instructions to Customs inspectors at the Otay Mesa Port of Entry to give easy clearance to a trucking company suspected of drug smuggling for a Mexican cartel.

Wallace never bothered to interview Camacho before broadcasting the allegations. Though Camacho later sued Wallace and won, the case got almost no national publicity. As part of its settlement, *60 Minutes* apologized on the air for making the allegations about Camacho.

Still, Wallace, who made his career demanding others answer his questions, has been ducking questions from the press about the Camacho controversy.

Wallace's deceptive use of the fabricated document, which could have been vetted with a minimum of journalistic footwork, fits a pattern with the veteran broadcaster.

Earlier this year, NewsMax.com reported on Wallace's *60 Minutes* attack piece on the 5-million-member Farm Bureau, a group he said had a conservative political agenda. Wallace didn't disclose that his *60 Minutes* segment had been produced with the help of a radical animal rights group that has opposed the Farm Bureau.

Wallace has openly admitted he lies when it suits his purposes.

During the controversy over tobacco whistleblower Jeffrey Wigand, Wallace appeared on *The Charlie Rose Show* with colleague Morley Safer. Wallace was asked point-blank by Rose if he or *60 Minutes* had paid Wigand for his cooperation. Wallace denied doing so.

Later, after documents in a legal case showed that *60 Minutes* and Wallace had indeed paid Wigand $13,000 as a consultant, Wallace admitted he had lied on Rose's program.

Liberal Fascism and Donato Dalrymple

By Lawrence Auster

NewsMax.com Vortex, June 2000 — The armed seizure of Elian Gonzalez was not only a lawless act of tyranny by the Clinton government, it was an announcement, for those with eyes to see, of the beginning of an age of tyranny in America. It is a tyranny that has been taking shape imperceptibly and informally over many years, but now is becoming so blatant and systematic that it virtually amounts to a new — if unofficial — form of government.

Under this regime, the executive, liberated from the Constitution and from any fear of genuine political opposition, does whatever it feels like doing, from character assassination campaigns against witnesses and prosecutors to missile attacks on foreign aspirin factories to the terror bombing of foreign civilian populations, while the major media, functioning in effect as a state organ, shape an ignorant and malleable public into agreement with whatever the executive is doing.

Each act of tyranny requires further acts of tyranny, namely the discrediting and dehumanizing of anyone who opposes the executive's will. Such attacks serve two functions: They justify the tyranny by showing that the "enemies of the state" were the ones who provoked it, and they send the unmistakable message to everyone in the society that this is what we're going to do to you if you get in our way.

Dissidents do not need to be crushed physically, as under a fully totalitarian regime, nor do they need to be framed on criminal charges, as has happened to Linda Tripp. It is enough to cast them outside the community of the "good, right-thinking" people.

This is especially easy when the dissident is not a public figure but simply some poor slob whom fate has placed in the path of the left. Since the legions of the politically correct do not regard such a person as a human being like themselves, they don't have to observe even minimal decency toward him.

This may sound extreme, but experience is bearing it out. Just as prop-

211

erty owners had no intrinsic value in the eyes of the Bolsheviks, and just as Jews had no intrinsic human value in the eyes of the Nazis, anyone who doesn't dance to the tune of America's dominant left has no intrinsic human value.

These are some of the thoughts triggered by the *Washington Post*'s front-page hit job against Donato Dalrymple four days after machine gun-toting INS agents grabbed Elian Gonzalez from his arms.

Dalrymple, writes reporter Michael Leahy, "seemed the one pure, likable character in this custody tug-of-war." Well, Leahy sure takes care of that little oversight. Writing with a combination of gossip-column salaciousness and a Stalinoid impulse to dehumanize an enemy of the people, Leahy exploits Dalrymple's naive and ingenuous comments to portray him as a shameless publicity hound and a pervert.

I won't go into the details of this unbelievably filthy piece of "journalism," which has been adequately discussed elsewhere. What I want to emphasize here is what the article tells us about the liberals' devotion to the "little people." It turns out that the liberals care about the little people only when they serve the liberals' own political purposes, either as objects for their conspicuous compassion, or as "victims of oppression" with which they can flay the "right."

But as soon as the little people are unfortunate enough to find themselves on the other side of an issue from the left, they become inconveniences to be swept aside. Their very insignificance — their relative lack of success in life, their lack of sophistication and media savvy, their quirks, their immaturities, even their very innocence — becomes the means the left uses to isolate and humiliate them.

The media's and public's contempt for Elian's Miami relatives and their supporters shows how hollow are this country's liberal ideals. This country, which is so pro-immigration — even to the point of allowing its national identity to be erased in the name of open borders — suddenly turns against a family of immigrants when they are anti-Communist and standing up to the Clinton government.

This country, which makes such a show of supporting the oppressed against the oppressors, treats the Miami relatives in their modest bungalow home — these people who have nothing to stand on but their humanity and their sense of what is right — with contempt.

This country, which gobbles up one Hollywood thriller after another in which people who fight against authority for a cause they believe in are regarded as heroes, regards the good Marisleysis as a joke and the heroic Lazaro as a lowlife.

How dead are the souls of the millions of Americans who, far from sympathizing with these good people, agree with those who callously mock and dismiss them.

How dead are their souls that they can't understand that a person who has saved a child's life feels forever a special bond and obligation to the one he saved. How contemptuous are they to a man who did nothing but good, a "fisher of men" who rescued a lost soul from the wide ocean.

Most of all, how lost are they that they cannot see the symbolic evil of what the Clinton government is doing with their support — grabbing at gunpoint from the man who saved him the boy he miraculously saved, seizing him from his surrogate mother, whom he called "Mari," seizing him through the despicable ruse of negotiations, seizing him in the early morning hours of Holy Saturday for fear of acting in broad daylight before the eyes of the people. If the feds had done their deed just 24 hours earlier, in the early morning hours of Good Friday, the parallel with the arrest of Jesus would have been complete.

The more tyrannical and evil a government becomes, the more it must tell lies about its victims so as to justify its tyranny. The providence that placed Elian, at the moment of his arrest, in the arms of the very man who had pulled him from the sea was such an undeniable symbol of good being victimized by evil that the only way the left could overcome that image was by more evil and lies. Donato must be made to appear like a creep.

Lawrence Auster lives in New York City.

ELIAN: Implications for America

By Miguel A. Faria Jr., M.D.

NewsMax.com Vortex, June, 2000—With the latest court rulings, it's obvious the political and legal battle for the fate of Elian Gonzalez is no longer about whether "he belongs with his father" or parental custody, as has been cleverly sold to the American people by the liberal media.

He has been forcibly reunited with his "father" and has now been deported. The conflict really was always about something deeper, between freedom and oppression, and, distilled to its essence, about the perpetual struggle between good and evil that every generation must face.

He was forcibly reunited with Juan Miguel, his purported biological father and a very deficient sort of father, the type that had been carried away with the tide of the revolution, a Marxist revolution that has resulted in the longest ruling dictator in the entire century — over 40 years of communist tyranny and slavery.

The media has described Juan Miguel as "fit and loving of his son," but was he really? In a fit of angry machismo, while still in Cuba, he threatened to come to Miami and shoot as many people as he could. It took him four months to get here and he then insisted, surrounded by Cuban agents, that he wanted to take Elian back to Cuba.

All this time after arriving here from Cuba, he stayed in the Cuban Interest Section near Washington, D.C., in a known nest of Cuban spies and communist agents who have nothing but hatred for the United States (or at the house of an alleged Cuban diplomat in Maryland, which amounts to the same thing).

Is that the normal behavior of a "fit and loving father"?

And to do so, the powers that be ordered that the child be taken away forcibly and violently. Why was it done this way? Because Juan Miguel refused to go to Miami to pick up his son.

As fate would have it, the menacing INS agents, at gunpoint, wrestled the frightened child from the fisherman who rescued him from the waters. And as fate would have it, the forceful removal was captured on film and most dramatically and graphically showed federal agents with automatic weapons, in an image that can only be compared to rogue storm troopers in Nazi Germany.

The scene of bucket-helmeted, jack-booted federal agents seizing a young child from a loving family is something I never expected to see in America.

The scene, graphically depicted in the dramatic and telling photograph by Associated Press photojournalist, Alan Diaz, nevertheless has not made an impression on the American public. Americans in their comfortable homes must think this only happens to refugee children of illegal aliens, not to American families.

Miguel A. Faria Jr., M.D. is Editor in Chief of the Medical Sentinel *of the Association of American Physicians and Surgeons (AAPS)*

Bush and GOP Abandon Elian

By John LeBoutillier

NewsMax.com Vortex, June 2000 — Here are two paragraphs from two recent news stories about the Elian affair that portend badly for George W. Bush and the Republican Party:

1. From the *New York Daily News:* "A top Republican Party official told the *Daily News* that Bush campaign manager Joe Allbaugh informed Senate Republicans on Thursday that the candidate wanted the hearings scrapped because the issue is a political loser."

2. From the *Washington Post*: "A key Senate Republican acknowledged Sunday that Congress may never hold hearings on whether the government used excessive force to seize Elian Gonzalez and return him to his father."

What this means is that the Republican leadership is listening to George W. Bush's campaign strategists so closely that they are ignoring their constitutional duty to oversee the executive branch.

In other words, Bush is willing to sacrifice Elian in order to have a better chance to win in November.

This is the kind of thinking that was exactly why his father lost and why he may lose, too.

Indeed, polls may show that a majority of people favor the raid and the forced return of Elian to his Cuban masters, but those polls do not measure intensity of conviction. In other words, maybe only 35 percent favor keeping Elian here, but those 35 percent really want to win this issue.

Bush, like his father before him, secretly has disdain for "com mitted conservatives." The Bushes are NOT conservative, even though W. has had to embrace the right like a lifesaver during his tussle with John McCain.

In fact, the Bushes are mere opportunists. Anyone who fell for President Bush's alleged love of pork rinds and country music was a gullible fool. How could a preppie who wears interchangeable madras watchbands truly love country music?

President Bush deliberately lied when he adopted a Reaganesque tone and promised, "Read my lips: no new taxes." That approach was simply to get the conservatives to support him. Then, once in office, he disdainfully raised taxes with no announcement other than a press release posted on the wall of the White House Press Room.

W. Bush is no different. All the previous talk about Elian was just that — all talk. Now that Bush and his party can dig into this issue through congressional hearings, he suddenly believes that it is a "political loser."

This opportunism and cynicism is positively Clintonian!

Why do Bush and the congressional leaders such as Trent Lott and Speaker Dennis Hastert think they are in office? To merely keep those offices — or to do something while in office?

There are two kinds of people who go into politics: those who want to be a somebody and those who want to do something.

The Bushes, father and son, do not particularly care about doing something. They are more interested in getting power. But I ask you, what is the point of devoting years and years of effort, campaigning, fund raising and traveling — all to obtain power — if you will not use that power to change things for the better?

Ronald Reagan was the exact opposite of the Bushes. "Dutch" was in politics totally to do something. He was secure enough that he did not need politics to salve his ego.

Not so the Bushes. Their entire purpose is to acquire power just to have done it. President Bush wanted to prove his mettle by becoming president. Now his namesake wants to prove himself Dad's equal by also becoming president.

What a waste!

The Republican Party used as a plaything for adult adolescents with an identity crisis!

Meanwhile Elian's fate rests with those of us who want to fight for him.

What a shame that the Republican Party does not want to join that fight.

John LeBoutillier is a former U.S. congressman from New York.

The Lesson of Elian:
Is America Still Worthy?

NewsMax.com Vortex, June 2000 — In the midst of all the furor over the Elian case is a most important question. Why do those of us who are fighting to keep Elian here in America care so passionately about this one little boy? The answer reveals much about each of us.

First of all, if you are an American you should be thanking God or your lucky stars about a million times a day for having the good fortune and destiny to be here in this country at this propitious time in history. Never have any people had it any better in any nation than we Americans have it today.

Now, if you have a generous soul and a good conscience, you must also wish that other people could be as fortunate as we are.

The Founding Fathers believed that everyone in this country was given certain rights. No mention was ever made of origin of birth. If you were here, you had these rights. The Constitution was designed to protect these rights from a potentially intrusive government!

Your rights include "life, liberty and the pursuit of happiness."

Our nation believes you have these rights — and no one can ever take them away from you unless, of course, you commit felonies and are tried, convicted and imprisoned. Even in jail, by the way, you still have some rights.

OK, now to little Elian. This seemingly insignificant little Cuban child touched the hearts of many Americans because in him we can see the innocence and purity of youth threatened by danger and evil.

First came the cruel seas of the rough Atlantic Ocean followed by the obviously dangerous threat of sharks. Then his mother died right in front of him. Can you imagine that scene? The drowning, the screaming, the shouting, the despair? The tears? The not knowing what had happened? The unfulfilled hope that perhaps she would still show up?

Not enough people have seriously tried to picture this horrifying ordeal — and what a miracle that Elian is alive here in America.

His next threat came from Fidel Castro, who declared an all-out effort to bring the boy back to his island prison. Inside that threat is the unstated but obvious plan to "re-educate" Elian, make a terrible example of him and then have him "disappear," as Castro's daughter has predicted.

And last but not least came the direct and dangerous raid to take a screaming Elian away from Miami and back into the hands of Cuban needle-wielding doctors and brainwashers and security men trained to manipulate and terrify.

In the face of all these threats and adversity, Elian remains here in America, at least temporarily protected by the very Constitution that Castro deplores. An infant foreigner protected against a president of the United States, an attorney general and an evil and corrupt foreign tyrant — all by a few pages of writing more than two hundred years old!

Those of us who believe that Elian must be allowed to remain here — despite the good arguments made in favor of the father-son relationship — recognize a simple fact: Elian's rights cannot be taken away from him.

If he is sent back to Havana, he will have no rights. He will be a slave consigned to a life of hardship, persecution and suffering.

America should not be in the business of sending refugees back to that system.

Those who want to send him back are saying, in effect, that they have more God-given rights than does Elian.

I reject that notion just as I condemn many Right-to-Lifers who favor sending Elian back to Cuba. If aborting an unborn child is, as these Right-to-Lifers sincerely believe, tantamount to depriving a human being of his or her "right to life," then so, too, is sending Elian back to a system that believes you have no rights.

Many of those who want to send Elian back speak of the "inconsistency" of this position. "Why do we send children back to Haiti and the Dominican Republic?" they ask.

They forget the unique history of Castro's Cuba and the United States. Life may be awful in Haiti, but it is not the same as Cuba. Haiti is indeed corrupt and poor and ruled by a series of awful despots. But Castro is a declared and avowed enemy of the United States. He has aimed nuclear missiles at our shores, run narcotics across our borders, discriminated against Jews, and persecuted those who dared to speak their minds.

We who are fighting for Elian believe his case is a test. In a time of unmatched freedom and abundance, has America actually lost something more valuable than material wealth? Have we lost that special quality that made America the leading nation of all time? Have we grown complacent and selfish? Have we grown so self-satisfied with our own lot in life that we cannot empathize with others less fortunate?

The ultimate outcome of Elian's case will give us an indication of whether the American people are still worthy of those special rights granted to us all.

Cuban Doctor Caught Taking Tranquilizers to Elian

NewsMax.com Vortex, June 2000 — U.S. Customs officials at Washington's Dulles International Airport confiscated several medications carried by Elian Gonzalez's Cuban pediatrician, who was en route to the 6-year-old's temporary residence at Maryland's Wye River Plantation.

Among the seized pharmaceuticals were two powerful tranquilizers that could be used to make Elian appear happier in the wake of the reunion with his father, Juan Miguel Gonzalez.

MSNBC Psychologist: Abduction Was 'Brutal and Frightening'

NewsMax.com Vortex, June 2000 — Dr. Robert R. Butterworth, a noted psychologist who has been a regular commentator on CNBC and MSNBC, said the federal raid on Elian's Miami home has "made me really reassess my position."

Dr. Butterworth said, "The Justice Department 'rescue' of Elian Gonzalez . . . was brutal and frightening, with little sensitivity for this child's psychological health.

"Using guns and force in the middle of the night to tear Elian from his Miami home, with his caretakers hysterical and screaming, will no doubt add to this child's long-term trauma."

Dr. Butterworth, who had been calling for a peaceful transition between both parties and was in favor of the reunification of Elian with his father, was shocked at the government's tactics used to remove Elian in a forceful manner.

"I cannot believe that a government psychologist would have approved this plan. This sounds like tactics used by Castro," Dr. Butterworth said.

Dr. Butterworth told Brian Williams on MSNBC that the sheer terror of the invasion by a strange man with a machine gun into Elian's bedroom — and his forced removal — will cause tremendous trauma to the boy.

Elian will relive this trauma "over and over" again for the rest of his life, Dr. Butterworth said, adding that he was not impressed by the photos of a smiling Elian that have also been released.

NBC Cameraman Hospitalized After Elian Raid Beating

NewsMax.com Vortex, June 2000 — Freelance NBC cameraman Tony Zumbado was hospitalized as a result of injuries sustained when agents for the Immigration and Naturalization Service (INS) and Border Patrol beat him and his soundman, Gustavo Moller, as they were trying to film the Clinton administration's gunpoint abduction of 6-year-old Elian Gonzalez.

Zumbado was the scene's designated pool reporter, whose video footage from inside the Gonzalez home was to be fed to all major broadcast and cable television networks.

But the beating by gun-toting federal agents left both Zumbado and Moller incapacitated for the duration of the three-minute raid, depriving television audiences around the world of live video coverage of the dramatic confrontation.

Zumbado's NBC colleague, reporter Kerry Sanders, was outside the Gonzalez house in the predawn hours that Saturday and talked to Zumbado and Moller seconds after the raid ended.

In an exclusive interview with NewsMax.com, Sanders said that Zumbado began to experience back pain over the weekend as a result of the attack. "I just got off the phone with Tony. Now he can't move really all that well." The NBC cameraman was removed from his home on a stretcher early Wednesday [four days after the raid] and was admitted to a Miami area hospital for an MRI and other tests to determine the extent of his injuries.

Sanders gave NewsMax.com this account of the attack that led to Zumbado's hospitalization:

"Tony and Gustavo had parked themselves for five months now at the corner of the house just outside the house. The family had said all along that they would invite cameras into the house to document what happened. As this is all going down, one of our cameramen by the name of Roger Prehoda was coming in at around 5 o'clock.

"He was a little bit late that morning. And so he's walking down the street and he sees the vans coming. And he's thinking, 'Oh my God, this is it.'

"So he grabs his two-way radio and he says, 'It's going down, it's going down.' That gets transmitted to Gustavo and Tony before the vans even come down the street. So they jump the fence, get into the yard and they race to the door. It's a race to beat the agents because he knows they're going to be there any second."

Unknown to the NBC camera crew, INS agents had already entered the house by the back door, Sanders said, and were inside when Zumbado opened the front door.

"As Tony makes it to the door, somebody inside the house grabs him and pulls him in and slams the door. Gustavo doesn't make it in. Gustavo's outside. He said one of the agents takes the butt of his gun and bangs it right into his forehead, causing him to fall down. I saw the blood on his forehead.

"Tony is in the house, but the plan all along had been that the camera was a pool camera and it was a live pool camera. So he's got cables that are dangling off the back of his camera that are now going into the house, slammed in the door. This is television equipment, this isn't your little home video camera.

"As the door reopens, which is only a matter of seconds, somebody is grabbing the cables, yanking them back. Tony's got the camera on his shoulder. They yank it back and pull it down. One of the cables gets pulled out of the camera, which is the audio cable. The video cable hangs on to the camera but it sends Tony falling backwards.

"At that point, somebody smacks him in the stomach. Tony is hit in the stomach and goes down. And then the agent puts his foot on Tony's back and puts a gun to him and says, 'Don't move or I'll shoot.'

"So, the camera is out of commission. Tony is now down and out of commission. Tony tells me that as he looks around, he sees the family there and he sees these little red dots on Lazaro's forehead, on Marisleysis' forehead. Which of course are the laser sights from the machine guns. He sees them all trained there and then he hears what's going on in the back room. But he's not in that back bedroom because he's now down on the floor with a foot in his back and a gun to his head saying, 'Don't move.' "

Sanders said that Zumbado has family members with law enforcement background and has actually undergone police SWAT training himself. As a former cameraman for the Fox TV show *Cops,* Zumbado had filmed hundreds of police raids prior to the abduction of Elian.

In fact, said Sanders, NBC selected Zumbado for the key job of videotaping Elian's abduction because of his film work on *Cops.* "He knows exactly what these people are supposed to do when they go in because he's trained to do it."

The attack on Elian's home, however, was different, Zumbado admitted to Sanders.

" 'Kerry,' he told me, 'it's amazing how humbling it is. You think you know how it goes down. I've been through the door with *Cops* plenty of times on raids. I know what it is. But it's such a different feeling when you're on the receiving end.' "

Analysis: Why Elian Lost

By Christopher Ruddy

NewsMax.com Vortex, June 2000 — When I arrived at the scene outside Elian's home, the smell of tear gas was still in the air.

I was there just minutes after federal marshals conducted a Gestapo raid on the home of law-abiding citizens — to snatch a young child. This is the first time in the history of the United States that federal agents used machine guns to settle a custody case.

I had gotten up about 5 a.m. and was planning to pick up syndicated radio host Michael Reagan at his hotel to take him to Elian's home.

Michael had told me the night before that he had brought with him cuff links worn by his father as president. This cherished gift from his father Michael planned to give to Elian.

This reminded me of a speech Ronald Reagan once gave in Miami. He promised that Cuba would be liberated. He reportedly brought the house down with cheers.

Though Reagan tore down the Berlin Wall, Cuba is still not free.

In fact, Castro's Cuba is among the few Stalinist regimes left on the planet.

That's why Elian's mother risked the shark-infested waters to bring her son here. This is why so many — and we still don't how many — have died escaping Fidel's "paradise."

The problem was never Elian, the father, custody issues, etc. The issue was, and is, Castro. For four decades the American press has looked the other way as his brutal regime represses the most basic human rights every man and woman desires.

Elian will now be returned to Castro.

John LeBoutillier, writing in NewsMax.com, foretold the snatching of Elian.

After the joyous court ruling, when everyone was celebrating, John concluded they were going to seize the kid. John's logic was simple:

Reno and friends had to get control of the kid to have him change his mind before his asylum hearing.

Reno claimed she worried the kid would be abused.

I worry now what will happen to the child in the hands of Castro's men. That same fear caused Sister Jean to turn her mind 180 degrees. A bona fide liberal, she saw through Clinton's machinations on behalf of Castro.

What more abuse could you cause a child than to have armed men in black suits come storming into his bedroom, with automatic rifles, to steal him from his loving environment and to whisk him away by still more strange men.

Janet Reno has always operated on the basis of twisted logic. She justified the federal holocaust at Waco because, she claimed, there was evidence of child abuse.

Child abuse is a constant theme in her career and, in her mind, allows for even the killing of the person being abused!

Reno got away with Waco. She has gotten away with covering for one Clinton scandal after another. She got away with covering up for the Chinagate scandal.

Without accountability, why should she stop acting recklessly?

After repeated visits to Little Havana during this crisis, after conferring with Jack Thompson, our reporter on the scene, and after meeting several times with the Cuban leadership there, it became too apparent to me that Elian's situation was very bad. Let me explain the basic reasons why I thought Elian was in deep trouble.

1. No Strategy.

The Miami relatives and Cuban-American leadership never had a clear strategy and were constantly reacting.

David Horowitz, in his booklet *The Art of Political Warfare,* writes that the side that has a strategy — when fighting against a side that doesn't have one — will always win.

Clinton and company clearly had a strategy. For weeks they laid the groundwork for the raid. The father was brought to the United States with wife and child — creating a powerful family image. (The press gave almost no attention to the fact that both of Elian's grandmothers were in detention and apparently being held hostage.)

Meanwhile, administration-friendly press conducted poll after poll indicating most Americans wanted Elian "returned to his father." (Who would be against that? The fact is the child is being returned to Castro, where Castro has a "re-adaptation" center prepared for him.) Later polls supported taking the child by force.

The administration stragegy continued: A government-paid psychologist close to Hillary Clinton, who had never met with the boy, determined he was being abused and likened his situation to being held hostage. This "doctor" recommended the boy be rescued immediately.

Then there was Mr. Smoothie, Gregory Craig, the same legal eagle brought in to get the president off his impeachment charges, demanding that poor Juan Gonzalez should have his son returned.

As the administration laid the groundwork for this horrific sciizure, the Cuban-Americans had an elderly, heavily accented man act as their spokesman.

They made mistake after mistake. For example, they gave hostile press like ABC News an exclusive interview with the boy. ABC then carefully edited and downplayed the interview. Later the family made a bold and wise move to release a home video of the boy saying he wanted to stay in America, but it was too late.

2. Conflicted Loyalties.

I was surpised to see how factionalized the Cuban-American community was here.

The "Democracy Movement" led by Ramon Sanchez was calling the shots, but the much more influential Cuban-American Foundation, I sensed, was not so gung-ho for confrontation over this issue, perhaps because of Sanchez's lead role.

A former Reagan official who dealt with the Cuban-American community during the 1980s explained to me that she was always quite surprised by how divided the Cuban-Americans were.

It was a common belief in the Reagan White House that Castro had thoroughly infiltrated most of the groups in Miami to create as much dissension among them as possible. "This was the model used by the East European satellite nations — putting agents in the exile movements — and Castro did the same thing," the Reagan aide explained.

There were other conflicting loyalties.

Alex Penelas, the Mayor of Miami-Dade, is Cuban-American, but he is also a rising star in the Democratic Party. He has been a major fund-raiser for Bill Clinton, Hillary Clinton and Al Gore. Penelas made some strong statements at the outset of the crisis, but has been backpedaling ever since.

Members of the Dade County Democratic Party played key roles in counseling the family through the crisis, including individuals close to Penelas and Reno. Who's kidding whom? Where are the loyalties of such people?

Obviously the Democrats in Miami-Dade have made their bed with Clinton and they are still sharing it.

When Penelas and Miami City Mayor Joe Carollo visited Washington, it was again clear to me the Clinton administration strategy was at work.

The Justice Department needed the cooperation of the local police. I am sure that was the real reason for the meeting. I asked Carollo point-blank if he had any idea the raid would take place, or if the police cooperated in any way. He said "No," and shook his head. He had to say that.

When Penelas arrived, the crowd swarmed around him, not to welcome him, but to shout at him. They were chanting, "Renounce the Democratic ticket!" The people here know exactly what the score was with Penelas and the leadership.

3. Timid Republicans.

As has become typical with the Republican leadership during the Clinton reign, they have been out to lunch in times of crisis.

Despite the usual lip service, George W. Bush has been quiet in Austin and ditto for his brother Jeb in Tallahassee. The Republicans in Congress remain as hopeless as ever. They were much more effective as a minority.

Like all politicians, they are looking at polls. The polls may show a majority of Americans want Elian to be "returned to his father" — but they also show at least a third of the country opposed such a move.

This one-third of America is largely the base of the Republican Party. Elections are not always won by majorities (Clinton won two in a row with less than 50 percent of the vote), but they are always won by a margin. Republican voters may just do what they did in the 1998 congressional elections — stay home.

Since the Republicans never really held anyone accountable for the massive federal abuse of power at Ruby Ridge, Waco or even with the president's crimes laid out in the impeachment, don't count on it happening here. The Cuban-Americans clearly failed to hold the Republicans' feet to the fire.

4. People power.

The biggest thing Elian and his Miami relatives had going for them was "people power" — the raw showing of popular democracy. For all their talk of "human shields," the Cuban-American leadership here never really created one around Elian's home. I remember when Jack Thompson and I first visited the area outside the home. Jack turned to me and said, "This is a joke; the Feds can come any time and take this kid."

We both noted that the so-called human shield was barricaded a hundred feet away at one end of the street. The other end had no protesters, was closed by the police and gave ample opportunity for anyone to ride right up to the house.

The feds did just that. Since they still feared "people power," they came in the dark of the night — much like the Roman centurians who feared the masses around Jesus.

John LeBoutillier wrote urgently the week before the raid that the feds were coming — and that people power would work by putting Elian in a Catholic Church. It is doubtful federal agents would have stormed a church building with automatic rifles.

Still, if the Cuban-American leadership had just a row or two of people around Elian's home, I doubt the feds would have stormed it. It was apparent from casual observation that the boy was for the taking. Penelas knew that. The Cuban-Amercian leadership obviously knew that and did not take steps to avoid it.

5. Cuban Issue.

In failing to strategize, the Cuban-Americans failed to demonstrate this was not a Cuban-American issue. The press was quick to pin this on the Cuban-Americans and to demonize them. Many members of the press wore "Camp Elian" press cards that depicted a banana with a Cuban flag sticking out of it.

Instead of bringing in non-Cubans to speak in Elian's favor, the leadership stuck with Cuban-American stars like Gloria Estefan and Andy Garcia. What they really needed was an actor like Charlton Heston, and political figures like George Bush and Jeb Bush, and other famous political, church and media personalities.

The battle for custody of Elian was lost, but much good has come out of this and more still may.

For one thing, more people have focused on Castro and his corrupt regime. And with the photo of Elian being taken at gunpoint, we can graphically understand the meaning of "child abuse" and of a government gone berserk.

The Cuban-American leadership has had many shortcomings, but it is incumbent on Americans everywhere to recognize this is much more than a "Cuban" story. It is one about freedom and one that should concern every decent American.

Feds Now Using 'Peeping Tom' Super X-Ray Machines

By Christopher Ruddy

NewsMax.com Vortex, April 2000 — At six major airports around the country the federal government is using highly sensitive X-ray machines that can view a person naked — including revealing private body parts.

Customs Service officials say they use the "Peeping Tom" machines only with travelers they consider possible drug smugglers.

Not all suspects are examined by the machine — only suspects who don't want to be frisked. Frisking typically includes a hands-on "pat down" of the person, a "strip search" — removal of a person's clothing for inspection — or a more intrusive body-cavity search.

"This technology will allow Customs to offer passengers an alternative, non-intrusive search method," Raymond Kelly, commissioner

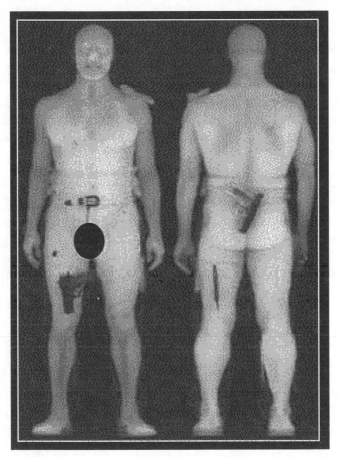

X-ray taken by the BodySearch machine. BodySearch creates a permanent image that can be transferred from the X-ray machine, prompting fears that some employees may save the images of naked people, including celebrities, and hawk them to magazines or publish them over the Internet.

of customs, said when the machines were first introduced at airports last year.

The use of the new machines, called BodySearch, has privacy advocates reeling.

"It's an electronic strip search, and it's extremely graphic," Barry Steinhardt, associate director of the American Civil Liberties Union, told the *Wall Street Journal.*

The federal government says it is placing strict limits on the usage of the machines — and hopes it will reduce the rising number of complaints from travelers about physical body searches. Customs has been sued numerous times over its body searches. A group of African-American women in Chicago filed a class action suit against the agency for racial profiling.

Critics also fear the machines will be rampantly abused.

Already Mexican authorities have been widely and covertly using BodySearch to catch drug smugglers. The *Journal* reports that one African leader uses the BodySearch X-ray without the consent of visitors to see if they have concealed weapons.

American Science & Technology, the Massachusetts firm that makes BodySearch, touts the machine's use for "correctional facilities, VIP security, border crossings and force protection."

BodySearch creates a permanent image that can be transferred from the X-ray machine, prompting fears that some employees may save the images of naked people, including celebrities, and hawk them to magazines or publish them over the Internet.

Customs officials have already deployed the machines at John F. Kennedy Airport in New York, Miami International Airport, Chicago's O'Hare Airport, Atlanta's Hartsfield International Airport, Houston Intercontinental Airport and Los Angeles International Airport.

Customs says it plans to expand the use of the BodySearch machines to as many as 20 other major airports in the near future.

Previously, the Federal Aviation Administration considered using the BodySearch machines for all airport travelers, but decided against its deployment for the time being because of the explicit nature of the images.

Nazi Chasers Should Turn to 'One of Our Own'

NewsMax.com Vortex, September 1999

An open letter to the Wiesenthal Center

By C. H. "Max" Freedman

> *"[Professor Peter Singer is] the most dangerous man in the world today."*
>
> — an activist for the disabled

Simon Wiesenthal Center
9760 West Pico Boulevard
Los Angeles, California 90035

Gentlemen:

According to a news report the other day, you were distressed to learn of recently uncovered evidence that American officials knew, as early as the autumn of 1940, of killings by the Third Reich of inmates in an asylum in southwestern Germany.

Had America condemned those killings, your director claimed, "thousands of lives would have been saved" and possibly the oncoming Holocaust itself might have been at least partly stayed.

Gentlemen, I'm sure you mean well, but given the chillingly similar activities presently occurring here and elsewhere — which are acquiesced in by most Jewish groups — this strikes me as an egregious case of misdirection of efforts.

Surely, gentlemen, you're familiar with prestigious Princeton University's appointment of the notorious euthanasia and infanticide champion Peter Singer to a chair in bioethics. Bioethics!

Professor Singer advocates, in certain circumstances, not just putting to death terminally ill adults, but severely disabled infants as well.

He would give parents and doctors the right to actually kill — not just to withhold treatment — newborns with, for example, Spina Bifida; even to kill those infants who suffer only from hemophilia (which is now almost completely treatable).

According to a news report, Singer thinks "a newborn has no greater right to life than any other being of comparable rationality and capacity

232 • *At Home*

for emotion, including pigs, cows and dogs."

It is ironic — or maybe, on reflection, not so ironic — that the fiercest opposition to the intellectually gifted but obviously evil and deranged Singer has been in German-speaking countries, where activists for the disabled have rightly denounced his views as "fascist and murderous."

Forgive me, but does this not embarrass you of the Wiesenthal Center?

Where has your comparable outrage been to what those decent Germans are expressing? Gentlemen, have you not contemplated the possibility of a future generation looking back at you with the same disdain with which you now look back at those who failed to act in the early stages of World War II?

Gentlemen, there are routine state-sanctioned killings taking place in the Netherlands — killings that are rapidly working their way into this country, as well as other lands — that might well have appalled some of the more moderate architects of the Third Reich in its early stages.

Every year in the Netherlands, some 1,000 people (a percentage of the population equivalent to perhaps 16,000 Americans) are being put to death without their consent.

And if there are any protests going on here against official Dutch policy, in all likelihood they are centered on such things as the high price of tulips.

While America is not — yet — at the point the Dutch are, so common is the practice of "pulling the plug" on those who wish to continue living that even Henry Kissinger's late mother narrowly escaped such an end. Thanks to Henry's stature, he was able to prevail over the doctors who wanted to relegate his mother to the fate from which she'd escaped at the hands of the Nazis. She thus recovered to a normal life.

Obviously, most Americans don't have Henry's influence, and so untold numbers are done away with against their will. This writer happened to have been personally acquainted with one such victim.

Taking all those critical differences into account, gentlemen, which silences, about which death-dispensing policies, are worse?

It's very easy to denounce, in hindsight, aged and long-dead men for questionable decisions made during the terror and bedlam of a worldwide conflagration — at a time when even the most active of imaginations couldn't conceive of an Auschwitz. It's quite another thing to recognize the evil in one's own generation — which is invariably self-described as "the most enlightened generation ever" — and to act appropriately.

It would thus behoove you of the Simon Wiesenthal Center to raise at least as big a storm against the very real and present danger of Peter Singer as you would against, say, the discovery of an ex-Nazi official living out his days luxuriously and peacefully, but quite harmlessly. Even though — no, make that especially because — Singer is, to our almost unbearable mortification, the son of Viennese Jews.

This article originally appeared in the Jewish Herald. *Max Freedman is a freelance writer. An Orthodox Jew, he lives in Brooklyn, New York.*

McCain's Mother Loved 'Falwell Tape'

NewsMax.com Vortex, April 2000 — John McCain ignited a small firestorm during one of his televised debates with George W. Bush. McCain charged that Falwell, who supports Bush, promoted a videotape that accused President Clinton of being a murderer. "I voted to impeach President Clinton, but I don't think President Clinton is a murderer," McCain said.

McCain had made similar remarks on the Don Imus radio show. Referring to a series of videotapes, he told Imus, "I voted to convict the guy [Clinton] . . . but a murderer?" McCain was referring to the 1993 video *The Clinton Chronicles* — an hour-long documentary of allegations made about the president during his days as Arkansas governor.

One of the persons appearing in the video is Gary Parks, the son of Jerry Luther Parks. Jerry Parks had headed up campaign office security for the Clinton-Gore team in Little Rock. In September 1993, just two months after Vince Foster's death, assassins killed Jerry Parks at a Little Rock intersection — gangland style.

The *Chronicles* video made numerous other charges about Bill Clinton. One of the biggest fans of the video, NewsMax.com has learned, was John McCain's mother, Roberta McCain. Mother McCain,

88, is still active on the Washington social circuit.

A friend of Mrs. McCain tells us that she has been touting *The Clinton Chronicles* around Washington for years. "She told me Bill Clinton is involved in all these criminal activities, murders, drugs," the friend said. Mrs. McCain told her that she "had to watch this video."

According to the friend, Mrs. McCain, through the Clinton years, has been talking to many people about the "Falwell tape," encouraging them to watch it.

Jerry Falwell Suing White House, Justice

NewsMax.com Vortex, April 2000 — Judicial Watch reports that it has learned that the Clinton Justice Department — run by Attorney General Janet Reno — has been keeping a secret database against religious and pro-life leaders.

The covert database is called "VAAPCON." When Judicial Watch learned of this secret illegal database, it filed a Freedom of Information Act request and confirmed that indeed VAAPCON existed.

Because he believed himself to be a likely target of the Clinton administration, Dr. Jerry Falwell, chancellor of Liberty University and founder of the Moral Majority, filed a Privacy Act request to determine whether the White House and Clinton Justice Department had files on him and his ministries.

Typically, both entities stonewalled — effectively confirming that illegal files are being kept on Dr. Falwell and his ministries.

To get at the truth, Judicial Watch and Jerry Falwell Jr., an attorney in Lynchburg, Virginia, and son of Dr. Falwell, filed suit in the United States District Court for the Western District of Virginia.

Dr. Falwell stated: "Over the years, my ministries and I have been subjected to a number of attempts to not only inhibit our free speech, but to subvert our pro-life advocacy.

"When I learned of this illegal VAAPCON database, I felt obliged to take action to stand up for the rights of all Americans to be free to express their religious beliefs, as people of faith should not be intimidated by a corrupt and immoral Clinton administration."

Is Low U.S. Inflation Rate More Clinton Fiction?

NewsMax.com Vortex, February 2000 — Inflation, the word that has ignited so much passion by Fed decision-makers for decades, practically doesn't exist today . . . if you believe the numbers.

In December 1999, the inflation rate — as measured by the consumer price index — was up just 0.1 percent. This is an annual rate of about half a percent — in real terms, just about zero.

The inflation rate is key for continuing the booming economy. Alan Greenspan, Federal Reserve chairman, has said he will move swiftly to crush any incipient inflation. For most of the Clinton era he has not had to use interest rates to tame inflation.

Inflation usually goes hand in hand with easy credit. Oddly, public and private debt has been expanding with no inflationary effects. And loose credit has also been feeding the bull market.

Last quarter, margin debt for equities surpassed the amount for debt issued to consumer borrowers.

Low interest rates and loose credit by the Fed have been predicated on low inflation numbers. And, if you believe the numbers, inflation is almost extinct.

Can we believe the inflation numbers put out by the Clinton administration?

Consider that oil prices — the fuel of 1970s stagflation — have more than doubled in the past year. Still, the inflation rate barely registers this.

Then take a look at monetary growth this past year. The three-month annualized growth rate of United States monetary growth at the end of 1999 shows a phenomenal growth rate of 27 percent. This growth rate is almost triple the highest rates in the past 50 years.

Inflation used to be defined as too many dollars chasing too few goods. But the money supply growth would suggest wild inflation.

Fed apologists argue that the large increase in monetary growth was a temporary measure to inject cash liquidity just in case the Y2K bug caused a bank panic.

The same apologists say that with Y2K behind us the money supply can be deflated and inflation will never appear. (This belief is like saying you can fill a balloon with water, and because you know it will be emptied soon, it will have no effect on the balloon.)

Who's kidding whom? Of course money supply growth affects the inflation rate. And so does the increased price of oil.

Last we checked, the United States is still dependent on electric power supplied by oil, heating by oil, transport by cars and trucks, airplanes fed by jet fuel and so on.

No effect? Huh?

Obviously, somebody has been trying to explain away common sense. On December 15, 1999, the *New York Times* business section and the *Wall Street Journal* both led with Page One stories explaining why inflation has almost disappeared.

The *Times* quoted experts as saying inflation has disappeared largely because of telecommunications, the Internet and deregulation of major industries.

The *Journal* tackled the oil problem head-on, headlining that "Petroleum Is Less Relevant in New Economy." Stated differently: A nation of hamburger flippers is no longer affected by oil producers the same way as a country whose economy manufactures steel. America no longer produces steel. We flip hamburgers.

That may be true, but even though we are not making the steel, it doesn't mean we have stopped using it, and somebody in the world who produces steel is now paying double for the same oil they were using a year ago.

Those costs will inevitably be passed along to American consumers. That's called inflation.

Not everyone is sanguine about the "non-inflationary" money supply growth.

Michael Belkin, president of Belkin Limited, an economic forecasting firm, wrote that the if the Fed "intentionally pumps up the monetary base at the fastest rate in history [as has been the case] — the U.S. equity market speculative bubble will obediently expand further.

"But this is only a temporary monetary boost designed to thwart Y2K panic in financial markets. So the flipside of a stock market rally [in December 1999] based on Fed Y2K credit expansion should be a collapse [early in 2000] when the excess credit is removed."

Clinton Corruption Too Much for Mafia Don

NewsMax.com Vortex, September 1999 — Lost in the rush of news emanating from Hillary Clinton's recent burst of candor in *Talk* magazine was this amazing tidbit in the *New York Daily News*:

Don Addicted to Monicagate

John Gotti is a news junkie, and he found a feast in the Bill Clinton-Monica Lewinsky scandal. He says Clinton got away with conduct a Mafia gangster would never be allowed to get away with.

He told his brother Peter that, based on what he heard Clinton say in tape-recorded conversations with one-time lover Gennifer Flowers, it sounded like Clinton was telling her to lie.

"He's telling her, 'Why would you want to bring this out? If anybody investigates, you lie.' "

The tapes, made in 1991 when Clinton was making his first White House bid and Flowers was thinking about telling her story, surfaced in 1992 and were picked up by the media again when the Clinton-Lewinsky matter began to brew early last year.

Gotti heard them on January 29. The next day, he said, they showed that Clinton implied to Flowers she wouldn't get in trouble if she lied because he could "get to" any judge.

Gotti's verdict on the president? "If he had an Italian last name, they would've electrocuted him."

Some see an amazing bit of prognostication in the jailed Mafia don's *Daily News* quote about Clinton being able to "get to" any judge.

Maryland state prosecutor Stephen Montanarelli indicted White House nemesis Linda Tripp for taping Monica Lewinsky's tell-all phone calls, after judge Norma Holloway Johnson ruled that Tripp's tapes had to be handed over to Montanarelli despite her grant of federal immunity.

A day later, news emerged that potentially damaging cases against the White House got special treatment by the same Monicagate judge. Turns out, Judge Johnson voided normal judicial procedure to make sure that charges against Clinton pals Charlie Trie and Webster Hubbell were tried only by judges appointed by the president.

Carville Confesses to Cigarette Habit

NewsMax.com Vortex, August 1999 — After spending years demonizing independent counsel Ken Starr for representing tobacco companies, White House attack dog James Carville has confessed that he regularly smokes cigarettes.

The Democratic Party strategist and Clinton insider made the admission during a joint appearance with his wife, GOP consultant Mary Matalin, on Don Imus' nationally syndicated radio show.

The topic of cigarettes inadvertently came up when Imus explained to a curious Matalin why he chewed gum during commercial breaks. Imus recounted how he'd picked up the gum habit to kick his former heavy smoking habit, then asked Matalin if she had ever smoked herself:

MATALIN: Yes.

IMUS: Did you, James, ever smoke?

CARVILLE: Ah, yeah. But I can — not very much. You know, that's never — that's never been one of my problems. I'll sneak a cigarette at night, that's all.

MATALIN: And he complains about me. Why smoke a cigarette a day?

Imus quickly changed the subject to Carville's recent involvement in the Israeli election, and Matalin, who has never made a secret of her own smoking, never got an answer to her question — at least not on the air.

But news of James Carville's secret smoking habit comes as something of a stunner for those who recall the contempt with which he so often described Ken Starr as "nothing but a shill for the tobacco companies." One of the first lady's favorite "vast right-wing conspiracy" theories was that tobacco money somehow bankrolled the myriad investigations into her and her husband's past.

Rambo and the Bogus War Heroes: Actor Brian Dennehy Fabricated War Record

By B. G. Burkett and Glenna Whitley

NewsMax.com Vortex, August 1999 — *The men and women of the Vietnam War deserved more than America was willing to give.*

Three decades later, the war, which never left our collective consciousness, still ignites passion among its participants.

Slowly, the war has come back to haunt us. Legions of homeless Vietnam veterans are in streets, hundreds of thousands of them are suffering from Agent Orange or Post Traumatic Stress Disorder, and more of them have died from suicide than died in the war . . . or so the social advocates and the media tell us.

B. G. Burkett, in over ten years of research in the National Archives, filing hundreds of requests for military documents under the Freedom of Information Act, uncovered a massive distortion of history, a distortion than cost the U.S. taxpayers billions of dollars. Mr. Burkett's work has toppled national political leaders and put criminals in jail.

The authors show killers who have fooled the most astute prosecutors and gotten away with murder, phony heroes who have become the object of award-winning documentaries on national network television, and liars and fabricators who have flooded major publishing houses with false tales of heroism that have become best-selling biographies.

Not only do Burkett and Whitley show that the price of the myth has become enormous for society, they also spotlight how it has severely denigrated the service, patriotism and gallantry of the best warriors America ever produced.

Scruffy John Rambo, carrying a bedroll and wearing a field jacket emblazoned with an American flag, stares down at a quaint country house by the side of a sparkling lake, with snow-capped mountains in the distance. A black woman hangs freshly laundered clothes on a line.

The first scene in the 1982 movie *First Blood* appears idyllic. But tension lurks beneath the surface. Rambo tells the woman he's looking for a friend; they served on the same team in Vietnam. She looks at the picture he gives her with bitterness. "Delmar's dead," she says with quiet pain. "Cancer. Brought it back from 'Nam. All that orange stuff they spread around."

Stunned, bewildered, resigned, Rambo heads for the highway and walks toward the small town of Hope. He's just looking for something to eat when he's accosted by Sheriff Will Teasle. Burly, blustering, Teasle literally runs the unshaven, longhaired veteran out of town. But Rambo refuses to be bullied. Deliberately, he walks back toward Hope (get it?), only to have the hard-assed sheriff toss his butt in jail.

As a deputy takes Rambo's fingerprints, the falsely accused vet catches a glimpse of a window crisscrossed with bars. Flashback to Vietnam—Rambo in a bamboo cage, being abused by his North Vietnamese captors. Following Teasle's orders to clean up Rambo, a deputy orders him to strip, gaping as Rambo removes his shirt to reveal a sculpted back and chest viciously scarred by a whip, a legacy of his days as a pow. Pounded by water from a fire hose, unnerved by the flashbacks, pushed to his limit by the sadistic sheriff, Rambo goes berserk, attacking the deputies, fighting his way to freedom.

But the war has just begun. Rambo, using nothing more than his wits and a hunting knife, takes on the sheriff's posse. He survives a leap from a cliff, evades a park of hunting hounds, kills a helicopter sniper using only a rock, rigs booby traps in the forest to incapacitate (but not kill) the sheriff and his deputies, and escapes from an abandoned mine, collapsed by a bunch of weekend warriors with a rocket launcher.

Through the wilderness of the Pacific Northwest, clearly a metaphor for the jungles of Vietnam, Sheriff Teasle and his deputies pursue their resourceful quarry, but they become the hunted.

Exciting, suspenseful, with spectacular stunts, *First Blood* is a stunning film, an adolescent male's fantasy of the super war hero, misunderstood by the society that turned him into a killer and then abandoned him—first by refusing to let him win the war they sent him to fight, then by rejecting him when he returned to the nation he loves.

Rambo can see no life for himself in the real world. "You just can't turn it off!" Rambo howls. "Back there I flew helicopters. I could drive a tank. I was in charge of million-dollar equipment. Here, I can't get a job!" Flashing back to the horror when a friend was blown up at his side, Rambo the Green Beret, the hardened combat hero—dissolves into an incoherent mess.

First Blood was a turning point. Before 1982, other movies about Vietnam featured the victimized, suicidal Vietnam veteran, traumatized by his memories. He was often portrayed as a vagrant, dirty, drifting through life. The other option: He was crazy as a loon. Prior to *Rambo*, the two most successful Vietnam movies were not likely to encourage anyone to identify with the soldiers in them. *The Deer Hunter*, winner of five Oscars, was not a hero's story. And *Apocalypse Now* was a surrealist exercise in absurdist excess.

But *First Blood* perfectly captured the hero as victim of society, of war, of his own inner demons. It was because he is the perfect fighting machine that the Vietnam veteran can't cope with the world, because he is a real man. Rambo's ire was directed toward the government, always a safe target. The government is evil. The government betrayed us. Hollywood finally caught up with the image of the dysfunctional vet created first by the anti-war movement and veterans' advocates and added its own mythic twist: Vietnam vet as dysfunctional superman.

There are several ironies about the movie and its two sequels, *Rambo: First Blood Part II* and *Rambo III*. They introduced a new word in the American lexicon: "He's a Rambo." Now Vietnam veterans are forever identified with macho-gone-berserk.

And both actors who starred in the original film are, to be charitable, pretenders. Sylvester Stallone, who played steroidal fighting machine John Rambo, now the epitome of the Vietnam veteran, managed to avoid military service and spent 1965 to 1967 as girls' athletic coach at the American College of Switzerland in Leysin. (Ironically, in one of his earliest movies, the 1969 *Rebel*, Stallone portrayed Jerry Savage, a college student and "modern-day, urban rebel" who drops out of school to protest the Vietnam War.)

And the sadistic sheriff is portrayed by character actor Brian Dennehy, who appeared in dozens of movies, such as *Presumed Innocent*, *Cocoon*, *Semi-Tough*, *Foul Play*, *Gorky Park*, *Silverado*, *F/X*, *Legal Eagles*, *Best Seller*, and *Street Legal*, as well as numerous TV movies and the series *Birdland*.

The actor publicly maintained for years that he was a Vietnam veteran. Dennehy told a *New York Times* reporter in 1989 that he had suffered a concussion and shrapnel wounds during combat. In a *Playboy* interview in 1993, Dennehy was described as serving a "five-year" tour as a Marine in Vietnam, where he suffered minor wounds in combat.

"Ever kill anyone?" asked *Playboy.* "Is there a Vietnam movie that nails the experience?"

"As for killing someone, anyone in combat would agree that it's pretty much accidental," Dennehy said. "It's not what you're thinking about. You spend a considerable amount of time just trying not to be in a combat situation. You're trying to avoid coming face-to-face with anything. So when something bad happens, it's usually accidental. But the implication in war movies is that war has this rational beginning, middle, and end. And of course none of it does. It's absolutely fucking chaos. *Apocalypse Now* is the movie. Even more interesting is that it was made so soon after the war was over. It was about the war and a parable about the war. It was and is the most sophisticated overview of the experience."

Dennehy seems like a nice guy, and he is a terrific actor. At six foot three, with the build and the craggy face of an Irish boxer, Dennehy looks the part of the combat-hardened Marine. (He played the tough Marine gunny sergeant in *A Rumor of War.*) But he's not a Vietnam veteran. A scholar athlete while attending Columbia University, Brian Manion Dennehy was on active duty from September 15, 1959, to June 4, 1963. His military record contains no Vietnam Service Medal, no Armed Forces Expeditionary Medal, no Combat Action Ribbon, no Purple Heart, and no transit orders showing him going to Vietnam. His records show no indication Dennehy was ever wounded, unless he suffered a sprained knee from his duty on his only overseas assignment — as a Marine football player in Okinawa during 1962.

After obtaining the record, I contacted Dennehy's agent and told him there were discrepancies. At his suggestion, I wrote Dennehy a letter; there was no immediate response. I suspected that Dennehy's exaggeration of his military experience started as a way for the actor to gain credibility as a tough guy for the movies.

Just before my book went to publication I did hear from Dennehy. A handwritten, six page letter from him appeared in my mailbox. In his letter Dennehy confessed to having completely fabricated his military war record. Dennehy admitted he never set foot in Vietnam. Still, he pleaded with me to keep his name out of my book, or any mention of his decades-long deception about being a war hero. I reread Dennehy's letter several times. Dennehy argued that his war stories were nothing more than an attempt to actually help the true Vietnam vets. He wrote that his make-believe war experiences were intended to give himself credibility when arguing with anti-war liberals in, and out of, the media business. While Dennehy's sentiments were apparently noble, they were also somewhat difficult to believe. A struggling Hollywood actor would take up the cause of the real Vietnam vets, especially when supporting the war was not in vogue in Hollywood?

Dennehy's letter to me was written by a brilliant actor. His explanation was a new twist from the many explanations given by bogus Vietnam war heroes. Dennehy was essentially saying he acted as a Vietnam vet to help us guys.

Dennehy's arguments didn't resonate with me. For one thing, Dennehy's public comments about the war were not about setting the record straight. In his 1993 interview with *Playboy*, Dennehy said the war was just like the film *Apocalypse Now*. Of course, anyone who served in Vietnam knew that film didn't represent what really transpired there. Instead, *Apocalyspse Now* fed into almost every negative stereotype about the war.

Soon after the publication of my book, Dennehy tried to get in front of my story about his phony record by confessing. He did so in an exclusive interview with the supermarket tabloid the *Globe*. Dennehy told the *Globe*, "[Burkett] was right in what he said. I did steal valor. That was very wrong of me. There is no real excuse for that. I was a peacetime Marine and I got out in 1963 without ever serving in Vietnam."

Dennehy's confession to the *Globe* was a smart maneuver. He lanced the boil of his dishonesty, while making the revelation in a supermarket tabloid not taken seriously by the mainstream press.

Dennehy also told the *Globe* he did not fabricate the stories to help his career or make an image for himself in Hollywood. He told the *Globe*, "I thought the veterans should have been treated better. I figured it sounded better when I spoke out about that if I said I'd been there."

Dennehy's "I lied to help them" defense still doesn't wash. Just months before this book went to publication, Dennehy called a highly decorated Vietnam veteran who had written a best-selling book that was to be made into a movie. Dennehy called the author, indicating an interest in directing the film. Dennehy began the conversation regaling the author about his experiences as a Marine in Vietnam. Dennehy has included his Vietnam experience in recent biographical entries in *Who's Who*. These facts don't jibe with his claims today that his Vietnam lies "started when I was shooting my mouth off in bars 35 years ago. . . . It was just something I did when I was young and stupid — to impress people."

Rambos 'R' Us

First Blood became a touchstone for pretenders, a pattern to follow consciously and unconsciously. Released one year after the completion of the national Vietnam Veterans Memorial, the movie marked a change in our nation's perception of Vietnam veterans.

During the decade after the war, few real Vietnam veterans wanted to identify themselves as such. The divisiveness, the anger, the confusion made it safer, wiser to file that part of ourselves away. As a Vietnam veteran, society rejected me. But as long as I did not identify myself as a Vietnam veteran, I was accepted. So I assumed my other identities: Vanderbilt graduate, golfer, stockbroker, husband, father.

But Rambo made it okay, even heroic, to be a Vietnam vet. Politicians began to claim Vietnam service while campaigning for office. Senator John Kerry, who had made a dramatic public splash with his anti-war stand, now wrapped himself in his Vietnam veteran status.

After the release of the second Rambo movie in 1985, counselors in vet centers across the country saw an influx of Vietnam veterans seeking help to vanquish their inner demons. Even to counselors who had never been in the military, some were clearly impostors, like the man who went into a Pittsburgh vet center in 1988 wearing a Marine Corps shirt and claiming he had served in Da Nang. He was not a day over thirty, making him a pre-teen during the war. Others wove their stories so well genuine combat veterans were fooled.

Many of these pretenders became "professional" Vietnam vets. Today, they fool psychiatrists, reporters, editors, even the military hierarchy. They learn how from Hollywood and from journalists and authors who swallow their tales and print them for others to study.

B. G. Burkett, a military researcher, was co-chairman of the Texas Vietnam Memorial with President George Bush as Honorary chairman. Mr. Burkett has been the object of an award-winning segment on ABC's 20/20, *as well as much-acclaimed articles in* Texas Monthly *and* Reader's Digest. *He is a graduate of Vanderbilt University and the University of Tennessee. He served in Vietnam with the 199th Light Infantry Brigade, and was awarded the Bronze Star Medal, Vietnamese Honor Medal, and Vietnamese Cross of Gallantry with Palm.*

Glenna Whitley, an award-winning investigative reporter, specializes in writing about crime and the legal system. A graduate of Texas A&M University, her work has appeared in the Dallas Morning News, D Magazine, Texas Monthly *and* Redbook, *as well as numerous other magazines and newspapers. Whitley currently is senior editor at* D Magazine *in Dallas, where she lives with her husband and two sons.*

FOBs*: Tom Hanks and Tony Bennett

NewsMax.com Vortex, April 1999 — By the time President Clinton and the first lady leave the White House, they will face staggering legal bills of up to $10 million. But on an annual salary of $200,000, sympathetic supporters are asking, "how's a president to pay?" But Bill Clinton has what no previous president ever had: a legal expense trust fund. Since 1998, fund trustees have collected $4.5 million. Gary Ruskin of the Congressional Accountability Project, says the fund may be legal, but that doesn't make it ethical. "Many of these donors work for major law firms that have major interests pending before the executive branch or Congress. Consequently, there is plainly the appearance that the president might do political favors for people who gave to his fund." The Clintons' current fund, which caps donations at $10,000, reads like a Hollywood A-list: it includes movie moguls like Steven Spielberg and Jeffrey Katzenberg, actors Michael Douglas and Tom Hanks, and singers Barbra Streisand and Tony Bennett. "To the best of my knowledge the first family is not involved in any direct solicitation," says Democratic consultant Vic Kamber.

— www.cbn.org/

Friends of Bill

Is America Becoming a Pagan Nation?

By Paul M. Weyrich

NewsMax.com Vortex, August 1999 — A few weeks ago the Free Congress Foundation stood up for our Judeo-Christian heritage and opposed the decision by the U.S. Army to permit the Wiccan religion to hold services on base. The Army is even considering chaplains for the Wiccans.

The Wiccans are an ancient pagan religion run by covens of witches. They invoke pagan "gods" to support their causes. If that's not bad enough, the Army has even listed the Church of Satan among its approved religions for holding services on base.

A few organizations joined us in our call for a boycott of Army recruitment until this matter is settled. We are, after all, a country where military service is voluntary. Do Christian or religious Jewish parents want to send their kids off to the military only to have them proselytized by a pagan religion? I think not. When we go to war, even a war we dislike such as the war in Kosovo, we implore the God of our fathers to watch over our men and women in the armed services. If the Army permits prayers to pagan "gods" how long will it be that God's blessing will continue to be upon His people?

I have heard from every Wiccan in the country about this. They may be a small group but they are well organized.

Christians and religious Jews, with the exception of the few organizations that have joined us, have been silent on this issue until now.

Rev. Pat Robertson has acted and spoken. First off, his representative signed on to our statement on the Wiccans. But the next day, the Washington office pulled their name from the list of organizations supporting the boycott. That order came from headquarters. Now that former Interior Secretary Don Hodel is no longer running Christian Coalition, decisions like that are being made by Robertson himself. Robertson wasn't content to be neutral on the subject. No, he has now supported the right of Wiccans to hold their services on military bases.

"I'm not worried about a little coven of witches running around. . . .[R]ather than suppress us all, we might give them their freedom," said Robertson. There we have it. Moral equivalency. Robertson's *700 Club* television program sent a crew to cover the Military Pagan Network's full moon prayer circle near the Jefferson Memorial, according to the PR Newswire. John Machete of the Military Pagan Network said, "Religious tolerance is the price of religious freedom for all. We are pleased that the Christian Broadcasting Network attended our press event. Their story was fair and balanced. We thank Rev. Robertson for his support of religious freedom," Machete told the PR newswire.

Christians, it seems, should not speak with a loud voice against pagan practices. Christians should be tolerant of what historically has been considered evil. I have news for Pat Robertson and the rest of the feminized Christians out there. When good remains silent in the face of evil, evil eventually triumphs over good.

For over 220 years we did not depend on the approbation of witches to assert the Jewish or Christians faiths in our military. Why now? What is next, you ask? Representative Bob Barr of Georgia has the answer. The Army is now going to permit so-called Indian religions to use peyote, a controlled illegal substance, in the conduct of their services on military bases. How would you like to send your son up in a military plane piloted by someone who just used peyote in his so called religious service?

No, paganism isn't just another religion. If you doubt this, read the Old Testament. Who are the witnesses? Moses proved more than once to Pharaoh whose God was the real God. Or ask Shadrach, Meshach and Abednego. There are many, many other witnesses as well. You get the point.

If those of us who believe in the one true God tolerate this, we will have taken another step toward becoming a pagan nation. We might recall that the pagans held the Jews captive for centuries. We might recall how the pagans tortured the Christians for centuries until the Emperor Constantine, equal to the Apostles, legalized Christianity.

Do we really want to go down this road? I'll make this prediction. If we do, Reverend Robertson will be the first to be persecuted when the time comes.

Paul Weyrich is president of the Free Congress Foundation. Contact Robert McFarland at 202-546-3000 or by email at rmcfarland@freecongress.org.

Gephardt Tied to White-Rights Group

By Carl Limbacher

NewsMax.com Vortex, April 1999 — House Minority Leader Richard Gephardt spoke before a prominent St. Louis white-rights organization during his first run for Congress and attended two of the group's picnics after his election, says Gordon Baum, head of the Council of Conservative Citizens.

Interviewed by NewsMax.com, Baum explained that Gephardt had come to a meeting of the Metro South Citizens Council to debate his primary-election opponent.

"The hall was adorned on one side of the speaker's platform with the Confederate flag, and on the other side was the American flag," said Baum. "And Dick Gephardt addressed the group and asked them openly for their endorsement."

"Gephardt is one of many local officials who dropped by the Metro South Citizens Council's gatherings in the early 1980s," according to a March 7, 1999, report in the *St. Louis Post-Dispatch*.

Baum told NewsMax.com that the Metro South Citizens Council was a group concerned primarily with "states' rights" and forced busing. When it disbanded, many of the members joined his Council of Conservative Citizens, which, Baum says, addresses broader interests like taxes, gun control, and general moral decay.

But groups like the Southern Poverty Law Center, the Anti-Defamation League of B'nai B'rith, and the National Democratic Senatorial Campaign Committee contend that the CCC's conservative message is just camouflage for a hidden white supremacist agenda.

And many of Gephardt's House colleagues apparently agree, though they don't seem to know about the Missouri Democrat's past association with the group.

Last year, in the heat of the impeachment battle, Harvard law professor Alan Dershowitz defended the president by linking Republicans favoring Clinton's conviction to Baum's group. Representative Bob Barr, Georgia Republican, and Senator Trent Lott, Mississippi Republican, were singled out by Dershowitz for having contact with the CCC in the recent past.

Both Barr and Lott distanced themselves immediately from the group's philosophy, but Democrats continue to criticize the pair for what Dershowitz calls their "racist" affiliations. The two Republicans were raked over the coals for months on the nation's op-ed pages and on political TV chat shows, with some pundits calling for their resignation.

But the press and Dershowitz have failed to note Gephardt's almost identical connection to the more extreme precursor to the CCC. NewsMax.com faxed the *Post-Dispatch* report to the Harvard law professor's office recently with a request for comment. The usually vocal and combative champion of racial tolerance has so far declined to respond.

In 1988, then–presidential candidate Gephardt denounced the organization, the *Post-Dispatch* reported, noting that he couldn't recall his own visit to the Metro South Citizens Council.

But Baum says, "If he denounced us back then, he must have whispered it in somebody's ear, 'cause it was never covered down here."

The St. Louis paper reported that two weeks ago the Missouri Democrat issued a statement saying that any group "who practices a brand of racially motivated politics has no place in the country we live in today." But nothing in Gephardt's statement clarifies his own contacts with the St. Louis white-rights group.

One source familiar with the matter told NewsMax.com that Gephardt privately does not dispute the allegations but that his press office is very unhappy that the issue has been revived at this late date. A recent call requesting comment from Gephardt spokesperson Laura Nichols went unreturned.

Last month, the House minority leader dropped his plans to seek the presidency in the year 2000, hoping instead that presumptive Democratic nominee Vice President Al Gore will help win back the House and make Gephardt Speaker. Gore has welcomed Gephardt's formal endorsement, though it is not clear whether the vice president is aware of Gephardt's history with the white-rights group.

Prompted by media outrage targeting Barr and Lott, Representative Robert Wexler, Florida Democrat, has introduced a House resolution condemning the Council of Conservative Citizens. Apparently unaware of Gephardt's one-time cultivation of a related group, Wexler's proposal attacks the CCC for providing "access to, and opportunities for the promotion of, extremist neo-Nazi ideology and propaganda that incites hate crimes and violence."

Baum told NewsMax.com that the rhetorical broadsides directed against his group are overblown and inaccurate. He insists, "We don't hate anybody." And he defended the Missouri Democrat's right to address the Metro South Citizens Council, explaining that "there was nothing wrong with Gephardt coming to speak to us. Politicians came to us because we represented a significant percentage of the voters."

But the CCC chief believes the press was wrong to single out conservative Republicans while giving Gephardt a pass, telling NewsMax.com that journalists used his group as a partisan billy club:

"The only reason they used us to beat up on guys like Barr and Lott is to save Clinton. It's just another case of liberal media hypocrisy," said Baum.

Disney's Eisner Set to Defame Christians — Again

NewsMax.com Vortex, April 1999 — Michael Eisner and his Disney Corporation, parent company to Miramax Films, seems to have an obsession with defaming Jesus Christ.

At least that's the way it looks by the advance word on the next Miramax movie release, *Dogma*.

The controversial *Dogma* is already making some Miramax executives nervous. So much so that *Dogma* star Ben Affleck, who appears in the film with Chris Rock and Matt Damon, has been begging Miramax chief Harvey Weinstein to make sure the project makes it into movie theaters.

Disney and Miramax enjoy antagonizing Christians with blasphemy, having produced 1995's *Priest* and last year's TV sitcom *Nothing Sacred* on Disney-owned ABC.

Nothing Sacred caused a fireball of protest from Catholic groups. Now comes *Dogma*, the latest Miramax production, in which Disney's movie studio stepchild apparently outdoes itself.

An article in the *New York Post* reports that "Among [*Dogma*'s] elements are a trash-talking 13th apostle, the notion that Joseph and Mary had sex, a female descendant of Jesus who works in an abortion clinic, a Skee-ball-obsessed God and an updated Christ who no longer hangs from the cross but instead offers a thumbs-up salute."

William Donohue, president of the New York–based Catholic League for Religious and Civil Rights, tells *Inside Cover* that he tried to contact Disney chief Eisner about *Dogma* last year but got no response.

Now Donohue warns that if the movie is as bad as early reports indicate, he'll take on *Dogma* the way he did Disney's *Nothing Sacred*.

"We had a lot of problems with that show and worked successfully to kill it. We got 37 corporate advertisers to withdraw their sponsorship of the program," Donohue told *Inside Cover*.

The Catholic League chief explained that he's trying to be tolerant of Disney's artistic license — as with the role of one of *Dogma*'s stars, Alanis Morrisette. She plays God.

"We have no objection to God being played by a female," Donohue told *Inside Cover*.

"But this is a woman who has come straight from doing a nude music video where the lyrics are about oral sex." The Catholic rights spokesman added, "And Miramax has some of the apostles doubling as drug dealers."

"There's obviously an agenda at work here," says Donohue.

Disney Dumps *Dogma*

NewsMax.com Vortex, April 1999 — Maybe Disney is reading NewsMax.com as many millions are.

Latest stats show that NewsMax.com now surpasses, in monthly viewers, the online editions of the *Los Angeles Times*, the *Wall Street*

Journal, Slate.com and the *New York Post* — and is within spitting distance of both the *New York Times* and *Washington Post*.

We note that only after lead coverage in NewsMax.com's *Inside Cover* did mega media giant Disney decide to drop plans to distribute the controversial anti-Christian film *Dogma*.

The movie, which was to be distributed through its Miramax studios, is bound to offend even the least devout Christians with a script that satirizes the Immaculate Conception, has Christ's descendant helping out in an abortion clinic and even portrays several of the Apostles as drug dealers.

Dogma stars Ben Affleck, Matt Damon, Chris Rock and, playing the role of God, Alanis Morrisette.

Affleck, a fallen angel in *Dogma*, admits the flick pushes the envelope.

Mr. Showbiz reported, "In Affleck's words, the film offers the notion that 'Mary and Joseph had sex, and they had a kid, and therefore there's a [female] descendant of Christ on earth who works at an abortion clinic.' The subject matter, he said, is 'definitely meant to push buttons. There are clearly things about it that will be incendiary.' "

Dogma won't have the Disney seal of approval because Disney chief Michael Eisner is worried about bottom-line implications for his company. Disney has already been a target for Christian groups upset with Disney's perceived anti-Christian bias.

Still, Disney's honchos at Miramax, co-chairs Bob and Harvey Weinstein, seemed to be undeterred in making the blasphemous flick a success.

"We intend to work with a distributor that shares our vision of the film," Harvey Weinstein told the *New York Times*. The *Times* reported that the Weinsteins had purchased the distribution rights for the film.

Kevin Smith, the film's director, who describes himself as a practicing Catholic, said the film is "from first to last always intended as a love letter to both faith and God Almightly."

Too bad the film's star, Affleck, didn't see it that way.

Nor did many Christian groups.

A press release from the Catholic League for Religious and Civil Rights quotes Catholic League president William Donohue as saying, "Michael Eisner made the right move to dump *Dogma*. As a result the Catholic League will not target Disney."

Dr. Laura Beefs Up Security in Wake of Death Threats

NewsMax.com Vortex, December 1998 — She may be the No. 1 talk show host in America, but Dr. Laura Schlessinger doesn't feel safe.

The advice guru has already become the target of establishment media types not happy with her old-fashioned, homespun "I'm my kids' mom" moralism. Add to that, a bitter old boyfriend has been dishing the dirt about her youthful wild days (along with some X-rated photos).

If all that wasn't bad enough, Dr. Laura has gone into the red zone of danger.

Inside Cover hears that Dr. Laura has been receiving death threats. Not the normal, crazy, wacko stuff. But real, serious, not-to-be-dismissed death threats.

Dr. Laura has recently hired round-the-clock, gun-toting bodyguards.

Inside Cover has also learned that one Dr. Laura stalker set off all the alarm bells with some threatening communications. The threat was deemed serious enough that the FBI has been called in to investigate, and FBI agents were spotted at Dr. Laura's Los Angeles studios.

Court Rejects Ohio's 'God' Motto

NewsMax.com Vortex, June 2000 — A federal appeals court struck down Ohio's state motto, "With God, All Things Are Possible," saying it illegally shows a governmental preference for Christianity over other religions. The 6th U.S. Circuit Court of Appeals overturned a federal judge in Columbus, who upheld the motto, which was posted on the Capitol during the tenure of Governor George Voinovich.

Voinovich, now a senator from Ohio, said he got the idea to place the motto on the Ohio Statehouse during a trade mission to India, where he saw a government building with the slogan "Government Work Is God's Work."

The appeals court noted the Ohio motto is based on a quotation attributed to Christ in the book of Matthew. The court rejected the circuit judge's opinion that the Ohio motto was as generic as the "In God We Trust" motto on U.S. currency.

254 • *At Home*

"While the words of the motto may not overtly favor Christianity, as the words of Jesus, they, at a minimum, demonstrate a particular affinity toward Christianity in the eyes and ears of a reasonable observer," the opinion reads.

The opinion was in response to a lawsuit filed by the American Civil Liberties Union on behalf of the Reverend Matthew Peterson, a Presbyterian minister from the Cleveland suburbs who challenged all uses of the motto.

Although on the Ohio Statehouse only since 1995, the motto has appeared on government stationery, some state reports and Ohio tax returns since 1959.

State officials argued against the lawsuit, saying the motto may have no religious connotation to some people.

In a written dissent, Justice David Nelson agreed with that view.

"I confess that prior to this lawsuit I could not have identified the source of either motto, and I doubt that it is vanity alone which prompts me to suggest that my ignorance is far from atypical," he wrote.

Stephanie Beougher, a spokeswoman for the Ohio attorney general's office, said attorneys are reviewing the opinion and trying to decide whether to appeal it to the U.S. Supreme Court.

Survey Says Frequent Sex Helps Keep You Young

NewsMax.com Vortex, April 1999 — Sex at least three times a week can make people look 10 years younger, according to new survey. "It's not a case of these people having more sex because they look younger, they actually look younger because they are having more sex in loving, stable relationships," said Dr. David Weeks, a neuropsychologist at the Royal Edinburgh Hospital. How does making love tap the fountain of youth? The human body produces growth hormones and other chemicals like endorphins during sex that enhance the body and mind, Weeks said. Casual sex with different partners did not help prevent wrinkles. If anything, Weeks said, the stress and pressure made for premature aging.

—dailynews.yahoo.com

Rabbi Reflects: My Last Letter From the Cardinal

By Rabbi Dr. Morton H. Pomerantz

NewsMax.com Vortex, June 2000 — During the Vietnam War, I served as a United States Navy and Marine Corps chaplain.

It was my good fortune to meet a senior chaplain, a Catholic priest named Father John O'Connor.

During my service our paths crossed many times, particularly while I was stationed in San Diego.

Some may think it odd that Catholic Father John Joseph O'Connor became a friend and a mentor to a young rabbi.

I remember well his saying, "Rabbi, make sure that you are aware of all the bars in your area, especially the disreputable ones."

I looked up in surprise. Father O'Connor continued, "You will be spending a good deal of time there" — pausing then quickly adding — "pulling sailors out of these locations."

As it turned out I spent many a weekend down in Tijuana fishing Marines and sailors out of the local police stations. A military chaplain's job is not just for the battlefield.

But Chaplain O'Connor was much more than a social worker. He had in fact voluntarily served with our combat troops at the front lines in Vietnam.

He was courageous, competent, dedicated and faithful to his calling, and he unfailingly displayed a marvelous sense of humor.

Through the years we kept up a casual contact and you can understand my delight when I learned that my old Navy colleague, Admiral John O'Connor, had been appointed Archbishop of New York.

At that time, I sent to him a congratulatory letter, and was soon asked to join several interfaith committees sponsored by the Archdiocese.

No matter how difficult the situation, no matter how severe the criticism, no matter how vicious the sneers emanating from the press, Cardinal O'Connor remained firm in his convictions.

I believe the most important virtue this man had was moral courage.

I recall that when he first came to New York a group of Orthodox Rabbis with long beards came to him and asked that he be a leader in the fight for family values in New York City. John O'Connor promised them that he would lead them in the good fight and that he would not let them down. He never did.

The last time I saw Cardinal O'Connor was at a mass for world peace at St. Patrick's Cathedral.

The Cathedral was filled with diplomats; the wife of the Secretary General of the United Nations was in attendance, and many dignitaries were there.

The Cardinal was kind enough to send me an invitation. After the mass there was a reception at the Cardinal's residence.

Instead of his usual manner of walking around the room and seeing everyone, the Cardinal sat in a chair and greeted people as they entered for the reception. He did not look well.

Nevertheless, he greeted me warmly and with the friendship that I had come to know from him. He expressed delight that I had agreed to sign an ad that a group of people were taking out attacking the barbarity that is called "partial birth abortion."

I left with concerns about his health, but no concerns at all about his fighting spirit.

On April 17th of this year, the Cardinal sent me what was to be the last letter I was to receive from him. There is nothing in it he would not mind me sharing, so I will quote most of it for you:

Dear Rabbi Pomerantz,

By God's grace, I have the delightful pleasure of sending you my heartfelt greetings yet once again for a joyful celebration of Passover.

It also gives me the opportunity to express my sincere thanks for the prayers you have offered for my recovery during my time of illness.

No matter what the days ahead may bring, the love and support you have given me are signs of everlasting friendship and endless encouragement. . . .

As you and your family join together at the Seder table, recalling through the Haggadah the liberation of the Jewish people and the giving of the Torah, I humbly ask that you remember me as one who wishes to be in your midst and receive blessing.

Passover is a gift for the whole world. Be assured you are in my prayers and very much in my heart.

Faithfully, John Cardinal O'Connor, Archbishop of New York

My mentor, my teacher, my friend, Cardinal O'Connor, has gone to a world far better than our own.

In Judaism we believe that if a person saves but one life, he has saved the whole world.

John O'Connor saved many lives. People of all faiths should emulate this man's example — his moral courage — in this way we may be saved and the whole world too.

Requiescat In Pace, Your Eminence.

Rabbi Dr. Morton H. Pomerantz, a member of the Reform movement of Judaism, is a state chaplain with the State of New York.

Quietly, State Department Turns Over American Islands to Russia, Others

By Stephan Archer

NewsMax.com Vortex, June 2000 — In recent years several United States islands have been ceded to Russia and other countries, without congressional approval or public debate.

These islands, many uninhabited, are significant because they hold potential mineral, gas, oil and fishing rights — not to mention potential strategic military value.

So where exactly are these disputed islands?

The Arctic Islands, which lie west of Alaska and north of Siberia, include the islands of Wrangell, Herald, Bennett, Jeannette and Henrietta.

The islands in the Bering Sea make up the westernmost point in Alaska's Aleutian chain and include Copper Island, Sea Otter Rock and Sea Lion Rock. These islands together have more square mileage than the states of Rhode Island and Delaware combined.

Though the United States had staked claim to these islands for more than a century, the State Department has been eager to turn them over to Russia.

The transfer would have gone unnoticed were it not for State Department Watch, a Washington-based group that monitors State Department activities. Retired U.S. Navy Lt. Commander Carl Olson, who heads State Department Watch, recently checked with the Census Bureau, asking if it had plans to count the inhabitants of these disputed islands in the current census.

He was stunned by the response he received.

"Census Bureau officials were informed by the U.S. Department of State that these islands remain under the jurisdiction of Russia," wrote Kenneth Prewitt, director of the Census Bureau in a letter to Olson.

"Without confirmation and appropriate documentation from the Department of State to the contrary, the Census Bureau cannot include these islands as part of the State of Alaska," Prewitt concluded.

Americans Become Russians

Olson notes that the Census Bureau, with the approval of the State Department, has just stripped Americans of their citizenship.

Consider the inhabitants of Wrangell Island, the largest of eight disputed islands — five in the Arctic Ocean and three in the Bering Sea. Geographically speaking, the island's inhabitants would also be citizens of Alaska since no other American state comes even close to the proximity of the islands.

But if anyone desired to visit Wrangell Island, they would be greeted not by the Stars and Stripes waving proudly in the brisk air but by a Russian military tower.

According to Olson, the islands, including Wrangell, have 18 Russian soldiers and one officer and 50 to 100 inhabitants.

Olson insists these people have been made to endure foreign occupation by the Russian military and believes the U.S. government should do something about taking the islands back.

NewsMax.com contacted Mark Seidenberg, a former senior traffic management specialist within the U.S. Department of Agriculture and asked him if he believed the United States should pursue its sovereignty on the islands. Seidenberg, without hesitation, said "yes."

U.S. Territory for Long Time

U.S. claims for these islands are strong. When the United States purchased Alaska from Russia in 1867, the impending treaty included all of the Aleutian Islands, including Copper Island, Sea Otter Rock and Sea Lion Rock.

A number of years later, in 1881, U.S. Captain Calvin L. Hooper landed on Wrangell Island and claimed it for the United States. One of the landing party was famed explorer John Muir. Also in 1881, the U.S. Navy claimed Bennett, Jeannette and Henrietta Islands for the United States. Later that century, the British gave up their claim to Herald Island, allowing the Americans to take it over.

Claims on these islands, however, didn't become an important issue between the former Soviet Union and the United States until the 1970s, when the concept of international fishing zones 200 miles from national coastlines went into effect.

With both the Soviet Union and Alaska having coastlines within a much closer proximity than the needed 400-mile buffer zone, a maritime boundary had to be established.

Secret Transfer

The resulting U.S.-U.S.S.R. Maritime Boundary Treaty was passed by the Senate and ratified by former President George Bush in 1991. The Soviet Union, however, never ratified the treaty because its leaders complained that the U.S.S.R. didn't benefit enough from it.

Nevertheless, former U.S. Secretary of State Jim Baker and the Soviet Union's Foreign Minister, Eduard Shevardnadze, signed a secretive executive agreement the year before that bound both governments to the treaty.

Currently, Russia is demanding hundreds of millions of pounds more fishing rights from the United States that would undermine the Alaskan fish industry and, subsequently, the state's economy.

A wealth of petroleum and natural gas hang in the balance as well.

When NewsMax.com contacted the State Department for an explanation, a spokesman said he wasn't aware of any issue involving the Wrangell Islands and the U.S. government and that it was his belief that the islands have been recognized as a part of Russia since the 1800s.

During the course of the interview, the State Department official asked if he was being "put on."

Even though now recognizing Russian jurisdiction over the islands, the State Department had testified at the June 13, 1991, treaty hearing that the maritime boundary agreement "does not recognize Soviet sovereignty over these [five Arctic] islands."

Enraged by the turnover of Alaska's sovereign land, Representative John Coghill Jr. of that state's legislature sponsored House Joint Resolution 27, which beseeches the Department of State to inform the Alaska legislature of any decisions regarding the maritime agreement. The resolution further points out that setting a maritime boundary between Alaska and Russia is a "constitutional issue of states' rights."

Two of the issues over these islands and the surrounding waters are the fishing rights of Alaskan fishermen and oil. Alaska has the largest national reserve of oil, which may be abundant in the disputed territory.

Military Value

Olson notes the area's strategic value as well. Beneath the icy waters around the islands, submarine warfare has taken place in the past between the former Soviet Union and the United States. The ice is now one of the last places for submarines to hide. The islands could also be hosts to vital facilities tracking hostile government movements.

"Everybody knows that the shortest distance between the U.S. mainland and Asia is the polar route, giving easy access to aircraft and whatever else," Olson explained. "And the Asian mainland doesn't just consist of Russia. It includes China."

More American Islands Lost

Olson adds that the Arctic islands are not the only American islands the State Department has been giving away without congressional approval or treaty.

In recent years four American Pacific Islands — Washington, Fanning, Makin and Little Makin — have been ceded to the island nation of Kiribati without a treaty.

"Lost" islands include Nassau Island in the Pacific Ocean and Bajo Nuevo and Serranilla Bank in the Caribbean Sea. The islands became American territory under the Guano Act in the late 1800s.

Regarding these three lost islands, the Census Bureau's Prewitt, in a letter dated March 15, stated, "With respect to Nassau Island, Bajo Nuevo, or Serranilla Bank, the Department of State has not informed the Census Bureau that claims to these islands have been certified."

In addition to the abandonment of the islands is the loss of all resources within a 200-mile economic zone of each island. As is the case with most of the Arctic Islands, the economic zones around each of the islands may be more important than the islands themselves.

Stephan Archer is a staff writer for NewsMax.com.

NewsMax.com Readers Vote Brit Hume 'Most Trusted Journalist in America'

NewsMax.com Vortex, February 2000 — Brit Hume is the most trusted journalist in America, according to an online survey of readers of NewsMax.com

The national survey asked Internet users to vote for the journalist who they believe is "the most trusted journalist in America."

A total of 96,217 users responded to the unscientific poll that was conducted between December 26, 1999, and January 7, 2000.

Hume, managing editor and chief Washington correspondent for Fox News, received the most votes.

Hume has a distinguished career in journalism spanning almost three decades. He joined ABC News in 1973, and was named the network's chief White House correspondent in 1989.

Hume received an Emmy for his coverage of the Gulf War in 1991. In 1996, he left ABC News for the then-fledgling Fox News Network.

In addition to serving as Fox's Washington chief correspondent, Hume hosts the political news program "Special Report With Brit Hume."

He serves as a regular panelist on "Fox News Sunday," hosted by Tony Snow, and is also a regular contributor to the broadcast network's cable network, Fox News Channel.

Hume is known for a crisp, matter-of-fact reporting style that offers the public a balanced presentation of the news. The *American Journalism Review* honored Hume by naming him "The Best in the Business."

"He is the best. In Washington there is no better than Brit Hume," said Arnaud de Borchgrave, CEO of United Press International.

De Borchgrave, a director of NewsMax.com, added that Hume's reporting style resonates with Americans because "he comes off as a straight and honest reporter. He's not married to any side, conservative or liberal."

William Rees-Mogg, former editor of the *Times* of London and a member of NewsMax.com's International Advisory Board, said Hume is an internationally respected journalist.

"There is a perception that the major TV networks in America were reporting one view, the liberal East Coast line of thinking," Rees-Mogg said.

"Brit Hume and Fox News have made a difference by giving the American people a diversity of views."

"NewsMax.com is proud to name such a remarkable and fair-minded journalist as Brit Hume as 'The Most Trusted Journalist in America,'" said Dana Allen, chairman of NewsMax.com.

NewsMax.com, a major news portal on the World Wide Web, was recently rated by users of Deja.com as the No. 1 Internet news source.

Prudential Securities' *Washington Research Newsletter* recently described NewsMax.com as the "must read" news site on the World Wide Web.

Americans Say: 'Don't Defend Taiwan, Israel, South Korea'

By Christopher Ruddy

NewsMax.com Vortex, April 2000 — A recent NewsMax.com/Zogby poll indicates Americans, by large majorities, oppose the United States' defending militarily several key allies, including Taiwan, Israel and South Korea.

The poll asked 1,155 Americans: "If attacked by another country, should the U.S. help defend militarily, even though it could cost American soldiers their lives," such hot spots as Kosovo, Israel, Taiwan, South Korea and Kuwait?

In each case, a significant majority of respondents said they would oppose using the U.S. military to aid these countries, some longtime U.S. allies. The poll had a statistical margin of error of +/- 3 percent.

The NewsMax.com poll results should be particularly troubling for the Taiwanese government. The Chinese leadership recently stepped up rhetoric toward Taiwan and stated categorically they would not renounce the use of force to take the island. Taiwan's jittery stock market slumped.

Previously, the Chinese leadership has warned American officials to stay out of their conflict, which it believes to be an internal one. The Chinese have made veiled threats of military attacks against the United States if it interfered.

Only 31 percent of respondents said they believed the United States should defend Taiwan, with almost 69 percent saying it should not aid Taiwan.

In February, the House of Representatives passed overwhelmingly a resolution calling for closer U.S. military ties with Taiwan. The Taiwan Relations Act already states the United States will aid in Taiwan's defense if it is attacked.

The NewsMax.com poll shows that Democrats, Republicans and independents all oppose U.S. military assistance to Taiwan in a time of war, though Republicans are more inclined to intervene military than Democrats.

Some 37 percent of Republicans responding believe the United States should defend Taiwan, while only 29 percent of Democrats agree. The poll numbers against U.S. military action to defend other hot spots were equally compelling:

• Seventy-four percent of respondents oppose defending Kosovo militarily.

These numbers may reflect continuing apathy to President Clinton's NATO-led effort to remove Serbian forces from the province. A NATO peacekeeping force currently polices Kosovo.

• Seventy-one percent don't believe the United States should defend Kuwait if it is attacked.

In 1991, President Bush's Operation Desert Storm, the largest U.S. deployment since Vietnam, successfully liberated Kuwait from Iraqi control.

• Seventy-two percent also don't want to use U.S. forces to defend democratic South Korea if it is attacked.

A large U.S. deployment of 30,000 troops still remains in South Korea.

• Fifty-nine percent agree that the U.S. military should not defend Israel if it is attacked.

Of the five hot spots surveyed, Israel received the strongest support for military help in time of war, with 41 percent responding that the U.S. should support Israel.

• Support for Israel was strongest among Republicans (48 percent agreed the United States should defend Israel), Southerners and Westerners and among individuals describing their religious beliefs as "born again."

Military Disillusioned Yet Still Loyal, Proud

NewsMax.com Vortex, February 2000 — Morale in America's armed forces is the lowest in a decade, yet its men and women in uniform continue steadfast in their sense of devotion.

That is the finding of the broadest survey in recent years of how the military views itself.

It is backed up by the Army's own internal study of its best future field commanders.

The two reports agreed that the greatest cause of dissatisfaction is the Clinton-Gore administration's policy of converting United States fighting forces into overseas policemen in so-called peacekeeping missions.

That ranks even higher than their frustration over inadequate pay, brief time with families, insufficient equipment and training for actual combat and lack of confidence in superiors.

According to the *Washington Times*, the Army's own survey of why it is losing so many captains, traditionally its source of future leaders, found:

• "Pay is not a major factor . . . a strong civilian economy enables career change but does not cause it."

• The reasons cited most often were President Clinton's repetitive use of the nation's military for non-traditional "peacekeeping" purposes, inadequate training and equipment and micromanagement from above.

• Captains repeatedly said that "is not what they came into the Army to do."

• Attrition rate for captains is now at 11 percent, up from 6.7 percent a decade ago — an increase of 3 percent in the past three years.

• This depletes the pool of the very officers the Army draws upon to become future commanders of combat battalions and brigades.

That survey was conducted by the Army Research Institute at the site where the Army historically trains its infantry troops, Fort Benning, Georgia.

A preliminary draft obtained by the *Times* reinforced similar findings released the same day by the independent Center for Strategic and International Studies, a conservative think tank.

Based on a study of 12,000 armed-services personnel throughout the world and 125 focus groups of both officers and non-coms, it found:

• Military careers continue to fall "significantly short" of expectations of soldiers, sailors and airmen for their families and themselves.

• The Clinton administration's repeated overseas assignments of troops on long peacekeeping missions contribute most to their dissatisfaction, by keeping them away from their families for longer periods of time than expected.

• "America's military is facing potentially serious rifts in the fabric of its culture, with attending damage to future operational effectiveness."

• Although military service by homosexuals is the subject of intense political debate in the 2000 presidential campaign, "the issue of gays in uniform was hardly ever flagged as a key concern by a man or woman in uniform."

• "There is little doubt in the minds of the study participants that conditions within the armed forces are far less favorable than they were a decade ago."

• Even so, members of the military continue to hold a fierce pride in their branch of the armed forces, and would put their lives on the line for their country.

U.S. a Sitting Duck For Bioterrorism

NewsMax.com Vortex, February 2000 — America is unprepared to cope with a large-scale biological or chemical assault upon its cities, according to the respected *Journal of the American Medical Association*.

And Cable News Network reported terrorism experts say "it's not so much a matter of if or when it will happen, as it is a question of where the attack will take place."

In its latest issue, *JAMA* reported the results of its survey:

• The United States has no practical contingency plan to handle catastrophic chemical terrorism.

• Fewer than one hospital in four of the nation's 6,000 hospitals is at some state of readiness, according to the American Medical Association.

• Most hospitals and other health care facilities, which are critical to the nation's ability to respond, are "poorly prepared" to care for victims.

• They are largely ill-equipped in the key areas of triage and decontamination, medical therapy and coordination with public health agencies and emergency-response personnel.

Parkland Hospital in Dallas was cited as one example:

Although it has a stockpile of antidote drugs to combat sarin nerve gas and anthrax, administrators say these would soon be depleted.

"We could be dealing with 10 to 100 times what we've planned for," said Dr. Kathy Rinnert.

"While the frequency of risk is low, when an event occurs, the casualty numbers and the mortality — the number of people that die — will be very, very large."

'Nuke L.A.' General Comes Calling in D.C.

NewsMax.com Vortex, February 2000 — A high-ranking Communist Chinese general, who threatened to vaporize Los Angeles with a nuclear attack in 1996, was scheduled to arrive for a two-day visit to Washington, D.C., in January.

Lt. Gen. Xiong Guangkai, deputy chief of the People's Liberation Army (PLA) General Staff, was scheduled to meet with senior Pentagon officials to discuss "military ties" and a possible visit to Beijing by Secretary of Defense William Cohen later this year, Reuters news service reported.

Four years ago, when Sino-American relations unraveled after the PLA fired nuclear-capable missiles over Taiwan in a clear attempt to intimidate an American ally, Xiong was hardly the model of diplomacy.

Then the People's Liberation Army deputy chief of staff for intelligence, he began his nuclear saber rattling in a meeting with former Assistant Secretary of Defense Charles Freeman.

"Taiwan is a matter of vital interest to us," Xiong told Freeman. Then the general warned that the days when China could be intimidated by America's overwhelming military power were over.

"[Y]ou could do that then because you knew we couldn't hit back," he said. "Now we can. So you are not going to threaten us again because, in the end, you care a lot more about Los Angeles than Taipei."

In his chilling best-selling book *Betrayal,* national security writer Bill Gertz reports that Xiong's threat was dismissed by Clinton administration officials.

"There is no outstanding nuclear threat against the United States from China, and it's silly to build this up into anything more than it is," said State Department spokesman Glyn Davis at the time.

That was three years before the Cox Report and revelations that China had obtained nearly all of America's nuclear secrets, thanks in part to the Clinton administration's casual attitude toward national security.

The same year Xiong issued his nuclear threat, his deputy, Gen. Ji Shengde, met with Johnny Chung, then a Democratic Party fund-raiser who had developed high-level ties to both Beijing and the Clinton White House.

"We like your president," Ji told Chung. "We want to see him re-elected."

The fund-raiser later turned whistleblower and told investigators in 1998 that Ji offered him $300,000 at that meeting to help Clinton retain the White House in 1996.

Americans Reject Pullout of U.S. From Panama Canal

NewsMax.com Vortex, January 2000 — Most Americans oppose the transfer of the Panama Canal and fear Chinese influence over the strategic waterway.

In a NewsMax.com/Zogby International poll, nearly 50 percent of Americans polled oppose the turnover of the Panama Canal to the Panamanian government. Only 29 percent of respondents thought turning the Canal over to the government of Panama was a good idea.

The NewsMax.com/Zogby poll also found that Americans are deeply worried that a Chinese-controlled company, Hutchison Whampoa, will control and operate the Canal and its facilities.

A majority, 58 percent, agreed that Hutchison Whampoa's influence over the Canal "threatens U.S. national security."

The survey — which sampled the opinions of 1,005 registered voters — indicated Americans are far more concerned about the Panama Canal than official Washington or the media pretend to be.

Administration officials, however, may have quietly done their own polling and also discovered voters were not so happy about the December 31, 1999, Canal transfer.

When Panamanian and U.S. officials held a ceremony on December 14 in Panama marking the turnover, Panamanian officials openly expressed disappointment that no ranking American official — President Clinton, Vice President Al Gore, Secretary of State Madeleine Albright or any Cabinet member, for that matter — bothered to show.

Former President Jimmy Carter, who shepherded the 1977 treaty that led to the transfer of the Canal, headed the U.S. delegation to the ceremony.

Critics of the transfer have cited increasing concerns about the military dangers posed by the American withdrawal. Panamanian polls show that the citizens there wish the United States had not withdrawn, and have voiced concerns that Marxist guerrillas in Colombia, backed by Cuba and China, have been making incursions into Panama's southern provinces. Panama has no standing army.

American groups have also expressed fears that Hutchison Whampoa, a company with close ties to China's military and intelligence agencies, will have *de facto* control of the Canal.

Admiral Thomas Moorer, former chairman of the Joint Chiefs of Staff, has testified before Congress that by turning over the Canal, the United States may lose critical time in deploying forces if war erupts in Korea, Taiwan or elsewhere in the world.

Howard Phillips, chairman of the Conservative Caucus, a group that has been spearheading efforts to maintain U.S. control of the Canal, said that it is "in the common interest of both the United States and Panama to restore a U.S. military presence in Panama."

Phillips is calling on Congress to intervene and force Hutchison Whampoa's contract for the canal to be revoked, and for U.S. troops to be permanently stationed there.

New Marine Commandant Wants Troops to 'Have Fun'

NewsMax.com Vortex, November 1999 — If it ain't broke, don't fix it — or so the saying goes.

Still, though the Marine Corps has managed to escape so many of the discipline and recruitment problems that have plagued the other branches of the U.S. military lately, the corps' new commandant wants to revamp its stern image.

The *London Telegraph* reported that General James Jones, who took command of the military's most aggressive fighting force in June, has announced plans for a "softening of the corps."

Under Jones, "the image of service in the Marines as hard, sternly disciplined and incompatible with family life will change," reports the paper. The general's plans include introducing the corps to new training concepts such as "holistic readiness."

Out with the old esprit de corps, which was based on self-sacrifice and single-minded dedication to a rigorous code of discipline, and in with a new approach, which General Jones hopes will "empower" the lower ranks to give him "feedback" about how to run the corps.

"I think it's important that, while people do these very demanding and difficult things, that we also find ways in which to allow them to have some fun," the general said. "We need leaders who will take leave, go on vacation, so that some of their subordinates will."

1990s: The Socialist Decade

By Christopher Ruddy

NewsMax.com Vortex, November 1999 — Sometimes we live so close to the trees, we can't see the forest.

Let me ask you to take a little quiz.

Question: The greatest expansion in federal social spending took place during which period:

a. Franklin Roosevelt's New Deal – 1930s
b. Lyndon Johnson's Great Society – 1960s
c. The Clinton Years/Republican-dominated Congress – 1990s

If you answered a or b, you are wrong.

We have lived through the greatest expansion of social welfare spending, in real dollars, in the history of the country. This spending spree took place without a major headline from the establishment press, without any significant debate, and with the complicity of a Congress dominated for most of the decade by Republicans.

How could such a momentous shift have occurred with little fanfare?

Here's how.

Remember the fall of the Soviet Union, the tearing down of the Berlin Wall in 1989, and what appeared to be an era of American dominance in the world?

Policy-makers and pundits concluded that the West had won the Cold War. Heavy military spending that had marked every federal budget since the end of World War II — including the large increases of the Reagan years — was no longer needed.

At that time, someone coined the term "peace dividend" — referring to federal budget money that would be freed up as defense spending fell.

In the early 1990s, for a brief period, it was a subject of discussion: how was Congress going to use the peace dividend money?

Democrats and the Left argued that the money should be used to fund social programs, new ones and old ones. There was a feeling that defense spending requirements and the increasing federal deficit had strangled any idea of the expansion of welfare spending. But with the peace dividend, the Left saw an opportunity to let the blood of social economics flow freely.

Conservative pundits and Republicans did not argue against the cuts in military spending. They did disagree with the Democrats, however, on the re-allocation of the peace dividend. Some Republicans wanted to use the peace dividend money to reduce the annual deficit and begin paying off the national debt. Still, the supply-siders called for Reaganesque tax cuts to continue the economic boom that began soon after Ronald Reagan took office.

As it turned out, the debate between Left and Right over the peace dividend was short-lived.

The budget numbers — readily available out of any current almanac — tell the tale of how the peace dividend was spent.

In 1990, total defense spending represented nearly 30 percent of the federal budget for that year. By 1997, federal outlays for defense fell to almost half, 16 percent.

Similarly in 1990, defense spending represented 6 percent of GDP (gross domestic product). By 1997, it was only 3 percent.

As defense spending dwindled, Congress — Republicans and Democrats — spent money faster than drunken sailors.

Huge sums of money were made available as a result of the peace dividend — and those funds went almost entirely to social welfare spending.

It is no secret who the spending spree beneficiaries were. From 1990 to 1997, Medicare spending rose by 94 percent. Social Security spending rose by an incredible 81 percent.

It is also important to note that increases in Social Security retirement incomes are tied to the inflation rate, so spending increases should have trailed fairly close to the increase in CPI (Consumer Price Index) for the period — 30 percent.

How can the massive run-up in Social Security spending be explained? Easy. During the Clinton years the administration allowed a monstrous increase in spending on Social Security disability programs. Social Security disability pensions became easy money during the 1990s — from drug addicts and alcoholics who were welcomed on to the rolls — to immigrants who were advised to sign up at U.S. embassies abroad even before they arrived as citizens on shores.

When President Clinton signed Republican legislation to "abolish" welfare in 1996, it was greeted as the most important conservative social victory in a generation. It was little more than a bad joke.

Welfare rolls have declined since then. But the punch line is that the politicians did this by legerdemain. State and local governments have been working with the federal government in moving many welfare recipients onto the Social Security disability rolls.

The politicians like the fact that welfare recipients have been moved onto Social Security rolls. During election season, the politicians can say they reduced the welfare rolls.

The former welfare recipients love it because the cash benefits for disability are much higher. For instance, a family of four can receive twice as much cash on Social Security than the same family on welfare.

Claiming a minor psychological malady can get you on disability. Once on the Social Security rolls it's a welfare cheat's paradise because there are practically no reviews from the government. Welfare recipients are more carefully scrutinized, as many states have aggressive welfare fraud units.

Thus, when President Clinton tells Congress the anticipated budget surplus needs to help fund the depleting Social Security trust funds, he knows what he is speaking about. Some of those funds have been used to cover the huge run-up in disability spending.

To be sure, the heavy social spending of the 1990s helped fuel the country's great economic expansion. But like many such government-fed booms, it may end up with a big hangover.

Even Alan Greenspan understands the role of the peace dividend in having made the boom possible. He also understands that eventually we cannot count on stealing additional spending dollars by taking from defense.

In 1997 he told Congress: "The payout of the peace dividend is coming to an end. Defense outlays have fallen from 6.2 percent of GDP in 1985 to 3.4 percent this year. Further cuts may be difficult to achieve, for even if we are fortunate enough to enjoy a relatively tranquil world, spending will tend to be buoyed by the need to replace technological obsolescent equipment, as well as by the usual political pressures."

Since Greenspan's comments in 1997 there has been increased political pressure in Congress to increase military spending for servicemen's salaries and to replace old equipment. Congress also wants to develop a costly missile defense system.

Additionally, the world may soon become less "tranquil" with the likes of North Korea, Saddam Hussein, Communist China, Miloevich and North Korea. Defense spending will need to increase, and Congress has recognized that fact.

If the economy weakens, watch out. The country may be hit with a double whammy. Congress may need to increase defense spending during a recession.

Typically recessions increase social spending on things like welfare and unemployment. Add to that an already bloated social budget and you have a recipe for disaster. Faced with such a situation, Congress will do what it usually does and raise taxes — no doubt further weakening the economy.

Administration Proposes Stripping Subs of Ballistic Missiles

NewsMax.com Vortex, September 1999 — The Trident nuclear submarine, the mainstay of America's nuclear deterrence, may be further undermined by Clinton administration plans. Congress this summer voted $16 million for administration plans to study the conversion of four Ohio-class Trident ballistic missile submarines to be cruise missile platforms. The study calls for stripping the Tridents of ballistic missiles, leaving the ship with only seven missile tubes for carrying short-range, tactical cruise missiles only. The submarines also would be modified to carry Navy SEAL forces. The Navy says the changes would cost $500 million a ship.

— Aviation Week

Stigmatized by Navy Secretary, Submarines Targeted for Social Change

NewsMax.com Vortex, August 1999 — The Center for Military Readiness has learned that despite frequent denials, the Navy is planning an informal test of the feasibility of female sailors on submarines. In response to CMR's inquiry, the Navy's Chief of Information Office (CHINFO) confirmed that a group of 144 female and 218 ROTC midshipmen are going to sea this summer on five Trident nuclear submarines.

The women will sail this summer on two-day "Career Orientation and Training" (CORTRAMID) trips. Groups of up to 27 will embark nine at a time, over a period of six days. The five Ohio Class "boomer" submarines involved in the program are the USS Pennsylvania, West Virginia, Maryland, Kentucky, and Rhode Island.

Military and individual civilian women have gone on single-day or longer trips on submarines, berthed in separate officers' quarters. Two-day overnight cruises with substantial groups of female midshipmen are something new and inexplicable.

For many compelling reasons, women have not been assigned to submarines in this or any country, except Norway — hardly a world power. Nevertheless, in a June 3 speech before the Naval Submarine League, Navy Secretary Richard Danzig said that he didn't foresee coed crews within the next year, but that the submarine force should prepare to mirror gender integration in the rest of society.

Adding insult to injury, Danzig said the sub force will have to deal with more female politicians, who may be hesitant to send money to a "white male bastion."

—*Navy Times*

PART II:

NewsMax.com Vortex Abroad: The Growing Risk of War

Soviet Germ Warfare Still Threatens U.S.

NewsMax.com Vortex, June 2000 — A U.S. program to help defang the old, largely defunct Soviet biological weapons program could actually be keeping it alive to threaten the United States in the future, according to a new study from the General Accounting Office.

The Clinton administration is asking Congress for $220 million — a 10-fold increase over the last five years — to address the threat between 2000 and 2004. About half of it would be awarded to underpaid Russian scientists to do legitimate work in the civilian sector. That program includes $36 million to fund collaborative research with Russian institutes on dangerous pathogens, an attempt to improve U.S. defenses against biological weapons, according to the GAO.

The GAO warns, however, that same program might actually be increasing the risk to the United States by furthering Russia's research in biological weapons and keeping scientists' skill levels high. Further, without proper oversight, the funds or research could be diverted into a new offensive weapons program.

There may be as many as 5,000 senior former Soviet biological weapons scientists who could pose significant proliferation risks and 10,000 personnel who have weapons skills, Russian officials told GAO investigators.

The buying power of scientists' salaries has dropped by 75 percent on average, according to Russian officials. Many earn between $40 and $80 a month. Russian institutes' operating budgets have dropped precipitously. One had a budget of $25 million in 1991 that has now dropped to $2.5 million, according to the report.

That these scientists could be tempted to sell their services to another country or terrorist organization is not the only reason the United States should be concerned, according to the GAO. These same workers have access to viruses and pathogens that could easily be slipped out of laboratories and smuggled abroad.

No steps the United States is taking to mitigate that risk "would prevent Russian project participants or institutes from using their skills or research outputs to later work on offensive weapons activities at any of the Russian military institutes that remain closed to the United States," the report states.

Russia has granted American scientists and military officials access to 30 of the roughly 50 civilian biological weapons institutes in Russia. But 15 remain closed to the United States, largely because it has not funded programs for those institutes.

The Russian Ministry of Defense still has at least four military biological weapons institutes to which the United States has not been granted access.

"Dire financial conditions at former Soviet biological weapons institutes could encourage the proliferation of weapons expertise to countries or groups of concern," according to the April 28 report.

According to the CIA, Russia is a "significant source of biotechnology expertise for Iran," and Iran has intensified its efforts over the last three years to acquire biological and weapons expertise and materials from at least 15 former Soviet institutes, the GAO reports.

The United States halted its biological weapons program in 1969. In 1972, the United States and the Soviet Union as well as other countries agreed not to produce or stockpile biological agents for offensive purposes. The same year, the Soviet Union established the Biopreparat, a civilian agency that ultimately employed 60,000 and produced weapons employing smallpox, anthrax, the plague and other pathogens.

Then–Russian President Boris Yeltsin acknowledged the program in 1992 and pledged to follow the terms of the 1992 agreement. By 1994, the United States established two programs to fund former weapons scientists to do research. They have received about $20 million over the last five years.

The institutes maintain thousands of strains of viruses, including Ebola, anthrax and Marburg, ostensibly for public health research. The same viruses, however, could be the basis for a new biological weapons program, the GAO warns.

—UPI

Defector: Large Number of Spies

By Christopher Ruddy

NewsMax.com Vortex, June 2000 — Russia's highest-ranking defector says State Department claims that no foreign or American journalists are engaged in espionage is absolute nonsense.

Colonel Stanislav Lunev reveals that many journalists from Russia and other countries are, in reality, spies. He also says that many Russian journalists have recruited leading American reporters to engage in espionage as well.

Colonel Lunev was the highest-ranking spy ever to defect from the GRU, Russia's military intelligence unit. He did so while living and working in Washington as a TASS correspondent.

His story was deemed so vital by the CIA and FBI that he remains under the Witness Protection Program. He currently writes a column for NewsMax.com.

When Lunev defected to U.S. intelligence, he revealed that at least half of all Russian journalists working in Washington and the United States were either GRU or KGB officers.

Questions about journalists posing as spies have erupted after security concerns were raised at State Department headquarters in Washington.

Listening devices have been found at the State Department This winter a laptop computer that held classified information on nuclear, biological and chemical weapons was stolen.

FBI officials have told Congress that security problems may emanate from the high number of journalists that have wide access within the State Department building.

According to the State Department, more than 467 Americans and 56 foreign journalists are credentialed with the department.

Secretary of State Madeleine Albright seemed baffled by the allegations and demanded, "If you are spies, then identify yourselves."

Apparently no one, so far, has responded to her order.

And Albright's own spokesman has thrown cold water over the allegations.

"At this time, we are not aware of any information that any members of the foreign press are utilizing the media as cover for intelligence activities at the State Department," explained State Department spokesman Richard Boucher.

"There's no question that Russia is using her best spies, her best assets here in the U.S., as journalists," Lunev countered.

He said the reasoning for using journalists as a cover is simple. "There's no big difference between a spy and a journalist — both are trying to get information," he said.

Lunev added that Russia has used journalists to target agencies with national security and defense information, including the State Department, the Pentagon, Congress and other agencies.

He noted that of 10 Russian journalists working in Washington when he defected, six were spies for the GRU and KGB, now the SVR.

He said his defection was no surprise for the FBI.

Lunev said the FBI keeps all Russian journalists under permanent surveillance. And the FBI is not just worried about Russian journalists, he said. Many countries use journalists as spies, including the British, French and Germans.

Though the number of Russian spies might be small, their reach is far wider, Lunev said, because they recruit American journalists to do espionage work.

Lunev himself had several American journalists working on Russia's behalf, and based on his experience, the number of American journalists spying for Russia is "very big."

He believes Russia has penetrated, and continues to penetrate, all the major press outlets in the United States.

"American journalists have access to a wide array of contacts: politicians, military, intelligence — it's top-of-the-line access, on-time intelligence — that foreign journalists would not have readily available," Lunev said.

Though he defected in 1992, he doubts little has changed. If anything, foreign spies operating as journalists may have latitude, he believes, because Americans have let down their guard since the end of the Cold War.

Russia's Mighty Nuclear Arsenal Remains a Menace

NewsMax.com Vortex, April 2000 — Seven years and several hundred million dollars later, a new Harvard University report reveals the United States has helped reduce only one-tenth of Russia's highly enriched, weapons-grade uranium.

According to the *Boston Globe:*

Former White House nonproliferation specialist Matthew Bunn, the author of the report, expresses a two-fold concern regarding Russia's aging nuclear arsenal. His fears include the Clinton administration's haphazard approach in funding the problem and the lack of security surrounding the nuclear stockpiles.

"If plutonium or highly enriched uranium became available on the black market, virtually any state, or well-organized terrorist group, might be able to make a nuclear bomb, and they could do so with virtually no warning to the international community," said a concerned Bunn. "It could come out of nowhere."

With more and more terrorist groups and anti-United States nations waiting to get their hands on nuclear material and with Russia's aging facilities and torn economy, "the problem is probably worse today than when we started working on it," said Graham Allison, a Russian specialist at Harvard's Kennedy School of Government.

"This is the biggest single threat to American lives today," Allison said.

The report recommends that the annual U.S. budget of $500 million to safeguard Russia's nuclear weaponry and materials be doubled or tripled.

Russia is said to have more than 1,000 tons of highly enriched uranium (HEU) stockpiled in 300 or more buildings at 40 or more sites.

The country is also believed to have up to 160 tons of plutonium. Thus far, the HEU-reduction program, begun in 1993, has eliminated 75 tons of the uranum stockpile.

"If you ask me, what's the main reason New York City hasn't gone up in a mushroom cloud, I'd say the main reason is we've been lucky," said John B. Wolfsthal, a former official on nonproliferation at the Department of Energy.

Bunn expressed concerns that with tension between Russia and the United States on a number of issues, including the war in Chechnya and a passed Senate bill that would put a hold on some payments to Russia due to the country's suspected sales of technology for biological and nuclear weapons to Iran, the "window of opportunity" to help Russia safeguard its nuclear arsenal is getting smaller.

Latest Russian ICBM Launched as Warning

NewsMax.com Vortex, January 2000 — In a calculated warning for the United States to butt out of its internal affairs, Russia has launched with fanfare its newest strategic nuclear weapon.

It soared eastward across 3,400 miles and seven time zones, landing as programmed in a target range on Russia's Kamchatka Peninsula just short of Alaska on December 14.

But its true impact was directed westward toward the American heartland, now shown to be within easy range of the versatile Topol-M intercontinental ballistic missile.

This awesome display of force came only four days after President Boris Yeltsin — outraged at President Clinton's criticism of his war to suppress the breakaway Caucasian republic of Chechnya — placed Russia's nuclear missiles on full war footing.

In a move intended to signal that Russia means business, Prime Minister Valdimir Putin, who is strongly prosecuting the Chechen war, made a display of being on hand to witness the Topol-M blastoff.

He issued a blast of his own when he said Russia "will use all diplomatic and military-political levers in its disposal" to resist the American president's "interfering" in Chechnya.

"The diplomatic levers are clear," Putin said, "and as for the military ones, Tuesday's successful launch of the Topol-M intercontinental ballistic missile is one of them.

"No one can accuse the government of inappropriate use of antiterrorist measures in Chechnya [or], call Russia an aggressor or an occupier.

"Some nations and blocs under cover of international organizations are interfering into affairs of independent states, and trying to speak to them in the language of force."

This was an abrupt reversal of Putin's conciliatory language only a few days earlier, when he tried to modify an angry statement by Yeltsin reminding Clinton that "Russia is a great power that possesses a nuclear arsenal."

Putin also took the occasion at the Topol-M launchpad to warn Clinton one more time that Russia will not tolerate his efforts to modify or scrap the 1972 Anti-Ballistic Missile Treaty in order to build an American anti-missile defense system.

The Clinton administration says such a shield is needed to protect its territory against a limited missile attack by a "rogue nation," not a nuclear onslaught such as Russia can inflict.

But Russia, for decades fearful of becoming vulnerable to a U.S. first strike, has regarded the ABM Treaty as its only effective nuclear shield.

If the U.S. goes that route, Russia says, its response will be to fit its Topol-M missiles with multiple nuclear warheads capable of penetrating any defensive screen.

With its earlier long-range missiles obsolete, Russia is betting the farm on its vaunted new Topol-M.

Unlike previous Russian ICBMs, with their massive payloads and launch power, Topol-Ms are relatively small, highly mobile on trucks, and very difficult to detect and track before they could deliver a crippling blow.

Moscow: 'Will Nuke in Local War'

NewsMax.com Vortex, January 2000 — Russia has announced it wants opponents to understand it has changed its military policy and will now use nuclear weapons in "smaller-scale conflicts."

It was a clear-cut warning to the United States and European nations that if they intervene in its war in Chechnya they may expect nuclear war in return.

At the same time, Russia announced it is also increasing its capability — by three-fold — to engage in strategic intercontinental- ballistic-missile nuclear warfare with America.

This news came out of Moscow in conjunction with the celebration of the 40th anniversary of its nuclear-missile forces.

In carefully timed interviews in *Krasnaya Zvezda* and the weekly *Nezavisimoye Voyennoye Obozreniye*, the chief of the missile force, Colonel-General Vladimir Yakovlev, said Russia had been compelled to rethink dramatically its nuclear-deterrent program.

"Russia, for objective reasons, is forced to lower the threshold for using nuclear weapons, extend the nuclear deterrent to smaller-scale conflicts and openly warn potential opponents about this," Yakovlev said.

Those reasons, he said, were the under-funding of Russia's rocket forces, due to the country's financial crisis, and the emergence of regional powers armed with missiles and nuclear technology.

Yakovlev made it clear Moscow will use its nuclear arms if attacked with chemical or biological weapons or outnumbered by conventional forces, Reuters news agency reported.

He told *Nezavisimoye Voyennoye Obozreniye* that Russia will continue to replace its existing intercontinental ballistic missiles with its new Topol-M ICBMs.

Topol-M is a highly mobile rocket with a multiple nuclear warhead that the Russian military has boasted can penetrate any missile defense shield the United States can create.

Yakovlev forecast that Russia will also produce an aircraft-based cruise version of the Topol-M and place greater emphasis on space technology, Reuters said.

Although not the superpower the old Soviet Union was during the Cold War, Russia still has the world's second-largest nuclear arsenal of hundreds of missiles based on land, in prowling submarines and aboard long-range aircraft.

The newspaper *Izvestia* reported Russia will double Topol-M production from the rate of 10 a year, as in 1998 and 1999, to 20 in 2000 and 30 in 2001 — giving it a total of 70 by 2002.

Izvestia said Russia will use the new Topol-Ms to replace its aging, almost-obsolete ICBMs as fast as the new models come off the production line.

This would deprive Russia of millions of dollars of U.S. tax funds, conditioned on being used only to help it dismantle and destroy, but not replace, its old ICBM fleet.

Those funds were appropriated under the 1992 Nunn-Lugar Act, steered through Congress by former senators Sam Nunn, D-Ga., and Richard G. Lugar, R-Ind.

The Russian Military: In Bad Shape?

By Colonel Stanislav Lunev

NewsMax.com Vortex, December 1999 — On October 25 Nikolai Mikhailov, first defense minister of the R.F. (Russian Federation) shocked the international community by his strong statements to the press. At a time when the R.F. is still in dire economic straits, dependent on Western money for its very survival, Mikhailov warned that his country's military has enough weaponry to overwhelm any antiballistic missile system in the U.S. He warned further that the R.F. will deploy more nuclear warheads if the U.S. continues its efforts to develop an anti-missile defense system. Mikhailov stated categorically, "This technology can realistically be used and will be used if the United States pushes us to it."

The U.S. reaction to these words came from Secretary of State Madeleine K. Albright. In her speech to the Chicago Council on Foreign Relations on November 10, she disclosed, "A Russian defense official recently proclaimed that his nation has the ability to overwhelm the missile defense system we are planning. . . . [T]hat is true — and part of our point."

These statements run counter to the standard reports in the U.S. about the supposed deterioration of the Russian military and its demise as a major threat to the international community. Evidently the U.S. media have been negligent in investigating the true state of the Russian war machine. Mikhailov, however, is an expert in these matters. Before his appointment as R.F. deputy defense minister he had spent 35 years working in both the Soviet and Russian military-industrial complexes.

He has inside knowledge, then, that the Russian defense industry is accelerating its buildup of a new generation of weapons systems. Mikhailov, after all, is a primary mover behind the Russian General Staff's plan to implement the new 10-year arms-development program for completion by 2010.

The Russian military has already begun operational deployment of the second-generation mobile-launch-based Topol-M ICBM, a weapon the U.S. does not possess and also has not yet allocated funds to develop. The Russian VPK (Voenno Promishlenni Komplex — Military Industrial Complex) has also introduced a new generation of nuclear warheads as well as a new stealth bomber and a stealth cruise missile — which could reach U.S. territory over the Polar Circle.

As further examples, the R.F. has under construction (1) the fifth-generation Borei-class ballistic-missile submarine, (2) a new submarine-based ballistic missile, (3) the Akula-2-class nuclear attack submarine (Shark), and (4) the new Severodvinsk-class nuclear attack submarine. The VPK is likewise continuing to modernize its army, navy and air force, not to mention further developing chemical, biological, nuclear, and other types of mass-destruction weapons.

The list of Russian weaponry could be extended many pages. Some of the new weapons do not have any counterparts in the arsenals of the West. According to the Russian General Staff these programs are to be in place by 2010 so that Moscow can regain the former stature of the U.S.S.R. Russia is determined to gain pre-eminence in unique nuclear and laser technologies for new types of systems.

With the war in Chechnya, Russian military spending has increased about 1.5 times, and the increases are expected to continue. The Russian General Staff is requesting a gradual increase in military expenditures from 2.8 percent of GDP (gross domestic product) in 1999 to between 6 and 6.5 percent by 2005.

The war in Chechnya has led also to an increase in military and special-services personnel, especially in the number and quality of the ground forces, which had been lacking in well trained professionals. During the last few months the Russian units in Chechnya have received new weaponry in such quantities as to represent a violation of the CFET (Conventional Forces in Europe Treaty).

Obviously, the R.F. does not need state-of-the-art weapons systems for the military action in Chechnya. They are ultimately intended for future full-scale wars against countries considered by the Russian General Staff to be "major potential military adversaries." This intention is clear from recent "West-99" field exercises, the largest since 1985, during which Russian military commanders ordered simulated nuclear strikes against NATO countries, including the continental United States.

This intention is also evident in a recent statement of R.F. Defense Minister Igor Sergeev, who on November 12 accused the United States of stirring up the war in Chechnya as part of a plot to weaken its former superpower adversary. He is quoted as saying, "U.S. national interests require that the military conflict in the North Caucasus, fanned from the outside, keeps constantly smoldering."

It is interesting to note here that Sergeev didn't speak about fighting against "international terrorism" in Chechnya, which is the official pretext for the war, but speaks instead about the conflict as being "fanned from outside." About which "outside" is he speaking? There is no question that he means the United States.

But who is footing the bill for these enormous Russian military outlays? Isn't Russia broke? The answer to this simple question is not easy to comprehend, for it defies common sense. The money is coming from America and other Western countries; or, more precisely, it comes chiefly out of the pockets of American taxpayers. The International Monetary Fund (IMF), the World Bank, and other financial institutions, which heavily depend on American money, have funneled tens of billions into Russia's corrupted economy. Some of these billions have vanished, only to magically reappear in the private accounts of so-called New Russians in Western banks.

But some of it has also been diverted into improving the Russian military-industrial complex. Even the portion of this money that has actually been used to service debt, its original purpose, makes it possible for Russia to spend more of its own resources on military and armaments development.

Much of this money ends up in VPK coffers via the special-assistance programs implemented by the West. For example, the United States has also initiated several bilateral assistance programs for Russia. After spending $1.7 billion, the Nunn-Lugar "Cooperative Threat Reduction Act" received a seven-year extension in mid-June 1999, which will cost an additional $2.8 billion to help secure R.F. fissionable materials and nuclear warheads.

Another program, begun in 1993 by the U.S. Department of Energy, will disburse an estimated $11.5 billion over a 20-year period to purchase 500 metric tons of highly enriched uranium, which should have been, according to the original agreement, diluted in the U.S. for sale to private nuclear power plants. In violation of this agreement, the R.F. claims to be diluting this uranium itself, and the U.S. has credulously agreed to accept this change in the procedure. This modified agreement will be in effect through the year 2003.

Over the next five years the U.S. Department of Energy will pay $500 million in salaries to Russian scientists employed in closed, nuclear cities. Many of them are working secretly on weapons of mass destruction. According to a U.S. General Accounting Office report, American officials "do not always know how many scientists are receiving funding."

On November 1 of this year, American and Russian officials observed the opening of a U.S.-financed building in the city of Sergiev Posad to help improve security at Russia's nuclear weapons sites. This Security Assessment and Training Center is a cooperative venture between the Pentagon and the Russian military, and will serve as a test site for security technologies. In other words, this center will serve to improve security for the Russian nuclear arsenal and its further development.

Is any of this of benefit to the United States? Obviously, it is not. Americans have spent billions of dollars to help establish a democratic Russia but certainly not to help it secretly overtake the U.S. in military capabilities or to line the pockets of gangster bureaucrats. When will Americans finally realize that the much-touted "strategic relationship" with Moscow exists only in the minds of a few misguided, or opportunistic, American politicians? By now it should be obvious to all that the billions of U.S. taxpayer dollars squandered on the Machiavellian ambitions of Kremlin leaders should be spent on strengthening the security of the United States. Who but Americans would subsidize the armaments of admitted adversaries?

Colonel Stanislav Lunev is the highest-ranking Soviet military spy ever to defect to the United States. He is a regular contributor to NewsMax.com and Vortex.

FBI Director Admits Russians May Have Secret Weapons in U.S.

NewsMax.com Vortex, November 1999 — FBI Director Louis Freeh admitted that Russia may still have stored weapons — including nuclear suitcase bombs — at secret locations around the United States.

The stunning revelations appeared in the *New York Post.* The newspaper quoted Congressman Curt Weldon, R-Pa., as having had a conversation with Freeh in the past two weeks.

Weldon said that Freeh "acknowledged the possibility that hidden weapons caches exist in the United States." Weldon, a leading congressional expert on Russia and chairman of the House Armed Services subcommittee on military research and development, said, "There is no doubt that the Soviets stored material in this country. The question is what and where."

Congressional scrutiny has focused on dozens of nuclear suitcase bombs that have disappeared from Russia's nuclear arsenal. According to Russian sources, including Russian General Alexander Lebed, Russia produced 132 nuclear suitcase bombs, each carrying 10 kilotons of explosive material. Only 48 remain in Russia's inventory; the rest have disappeared.

The FBI has taken a nonchalant approach to locating the secret caches.

Congressional sources indicated that the FBI scoured the area around Brainerd, Minnesota — one area Russian agents were believed to have forward-deployed weapons in the event of a war.

But Weldon said the Clinton administration is not interested in pressing the Yeltsin government for fear of destabilizing his shaky position vis-à-vis the country's military leadership.

Concerns about the secret stockpiles have been fueled in recent years by revelations made by Russian defectors.

One KGB defector, Vasili Mitrokhin, provided information to British intelligence that secret weapons stockpiles are scattered throughout the U.S., including upstate New York, California, Texas, Montana and Minnesota.

Mitrokhin has also stated that such stockpiles were also made throughout Europe. Some Russian weapons caches have been located in Belgium and Switzerland.

Colonel Stanislav Lunev, the highest-ranking military spy ever to defect from Russia, has testified that the Soviet military developed elaborate plans for the use of weapons during the outset of a war with the U.S.

Lunev said Russian military plans include the destruction of military bases, command and control centers, and the assassination of top U.S. leaders, including the president and members of Congress. Lunev has also told members of Congress that suitcase nuclear devices may have already been forward-deployed into the U.S.

While the secret stockpiles appear to be remnants of the Cold War period, Lunev, a NewsMax.com columnist and author of *Through the Eyes of the Enemy,* has warned U.S. authorities that Soviet military strategy continues under the guise of Russian "democracy."

Lunev has stated that Russian military leaders continue to see a nuclear conflict between Russia and the United States as "inevitable."

In recent years, the Russian government has continued to invest heavily in strategic weapons. Russia is currently mass producing the Topol-M intercontinental missile — a weapon more sophisticated than anything produced by the U.S. military.

Russia also continues to invest billions in building large underground bunkers for use during a nuclear conflict. Last month, the Yelstin government announced plans to increase military spending by 50 percent in next year's budget.

Russia to Speed Development of Arms Systems

NewsMax.com Vortex, September 1999 — Colonel-General Anatoly Sitnov, who attended the international air show in Zhukovsky, said in an interview with Itar-Tass news agency that the Defense Ministry had passed the decision to hasten the development of new arms after NATO's assault on Yugoslavia.

"We have not seen anything principally new in terms of armaments of the NATO countries and of the tactic of their use in the Yugoslav conflict. On our part, we have made the decision to speed up the creation of the newest arm systems based on new physical principles," Sitnov said.

Asked why federal troops are not using the newest arms in fighting Islamic militants in Dagestan, Sitnov said the fighting was not a war but rather stopping bandit activity, which does not warrant sending the newest arms to the region.

— Itar-Tass

Russian PM Says Nuclear Weapons Still Important

NewsMax.com Vortex, September 1999 — Prime Minister Vladimir Putin vowed that Moscow would maintain its nuclear arsenal to protect Russia, a day after the country celebrated its 50th anniversary of the first atomic test.

"[Nuclear weapons] remain fundamental for the country's security, a guarantee for keeping peace in modern geopolitical conditions," Putin, whose country is the second largest nuclear power, was quoted as saying by Russia's Interfax news agency.

"The development and improvement of the nuclear arsenal is one of the most important demands for our government. . . . [I]f we do not keep [weapons] over the coming five to seven years, then the situation in our country will change in a radical way," he was quoted as saying at a ceremony commemorating the test.

—Yahoo

Report: Russia Has Smallpox Biological Weapon

NewsMax.com Vortex, September 1999 — American military scientists are developing defense vaccines against smallpox — a disease wiped out in nature, but one that still threatens, thanks to ongoing biological weapons programs.

Smallpox is caused by the variola virus. According to the *Washing-*

ton Times, "there are reports that Russia has created a biological weapon utilizing variola.

And U.S. intelligence suspects North Korea, Iran, Libya and Syria are among the nations that have hidden quantities of variola for possible weapons production. . . . Smallpox . . . is currently practically unstoppable."

— American Foreign Policy Council

China, Russia Vow to Thwart U.S. Domination

NewsMax.com Vortex, September 1999 — China, Russia and three Central Asian states have pledged to promote a "multi-polar" world and thwart global domination by the United States.

Capping a two-day summit, presidents Jiang Zemin, Boris Yeltsin and their counterparts from Kyrgyzstan, Kazakhstan and Tajikistan signed a formal declaration pledging to fight separatism and religious extremism. Jiang said in a speech at the fourth summit of the five nations held in Bishkek, Kyrgyzstan, that they should mobilize resources to "fight destabilizing factors to regional security such as religious extremism, national separatism, international terrorism and other international criminal activities."

He gained support from the four leaders against "a unipolar world order," a reference to alleged expansionism by a Washington-led NATO.

The declaration said the five states opposed the use or threat of force not sanctioned by the United Nations Security Council in international situations.

— *South China Morning Post*

'Russia-China,' the New World Superpower

By Colonel Stanislav Lunev

NewsMax.com Vortex, September 1999 — Seminal change has taken place in the balance of world power, and scant notice has been paid to this dramatic shift. Russia and China, for decades hostile enemies, are moving ever closer to forming a political and military alliance to challenge the United States and the West. Fearing an aggressive NATO in the wake of the Yugoslavia campaign right on Russia's doorstep, the Russian Federation seeks new military allies as a counterbalance to NATO. So the Russian elites are now turning to "the great neighbor to the East," China, as the foremost among their new partners.

China also fears NATO. Chinese leaders believe that NATO, especially after NATO bombed its embassy in Belgrade, is not genuinely a defensive organization. Also, President Clinton's justification for the Kosovo war, the human rights issue, has been worrisome for China. What is to stop the Western countries from attacking China for human rights abuses in Tibet and other areas with large national minorities, numbering in all close to 100 million people?

"Democratic" Russia and totalitarian Red China are proving to be natural allies. Both have buried the hatchet on the ideological differences that imbued hatred between the two states for almost three decades. And China continues to present to the whole world the prospect of "real socialism — Chinese style" under the leadership of the Chinese Communist Party (CCP). This, no doubt, has impressed Kremlin leaders, who never really wanted democracy, just the riches that come with it.

Economic ties between the two neighbors are stronger than ever and are continuing to stablilize. The shelves of Russian stores are filled with Chinese food products and industrial goods, and trains full of high-quality Russian raw materials cross the Chinese border every day, supplying Chinese industry and increasing its competitiveness on the world market.

Internationally both countries are standing together. This became apparent during the Kosovo crisis when China and the Russian Federation officially condemned NATO and supported Yugoslavia's ruling regime. The military ties between Russia and China began to develop in 1992. These were, and still are, characterized by active military sharing on the highest levels, with ongoing cooperation in the development and production of the most modern weapons systems. The Russian-Chinese Intergovernmental Commission on Military and Technical Co-operation is working quite well. It meets twice a year in Moscow and Beijing under the leadership of the Russian first deputy prime minister and the deputy chairman of the Chinese Central Military Commission. The last session of the Intergovernmental Commission took place in June and was attended by then–Russian Prime Minister Sergei Stepashin, who, on June 9, met privately with Chinese delegation head Zhang Wannian, deputy chief of the Central Military Commission of the CCP. According to the Russian press, Mr. Stepashin made it absolutely clear that building close ties with China is one of Russia's top foreign-policy priorities and that the two nations desire a strong strategic partnership. Also, he told his Chinese visitor that he was born in China, where his father was an adviser to the Chinese military. "Meeting you, I am in a way continuing my father's work," he told Zhang.

Clearly President Yeltsin, who has favored an alliance with China to counter Washington, looks with favor on these developments. And the military relationship is moving at great speed. Both nations have already introduced compatible weapons systems. By integrating the weapons systems of the Russian Armed Forces and the Chinese People's Liberation Army, the two countries are rapidly becoming a superpower.

Moreover, cooperation between Russia and Red China is expanding in the area of intelligence, which is laying the foundation for a climate of mutual trust in Russian-Chinese relations, including guarantees of each other's mutual security. Thus, all the necessary conditions for a strategic alliance between the Russian Federation and Communist China are in place. And this alliance could threaten the United States and the West much sooner than anyone thinks.

President Yeltsin is set to visit China sometime this fall (the precise date is not yet established). Perhaps a formalized treaty may come of the visit, or a verbal agreement, which is sometimes more important to the Chinese leadership.

The West should be alarmed by such an alliance. The two countries together would combine the largest conventional army, the Chinese army, with the largest atomic arsenal, the Russian nuclear stockpile. Again, this menacing shift of power, which will likely be realized in the next few months, will have dramatic consequences for our civilization that cannot be overestimated.

Colonel Stanislav Lunev is the highest-ranking Soviet military spy ever to defect to the United States. He is a regular contributor to NewsMax.com and Vortex.

Norwegian Paper: Russia Has Secret Chemical Weapons Store

NewsMax.com Vortex, August 1999 — The Norwegian daily *Verdens Gang* reported that for the last 15 years Russia has been operating a secret plant for producing and storing deadly chemical weapons just east of Murmansk on the Kola Peninsula. After a two-year search, *Verdens Gang* said it had uncovered the site in a forest just over a mile from Murmansk in northeastern Russia.

"An explosion at this plant could lead to an environmental catastrophe in the Nordic region. There would be damage up to 150 miles away," *Verdens Gang* said

Norway, which shares a 120-mile border with Russia at the Kola Peninsula, said it had approached Russian authorities over the article.

—Russia Today

Russia Plans Mini-Nuclear Bombs

NewsMax.com Vortex, July 1999 — Missiles that can strike battlefield targets with low-yield nuclear warheads are being developed by Russia to bolster its impoverished conventional forces in the face of NATO expansion.

The project to perfect such "pinpoint" weapons is being carried out by the Atomic Energy Ministry, whose chief says that Russia needs to regain its superpower status without bankrupting the country. Missiles armed with warheads ranging in explosive force from a few dozen to hundreds of tons of TNT could be used to knock out tanks, divisional headquarters and other targets. "Pinpoint nuclear attacks won't start a global nuclear war," Viktor Mikhailkov, the Atomic Energy minister, told the Moscow daily newspaper *Sevodnya*.

Developing such weapons would not cost very much, said Pavel Felgenhauer, a Moscow-based defense expert. He said NATO expansion and the bombing of Yugoslavia had spurred official sanction for the project.

—London Telegraph

Russia Will Sell New, More Accurate Grenade Launcher

NewsMax.com Vortex, July 1999 — Russia will soon put a new, highly accurate grenade launcher on the international arms market.

The 30-mm AGC-30 automatic launcher can fire up to 400 rounds per minute and is 150 percent more effective than comparable Western weapons.

The new launcher could be sold to countries in the Asia-Pacific region, the Middle East and Latin America.

The weapon has a range of up to 1.06 miles and is designed for use against armored targets by infantry and airborne units.

— Associated Press

Scientist Claims Russia Has Built Uniquely Fast Submarine Missile

NewsMax.com Vortex, July 1999 — Itar-Tass reports that Russia has built a uniquely fast submarine missile that can travel at more than 230 miles per hour and penetrate the defenses of all the world's fleets.

The new missile is both fast and very effective from a technical and tactical point of view. It has a built-in target-seeking system that would foil all attempts to escape the missile or repel it.

"Our missile can deliver a quick and devastating blow to the hull of its target and can be used in very shallow water," he said. "When it is seeking its target, the missile operates with its engines off," he said.

— *Agence France Presse*

Russians Finalize Test on New Generation Anti-AWACS Missile

NewsMax.com Vortex, July 1999 — Russia is finalizing tests on an advanced missile air defense system which experts say will have ballistic missiles and the U.S.-built AWACS early warning aircraft in its sights.

The S-400 system, due for delivery to the Moscow district air defense forces by year's end, can "effectively destroy all existing and future air attack systems," military experts said.

Some U.S. senators rate the Russian technology so highly that they have urged the Pentagon to buy the S-300 to replace the United States' own Patriot anti-missile system.

—Agence France Presse

Russia Develops Precision Air Bomb

NewsMax.com Vortex, July 1999 — Russia has developed a precision air bomb, said Yevgeny Shakhidzhanov, director general of the state-owned research and development enterprise Region, a leading company in precision weapons design. He said that Russian scientists had designed several generations of precision weapons with a high combat performance.

"One of the most modern ones, having no direct foreign analogues, can hit pinpoint [small-size] targets 'on the bull's eye'."

"The presence of such a warhead provides a pilot with the possibility to work on the 'drop-and-forget' principle, which is very important in escaping from the adversary's air defense system," Shakhidzhanov said.

—Itar-Tass

Russia Admits Famine Was Phony

NewsMax.com Vortex, July 1999 — There is no real need for Western food aid to Russia. The U.S. and European Union food aid to Russia will deal a tough blow to the country's agriculture, Professor Yevgeniya Serova, president of the Agrarian and Food Economy Center in the Institute of Economic Problems in a Transition Period, told Interfax.

It was obvious as early as last fall that asking the West for food aid was a mistake, because food stores have proved to be sufficient and there was no deficiency in the winter, she said. The import of grain as food aid will add up to 20 percent and meat will equal 11 percent of the average annual amounts of sales. Because the supplies did not begin arriving until the end of March, the fraction of aid in the amount of sales in the coming three months will be much above the average and will make it hard for Russian producers to sell their goods, Serova said.

"Foreign supplies will deliver an equally devastating blow to the grain market and to Russian grain producers," she said. Large-scale imports of grain began exactly when Russian producers had finished sowing and selling the remaining grain to empty the stores for the next harvest, Serova said. State Statistics Committee data show that the stores of marketable grain from last year amount to 2 million to 4 million tonnes [metric tons]. The figures, however, have to be revised and increased by at least 5 million tonnes, because the actual harvest in 1998 was larger than the official 47.8 million tonnes. "This confirms that there was no real need for centralized supplies of foreign grain," Serova said.

—Interfax

Russia Mobilizes, America Sleeps

By J. R. Nyquist and Christopher Ruddy

NewsMax.com Vortex, April 1999 — Bill Clinton's use of NATO forces to bomb Yugoslavia could trigger global war.

Before arriving on a state visit this month, Chinese Premier Zhu Rongji hinted that the crisis in Kosovo could lead to a world war. At the same time, Russia — a longtime ally of the Serbs — has begun a large-scale mobilization of its military forces.

While NATO countries are engaging in military operations, not one Western country is mobilizing for a larger war, as is Russia.

The New Strategic Partnership of Russia and China

NATO's soporific reaction to Russia's mobilization should also be viewed, not in the context of the Yugoslavia bombing, but in the broader context of the new China-Russia relationship — one that has dramatically altered the balance of power in the world.

In November 1998, Russia and China officially formed a "strategic partnership." According to the official Chinese news agency, this partnership is meant to challenge the "perceived global dominance of the U.S." In plain English, the primary enemy Russia and China plan to fight is the United States and its allies.

Together, Russia and China have the world's most powerful military, including over 30,000 nuclear weapons, armies of 6 million men with hundreds of battle-ready combat divisions, and thousands of tanks. Their new alliance should have rung warning bells throughout the world. Instead the Western media, Clinton and other Western leaders have ignored it, continuing to insist that Russia and China are our "friends."

While Clinton Diddles, Russia and China Prepare for War

In recent months, Russia and China have jointly demilitarized their 2,500-mile border. Three hundred Russian combat units were withdrawn from the Chinese frontier. A similar number of Chinese units were withdrawn.

China has also been rapidly building up its ballistic missile forces opposite Taiwan — forces that could be used against the U.S. military in the Far East. An attack against Taiwan could come at any time. Carl Ford of the Heritage Foundation, testifying before the Senate Foreign Relations Committee on March 25, said that the Chinese People's Liberation Army (PLA) has changed its military strategy from one of a slowly developed assault and blockade against Taiwan, to "more intense, quick-hitting attacks using ballistic missiles."

For many years, Russian military theory has held that ballistic missile weapons can be used to accelerate attacks, allowing for rapid victories over powerful opponents. The Chinese missile buildup together with its shift in military strategy suggests that China's generals have fallen under the spell of Russian military theory.

At the same time, the Russian units moved off the Chinese border are now free to threaten Europe.

As the NATO bombing began, Russia talked of moving heavy bombers and tactical nuclear weapons into Belarus, the traditional invasion route from Russia to Europe.

Still, NATO is oblivious to the tremendous shift in the global balance of power caused by the new Russia-China military alliance.

North Korea Joins the Russia-China Axis

There are strong indications that the Russia-China alliance also includes other sworn enemies of the West, including the North Korean military dictatorship. During the Korean War, tens of thousands of Chinese troops fought against the U.S. in support of the North Korean dictatorship, and China continues to be North Korea's principal ally. It is virtually unthinkable that the North Koreans would launch a new war against South Korea or the West without Chinese approval and support.

In the past year, North Korea has become increasingly bellicose, repeatedly threatening to launch nuclear weapons against U.S. cities if we interfere with their activities on the Korean Peninsula. In just the last month, Korea has also deployed a new three-stage missile capable of hitting most U.S. cities.

A major obstacle in any war launched by North Korea is America's ally, Japan. According to the nationally circulated Japanese newspaper *Sankei*, on March 23, North Korea used a naval diversion to cover the insertion "dozens" of special operations commandos into Japan. According to unidentified sources, these North Korean infiltrators are trained in the sabotage of trains, bridges, and communications.

Such a move by the North Koreans could mean that an attack by North Korea against the South is imminent.

American Forces Spread Thin and Vulnerable to Russian or Chinese Aggression

The bulk of front-line American combat troops are now dispersed abroad. As the Balkans conflict escalates even further with the likely introduction of NATO ground forces, the West is ill prepared to defend South Korea, Taiwan, or even America.

The NATO blitz against Yugoslavia is already sapping U.S. military strength needed in the Middle East to check Saddam Hussein. If war were to intensify in the Balkans, or if war broke out in Korea, with our current commitment in Iraq, America doesn't have the resources to cope.

The logic of this is apparent to our enemies, and could well be exploited to inflict a major defeat on American forces in one or two hot spots simultaneously.

Still, the main threat to America is Russia, which now has more nuclear weapons than every other nation on earth combined.

For the past three months NewsMax.com has been sounding the alarm about growing war preparations against the West by a new Russia-China axis. The very timing of the Russian-Chinese alliance — when U.S. forces are at a low — is extremely ominous.

But the establishment media have ignored this story. Now NATO's attack against Yugoslavia has provoked bitter condemnation from Russia and China and the military threat is apparent for all to see.

Preparing the Russian People for War

As we reported in Newsmax.com four months ago, before it would be politically possible for the Russians to launch a war against the West, the Russian people would first have to be psychologically prepared for war. Clinton's war on Yugoslavia has provided precisely the stimulus needed to create massive war hysteria among the Russian people.

Recently, hundreds of furious Russian demonstrators marched through Moscow calling for Russia to go to war against NATO. One banner said: "It's time to bomb the military bases of the United States." That banner becomes much more ominous when you realize that the demonstration was either sponsored by the Russian government or at least had its tacit approval.

Equally ominous was the singling out of U.S. military bases, the first-strike target in any war against the West, essential for destroying America's retaliatory nuclear capability.

'Clinton Has Single-Handedly Revived the Cold War'

The sentiment expressed by Russian war protesters isn't just the opinion of a few extremists. A recent opinion survey found that in the wake of NATO bombing of their traditional allies, the Serbs, an incredible 64 percent of all Russians now believe that NATO intends to attack Russia.

Russian officials have also issued increasingly ominous pronouncements against America and the West. Foreign Minister Igor Ivanov spoke of "new tasks" for Russia's military. Defense Minister Igor Sergeyev likened the crisis to "a whirlpool which is drawing more countries into it." Former Russian Premier Gorbachev said, "Clinton has managed to single-handedly revive the Cold War."

Russia Prepares for War

Obsessed with the carnage in Kosovo, NATO appears to be oblivious to the fact Russia has been engaging in a massive military mobilization.

In the two weeks since NATO launched its offensive against Yugoslavia:

• The Russian Defense Ministry began an enlarged draft, calling up 168,776 men from the ages of 18 to 27.

• The ministry recruited over 60,000 Russian "volunteers" to fight NATO troops in Serbia. On April 6, the first Russian volunteers arrived in the Serbian town of Novi Sad.

• It threatened to move tactical nuclear weapons and heavy bombers forward into Belarus — Russia's highway to NATO.

• It dispatched key elements of Russia's Northern fleet, including the aircraft cruiser Admiral Kuznetsov and the newly commissioned Peter the Great, the largest ballistic missile cruiser ever built.

Vice Admiral Popov, commander of the Northern Fleet, told Itar-Tass the Northern Fleet is "ready to fulfill any order of the supreme command to defend the interests of Russia."

The Northern Fleet has more ballistic missile submarines than the entire U.S. Navy.

• On March 30, Russia sent a battle group of over 20 warships to sea from its Pacific Fleet. Included in the fleet were ground forces from Russia's Far Eastern Military District.

• Russia dispatched ships from the Black Sea Fleet — including a missile cruiser, two anti-submarine warfare frigates, and support ships. A Russian reconnaissance ship has already entered the Mediterranean.

• Russian TV displayed pictures of ballistic missiles being loaded on cruisers in the Black Sea.

• Russia announced the successful launch of a ballistic missile during exercises of its Northern Fleet.

Despite these clear war preparations, Russian news agencies continue to repeat the Big Lie that Russia has no plans to get involved in military action in Yugoslavian war.

If that's true, why all the war preparations? How have the supposedly "economically desperate" Russians been able to mobilize so many naval ships and combat troops so quickly?

Russia's Pattern of Deception

Russia's growing preparation for war during the Kosovo crisis suggests a massive pattern of deception, which is being ignored by the clueless Western media and Clinton. This pattern of deception is just the most recent and blatant example of how Russia has been talking peace while preparing for war against the West. How else do you explain this behavior from a friend and ally of America:

• Russia continues to maintain the world's largest arsenal of nuclear weapons — over 30,000 — the overwhelming majority targeted against the West.

• During the past two years, Russia has engaged in several mock nuclear war exercises against the United States. These exercises have included the use of rockets as well as naval and airborne forces to wipe America from the map.

• For the past 18 months, Russia has been moving its nuclear weapons onto naval ships. Naval ships are considered to be less vulnerable to retaliation in a nuclear war.

• This past December, Russia's Strategic Rocket Forces deployed a regiment of state-of-the-art Topol-M missiles targeted against the West. These missiles are now rolling off Russian production lines and are more sophisticated than anything in America's arsenal.

• In January, Russia put its nuclear forces—strategic rockets, naval and air—under a unified command — essential for a coordinated first strike against the West.

• Russia appears to be hoarding food, fuel, gold, and other commodities — an essential preparation for a major war. Despite claims of poverty and famine, Russia is stockpiling millions of tons of food and urging its people to buy gold. It is interesting to note that the Kosovo crisis began just as the last shipments of billions of dollars of Western food aid reached Russia.

• Russia has built the world's largest network of fallout shelters — complete underground cities, some as large as Washington, D.C.

War Preparations in Russia Have Been Going On for Years

In order to mobilize their people against the West, and prepare them for the destruction it will bring, Russian leaders know that they must create massive hatred of the West.

The first step occurred during the summer of 1998 when Russia defaulted on its foreign loans, resulting in massive bank and business failures, bread lines throughout the country, and incredible suffering.

On the face of it, it made no sense for the Russian government to default, since just weeks before the default, the International Monetary Fund had given Moscow some $5 billion in new foreign aid. (According to the *Wall Street Journal*, these funds mysteriously "disappeared into the offshore accounts of Russia's oligarchy.")

Why would any regime in its right mind subject its own people to such massive suffering when it had the resources to prevent it?

The likely answer: Russia's leaders knew that "evil Western capitalists" — not themselves — would be blamed. Indeed, as a result of the 1998 Russian economic meltdown, millions of Russians demanded that communism be restored and corrupt Jewish tycoons be sent packing. The Russian economic meltdown, quite possibly engineered by Moscow, was in effect a bloodless coup that did more than any other single event to revive hatred of capitalism and anti-Semitism, and again set Russia on the path of tyranny and confrontation with the West.

Creating a New Soviet Empire

With Russia's economy in shambles, Russian leaders should have been preoccupied with domestic problems. Instead, the primary focus of Russia's energies and resources has been creating a new Soviet Empire.

Last November, China and Russia announced a new global alliance. Their intelligence services now share information. Their high commands have organized cooperative working groups.

The new Russian-Chinese Alliance represents the greatest shift in the balance of power since World War II, yet the Western press has virtually ignored it. Chinese leaders speak more and more openly about war with the West. In January, Chinese President Jiang Zemin told the

People's Liberation Army to get ready for two things: First, nuclear world war; and second, to suppress uprisings inside China.

Anti-American Hatred Is Reaching New Heights

In Russia, the government doesn't have to worry about uprisings. Thanks to Bill Clinton's bombing campaign in Yugoslavia, the Russians have rallied to the Kremlin.

Consider what Clinton has done: For the first time in its history, NATO has attacked a sovereign state, in direct violation of the NATO Charter, which forbids an offensive war against other countries.

The result of that attack, encouraged by the American leadership, may well be the collapse of the NATO alliance and the end of American leadership in Western Europe, particularly in Italy and Greece. At the very least, Clinton's use of NATO as an offensive tool of war has shifted public opinion against the U.S. in Russia, Eastern Europe, and much of the Third World.

Understandably, since both Russia and Serbia are Slavic nations with strong historical, religious and cultural ties, there is real anger among the Russian populace against the NATO bombing. After all, how would Americans feel if Russia bombed London because of the strife in Northern Ireland? Or if Russia bombed Canada or Mexico? NATO's bombing of Yugoslavia proves to the average Russian that NATO is an offensive military organization whose ultimate aim is the destruction of Russia — which is what they have been told by their leaders for generations.

Clinton's War Against Yugoslavia: A 'Royal Gift' to Communists and Kremlin Insiders

The present Russian anger over the NATO bombing is, as *Izvestia* called it, a "royal gift" to the communists and Kremlin insiders — some of whom have publicly advocated war with the West. There is growing pressure on even moderate Russian leaders to take "some action" against NATO to restore Russia's glory and pride.

Russia's Duma passed a resolution 366–4 that declared that NATO "aggression" is "a threat to Russia's national security" and called on the Russian government to begin war mobilization. Russia's foreign secretary Igor Ivanov said while Russia had no immediate military plans, it was "holding extreme measures in reserve."

As the *Christian Science Monitor* reports, Russian nationalists now repeat a mantra, "What is happening in Serbia today will happen in Russia tomorrow."

Itar-Tass reports that leading Russian intellectuals have formed a new movement called "Against World War III" to combat growing war hysteria in Russia.

Russian Leaders Consider Nuclear War Inevitable

Colonel Stanislav Lunev, the highest-ranking GRU officer ever to defect from Russia, has stated that the Russian General Staff considers nuclear war with America to be inevitable.

Lunev writes, "I spent 30 years preparing for war against America. Not a war against China. Not a war against Europe. A war against America."

In an interesting footnote, almost immediately after the NATO bombing campaign began, Russia canceled its cooperation with America on the Y2K computer virus. This cooperation is vital as the year 2000 rapidly approaches, and by rejecting U.S. help suggests the Russians have other plans and have no intention of ever opening up their defense systems to outside technicians — unlike the U.S. under Clinton, which has allowed Russian and Chinese military agents to roam our top-secret defense labs virtually at will.

'Wag the Dog' Global War?

As conservative commentator Lwellen Rockwell points out, Clinton's foreign policy can be summarized by a single word: Bombs!

Clinton's popularity dips and he bombs Iraq. Ken Starr issues a report recommending that Clinton be impeached, and he bombs Sudan and Afghanistan. The Senate prepares to vote on impeachment charges, and Clinton again bombs Iraq. Chinagate — Clinton's cynical selling of U.S. military secrets in exchange for campaign contributions — threatens to break in the popular press, and Clinton bombs Yugoslavia.

As in the movie *Wag the Dog*, whenever Clinton gets in trouble, he bombs someone to distract attention from his own scandals and crimes. Clinton's foreign policy reads like a script for a Hollywood B film.

Personal and political scandals have enveloped Bill Clinton's presidency since his first days in office. Just months after becoming president, he launched a bloody attack on the Branch Davidians in Waco, which ended with the immolation of some 80 innocent men, women and children. He blatantly used the military to "wag the dog" on the eve of the Senate impeachment vote with a cynical bombing of Iraq.

Those who claim, that with impeachment behind him, Clinton has no real reason to wag the dog by bombing Yugoslavia are dead wrong. Supreme egotist that he is, Clinton is consumed with remaining popular and securing his place in history — both of which are threatened by continuing public attention to previous and newly revealed scandals, like Chinagate. Some of those scandals could even have legally devastating consequences for Clinton and Hillary personally, after his presidency ends.

The Lewinsky scandal continues to percolate, and Monica has been on a high-profile book tour. Now a new and very serious rape allegation hangs over Clinton's head — and there could be more such allegations forthcoming. New revelations come out almost daily about Clinton's treasonous aid to the Chinese war machine, in exchange for campaign contributions.

Despite Clinton's claims to the contrary, no vital U.S. interests are at stake in Kosovo, and no NATO members have been attacked by Serbia. In fact, by attacking Yugoslavia, Clinton has created precisely the outrages he claimed he was acting to prevent:

• Mass murder of Albanian Serbs;
• Shoring up the power of the tyrant Milosevic;
• Destabilizing surrounding countries;
• Expanding the war — with the introduction of Russian "volun teers"— beyond Yugoslavia;
• Weakening NATO;
• Killing of innocent men, women and children in Yugoslavia.

Not to mention the flirtation with global war. By wagging the dog with a very hot war in Europe, Clinton has managed — for now — to bury growing accusations of treason against him. Clinton may go down in history as the first U.S. president willing to risk — or cause — global war to ensure his own popularity.

How Clinton Is Pushing Russia Toward War

The Russian people view the NATO bombing of Yugoslavia as almost a direct attack on their nation. American refusals to allow Russia to broker a peaceful settlement have led to further Russian war hysteria.

As the American-led assault began, Russian Prime Minister Yevgeny Primakov, an old-line KGB general, went to Belgrade and hours later had a peace deal. Waving a scrap of paper in his hand, he flew to Munich to meet with German Chancellor Schroeder. Germany is NATO's most important continental member. Germany and NATO rejected the offer. Russia, the peacemaker, was rebuffed by the Americans, the aggressors. So hostility grew in Russia.

Clinton's bombing of Yugoslavia encourages the most violent, extreme and anti-American factions in Russia. Russia's ailing leader and erstwhile U.S. friend, Boris Yeltsin, faces his own impeachment vote on April 15. He, too, desperately needs to wag the dog to distract attention from his own failures. His status weakened by NATO bombing, only after agreeing to oppose NATO and draft troops for Yugoslavia did Yeltsin partially recover his standing in the polls.

Will Russia Actually Go to War with the West?

Russian war preparations continue to accelerate.

When the Yugoslav crisis erupted, we were told that Russia's major fleets were going out to sea. A coincidence, the West was told. It has long been theorized that if Russia ever wanted to attack America, it would steer its ballistic missile submarines underneath its surface ships on their way to sea, making it difficult for U.S. sonar to detect the submarine deployment.

Once deployed, the submarines can sink to the bottom of the Atlantic and Pacific, where they can stay for months, quietly waiting for orders from the high command.

Convenience is joined by luck. Russia supposedly has no oil for its ships, one spokesman says. But miraculously, there's suddenly enough oil for its major fleets to engage in extensive maneuvers.

The Russians must have noted that their deployment causes no alarm from the West. After all, Russia is so weak it couldn't harm a fly — so the thinking goes. Russian spokesmen continually insist they have no plans to engage NATO militarily, but every action suggests a progressive mobilization for war.

So the Russians will continue mobilizing and gaining the advantage as America and the West sleeps. In Russia, hundreds of thousands of troops are called up. It will only take three months for the full conventional weight of the old Soviet army to be resurrected. It will have five times as many soldiers as the American Army.

Russia "has no intention of interfering in the current conflict around Yugoslavia," a government spokesman told Interfax. Meanwhile, Russia's leaders continually talk of war. They hint, they threaten, and they mobilize for it.

And good Republicans like Henry Kissinger, Donald Rumsfeld, Jeane Kirkpatrick and Senator McCain are actually calling for American ground troops to be sent into Serbia.

Those calling for a ground force in Yugoslavia — estimated to be at least 200,000 soldiers — are not considering the implications of such a move if a global war does break out. The NATO ground force would be vulnerable to a tactical nuclear strike and easily cut off from supply lines. Moreover, the continental U.S. would have no significant force to defend itself from invasion by China or Russia.

Such considerations and precautions are not being considered, because it is party time in the West. The Dow Jones rises past 10,000 as NATO bombs. The price of gold drops. People still plan their trips to Disney World instead of worrying about the nation's vulnerability to Russia's nuclear weapons.

There is no way to be certain if Russia will actually attack the United States, and there is one alternative plausible explanation of their actions: They may be getting ready for one big blackmail attempt, hopeful that Clinton will buckle under.

Instead of war, Russia could be preparing for global domination.

J. R. Nyquist is an expert on Russia.

Defector Warns of Russian War Plans

By Christopher Ruddy

NewsMax.com Vortex, February 1999 — Russia cannot threaten the United States. She is poor. She is weak. She is starving. She is in chaos. Think again, says Colonel Stanislav Lunev.

Colonel Lunev is the highest-ranking military intelligence officer ever to have defected from Russia. He did so in 1992, a year after the U.S.S.R. dissolved and Boris Yeltsin had come to power. At the time of his defection, Lunev was living in Washington with his wife, working a cover job as a journalist for Tass while doing his real job — spying on America.

Since Lunev was an officer in the GRU (Russian military intelligence), his spying related to military matters — gathering information on America's military plans, reporting on our vulnerabilities, devising special operations in the advent of war.

Last year, Lunev detailed just some of his activities in a new book he co-authored with Ira Winkler, *Through the Eyes of the Enemy: Russia's Highest-Ranking Military Defector Reveals Why Russia Is More Dangerous Than Ever* (NewsMax.com, 1-800-485-4345).

The book is a light read, with some sensational details about Russian plans to bring suitcase nuclear bombs into America and to use special forces to assassinate the president and congressional, military and other leaders during the initial phases of a war.

Lunev claims in *Through the Eyes of the Enemy* that Russian military leaders still view a war with the United States as "inevitable" and that the Cold War never really ended.

Save for some talk radio outlets and the Internet, Lunev's book received little media coverage. This comes as no surprise, since most Americans believe we won the Cold War. Russia is not a threat, most are convinced, and any suggestion that it is has to be written off as just paranoid jingoism.

Lunev is used to unfriendly receptions. When he did defect, higher-ups at the CIA and Pentagon did not accept what he had to say.

What he said was rather simple: Russia is continuing its old ways. The military is still preparing for war against the United States. A nuclear war.

In the era of fuzzy, warm feelings between the U.S. and Russia, American officials were not going to upset the apple cart no matter how much evidence Lunev offered.

In the intervening years, Russia has appeared to further disintegrate. Can she really be a threat? skeptics ask. Lunev most certainly has been proven wrong.

Lunev says think again. He retorts that Russia still retains a formidable military-industrial complex. She is one of the world's largest arms exporters. She makes quality products and delivers them on time.

Russia continues to build nuclear submarines, bombers, and missiles. Last year, President Yeltsin commissioned Peter the Great, the largest ballistic missile cruiser ever built by mankind. This past Christmas, Russia deployed a regiment of 10 Topol-M intercontinental ballistic missiles, missiles reportedly more sophisticated than anything we have.

Just this month, Russia unveiled her stealth bomber. The *New York Times* reports Russia continues to build huge underground bunkers, some as large as cities, in case of war. She also continues to build an arsenal of chemical and biological weapons. Russia's nuclear armory remains the world's largest. She continues testing her nuclear weapons.

Such facts demonstrate that Lunev is not to be dismissed.

Interview

QUESTION: Colonel Lunev, you were first and foremost a spy for Russia who posed as a journalist. In your book, you discuss the help you received from American journalists. How significant was the Russian penetration of the American press corps? How many American journalists were working for Russia?

ANSWER: In my book, I talk about myself. Keep this in mind, when I worked in Tass' Washington bureau, I had two colleagues from the KGB also working as agents.

So we had plenty of people undercover working as journalists. How many people they recruited? I don't know. But I can tell you that journalists, American journalists, and foreign journalists in this country were considered a major target. They were the same level of target as military, government personnel or Capitol Hill staff.

Q: When you say targets, you mean . . .?

A: Recruits.

Q: It has been acknowledged that the East German government had as many as 5,000 spies working for them in West Germany.

A: East German intelligence was very successful. Very successful. I don't know exactly how many people they recruited, but they were very successful. Not only in penetrations through western Germany and the European establishment, but through American institutions located in Western Europe.

Q: What do you think the degree of penetration is of the U.S. government by communist or former communist countries in the CIA, the FBI, and State Department?

A: It could be hundreds. But I don't know the exact number.

Recently, the FBI admitted there were a couple of hundred open cases of espionage they were investigating. These are the ones they know about. So you can multiply this number by many times to guess the number of people who are working as spies who the government does not know about.

Q: You were not only a spy but a military intelligence officer. Your work involved developing military plans, and learning of other countries' plans. What did you study when you were in military schools in Russia?

A: We had a lot of special subjects we needed to learn, including military science. We learned basic ways of commanding armies and how to conduct military operations.

Q: How much of your training and education was geared toward fighting a nuclear war?

A: All of our educational process and training was connected to the actual fulfillment of military plans in time of a nuclear war.

Q: Your book suggests that the whole Russian military structure, the whole society during the Soviet era, was geared for a nuclear war, and that that has not changed under the new regime.

A: Yes. The Soviet plan was the use of strategic forces to destroy strategic targets in America and the West, followed by the use of nuclear and conventional forces. This was the Soviet way, and the Russian military still thinks the same way today. They are much more dangerous now, because the Russian military is relying more on their nuclear weapons.

Q: What about a first strike on the United States?

A: The likely plan does not include use of missiles first. First, the

Russians would use their special operations forces, special troops, inside the United States to destroy targets like communications facilities, airfields, command centers, and other targets that might be difficult to destroy with a missile attack.

Suitcase nuclear bombs at strategic locations are just one small part of their arsenal. I mentioned this in my book, and I have been so surprised that the American public is so interested in this. Why? This is not something unusual for Russian military plans.

Q: One of your jobs here in the U.S. as a spy was to look for locations to hook up these suitcase nukes to electric power sources.

A: Its not really necessary to have an electric power source, because the devices can work on a battery. But not for very long.

Q: Are there such bombs in the United States already?

A: It's possible.

Q: How soon could this war come?

A: The Russian conventional forces are not in a state of readiness. Their rocket and nuclear forces are. This war scenario could be in place by the request of the Russian government in a short time.

Russia is a country on the edge of social explosion. The total decline of living conditions — human, industrial, political, social — and now the financial crisis. This could lead to war.

Q: It's dangerous because the Russians may consider their only option is to use the "gun." At the same time, the United States has been destroying its nuclear forces.

A: Yes! I am sorry, but let me ask you, "What's going on in this country?" Right now, the Russians are engaging in criminal extortion for money. This is the same method criminals use. Every other day, in conversations with Western leaders, the Russians are saying, "Show me the money, or something dangerous will happen in my country with tens of thousands of nuclear warheads." It's extortion.

There could be an explosion, a catastrophe. It could happen in Russia, and somebody like a major general or a one-star general or colonel will come to power without any international experience. If such a person would come to power, pushing the nuclear button would be no problem.

Q: If that happened, how long would it take for a strong leader to get the conventional forces ready if he wanted to start a nuclear war against the United States?

A: A few months. You have to remember that the Russians have the same number of submarines, nuclear missile submarines, ships, bombers, fighters, tanks, and the like as they did at the height of Soviet military power.

I know that the Russian military downsizing was connected with only army divisions, and these divisions could be rebuilt in weeks or months.

Q: China also is moving closer to Russia. China has the largest conventional army in the world. What danger does that pose?

A: If China and Russia would ally in a war against the United States, with Russia providing the strategic weapons and China the troops, they could begin the war tomorrow.

Q: Recent press reports state that the Russians have been helping the Chinese develop ballistic missile technology.

A: I would say that actually the Chinese missile industry was created by the Soviet Union, by Soviet specialists, by Soviet technology, and by education of Chinese engineers and scientists in Soviet institutions. So the Soviet Union, let's say, played the major role in the establishment of the Chinese missile industry. But this was in the '50s before the Sino-Russian split.

This split was healed in the late 1980s, and any ideological obstacle for helping China was removed. China, of course, pays real money to Russia for this technology.

Q: Well, it does seem that there are some steps the Russians are taking that suggest war preparations. They are building a huge underground complex in the Ural Mountains. Have you heard about that?

A: You ask about Yamantau Mountain. Well, this is a huge underground city that could be used in a time when many Russian cities are destroyed, but the military and political elite will survive and live until our planet will try to restore itself.

Q: The American military is downsizing because there is no Warsaw Pact anymore. We have let down our defenses. If the Russians were to launch a first strike, a surprise attack against the United States, they could wipe us almost off the map. European countries like Britain and France have small nuclear arsenals. If the U.S. does not exist, Russia rules the world, because after an attack, she

will still have a huge nuclear arsenal.

A: Yes.

Q: Is it possible that the Russian communists planned this? That the Russian intelligence agencies and the military establishment said, "Hey, if we give up Eastern Europe, if we throw open the economy, democratize, allow the country to seem in chaos, the Americans will let down their guard. We can get them to reduce their strategic nuclear forces, and they won't think of us as a threat."

A: I believe there was a plan. I cannot prove it to you. It is my hunch this is what happened. This is based on my experiences, things I saw going on. Because now, six years later, it looks like it was planned, but at that time we didn't have any idea that it's possible to plan all this activity.

Q: Well, it seems to me the most important information you have is that the Cold War isn't over, that the Russian military believes inevitably that there will be a war with the U.S.

A: In April of 1998, Russia used its strategic bombers in an exercise against the United States. These exercises were organized for the future war against America. Before that, there were several nuclear exercises.

In the fall of 1998, President Yeltsin commissioned Peter the Great, the worlds largest nuclear missile cruiser. They have been doing ground forces exercises. Airborne force exercises. All of these exercises are being conducted for a reason, for the future war against America.

Q: What do you think are the chances — I know this is highly speculative — that there will be a nuclear global war between Russia and the United States within the next five years?

A: I need to repeat myself. In a time of social explosion in Russia, nobody can exclude the possibility that it will begin. Preparations for this nuclear war are now being made in Russia.

Q: Would the Russian people support such a war?

A: In recent years and times, the feeling of the Russian people toward America has begun to change. The Russian people believe the United States is giving money to the corrupt Russian government, which never helps the ordinary Russians. America has identified herself so strongly with Yeltsin, and now Yeltsin and his government are viewed as corrupt.

There is a perception that America, who destroyed the old Soviet Union, is again trying to destroy Russia.

Q: A former American general, Benjamin Partin, suggested that after the Allies had beaten Hitler in World War II, if the new German government was filled with ex-Nazis in the Cabinet, ex-Nazis in the military, ex-Nazis in private businesses, would we believe we won? General Partin notes that in todays Russia, ex-Communists, many high-level Soviet officials, run most of the government and private businesses. Most of the republics are run by former Communists.

A: Well, almost all, yes. General Partin is correct in his concerns.

Q: It appears that in 1917, the Communists that came to power in Russia were not much more than organized-crime figures.

A: Yes, they are the same. They are together. There is no difference.

Q: It seems this permanent government will be always seeking domination, whether official or through organized-crime means.

A: And you are right. But how will you sell this idea to America?

Q: You can't sell it to America, because they believe all the bad guys just gave up with the end of the Cold War. One day it was all over, we won. End of story.

A: You should know this did not happen in one day, like on Christmas Day of 1991, when Gorbachev dissolved the Soviet Union. A long time before this, the KGB began to transfer Communist Party money to private accounts under the names of different people in Western countries.

At the same time, the KGB moved some of its very experienced people, including generals, sometimes four-star generals, into the new private businesses being formed in Russia. For example, former KGB agents joined financial and industrial groups. Since they had intelligence backgrounds, they could be placed in various positions, like vice president in charge of personnel or foreign operations.

The KGB established these private accounts, controlled by its own people using money from the CCCP — the Communist Party assets — for the future, for the future restoration of communism.

Q: The power of organized crime in Russia developed so quickly. What role did the KGB play in its rise to power?

A: The KGB and the old-line communists needed to use criminals in this phase because who had experience in money laundering? Who has connections with drug cartels? With other organized-crime groups in Western countries? The KGB worked closely with these groups and actually provided passports and permission for criminals to travel abroad.

Organized crime in Russia has existed for a long time, as long as anyone can remember. Yet the criminals never played any sufficient or important role in Russian or Soviet society until the so-called reforms were begun under Gorbachev.

Q: You mentioned earlier that the KGB transferred funds outside Russia for the future restoration of the Communist Party.

A: Yes, for the future.

Q: So people are thinking in terms of restoring the Communist Party there?

A: Yes, I think that they made plans to bring back the Communists. The Politburo accomplished this at the end of the 1980s and the early 90s when millions, if not billions, of dollars from Communist Party accounts were transferred by KGB officers with assistance and help from criminals.

Russia Aids Iranian Weapons Program

NewsMax.com Vortex, February 1999 — The Mossad estimates that up to 10,000 Russian experts are assisting Iran's biological, chemical and nuclear weapons programs, according to the newsletter *Foreign Report*, a London-based newsletter.

The government's dissatisfaction with Moscow's unreadiness to block leaks of weapons technologies to Iran has led to a chill in defense relations between Israel and Russia, defense sources said.

According to *Foreign Report*, Israel was attempting to put pressure on Russia by postponing a trip there by Defense Minister Yitzhak Mordechai, whose visit was to have coincided with the resumption of a defense cooperation agreement.

— www.jpost.com

War Preparations Continue in Russia: Nuclear Arms Put Under Unified Command

China's Clenched Fist: Premier Calls on Country to Prepare for War

By Jeffrey R. Nyquist

NewsMax.com Vortex, February 1999 — All around the globe, a pattern of belligerence toward the United States and her allies is emerging: from the Korean Peninsula down through the Spratly Islands near the Philippines, enveloping Taiwan, then reappearing in Central Asia, the Middle East, and the Balkans.

The rhetoric from Beijing, Moscow, Belgrade, Pyongyang, and Baghdad suggests possible coordination. Forward military deployments by China, Iraq, Serbia, and Russia, together with sinister construction projects and major troop movements, have been noted in East Asia, the Pacific, and the Middle East.

In the past month, numerous developments have taken place in Russia that suggest war preparations:

Russia Creates Unified Command of Nuclear Weapons

In January, the Russian General Staff announced that all of the country's nuclear forces — Strategic Rocket Forces, submarine-based weaponry, and nukes on their strategic bombers — would now be placed under one command.

ANALYSIS: This development was widely reported in Russia and by the Associated Press. The AP story indicated bafflement that Russia, in the middle of economic problems, would be reorganizing its armed forces, especially the nuclear forces. But this development fits the thesis that Russia is, in fact, preparing for war.

In war, the principle of "unity of command" is considered crucial. By moving to unify nuclear command, the Russian armed forces can now better coordinate a nuclear surprise attack involving all nuclear service branches, obviating the friction of interservice rivalry. In a strictly defensive situation, centralization of the nuclear forces is unnecessary, even counterproductive. Decentralization is better for defense. However, this is not true for attack. Coordinating an effective, disarming first strike requires a high degree of control and coordination, which a unified nuclear command facilitates. This move, coupled with the fact Russia has been moving its strategic warheads onto submarines in the past six months, should be viewed with alarm.

Top Generals Resign From Strategic Rocket Forces

In the second half of January, the commander of Russia's Strategic Rocket Forces, Col.-General Vladimir Yakovlev, resigned his post together with his three chief deputies, allegedly throwing Russia's nuclear forces into disarray.

After taking this unprecedented action, Yakovlev stated that the reason for his resignation was a personality conflict with General Sokolov, the commander of Russia's early warning service.

ANALYSIS: According to Colonel Stanislav Lunev, ranking defector from the Main Intelligence Directorate of the Russian General Staff, Yakovlev's retirement was planned some time ago.

"They already have civilian jobs waiting for them," Lunev said. "There will be no disruption of the rocket forces."

Lunev believes the resignations stem from the reorganization of Russia's nuclear forces under a single chief, but he nonetheless admits that Yakovlev and his deputies are hard-liners and careerists. After closer analysis, it is difficult to argue that they would resign in protest over a measure they themselves long advocated, as they were supporters and proteges of Defense Minister Igor Sergeyev, the man most responsible for the reorganization of the nuclear forces.

There are serious inconsistencies here that must not be passed over. Why did Yakovlev and his deputies resign? Has a secret nuclear command center been established? A centralized nuclear command would have to create alternate command posts in several bunkers, with many capable general officers at the ready.

Were these resignations made in protest over the reorganization of Russia's nuclear forces, or were they part of the reorganization itself?

Russia's Northern Fleet Put on Alert

When President Clinton bombed Iraq in December, Moscow

put its Northern Fleet on alert. **This curious move, which makes no sense in terms of reacting to a Middle East crisis, and coming at a supposed time of reduced superpower tensions, has serious implications that ought to be explored.**

ANALYSIS: Prior to a surprise nuclear attack on the United States, it is believed the Russians would attempt to put most of their nuclear missile submarines to sea. Therefore, the question that must be asked is whether the Russians used the alert to deploy their missile submarine forces. Despite what some analysts might say, any large-scale deployment to sea is a red flag.

The Northern Fleet contains the lion's share of Russia's naval strike capability, and any alerting of that fleet needs to be carefully scrutinized. In fact, any Russian fleet alert should be answered by a comparable U.S. fleet alert. It is alarming in and of itself that the United States did not respond in kind.

Russians Continue Nuke Testing

The Russians have abandoned the agreement to forgo underground nuclear tests. They have admitted to testing three tactical nuclear warheads in recent weeks. These are part of a new generation of tactical nuclear weapons that the Russian armed forces have developed.

In addition, during the period of the agreed suspension of underground tests, there have been suspicious earthquakes in Russia with signatures characteristic of strategic nuclear tests.

ANALYSIS: Nuclear readiness requires the occasional testing of nuclear warheads. New, more efficient weapons must be tested before they are deployed to the armed forces. The United States has not tested its nuclear stockpile in several years, while the Russians have been testing their weapons.

The importance of tactical nuclear weapons to the Russians lies in the fact that these cannot be kept track of by arms control specialists. The START agreements require Russia to destroy the bulk of its strategic nuclear stockpiles, which cannot be hidden.

But tactical nuclear weapons have a number of advantages over strategic ones. First and foremost, they are more efficient in terms of their use of nuclear fuel. Also, tactical nuclear weapons can be packed into

ICBMs, bombers, fighter-bombers, or artillery units, making them the most versatile type of nuclear weapon.

Last, but not least, tactical nuclear weapons can be delivered as a cluster, which is a more effective means for destroying large urban areas, and obviates the terms of the START treaties, which call for the elimination of multiple independently targeted re-entry vehicles (MIRVs).

The Russians Lie About Their Readiness

The chief of the Russian General Staff, Anatoly Kvashnin, a hardened professional known for his stony silence, now claims that Russia has halved its western military deployments, reducing its strike capability near Finland. On January 11, Kvashnin stated: "We have extremely low defense readiness."

ANALYSIS: These are curious words from an ordinarily obsessive, secretive, and paranoid functionary. Such a pronouncement is uncharacteristic and probably deceptive. Throughout history, when Russian forces have been weak or unready, no Russian general officer would dare to acknowledge the fact. Such acknowledgment, under normal conditions, would lead to immediate dismissal.

Russian military doctrine pays close attention to the dictum of Sun Tzu, the ancient Chinese strategist, who said: "All warfare is based on deception. Hence, when able to attack, we must seem unable; when using our forces, we must seem inactive; when we are near, we must make the enemy believe we are away. . . . Hold out baits to entice the enemy. Feign disorder, and crush him."

If Russia is really moving troops off its border with Europe, as well as troops away from its Chinese border, where are the troops being relocated?

Unprecedented Slaughter of Russian Fur Animals

Russia and Belarus have large collective farms dedicated to the breeding of polar foxes and minks. Russia is the world's largest fur consumer, annually buying 40 percent of the furs produced worldwide. But now, Russian officials claim that demand has stalled, and they are slaughtering their fox and mink herds because they cannot afford to feed them.

Slaughter is normal at the onset of winter, of course, but this slaughter is of unprecedented numbers of animals. At the same time,

Russia is importing fur from China, as well as coats, jackets, and boots. If Russian demand has stalled and the market for furs is flooded, why the imports?

ANALYSIS: Wherever we see an inconsistency in Russia's economy, we have to think twice. In World War II, Russian spies infiltrated all of the sheep ranches in Europe. Their mission: to watch and see if sheep were being sheared for 5 million sheepskin coats. Soviet military intelligence reasoned that if Hitler intended to invade Russia, he would need heavy winter clothing for his troops. The shearing of the sheep would be a dead giveaway.

Unfortunately for Hitler, he did not make the 5 million coats. And though he caught Soviet military intelligence off guard, his troops in Russia suffered frostbite and amputations once winter began. In fact, one of the medals struck for German soldiers during 1941–42 was called "The Order of the Frozen Meat."

Logistical preparations are a necessary part of war. National leaders ignore such preparations at great peril. In this context, what are we to make of this huge increase in the production and importation of furs and uniform clothing in Russia?

While this activity could indicate Russian economic miscalculation, one has to wonder why the fur herds were increased to such a size to begin with. Since these fur farms are state-controlled, an increase in production suggests an increase in projected consumption. But as civilian consumption has remained steady, the obvious conclusion is that somebody in Moscow was anticipating a huge increase in the military's demand for winter clothing. With the aforesaid cover story of a collapsed market, Moscow might well mask a planned troop mobilization of very large dimensions. If Russia called up her reserves either before or after a nuclear exchange, she would need winter coats, boots, and headgear (even if the attack took place in warm weather).

Russia's soldiers may have to confront winter weather conditions in North America if Russian military doctrine is followed. This doctrine calls for an invasion of America. Always cognizant of history, the Russian General Staff is well aware of Hitler's mistake in World War II and would never repeat that mistake in World War III.

As Russia openly makes moves for war, its new partner, China, has been taking equally dramatic steps.

Chinese Premier Calls for Nuclear War Preparations

On January 8, as if to prepare his people for war, Chinese President Jiang Zemin laid out the mission of the People's Liberation Army in a speech: "We must resolutely safeguard the unity of the motherland and the nation's territorial integrity."

Unity, of course, is the war cry of the Communists against Taiwan. Jiang also warned that the Chinese People's Liberation Army must prepare itself for nuclear war.

Soon thereafter, China conducted military exercises in which Chinese nuclear forces practiced targeting American troops in the Far East.

At the same time, the People's Republic announced radical changes in military policy. The Chinese air force was placed on "offensive mode" as opposed to "defensive mode," and China's army doctrine was altered to one of global warfighting.

China has also begun centralizing the distribution of supplies for all branches of the military in what the official media call the biggest streamlining effort in 50 years. In this context, China's new "strategic partnership" with the Russian Federation takes on sinister ramifications. China is also backing North Korea in its dispute with the U.S. alliance.

ANALYSIS: China is making serious war preparations. This enhances China's options against Taiwan, South Korea, the Philippines, and Japan. There is every reason to believe, from these moves, that China will support North Korea if war should break out in the Far East. In the context of a renewed war, Taiwan would almost certainly be subject to blockade, possibly sparking a naval action between China and the U.S. This is a dangerous situation that China seems ready to welcome. (Also, China now supports Saddam Hussein in the U.N.)

China Seizes Spratly Islands

In the Far East, China has invaded the Spratly Islands, more than 800 miles from China yet 140 miles from the Philippines. Manila has expressed alarm that the People's Liberation Army is erecting gun and anti-aircraft emplacements on Mischief Reef.

The Chinese ambassador to the Philippines, Guan Dengming, insisted that China was merely constructing "shelters for fishermen." But a leading Philippine official countered this, saying: "We strongly believe a fortress is being built."

Philippine Defense Secretary Orlando Mercado stated that concrete buildings in the Spratlys "are beginning to look more like military structures rather than the so-called fishermen's refuge the Chinese claimed it to be." Mercado further accused China of bullying the Philippines, referring to recent Chinese moves as "a creeping invasion."

ANALYSIS: China's invasion of the Spratlys may not be aimed at the Philippines. The Spratlys lie across a key waterway that is essential to Taiwan. The concrete structures, aside from the anti-aircraft emplacements, may be useful to mine-laying operations. The Mischief Reef operation may be the first step toward an eventual blockade of Taiwan, which is heavily fortified and would probably repel a direct Chinese assault.

Taiwan President Lee Teng-hui, taking note of Beijing's attempts to encircle his small island country, called on his citizens "to raise their vigilance against the military threat from China."

It's important to note the Clinton administration has been silent over this audacious move by Beijing. In previous administrations, America would have moved with military force to prevent China's expansionist plans. The failure of the United States to confront China in the Spratlys bodes ill for Taiwan.

Russia and Chinese war preparations are not isolated and involve communist client states around the world.

Saddam Has Renewed His War Machine

The Iraqi government has stepped up military activity in southern Iraq. The military governor of the Basra region, a Russian-trained Iraqi general, has confirmed the arrival of new air defense weapons, fully acknowledging that his orders are to shoot down American planes. On January 26, American warplanes pounded Iraqi artillery and anti-aircraft positions.

Throughout the second half of January, Iraq deployed troops toward the Kuwait border. In response, Kuwait has mobilized its army, claiming that Saddam is about to do something "dramatic." The Iraqi dictator, aside from asserting his territorial ambitions

against Kuwait, denounced Saudi and Egyptian leaders as "lackeys and stooges of the U.S."
ANALYSIS: Iraq is an old Soviet client state. The country's secret police was trained by Yuri Andropov's KGB. Its officer corps was trained by the Russian army. Nearly all of Iraq's military equipment is Russian. Russian Prime Minister Yevgeny Primakov, a fluent Arabic speaker and longtime supporter of Saddam Hussein, has intensified Moscow's diplomatic and military support for Saddam.

As Kosovo renews its civil war, as China tightens its noose around Taiwan, as North Korea girds for war, Saddam's threat to Kuwait keeps U.S. forces diverted and occupied. Saddam's provocations may be coordinated through Moscow with the provocations by China, North Korea, and Serbia.

North Korea's Extreme Behavior

The North Koreans, close allies of Moscow and Beijing, have recently declared that "the United States will [soon] be reduced to ashes and will no longer exist." North Korean headlines from the first week of 1999 proclaimed that "U.S. Imperialist Aggressors Will Be Unable to Avoid Annihilating Strikes."

Another North Korean source stated that the Americans would be wiped "from this planet for good." In the New Year's message of the North Korean government, the communists called on their citizens to "love rifles, earnestly learn military affairs, and turn the whole country into an impregnable fortress."

Kim Myong, an influential North Korean writer and editor who lives in Tokyo, was quoted as saying: "Maybe there will be a new war. Maybe everyone in Tokyo will die."

Kongdon On, a North Korean specialist at the Institute for Defense Analysis in Washington, says: "There is . . . strong frustration among a lot of people that North Korea is acting very strangely." Han Park, a political scientist specializing in North Korea at the University of Georgia, also stated: "The situation will be very, very dangerous in the next few months." South Korean President Kim Dae-jung, fearing the communist threat, warned his people to be ready for a surprise attack from the North.

ANALYSIS: North Korea has broken its agreement to desist from developing nuclear weapons. It is now suspected that North Korea has nuclear capability, and also has the missiles to deliver nuclear weapons. Able to threaten Tokyo as well as other Japanese cities with nuclear destruction, North Korea is now emboldened and may renew its struggle to conquer the South. With Chinese and perhaps Russian support, Pyongyang has mobilized its armed forces and is now ready to strike. Defectors from the North Korean military have stated that Pyongyang has a plan to conquer South Korea in seven days. Such a plan, if it exists, probably emphasizes the use of nuclear, biological, or chemical weapons of mass destruction, since the conventional firepower of the North Korean army (as it now stands) could not readily defeat the South in such a short time.

Civil War Looms In Kosovo

Violence has again erupted between Albanian separatists and Serbian forces in Kosovo, and, despite NATO warnings, the violence shows every sign of continuing. Russia has openly supported the Serbs, giving out subtle warnings about a "widened war in Europe."

ANALYSIS: More American troops and air units, including a carrier group, are pinned down. This crisis further stretches American military resources, and with no end in sight. American ground forces are said to trace their lines of supply through Hungary, a former Russian satellite with a dubious political leadership. This is an awkward position to be in, and with Russia's new belligerent stance we are in no position to challenge the Serbian communists.

Taking the above items as a whole, a pattern of war preparations and belligerence is clear. Nations of the old communist bloc are making provocative moves across the board. With America's armed forces at an all-time postwar low in readiness and strength, it is doubtful we can meet the challenges that lie ahead.

North Korea and China seem to sense our weakness. And add to this that all these provocative moves have come during the impeachment trial of President Clinton.

Jeffrey R. Nyquist is an expert on Russia.

Russia and China Prepare for War

By Christopher Ruddy

"If you don't look the facts in the face, they have a way of stabbing you in the back."

— Winston Churchill

NewsMax.com Vortex, January 1999 — While America has been preoccupied with Clinton's sexual shenanigans and Wall Street's gyrations, extremely ominous developments have been quietly taking place within Russia and Communist China.

These ominous developments have occurred during a time when President Bill Clinton has systematically moved to disarm the United States.

While it has gone largely unreported, President Clinton has overseen the destruction of nearly two-thirds of America's nuclear weapons stockpile. He has ordered that America no longer have a "launch on warning" policy and has replaced it with one that says America will retaliate only after it has been attacked. This nonsensical Clinton policy means that American cities and American military targets must first be destroyed before America retaliates. He has proposed taking computer circuitry out of land-based missiles, so that they could not be launched in an emergency. Clinton has proposed making it much more difficult for our submarines to launch their weapons, and even has suggested welding closed the missile hatches on our submarines.

Most Americans assume that the Cold War is long over, and that we have nothing to fear from our new "friends," Russia and China. Such a notion is completely contradicted by Russia's and China's expansion of their nuclear arsenals at breakneck speed, and deployment of dozens of new weapons systems. Target: America. (Now, I know you may be saying this can't be true; Russia is in chaos and China is just too weak to take on the United States. Please read on and then form your own opinion.)

Most Americans think war with these communist nations is now impossible. Unfortunately, Russia and China don't agree. These are the same nations that have murdered tens of millions of their own citizens and which continue to target America with tens of thousands of strategic and tactical nuclear weapons. Never before has the strategic balance been so much in favor of Russia and China.

Further, a series of unusual recent activities in these countries indicate that they are at least contemplating nuclear blackmail of the United States These activities include

- an enormous military buildup, including expansion of their arsenals of strategic nuclear weapons, and introduction of new biological and nuclear weapons with first-strike capability;
- a huge expansion of their navies (while the U.S. mothballs over half its ships);
- a new form of brinkmanship, in which Russia and China regularly probe America's defenses;
- huge new civil defense programs, including enormous fallout shelters in Russia (one new underground city is larger than Washington, D.C.).

At the same time, under Clinton, the U.S. military has been cut to the bone, leaving America more vulnerable to foreign attack than at any time since the Cold War. Specifically:

- Clinton has slashed troop levels in the Army, Navy and Marines by 30 percent to 40 percent. Most remaining battle troops are now deployed overseas, in the Middle East, Bosnia, South America and elsewhere.
- The U.S. arsenal of cruise missiles has dropped to a dangerously low number; just over 100 cruise missiles are left. Further, these few remaining missiles are being quickly thrown away in senseless engagements in the Middle East, and the administration is not building any more.
- Clinton has slashed defense spending, from 28 percent of the federal budget in 1988 to 17 percent today.
- The Navy has decommissioned almost half of its ships, down from 600 in 1991 to 336 today. That's the lowest level since 1938.
- The critical balance of nuclear weapons is now heavily in Russia's favor. The U.S. has about 10,000 to 11,000 nuclear weapons left, compared to over 30,000 for Russia. Further, thanks to Clinton, many of our remaining nuclear weapons are vulnerable to attack. For instance, the nuclear warheads for our strategic bombers are in the U.S., while many of the planes are in the Middle East and Europe.

Never before has America been so vulnerable to devastating attack by the worst mass murderers in human history, and never before has an American leader so jeopardized America's ability to defend itself.

Clinton's Sellout of America

It seems incredible, but it's true: Clinton has released classified missile technology to China after receiving political contributions from the communist Chinese; he has allowed China to take control of port cities on both ends of the strategically vital Panama Canal; and he has allowed the Russians and Chinese access to sensitive missile bases, command centers, and shipyards. Here are the shocking facts.

Clinton Urged Turnover of Long Beach Port to the Red Army

When I was in Long Beach a few years ago, local papers were filled with stories of leasing huge military facilities to the Communist Chinese. Here's how the deal was structured:

COSCO — the Chinese Overseas Shipping Company, a subsidiary of China's People's Liberation Army — would be allowed to lease the Navy shipyards in Long Beach, California, for 16 annual payments of $14.5 million a year (total: $232 million). The deal would also have required the Port of Long Beach to spend $235 million to modernize the facilities. In other words, the PLA would have been handed former U.S. naval facilities in Long Beach at a cut-rate cost while taxpayers forked over $235 million to upgrade the facility for the Chinese.

Under a Department of Transportation subsidy program, U.S. taxpayers would have also subsidized 87 percent of the $157 million cost of COSCO building four new container ships.

What do the Communist Chinese plan to do with the facilities and ships? Here's one example:

Authorized Importation of 100,000 Chinese Combat Rifles

In 1996, soon after Clinton had signed a law making it illegal to import foreign semiautomatic weapons into the U.S., he signed a waiver allowing COSCO to import 100,000 semiautomatic military rifles as well as millions of rounds of ammunition, into the U.S. Not content to bring in just semiautomatic weapons, COSCO also tried to smuggle in 2,000 illegal, fully automatic Chinese AK-47s. According to press reports, these weapons were destined to be sold to street gangs in Oakland. That seems like a phony cover story. We still need to know why

China tried to smuggle into California enough weapons to equip an army.

Opened U.S. to Russia and China

On May 13, 1997, Defense Secretary William Cohen signed a military cooperation agreement with Russia. Under the agreement, U.S. and Russian forces would work together on over 100 exercises in 1997 alone. These exercises included joint troop movements, "urban pacification," and U.S. advice for Russian forces killing rebels in Chechnya.

After signing the cooperation agreement, Russian Defense Minister Igor Rodionov toured the National Military Command Center and met with the Joint Chiefs of Staff in secret.

In January 1998, Secretary Cohen also signed an agreement to allow cooperation between the U.S. and Chinese militaries.

Allowed Russians to Photograph U.S. Military Bases

Under the Open Skies Treaty, Russian military planes began flying over and photographing U.S. military bases last year. Chinese military aircraft will be allowed to fly over U.S. military bases beginning in 1999. Information Russia and China obtain from these flyovers would be invaluable if they ever attack the U.S.

Control of the Panama Canal Gave to China

The Panama Canal is probably the single most strategically important piece of real estate in the Western Hemisphere. The U.S. has fought two wars — in which thousands of Panamanians and hundreds of Americas died — to control the Canal. Now it's being handed to the Communist Chinese on a silver platter.

President Clinton has allowed a company controlled by Chinese communists — Hutchison Whampoa Ltd. — to take control of the cities at both ends of the Canal. Further, under Panamanian Law No. 5, Hutchison Whampoa will determine which ships are allowed to enter the Canal and will control many of the Canal's operations. This is utterly absurd and frightening.

Admiral Thomas Moorer, former chairman of the Joint Chiefs, reminded Congress last summer that "the defense and use of the Panama Canal is wrapped inextricably with the overall global strategy of the United States and the security of the free world."

Moorer vehemently opposed the turnover of the canal to the Chinese, saying it was vital for U.S. oil supplies, and for the transit of U.S. ships and troops in a war, and described the Canal as "essential" in any "military conflict — past, present, or future."

U.S. Sells Strategic Weapons Technology to China

On March 23, 1998, the *Washington Times* revealed a secret Clinton administration proposal to sell advanced missile technology to China. Under Clinton, 47 supercomputers have been sold to China, most for use by the Red Army — the butchers of Tibet and Tiananmen Square. These U.S. computers can be used to target nuclear missiles at America and to build and design new and more powerful nuclear weapons.

Russia and China — Our Friends?

Many Americans find it unthinkable that Russia or China would launch an attack on the U.S. knowing that it would mean millions of casualties on their soil. But what Americans fail to take into account is the mind-set of the authoritarian communists, who still occupy every important military and political office in those countries.

These are the same people who gave the world brainwashing, the secret police, and the Gulag. Under these communist leaders and their predecessors, China and the Soviet Union became the most murderous regimes in the history of the human race, and the primary victims were their own citizens.

According to Professor R. J. Rummel, author of *Death by Government*:

"Almost 62 million people, nearly 54,800,000 of them citizens, have been murdered by the Communist Party — the government — of the Soviet Union.

"Old and young, healthy and sick, men and women, even infants and the infirm, were killed in cold blood. They were not combatants in civil war or rebellions; they were not criminals. Indeed, nearly all were guilty of . . . nothing."

[*Death by Government*, pp. 79–80]

Second only to the Soviet Union in mass murder is Communist China. At least 35,236,000 people have been killed in Red China. Rummel writes:

"*These poor souls have experienced every manner of death for ev-*

ery conceivable reason: genocide, politicide, mass murder, massacres, and individual directed assassination."

[*Death by Government*, p. 92]

Have Russia and China "reformed" and become peaceful lambs, as President Clinton would have us believe? The evidence to the contrary is overwhelming.

The Myth of Russian Democracy

Americans and the world would like to believe that the fall of the Berlin Wall ended the threat of international communism. For a few years that indeed seemed to be true, in at least parts of the former Soviet Union.

Free elections were promised. Multiple political parties were allowed. Captive nations — such as Latvia and Lithuania — were set free. Press censorship was scaled back. There was some attempt at free market reforms. And foreign capital was invited in.

However, the reforms were at best paltry. As Joel Carmichael, editor of *Midstream,* wrote last year, "Out of the 12 fragments of the former Soviet Union, only one — Russia — has received a popular election." And of those 12 countries, virtually every one is run by former high-ranking communist officials.

What of the highly touted free market "reforms"? While small, privately owned businesses were allowed, virtually all farming and manufacturing — including Russia's dominant defense industries — remain firmly in control of the state, as well as virtually all communications, transportation, and housing. (Last year, a measure to allow private ownership of homes was firmly defeated in the Duma, Russia's parliament — a parliament controlled by the Communist Party.)

In brief, the centralized apparatus of economic control remains firmly in the hands of "former" communists, both in Russia and China, and throughout the states of the former Soviet Union. And the same people are in charge of the economy. Richard Ebeling, professor of economics at Hillsdale College and a regular visitor to Russia (his wife is Russian), states bluntly, "The same people in the same offices are still running the economy. Only the names of their offices have changed."

What of the highly touted new free market "businesses" in Russia?

All but the smallest businesses are controlled and run by the Russian mafia, which in turn is controlled by former KGB (state security) agents and the Russian government. Even the U.S.S.R.'s Gulag — the concentration camps that were the epitome of totalitarian communism — remain and, in fact, have grown. Avraham Shifrin, author of *The First Guidebook to Prisons and Concentration Camps of the Soviet Union* and the world authority on the Gulag, stated in 1996:

"Basically the situation in the camps of Russia, the Ukraine (as well as other parts of the U.S.S.R. with the exception of the Baltic states) has not changed. As a matter of fact, the Russian authorities have had to transform their entire industry and base it on forced labor of prisoners; for this purpose, the camps — within the last few years — have been gradually enlarged. . . . " Shifrin noted ominously, "The West believes the Russian lies, as it wants to believe there will be a quiet life, but there won't be."

Russia's Commitment to Global Conquest

In 1996, I had the honor of interviewing Dr. Edward Teller, the former director of Lawrence Livermore National Laboratory. Teller is one of America's premier scientists, best known as "the father of the hydrogen bomb."

It was Teller who persuaded President Truman to develop the hydrogen bomb — a thermonuclear weapon 1,000 times more powerful than the bombs dropped on Hiroshima and Nagasaki. Teller's recommendation proved critical when Russia exploded its own thermonuclear device shortly after the United States. If the Soviets had had a monopoly on thermonuclear weapons, they might well have dominated the world.

In the 1980s, Teller also convinced President Reagan to begin development of the next generation of superweapons, known as "Star Wars."

When I spoke to Teller at his home, he was very worried about Clinton's military polices, which he called "extremely dangerous." According to Teller, under Clinton the U.S. has ceased the development of virtually all strategic weapons, especially nuclear ones.

Teller seemed perplexed that an American president would do such a thing, especially since the Russians and Chinese were building new and more powerful weapons at breakneck speed. If this goes on, Teller said, the U.S. military would witness no real improvement in its weapons systems for a decade — exposing America to pre-emptive attack. I asked Dr. Teller to quantify the risk of the United States becoming involved in a global nuclear war if Clinton's policies continued. He replied that in 1992 the chances of the United States becoming involved in a global war was at most one chance in a hundred, with the main risk being accidental war. However, under Clinton's military stagnation policies, Dr. Teller explained, the chance of global nuclear war will increase to 50-50 during the next few years.

Dr. Teller also stressed the importance of technologically advanced weapons in safeguarding our society. He noted that for centuries China's culture was considered more advanced than the West's, but the West was still able to dominate China and the world. Why? Because, Teller explained, the West had developed the technology to effectively use gunpowder — the first superweapon. This new weaponry, coupled with advanced navigation aides, gave the West dominance of the seas and control of the world.

The same principle holds today, Teller said. The nation that achieves dominance in superweapons of mass destruction dominates the world.

The U.S. may have dazzling gadgetry in the cockpit of an F-16, and formidable aircraft carriers, neither of which the Russians have. But in a nuclear war, such weapons are not that important, compared to nuclear weapons. (Saddam Hussein understands well this concept. By U.N. estimates, he has given up $120 billion in lost oil sales during the past decade rather than abandon his biological, chemical and nuclear programs.)

The Soviet strategy for the past three decades has been to achieve numerical superiority in superweapons while preventing the West from developing new superweapons.

President Clinton has been a willing accomplice to Russia's agenda. Not only has he refused to develop any major new weapons systems, he has halted underground testing of nuclear weapons, which is crucial to the development of new superweapons. At the same time, he did nothing when Russia conducted no fewer than five underground nuclear tests during the fall of 1998 alone.

To put it briefly, the West has been disarming, while the Russians and Chinese have been building their militaries rapidly — especially their strategic forces, or "superweapons."

Was the West Tricked?

Since its inception in 1917, the Soviet Union followed the policy of alternating periods of repression with relaxing of authority and opening to the West to attract Western capital and aid. Then, a few years later, revitalized by the infusion of Western money and technology, it would clamp down again, more brutally than ever. China has done the same.

Time and again, the West has been taken in by this trick. Indeed, throughout the 1920s and 1930s, the Soviet Union was the darling of myopic intellectuals in America and Europe who praised it for its "noble" ideology, donated funds and urged Western aid — while ignoring the mind-numbing repression, concentration camps and mass executions.

Anatoliy Golitsyn, an important KGB defector, warned the CIA that the U.S.S.R. would launch a massive "liberalization" movement, as a ruse to get the West to disarm.

Golitsyn's 1984 book, *Old Lies for New: The Communist Strategy of Deception and Disinformation*, eerily predicted that the Soviet Union would "collapse," that Eastern Europe would be "liberated," and that the Berlin Wall would be torn down — all as a way to deceive the West into disarming. All of these events have taken place, including massive Western disarmament under Clinton (described in detail below).

Golitsyn claims that the Western public has been fed a steady diet of disinformation about Russia. During this period, Golitsyn warned, Russia's military-industrial complex would not shrink but would rapidly expand. What is the purpose of this enormous military expansion?

Russia May Launch a Surprise Attack Against U.S.

Since 1917, "capitalist warmongers" in the U.S. and Europe have been the principal targets of hatred by Russians and the Chinese. Following the fall of the Berlin Wall, those campaigns of hate subsided briefly, and authoritarian communists stepped out of the spotlight. Today, with Russia reported in desperate economic straits, the Russian people are again being told "it's the fault of America and Europe." Brutal communist leaders are again publicly talking, dissent is again being banned, and hatred against the West is soaring. During the past year, my concerns about Russia have been greatly increased as a result of an interview I conducted with Jeffrey Nyquist, an independent researcher on Russia and author of *The Origins of the Fourth World War.*

Nyquist believes Russia has been planning a surprise nuclear attack against the United States, and that this attack will come sooner rather than later — quite possibly within the next year if the U.S. continues on its present reckless course. I would have scoffed at such suggestions had Nyquist not made such a convincing case and demonstrated such a powerful intellect.

During our conversations, Nyquist listed signs that would indicate a Russian attack was being planned.

Nyquist's Startling Predictions

In early 1998, Nyquist predicted that authorities in Russia would deliberately implode their own economy to advance their political and military agendas. There were several reasons. First, that would divert attention from the theft of billions of dollars by government officials from "privatized" companies and provide a convenient explanation why none of them were making any money. Second, by engendering Russia's economic collapse and blaming the West, the necessary psychological atmosphere for war against the U.S. would be created.

Another outcome of Russia's economic collapse, Nyquist said, would be the emergence of a series of progressively stronger and more militarist Russian leaders. Primakov — Yeltsin's prime minister — perfectly fits Nyquist's prediction. He's a former hard-line, anti-American KGB general.

Nyquist also predicted that Russia would ally with China. That, too, has now taken place, as you'll see below.

Finally, Nyquist predicted that Russia would stockpile huge quantities of food and other supplies for war, and begin moving its nuclear weapons on to its naval ships where they are much more difficult to monitor and deter. All of this has occurred.

Spy Warns of Russian War Plans

Nyquist is not the only astute observer of Russia who believes Russia may be preparing for war against the U.S. Stanislav Lunev — the highest-ranking GRU (Russian military intelligence) officer ever to defect from Russia — also warns that Russia is preparing for war against the United States.

Lunev's book *Through the Eyes of the Enemy* states categorically that the Cold War is not over and that Russia continues to plan for a nuclear war. "Russia remains terrified of the power of America, and Russian military intelligence does everything it can to prepare for a war that it considers inevitable," he wrote. This war, Lunev details, would employ nuclear, biological and chemical weapons against America.

Russian Plans: Kill U.S. Leaders, Use Biological Weapons Already in U.S.

Lunev explains war would begin with the infiltration of Russian special operations troops into the U.S., who would kill top political and military leaders. Lunev also warns that Russian GRU (military intelligence) agents have already deposited, near key water reservoirs, deadly poisons and toxins which would result in millions of civilians being ravaged by disease. Lunev says, for instance, that the Russians have determined that they could wipe out a significant part of the population of Florida by polluting water sources in the Carolinas.

Another part of Russia's plan, according to Lunev, is to deploy suitcase nuclear bombs at strategic points throughout the U.S. Lunev says he personally scouted a site in the Hudson Valley just above New York City for one such suitcase nuke.

Lunev has also told me that the democracy movement in Russia was a charade and part of "a plan" to get the West to disarm — achieving through deception what the Soviet Union was never able to achieve militarily. Lunev explained that China was pursuing parallel policies, absorbing as much Western aid and technology as possible before a final confrontation, which Lunev regarded as imminent.

Russia's Economic Collapse Increases Risk of War

The collapse of Russia's economy greatly increased the chances of war with the West. With 29 times Finland's population, Russia's budget barely matches theirs. According to news reports, millions of ordinary Russians are now struggling just to stay alive, selling family heirlooms and chopping up their furniture for kindling.

Russia's political leaders and economic czars, of course, will never admit that they and their failed totalitarian system are responsible for this widespread misery, and increasingly the West is being blamed.

This is particularly dangerous, because despite economic desperation, Russia is still a nuclear superpower. Victor Olove, director of Moscow's Center for Policy Studies, told the *Los Angeles Times*, "People who have nuclear warheads in their hands have not gotten their salaries for three or four months and are literally hungry."

Some press reports show how close to war we have already come. Britain's *Panorama* news program reported that in 1995 the Yeltsin government came within minutes of a full nuclear attack on the United States after Russian defense systems failed.

U.S. Destroys Nuclear Arsenal, Russian Arsenal Expands

Since the end of the Cold War, the United States has been systematically destroying its nuclear arsenal. In 1991, the U.S. had approximately 30,000 strategic and tactical nuclear weapons. Under Clinton, that arsenal has fallen nearly 60 percent. In 1997, the United States had only 12,500 tactical and strategic nuclear weapons. Of these, only 8,750 were active, 2500 more were on reserve, and 1,250 were slated to be destroyed. Moreover, our nuclear arsenal has a limited "shelf life," and year by year, more and more weapons become unusable. The Clinton administration has only recently taken belated steps to produce tritium, a necessary component for the maintenance of nuclear weapons.

In contrast, the Russians may now have as many as 50,000 strategic and tactical nuclear weapons — ranging from small suitcase bombs to large warheads suitable for intercontinental ballistic missiles (ICBMs). The lion's share of these weapons remain targeted at the U.S. And Russia is quickly building even more weapons.

Never before has the strategic nuclear balance been so greatly in Russia's favor. From a military standpoint, this creates a unique window of opportunity for Russia to launch a successful first strike against the United States at minimal cost to themselves.

"Use It or Lose It"

Like America's nuclear arsenal, Russia's is degrading as it gets older and requires expensive periodical servicing. The Russian government is well aware of this problem. In a recent report to the Duma (Russia's Congress), First Deputy Prime Minister Yuri Masluyokov (a former Soviet military-industrial planner) states that because of obsolescence, Russia's nuclear arsenal will decline quickly, and Russia may "be able to field only 800 to 900 nuclear warheads seven years from now."

Because of Russia's economic problems, Russia may never again enjoy the huge strategic advantage it now has over its old enemies in the West. For die-hard communists, the huge, but temporary, military advantage may represent an irresistible opportunity to "use them before we lose them." Indeed, Bruce Blair, a well known liberal from the Brookings Institution, stated last summer in *The National Interest*, "Russia's conventional forces have decline . . . and into this vacuum has rushed a growing reliance on nuclear weapons — including their first use in any serious conventional conflict."

Recognizing the limited shelf life of Russia's nuclear arsenal, Blair adds, "The nuclear forces themselves have become vulnerable. . . . Consequently Russia today faces far stronger pressures to 'use or lose' its nuclear arsenal than at any time since the early 1960s."

Thus, in an extremely ominous sign, on December 17, 1997, President Yeltsin issued a 37-page policy statement, reneging on previous pledges not to use nuclear weapons first.

Russia's Recent Military Buildup

How grave a threat to the West is Russia's military today? The perception in much of the West is that Russian conventional and strategic forces are in complete disarray, on the verge of breakdown or worse, like the civilian economy. Fears of a military meltdown in Russia have successfully been exploited by the Russians as a subtle form of blackmail. Either the U.S. and the West hand over billions in aid, or else.

The truth is that Russia's military-industrial complex did not collapse as a result of the dissolution of the Soviet Union — nor was its arsenal of strategic weapons dismantled.

In May of 1997, Reuters reported, citing French intelligence estimates, Russia maintains a stockpile of 18,000 to 20,000 tactical nuclear weapons — that is in addition to approximately 8,000 big, strategic nuclear weapons. Other estimates put the total number of nuclear weapons at between 30,000 and 50,000.

That is the largest nuclear arsenal Russia has ever had, equaling or exceeding what they possessed at the height of the Cold War.

Russia has also been modernizing its strategic weapons. Air Force General Eugene Habiger, commander of the U.S. Strategic Air Command in Nebraska, told the *Washington Times* last year that Russia and China have been engaging in a massive weapons modernization program.

Habiger told the *Times* that "Russia has begun producing its new SS-27 strategic missile (the Topol-M) and is building new submarines armed with multiple-warhead missiles and new bomber-launched cruise missiles."

Habiger continued, noting that "Russia is the only power with the capacity to destroy the United States. 'The anomaly that we're faced with is that the Cold War ended, and did the loser really lose?' he said. 'Did you see a demobilization? Did you see all those nuclear weapons come down in Russia? No.' "

The Air Force's National Intelligence Center concluded in a recent report to Congress that even with the economic and social problems of Russia, she "probably will retain the largest force of land-based strategic missiles in the world."

This is nothing new. Since the communists took over in 1917, Russia has had two economies: a military economy, which has consumed the country's top scientists, engineers and workers and up to 70 percent of the country's wealth — and its poor cousin, the civilian economy, which received the dregs. (Western media reports almost always focus on the civilian side of Russia's economy and ignore her military-industrial complex.)

Russia also continues to field a huge conventional army, with 100 combat divisions, compared to 10 fielded by the U.S. Russia also has some 100,000 airborne troops ready at a moment's notice for action. America would be hard pressed to field even 100,000 regular soldiers.

Russia: World Class Arms Maker

Russia's economic minister announced in December of 1998 that Russia plans to increase arms exports by some 20 percent in 1999, and Russia will remain in the top four of the world's major arms exporting nations. (Arms exports from the combined Commonwealth of Independent States makes Russia second in world export.) As the Associated Press noted, Russia's arms industry is "one of the few sectors where Russian industry continues to operate efficiently."

No doubt because few countries would buy from them if the Russians couldn't deliver quality products on time. This should be an ominous sign for those who believe Russia is in such "disarray" that they cannot remain a threat to the West. The military-industrial complex not only operates in Russia today, it operates well.

Russia Emphasizes "Superweapons"

According to the *Russia Reform Monitor:*

"During the past year, Russia has been deploying the ICBM Topol-M (SS-27), a missile that is both mobile (making it harder for us to hit) and orbital (goes into orbit) before hitting its target."

[Note: The U.S. has no strategic weapon that is either orbital or mobile.]

Further, according to the *Reform Monitor*, this past September Russia had its 58th test launch of the missile, a sign the *Monitor* said demonstrated that the missile was well into serial production. In late December of 1998, the *Monitor's* belief was confirmed when Russia publicly admitted to officially deploying ten Topol-M SS-27 missiles. (Please note that the common thread of Russia's military activities is its investment in developing, building and deploying strategic superweapons. News sources like CNN won't report on many of these Russian accomplishments. This does not alter the fact that the Russians are engaged in a buildup of such superweapons — the very same weapons Dr. Teller warned about.)

In addition, according to excepts from the *Monitor*, during the past two years Russia has:

- commissioned a new aircraft carrier, the Admiral Kuznetsov;
- commissioned the largest ballistic missile cruiser in the history of the world, called Peter the Great. According to *Pravda*, the ship has

an unsurpassed "missile and artillery system and radar optical target tracking system";

- begun construction of the fifth generation Borei class of ballistic missile submarines, beginning with the Yuri Dolgoruki, which has an ultramodern hull;
- built a new submarine-based ballistic missile;
- continued production of the Akula-II class nuclear attack submarine;
- begun construction of the new Severodvinsk class of nuclear attack submarines;
- refitted all Typhoon ballistic missile submarines to launch an upgrade of the SS-N-24/6 ballistic missile;
- introduced a new generation of nuclear warheads;
- modernized its Bear and Backfire strategic bombers, with the ability to carry updated cruise missiles;
- developed a new stealth bomber;
- begun development of a new strategic bomber;
- continued development of chemical, biological and nuclear weapons.

In 1997, Russia's Parliament allocated some $12.8 billion for new weapons development. *Pravda* (Russia's leading newspaper) cited a General Staff official who says that new weapons systems include directed-energy weapons, new "smart" weapons, deep penetration munitions, and electronic warfare technologies. Funding also went for the Topol-M, new tactical nuclear weapons, miniaturized nuclear weapons and seven new ballistic missile submarines.

Previous Russian spending has paid off. In February of 1996, the *Times* of London reported that Britain's Royal Navy was concerned about "Russian nuclear hunter-killer submarines" stalking British Trident submarines operating off Britain's coasts.

The British navy described these submarines as "larger, quieter and more deadly than anything Western navies can put to sea."

The *Times* also disclosed that Russia had deployed a new "Akula-class" submarine that carries SS-21 nuclear missiles aimed at American targets. The head of U.S. Naval Intelligence, Admiral Mike Cramer, said the new submarine "has demonstrated a capability that has never been demonstrated before to us. . . ."

Both British and U.S. military experts have been astounded by new Russian super-silent technology that allows their new submarines to avoid American sensors and early warning systems. Gone are the days of the big, noisy Russian subs. If Russia is "falling apart," how have they been able to do all of this? How will America know if Russia subs move close to the U.S. if our detectors are useless against this new Russian technology?

Russia's Deadly Chemical and Biological Weapons

Nyquist states that in a war with the United States, Russia will heavily utilize their extensive biological and chemical weapons — particularly during the initial strikes. These are comparatively cheap weapons of mass destruction, with a low "cost per kill." Because America has a large population dispersed over a wide area, biological and chemical weapons are an effective means of mass extermination.

Lunev concurs with much of what Nyquist says. In his book, *Through the Eyes of the Enemy*, he details how Russian GRU agents have been sent to the U.S. to scout out the best way to employ such weapons.

Russia has the ability to produce enormous quantities of deadly biological and chemical weapons quickly. The *International Herald Tribune* of December 29, 1998, describes one such factory:

"Six stories high and two football fields long, the central factory [Stepnogorsk] is filled with 10 giant fermentation vats, each meant to brew 5,000 gallons of anthrax microbes — enough to kill every man, woman and child in America many times over.

"Stepnogorsk's former director, who defected to the United States in 1992, says the plant was to produce up to 300 tons of final 'product' in a 200-day period if the order came to mobilize for war."

The Stepnogorsk human death factory has been closed. But there is no way to tell how many other factories continue to operate or how many tons of deadly poisons the Russians have stockpiled. For example, in February 1997, the *Washington Times* reported that a secret military intelligence document reported that Russia had developed a nerve gas called A-232. The report stated that Russia has the ability to mass produce the agent "within weeks"

In March of this year, the *New York Times* carried an article by Ken

Alibek, a chief deputy in Biopreparat, the military's biological weapons division. Alibek says Russia continues to develop new biological weapons, from anthrax to various plague strains. Alibek criticized U.S. aid to Russia, which does not allow full-scale inspection of the sites where these weapons are being developed.

Alibek's claims were substantiated in September of 1998 when the Defense Intelligence Agency reported to Congress that "key components of the former Soviet biological warfare program remain largely intact and may support a possible future mobilization capability for the production of biological agents and delivery systems."

America continues to play the fool. A December 28, 1998, report in the *New York Times* says that in 1972, after signing an international treaty banning such weapons, Russia "almost immediately, Soviet defectors say, . . . secretly redoubled its germ research and production."

Christopher Story, editor of *Soviet Analyst*, recounts that in the late 1980s Margaret Thatcher confronted Soviet Premier Gorbachev over intelligence reports that the U.S.S.R. had extensive biological and chemical weapons programs. Story said that Gorbachev promised to abolish such programs. Significant evidence shows such programs were not abolished.

Again, in 1992, President Yeltsin said he was abolishing all chemical and biological weapons programs. Rather than opening up the laboratories involved in such weapon-making, Yeltsin proceeded to "close" such installations and cities where weapons of mass destruction were being built so that visits by foreigners would be prohibited.

Alibek told the *New York Times* in December of 1998 that "Russia . . . will never entirely abandon a program in which it had military superiority, no matter how many treaties it signs or cooperative programs it joins."

"I say, 'Guys, don't be so gullible. They're lying to you,' " Alibek told the *Times*.

Why does "democratic" Russia close its cities to foreign visits, just as it did during the Soviet days? Why are "our friends," the Russians, continuing to develop these monstrous weapons of mass murder in blatant defiance of Russia's international treaties with the U.S. and other countries — and who do they plan to use them on? And why, oh why, does our government turn a blind eye to these Russian activities?

Eleven Signs of a Russian Surprise Attack

Here are 11 more disturbing signs Nyquist identifies as Russian war preparations:

1. Russia's alert status. As reported last year, Russia regularly put its missiles on a high state of alert, claiming their early warning systems did not work properly. Nyquist calls these periodic high alerts "one of the ominous signs of Russian duplicity."

As Nyquist explains, firing a missile is not as simple as "pushing a button." An alert status means, in real terms, increased activity around a missile base as fuel and other preparations are made for a launch. Putting missiles on high alert means Russia is capable of launching in a matter of hours or even minutes.

American intelligence analysts have scrupulously monitored such activity, largely through satellites. During Soviet days, an alert status would have been a huge red flag to U.S. intelligence, leading the U.S. to also heighten its alert status. The Russians' high state of alert and their frequent changes in alert status have made the U.S. military complacent. What normally would be a warning sign of an attack — Russia going on alert — is now viewed as business as usual.

2. Mock attacks. In the past two years, Russia has engaged in numerous mock attacks against the United States, including nuclear attacks.

On February 21, 1997, then–Russian Prime Minister Viktor Chernomyrdin "was at the Odinstovo nuclear command center, overseeing an exercise whose assignment was 'to destroy the U.S. in less than an hour,'" according to a press account in Segodnya.

In September of 1997 Russia's defense forces conducted a three-day nuclear attack exercise, which included a test firing of ICBMs, submarine-launched ballistic missiles, and bomber-launched cruise missiles.

The *Washington Times* reported that in the fall of 1997, a Russian attack submarine stalked "close enough to sink . . . with high speed cruise missiles" three carrier battle groups off the coast of Washington state.

In October of 1998, Tass news agency reported that Russias' Strategic Rocket Forces practiced a mock nuclear attack, firing an ICBM, against the United States. The exercise was coordinated with the Russians' strategic bomber force.

The *Washington Times* reported that in April of 1998, "Russia's strategic bomber forces recently carried out simulated nuclear bombing raids against the United States in an exercise that included test firings of long-range cruise missiles." During these exercises, Russian bombers flew to the polar regions, as they would in an attack against the United States.

These are the exercises that have been reported. Are these the actions of "America's friend"? In military strategy, mock attacks are a classic way to launch a real, surprise attack. Like high-alert status, such repeated exercises create complacency on the part of American analysts, who are being conditioned to view these exercises as normal.

3. Russia is stockpiling food in the midst of a supposed "famine."

Three years ago, Ambassador Richard Staar, a top Reagan administration arms control expert, writing in the *Wall Street Journal*, said that Russia had stockpiled some 362 million metric tons of wheat. (One economist calculated this was enough grain to feed the entire population of the former Soviet Union for three years.)

Recent Russian national budgets have also allotted large amounts for civil defense, including the purchase of provisional supplies like food stocks.

Such food stockpiles are crucial in fighting and winning a nuclear war. Russia has a much more sophisticated civil defense system than the United States. During a nuclear war, millions of Russians would be underground, unable to plant, harvest or process food. Russia also has always used its armed forces to harvest food, which would be difficult during a war.

A nuclear war would likely create a complete breakdown of the economy of the warring parties, and the rest of the world's economy. Any nation engaged in war would need food, oil and other vital supplies. A nation without such supplies would likely have no alternative but to surrender or be destroyed.

Nyquist noted to me six months ago that unusual changes in the food requirements of Russia could be a tip-off that war is close at hand. In the fall of this year, just months after Nyquist's comments, Russia announced that it had suffered its worse famine in more than 40 years. Russian authorities claimed, alternatively, there will be mass starvation later this winter, and near-famine is already taking place in some regions of Russia. There are good reasons to be skeptical of Russian claims of a "famine."

The government claims the harvest was half of what it was last year. Other press reports state it was 25 percent less than last year. In either case, as a result of these claims of famine, the U.S. and Europe are transferring huge quantities of food to Russia.

The European Community has agreed to send approximately $550 million in food. The aid package includes a million tons of wheat, 100,000 tons of pork, 150,000 tons of beef, and 50,000 tons of milk powder and rice.

The United States aid package was formalized just two days before Christmas 1998. The U.S. agreed to ship Russia $625 million in food. The package includes an outright gift of 1.5 million metric tons of wheat. The U.S. will also "lend" Russia funds to purchase an additional 1.5 million tons of other commodities — including corn, soybean meal, rice, beef, pork, and nonfat dry milk. (Note: Why, with a "wheat shortfall," does Russia desperately need everything from beef to milk?)

Is there really a famine in Russia, or is it a propaganda creation of the government? Interfax reported that by the fall of 1998, overall farming production was actually up ".4 percent higher than it was in 1996."

Russia's demand for wheat has also fallen considerably in recent years. Why? Russia has been slaughtering her herds during the past five years — another ominous sign.

In 1997, Russia had a bumper grain crop of nearly 90 million tons of wheat, with claimed reserves of 20 million tons. Since Russia has about 50 percent fewer livestock than five years ago, this should have left substantial reserves for this winter.

Major General Sergei Shoigu, minister of emergency situations, was quoted in the *Los Angeles Times* this past October stating, "I am totally sure that there will be no sort of famine at all, since there are sufficient reserves in the country."

As word of the "famine" spread from Russian sources this past September, Russian Agricultural Minister Viktor Semyonov also denied that Russia had a serious food problem.

"This campaign is being waged in the interests of foreign agricultural producers who, under the pretext of severe food shortages, are trying to gain advantages importing their products." Reuters reported that Semyonov said domestic producers "are still capable of filling the shops with food."

Another contradictory statement: Mikhail Zadornov, Russia's finance minister, said as late as October 22 that "Russia's financial situation is not such that it requires direct humanitarian aid. I would express gratitude for such [food aid] proposals, but I think food imports will continue on the normal market basis."

A poor, all-around harvest was then redefined. Russia is now claiming that its grain harvest was generally OK except "in wheat grown for animal feed."

"The food portion, of the milling quality [wheat], is just as large as last year," Gerald Rector, the head of USDA's wheat and food grains forecasting committee, reportedly told a USDA meeting.

Army to Get Food

In October Prime Minister Primakov announced that Russia was allocating some $600 million to purchase food stocks for "special consumers" and "certain regions." The Associated Press reported that Primakov's reference to "special consumers" referred to "soldiers."

Claims that the army urgently needs emergency food, and other reports that the army is starving or eating "dog food," seem far fetched. It is well known that the Russian army has generous funding for secure stockpiles of food and that troops are traditionally fed from food reserves, which in some cases are over six years old. Thus, a current food shortfall for the military would have to be the result of bad harvests in previous, recent years — which is not the case. The current claim of a bad harvest could affect the army's food supply sometime down the road, but would not require the emergency shipments of food that Russia says she desperately needs.

How Can Russian Promises Be Trusted?

As word was spreading of the Russian famine, Russia's second-highest-ranking auditor, Accounts Chamber chief Boldyrev, went public in Germany's *Der Spiegel,* with allegations of massive fraud of Western loans to Russia. Boldyrev claims there is massive fraud and misappropriation of funds and that he "does not know of a single case in which government activities were investigated and no gross violations were discovered."

The *Los Angeles Times* reported recently that the American negotiators were concerned whether food aid would actually get to the intended people and might instead end up on the black market, or simply disappear into a black hole, as had happened with previous food shipments.

According to news reports, the U.S.-Russian food deal had hit a snag because Russia did not want monitors overseeing the distribution of the food to make sure it is delivered to the Russian people. (It is important to note that such food supplies are fungible and that foreign food aid could be distributed to the population while domestic supplies are stockpiled.) Russia did, eventually, agree to monitors. As it turns out, the United States will have two — yes, just two — monitors in Moscow to oversee the $625 million food distribution program.

Food exchanges could endanger U.S. security, as Nyquist points out, because each ton of food shipped from the U.S. and Europe is one less ton America or Europe will have during the next war.

Quite remarkably, the Clinton administration is considering drawing down critical U.S. military food stocks to help Russia. According to a *Washington Times* report, "a retired Russian general has informally asked the U.S. government to ship defense food stockpiles," known as MREs, or meals-ready-to-eat. That move would be disastrous if war breaks out because, at current U.S. troop strength, the Pentagon only has 150 days of food reserves (a very low number in the event of war). According to the *Times*, the Clinton administration is actually considering this dangerous move.

If Russia is really in the midst of a famine and our friend, why is she building up military food stockpiles? This makes no sense, unless Nyquist's scenario is correct.

4. Russia is cutting back on planting. If the famine this year is for real, Russian planners should be seeking expanded planting and harvesting next year. But this is not the case.

In fact, according to Tass, the State Statistics committee reported on October 15 that Russia is dramatically reducing the number of acres to be planted next year, from 60 million acres this year to 54 million acres. As Nyquist points out, that doesn't make sense if Russia has a long-term food problem. It does make sense if Russian planners know that a large area of Russian farmland will be contaminated with fallout, or that the population will be underground during the planting or harvest season.

Another disturbing fact is that Russia's food situation is being handled by Andrei Kokoshin, secretary of Russia's Security Council. The Security Council is a military agency. Consider how such a food shortage in the United States might be handled. Would the Pentagon be handling the matter or would the Agricultural, Commerce or other civilian departments be used?

Also noteworthy is information that Russia had increased food imports well before any knowledge of the harvest was apparent. In August, Russian imports of chicken from the United States increased a dramatic 20 percent.

5. Russia has been slaughtering its herds. According to SovEkon, a Moscow think tank, during the past five years about half of Russia's cattle, sheep, goats, and chickens have been killed.

In the past year, the slaughtering of the herds, particularly of cattle and sheep, has dramatically increased. Interfax reported that as of October 1, 1998, Russia had 16 percent fewer sheep and goats and 9 percent fewer cattle than a year previous. These are extreme reductions, and it is difficult to rebuild those stocks.

Why the reduction? Nyquist believes that the Russians are canning the meat from their herds because they know that grazing herds, such as sheep and cattle, will be less valuable after a nuclear war begins. Fallout from such a war would contaminate livestock, making them useless for food. (And remember, last year Russia had a bumper harvest, so there should have been no shortage of animal feed, and it is still cheaper to raise livestock in Russia than it is to ship meat and poultry from United States or Europe.)

6. Russia is hoarding oil. Oil has been an important commodity for

Russia for decades, and a major source of hard foreign currency. Russia has long been a net exporter of oil.

In October 1998 Tass reported that Russia had "cut export of petroleum products by 26.6 percent to 30.2 million tons in 8 months of 1998." Why would cash-starved Russia cut back on exports of one of its best sources of hard currency in the midst of an economic crisis?

Though Russia has modernized its oil production capabilities in recent years thanks to a huge infusion of Western capital and expertise, Russia's First Vice Premier Yuri Maslyukov told Interfax (as reported in the *Wall Street Journal* November 4, 1998) that Russia was quickly "turning into an oil importing nation."

One of the nations Russia has been buying oil from is Iraq. In a six-month period in 1998, Russia purchased 107 million barrels of Iraqi oil, making Russia the largest purchaser under the U.N.'s "oil-for-food" program. Why does Russia find it necessary to buy so much oil and why from Iraq? Nyquist believes this is a payoff to Iraq and another big tip-off of an impending war.

Like food, a modern society cannot exist without oil. Nyquist notes that the Russian military is very aware of the lessons of World War II. They know that the German war machine was actually more productive at the height of allied bombing in 1944. Not until Russian troops physically occupied the Romanian oil fields, the lifeblood of the German war machine, did German war production grind to a halt.

In a global war in which nuclear weapons are used, the nation that has resources of food and oil will have a critical advantage. The nation that doesn't have significant reserves will likely be utterly destroyed — no matter how wealthy that nation is before the war starts.

7. Russia is moving its strategic nuclear weapons from land to sea. This is perhaps one of the most ominous developments to take place in Russia during the past six months.

Any military strategist knows that sea-based nuclear weapons, particularly those on submarines, are considerably less vulnerable to attack than land-based weapons. Strategists in both Russia and the United States also know that land-based missiles can be knocked out by ground-bursting nuclear weapons, making the need for sea-based weaponry critical. Russia has long had numerical superiority over the United States in both nuclear weapons and submarines. Russia has 42 ballistic missile submarines compared to 18 for the United States.

In July of 1998, the commander in chief of Russia's navy announced — as widely reported in the Russian press — that the Russian military was moving a huge number of their total land-based, strategic nuclear weapons onto naval ships, where they will be much less vulnerable to attack or counterattack. Previously, the Russian navy only controlled 30 percent of Russia's strategic nuclear weapons. That number will dramatically increase to 50 percent under the new plan.

Why is this being done? Why now? Why during a fiscal crisis when their whole country is supposedly in disarray and their soldiers are supposedly being fed dog food?

8. Russia is hoarding gold. Gold is a precious commodity, and in times of war it's even more precious. When war breaks out, the price of gold can go up three-, five-, even ten-fold overnight in a warring nation.

Russia has long been one of the world's largest gold-producing nations. At the end of the Soviet period, Russia was said to have had large reserves of gold, but these reserves mysteriously disappeared during the breakup of the U.S.S.R.

In recent months there has been more strange activity. In October of 1998, the Associated Press reported that Russia's gold production this year was approximately 120 tons, and that next year, the cash-strapped Russian government planned to spend $411 million to buy 50 tons of gold.

The Russian government announced that it would begin something that is highly unusual: It would mint and issue to the public $1.5 billion in gold and silver coins.

Still more interesting is the Interfax report just a month later. The Russian government approved legislation that abolished taxes on the sale of gold coins and ingots, giving its citizens a strong incentive to buy gold.

This is extremely odd because Russia is in the middle of a major currency crisis in which its currency has been repeatedly devalued. Typically during such a crisis, governments do everything they can to prevent their citizens from dumping the national currency and buying foreign currencies or gold.

Nyquist believes that the Russian government is encouraging its citizens to buy gold because it wants to have as much gold as possible within its borders in the event of war. The Russian government knows that gold would be the most stable currency in a wartime economy.

9. Russia has openly entered into an alliance with China and is increasingly working with other totalitarian powers hostile to the United States. During the last few years, Russia and China have increased their military ties and technology transfers, including the purchase of some $15 billion of Russian armaments by China.

In just the past few months, China and Russia have also sharply reduced troops along their mutual border. For instance, this fall alone, Russia removed 300 army units from the Chinese border.

In late 1998, Russia and China openly announced that the purpose of their new alliance was to challenge U.S. global dominance. Nyquist believes this could mean that Russia and China have agreed to war protocols along their border and are preparing to confront America with "one clenched fist."

The new alliance between China and Russia is a major blow to U.S. strategic deterrence. Since Nixon "opened up China" in the 1970s, the U.S. has regarded China as an important ally in containing Russian expansion. Time and again I was told that, as odious as strengthening China might be, it was essential to curbing Russia. Based on the belief that China was America's ally in Russian containment, the U.S. and Europe have given China tens of billions of dollars in aid, loans, and trade concessions. That Western aid and trade has made China the commercial tiger of Asia, and a world military power.

By allying with Russia, China has shattered decades of U.S. strategic planning — and incredibly this has not made headlines and no one in Congress or the media seems concerned.

This new alliance also means that in the event of war, America will probably have to fight both Russia and China, which together have both the world's largest nuclear arsenal and the world's largest conventional army. The 1998 *World Almanac* credits China with the world's largest armed forces with 2.9 million active troops and 1.2 million reserve troops. Including local militias (the equivalent of our National Guard), China could quickly field some 5 million troops, compared to less than 1 million for the U.S. Russia could field an additional 1.2 million troops and has an incredible 20 million reserve troops. Together, Russia and China could field 26 times as many troops as the U.S. In the past few months, Russia has also been making diplomatic overtures and formalizing treaties with a half-dozen militant rogue states, including North Korea, Iran and Iraq. Several analysts see this as the possible beginning of an immense and very sinister anti-American axis.

10. Russia has built Nuclear War Bunkers. Perhaps the clearest sign that Russia is planning on fighting and winning a nuclear war is its investment of billions of precious dollars to build a vast system of underground bunkers and shelters. This system has just one purpose: to enable millions of Russians to survive a nuclear war.

In 1996 the *New York Times* described just one of these huge underground facilities, which was being built under the Ural Mountains. Its size alone is staggering: Over 10 square miles of shops, homes, and storage facilities were being built underground — an area greater than that of the entire city of Washington, D.C. The *Times* reported that the facility includes railways, factories, and apartment complexes — everything hundreds of thousands of people need to survive a nuclear war. And this is just one of scores of such facilities throughout Russia and the CIS (Commonwealth of Independent States).

In 1997, the *Washington Times* reported that a CIA report detailed the vast underground network includes a subway from the Kremlin directly to facilities in the Ural Mountains. If the Cold War is really over and Russia is our friend, why have they built this enormous system of shelters?

11. Russia has a sophisticated anti-ballistic missile system. According to William Lee, a former Defense Intelligence Agency analyst, Russia has between 10,000 and 12,000 anti-ballistic missiles ringing Russia, controlled by 18 battle management radar systems. The only possible use for this system is to neutralize a nuclear counterattack by the United States. Under Russia's 1972 Anti-Ballistic Missile Treaty with the United States, this anti-missile system is completely illegal. Moreover, the system is widely believed to use nuclear weapons at the tips of its interceptor missiles, which could be exploded high above the atmosphere to knock out incoming U.S. missiles. Clinton has yet to utter one word of protest.

United States Is Unprepared for War

At the same time that Russia has been building an enormous war machine and making war preparations, the U.S. has been slashing its strategic nuclear arsenal, mothballing ships, and eliminating entire military battle groups.

Equally suicidal, Clinton has cut troop levels in the U.S. Army by 40 percent and the Air Force, Navy and Marines by over 30 percent. Clinton has also tied up many of America's best troops in endless and futile foreign quagmires, including "peacekeeping" in Bosnia and the Middle East, humanitarian projects in Africa, and drug interdiction in Latin America. Few troops are left to defend the United States.

Clinton has also been throwing away America's limited arsenal of cruise missiles. These missiles were primarily built to deliver strategic nuclear warheads deep into Russia. Russia is believed to be vulnerable to such weapons because they evade radar and fly low to the ground.

ABC News reports that before Operation Desert Fox (our recent, undeclared war on Iraq) the U.S. had just 239 cruise missiles left. In the first few days of Desert Fox Clinton ordered that over 90 of these precious cruise missiles be fired on Iraq against what has proven to be mainly empty warehouses and radar installations that were rebuilt in days. As this article is being written, additional cruise missiles have been launched in continuing confrontations with Iraq.

Each missile expended in Iraq is one less that can be used to defend the U.S. — and at the current rate of expenditure, the U.S. military would have none left in less than 30 days. Why is Bill Clinton squandering these crucial weapons? This question becomes even more serious when one considers that the U.S. is not currently making cruise missiles and has no plans to do so.

And this is just one way that, under Clinton, America is being stripped of its ability to defend itself. Never before has the U.S. been so ill prepared to defend its own territory and citizens. Here are the chilling facts:

1. The United States has practically no civil defense system to pro-

tect its citizens from a biological, chemical or nuclear attack.

2. The United States has no anti-ballistic missile system to protect against incoming missiles.

3. U.S. defense spending has been dramatically reduced, from about 28 percent of the federal budget in 1988 by almost half, to 17 percent today. Former Secretary of Defense Casper Weinberger states in his book *The Next War:*

". . . the United States has embarked on a massive disarmament. Since 1985, military budgets have declined 35 percent. Spending on research and development has been slashed by 57 percent, and procurement of newly produced weapons by a whopping 71 percent."

4. U.S. naval forces have been slashed. These forces are vital for protecting the U.S. against foreign threats such as Middle Eastern terrorism and potential attacks on allies like Taiwan and South Korea. Today the Navy only has 336 ships compared to over 600 in 1991. That's the lowest number of ships since the late 1930s.

More frightening is the fact that U.S. naval surface ships have been stripped of their tactical nuclear weapons. Even though the U.S. Navy is still much larger than Russia's or China's, without nuclear weapons the U.S. fleets are sitting ducks for Russian and Chinese nuclear weapons.

5. The critical balance of nuclear weapons between Russia and the United States has tilted in Russia's favor. If intelligence estimates are accurate, the U.S. and Russia share an almost equal number of strategic nuclear weapons, but Russia has a huge advantage in tactical nuclear weapons.

The Clinton administration has systematically destroyed the U.S. stockpile of tactical nuclear weapons. Under Clinton, the total number of tactical nukes has dropped from approximately 20,000 weapons in 1988 to a few thousand today. And every day, under Clinton's orders, the military destroys more tactical nuclear weapons.

Even with these cuts, the Clinton administration is still not happy, and has pushed the Pentagon to seek unilateral cuts well below the current Start I floor of 6,000 strategic weapons.

6. U.S. military preparedness is at the lowest level in 50 years. On March 20, 1998, the General Accounting Office reported to Congress on the preparedness of the five of the Army's 10 divisions that would deploy in the second wave of an overseas war. The results were grim: 1st Infantry Division — the division's 1st brigade had only 56 percent of the personnel needed to fill its armored vehicles. Many brigades were only partially filled or had no personnel at all assigned to them.

25th Infantry Division — 52 of 162 infantry squads were "minimally filled or had no personnel assigned."

1st Armored Division — only 16 of the unit's 116 tanks had full, battle-qualified four-man crews.

4th Infantry Division — 13 of 54 squads in the divisions engineer brigade either had no personnel assigned or fewer personnel than required.

7. America is paying for Russia's rearmament. Under programs like Nunn-Lugar, the U.S. has paid Russia billions to dismantle nuclear warheads because Russia said it did not have the money to pay for it (odd, since they have plenty of money to build new missiles, aircraft carriers, and submarines). By funding these expensive warhead dismantling programs for Russia's obsolete weapons, the U.S. has enabled the Russians to divert millions of dollars to building new weapons.

8. President Clinton has unilaterally changed more than four decades of U.S. defense policy of "launch on warning." Under a secret Clinton directive — known as a Presidential Decision Directive or PDD — issued in November of 1997, the United States would accept a first strike and only retaliate after millions of our citizens had been killed.

Some of the details of the PDD were leaked to the *Washington Post* (12/7/97). The *Post* reported that the Clinton administration was unilaterally changing America's nuclear defense posture. Clinton's PDD directed the U.S. military to no longer plan to win a nuclear war with Russia.

Just weeks after the *Washington Post* report, on December 23, Robert Bell gave an interview to *Arms Control Today*. Bell, senior director for defense policy and arms control at the National Security Council, helped draft the PDD.

Bell revealed more astounding details of the PDD and Clinton's new policy:

"In this PDD we direct our military forces to continue to posture themselves in such a way as to not rely on launch on warning — to be able to absorb a nuclear strike and still have enough force surviving to constitute credible deterrence," Bell said.

Bell continued, "Our policy is to confirm that we are under nuclear attack with actual detonations before retaliating."

In other words, Clinton is willing to wait until American cities, military installations, and our vulnerable land-based ICBMs are devastated before counterattacking. If, God forbid, such a surprise attack was launched, most of the U.S.'s strategic weapons would be destroyed and there would be little left to retaliate with.

Clinton's new launch policy is an invitation for Russia to attack. With the U.S. prevented from launching on warning, a Russian first strike could wipe out two of the three legs of America's strategic defense triad: land-based missiles and strategic bombers.

At any given time, six of America's 18 ballistic missile submarines are in port and would probably be destroyed in a Russian first strike under the Clinton doctrine. All that would be left to defend America would be 12 ballistic submarines with 180 megatons of warheads. That's over less than 50 percent of the 400 megatons required under MAD to deter Russia. (MAD refers to the policy of Mutually Assured Destruction, a policy that kept America safe in the nuclear age.)

Given Russia's missile defense system, modernized weapons and vast system of underground shelters, it is easy to see why Russia might find launching a first strike against America in 1999 tempting and any losses they would suffer "acceptable."

Russia could destroy every major American city and military target, and suffer only limited retaliation against its own cities even if America fired every surviving nuclear weapon. After America launched its handful of surviving missiles, Russia would still have tens of thousands of weapons in its arsenal, making it the only military superpower on Earth and the world's likely ruler.

Further evidence that Clinton has diabolically sought to undermine America's nuclear arsenal are his numerous proposals to "de-alert" U.S. nuclear forces. Clinton claims that the real risk of war is from the U.S. accidentally launching nuclear weapons. To prevent such an "accident," the *Washington Times* reports, the Clinton administration plans on "removing the integrated circuit boards from ICBMs and storing them hundreds of miles away, taking the warheads off the MX missile or possibly the Minuteman ICBMs, welding shut the missile hatches of some submarines, and doubling the number of orders a hard-to-communicate submarine would have to receive before it could launch a missile."

The purpose of these changes would be increase the time to launch a weapon "from minutes, to hours or even days." The truth is that in a nuclear war an unlaunched weapon may never be launched.

Since Clinton can make such policy changes by issuing a secret PDD, these dangerous moves can be made without informing the public or Congress. There are some indications that, in fact, Clinton has taken steps to make it more difficult for our submarines to launch their missiles.

9. America's land-based missiles are vulnerable. The Defense Department estimates that Russia would need to fire only about 15 percent of its ICBMs to destroy two-thirds to 85 percent of U.S. silos. In contrast, Peter Vincent Pry, a former CIA analyst, reports that Russia's ICBMs are "in harder silos and on mobile launchers" — making them less vulnerable to an American counterattack.

10. The United States has not sanctioned Russia for breaking the ABM Treaty and many other arms control treaties we have signed with them — including bans on biological and chemical weapons, weapons modernization, and construction of vast underground bunkers.

Why hasn't the Clinton administration made receipt of aid from the U.S., IMF and the World Bank (which are controlled by the U.S.) conditional upon Russian demilitarization or at least their abiding by the treaties they have signed? Why do the U.S. and U.N. continue to pour tens of billions of dollars into Russia while they are building a vast war machine and apparently preparing for war?

11. Foreign deployment of troops leaves the U.S. vulnerable to foreign military occupation. U.S. troops are currently deployed in some 160 countries, with large deployments in Bosnia and the Mideast.

Nyquist argues that foreign deployment is an ominous sign, since the United States would not have an army to protect the United States proper.

Since Nyquist made those comments, President Clinton has sent tens of thousands of U.S. troops to the Mideast, along with most of our naval forces and strategic bombers. This is extremely dangerous, since by deploying our strategic bombers overseas, they are cut off from their nuclear weapons and are sitting ducks for a Russian attack.

Why Are Most Americans Oblivious to These Terrifying Facts?

There are many reasons.

1. In today's society, where hundreds of stories compete for attention, a story must be reported over and over again and repeated by several different types of media (such as TV and newspapers and news magazines) before it penetrates the public consciousness.

2. The establishment press has not regularly reported on military developments in Russia. Most media have unthinkingly swallowed the Clinton line that "Russia and China are our friends," hook, line and sinker.

3. Media omissions and distortions, coupled with Clinton administration propaganda about "our friend, Russia" and "our friend, China," have left the overwhelming majority of those in Congress and the military totally ignorant of the new military threat posed by the Russians and Chinese.

4. U.S. military leaders who are aware of Russian rearmament and U.S. disarmament in their particular area of expertise (for instance strategic bombers) may be unaware of the big picture, i.e., how extensive those trends are.

Further, military officials who want to speak out may fear being fired or blacklisted from employment by defense contractors after they leave the military. Many probably also buy the official line that "the Cold War is over" so there's no reason to be concerned about Russian military exercises or overflights of the U.S. or the closure of U.S. military bases.

Others may believe, with some justification, there is no one in the mainstream they can turn to who will honestly report Russian rearmament and U.S. disarmament.

5. Russia appears to be making most of its preparations in the open, so as not to arouse suspicion, lulling U.S. observers into a false sense of security. After all, if the Russians are conducting military exercises out in the open and announcing redeployment of missiles to the seas, there can't be anything sinister about it, can there?

6. The idea of a REAL nuclear war that would destroy America is so alien to most Americans that most can't even imagine it, much less try to stop it. Unfortunately this is not the case in Russia, which discussed and threatened nuclear war against the United States for 50 years. Russian strategic military planning has been based on a nuclear war with the U.S. for decades. Unlike Americans who believe that "there are no winners in nuclear war," Russia's leaders believe they can win a nuclear confrontation. Having lived through repeated invasions by foreign enemies, such as the Nazi destruction of Stalingrad, the Russian people know from firsthand experience they and their nation can survive and recover from enormous military devastation.

7. America's intelligence agencies cannot be totally relied upon. Clinton has drastically reduced the number of CIA personnel in covert operations — the cloak-and-dagger spies necessary for getting first-hand information.

The United States has unquestioned technical spying ability. However, there are limits to what we can discern about Russian intentions and plans from spy satellites. That's when it counts to have a man in the Kremlin.

However, the U.S. has never had a top-level spy in Russia's intelligence services above the rank of colonel. No senior members of the Politburo or any members of the Russian General Staff have ever defected to the West. Even in East Germany and Cuba, all our "top" spies have all turned out to be double agents for the communists.

Spy agencies, like the CIA, also are often wrong. The CIA didn't know Saddam Hussein was planning to invade until his tanks were crushing Kuwait. The CIA was caught completely by surprise when India detonated several nuclear explosions. If we don't know for sure what Iraq and India are up to, how can we be sure about Russia?

Famous Russian Dissidents Warn America

Writing in the *Wall Street Journal* after the recent economic up-
heaval in Russia and resurgence of totalitarianism, former Russian chess
champion Garry Kasparov notes, "Strangely enough, few Western
policy makers seem willing to acknowledge the implications of the
drastic political changes under way in Russia. The immediate signs of
a shift are unmistakable."

Kasparov further notes that since the apparent breakup of the Soviet Union, no real "reforms" or "real liberalization" has taken place
in Russia. That is certainly not the perception of Russia here in the
West. Kasparov's views are not entirely different from those of
Alexander Solzhenitsyn, who wrote in 1997 that the West's perception of Russia is skewed and doesn't examine "Russia's overall condition and the forces at work in that country, but on the latest
developments, such as elections to the Duma, the firing of Alexander
Lebed and Boris Yeltsin's heart surgery. Any broad, deep view of what's
happening gets lost."

Solzhenitsyn sees clearly. He writes: "As far as I can judge, two
strongly held opinions are widely shared in the West: that during the
last few years democracy has unquestionably been established in Russia, albeit one under a dangerously weak national government, and that
effective economic reforms have been adapted to foster the creation of
a free market, to which the way is now open."

"Both views are mistaken," Solzhenitsyn concludes.

Totalitarians with nuclear weapons remain firmly in charge of Russia and the other states of the former Soviet Union. Communist governments in China and, most likely, North Korea, also have nuclear
weapons and have repeatedly threatened to use them against the United
States if we try to thwart their plans or do anything to diminish their
power. For instance, it was reported in the *New York Times* in 1996 that
China had warned that if the U.S. interfered in a showdown between
China and Taiwan, China would destroy Los Angeles and other American
cities.

There is growing evidence that Russia and China are planning for a
major war with the United States, and that they could deliver a killing
blow anytime in the next two years. The Y2K problem has signifi-

cantly increased the possibility of war during 1999 or just after the turn of the clock to the year 2000.

What the U.S. Can Do

The end of the Cold War, and U.S. victories against that third-rate dictator Saddam Hussein, have lulled America into a false sense of complacency. Most Americans — including our leaders in Congress and the military — believe that our power is unchallengeable and all-out war with communist nations is no longer possible. When you combine that misperception with a president who seems more concerned about the satisfaction of his libido than the fate of America, you have a recipe for disaster.

Russia may not launch an attack on the U.S., but the weaker the U.S., the stronger the temptation. How can we reduce that temptation? By bringing the troops home, returning to launch on warning, keeping more ballistic missile submarines operational and at sea, and returning our strategic bombers to the U.S. where they can be quickly armed with nuclear weapons. We should also return to our policy of keeping some strategic bombers airborne at all times. The removal from office of Bill Clinton will also be a positive step toward rebuilding America's defense posture and the morale of her troops.

Those steps would make the U.S. far better prepared for war and would make an attack on U.S. soil too costly for the Russians to even contemplate.

Russia Helps Syria's Chemical Weapons Program

NewsMax.com Vortex, February 1999 — Unofficial secret links have been uncovered between former Russian officials and Syria that are aimed at helping Damascus to produce advanced chemical weapons, according to intelligence sources.

Syria has been developing chemical agents since the mid-1980s, but it is now feared that sophisticated Russian technology has been passed to Syria by former members of Moscow's chemical weapons project.

British intelligence sources said they believed that, although many countries were developing chemical and biological weapons, there was as yet no indication that states were prepared to pass on the expertise to sponsored terrorist groups.

However, the alleged involvement of former members of the Russian chemical weapons project in passing on key technology to Damascus — in breach of the Chemical Weapons Convention, of which Russia is a signatory — has highlighted the increasing danger posed by these systems.

— *Times* of London

U.S. Held pow Info

NewsMax.com Vortex, December 1998 — Secretary of State Madeleine K. Albright waited months before asking the Russian government about a KGB document suggesting captured Americans were taken to the Soviet Union for intelligence purposes during the late 1960s, according to Clinton administration officials.

A document mentioning the KGB program was discovered by the Pentagon in January among the papers of a retired Russian general. President Clinton was notified in March about what investigators viewed as a major discovery that could shed light on the fate of nearly 2,000 missing Americans from the Vietnam War. A month later, the State Department was informed.

— www.washtimes.com

Russia: Spying Remains Priority

NewsMax.com Vortex, November 1998 — "First Deputy Prime Minister Yuri Maslyukov's announcement that he intends to actively revitalize the military-industrial complex by allocating it greater budget funding," according to former KGB officer Preobrazhensky, means that theft of military technology from Western countries will remain a Moscow priority. "Consequently, and just as in the Soviet years," he writes in the *Moscow Times,* "the Foreign Intelligence Service's 'T' Division [Directorate T], the scientific and technical intelligence wing that gathers technical military secrets from around the world, will enjoy a stable demand for its information, generating money to expand the service's foreign missions."

— *Russia Reform Monitor,* www.afpc.org

Moscow Still Uses Cuba as Base to Spy on U.S.

By Colonel Stanislav Lunev

NewsMax.com Vortex, April 2000 — Today's Cuba is one of the last strongholds of old-style communism. After the Union of Soviet Socialist Republics collapsed nine years ago and international communism suffered major setbacks elsewhere, it survives on the so-called freedom island and shows no signs of disappearing in the near future.

As is typical for totalitarian rule, everything in Cuba is under government control. Virtually all daily activities of Cuban citizens are dictated by the communist iron fist. No time is wasted on explaining to people the reasons behind the countless rules and regulations that are forced upon them. Blind obedience to endless restrictions is non-negotiable. The rights and liberties that Americans take for granted are non-existent. There are no freedoms of speech, assembly, travel, education or choice in Cuba.

Despite these ugly verities, with support from Communist China and "democratic" Russia, the Cuban regime is again strengthening its position in the Latin American countries by means of anti-American propaganda in addition to more aggressive strategies.

The Russian newspaper *Izvestia* has the following to report on Cuba's recent past:

"For nearly three decades Cuba ranked first among all foreign countries in terms of the density of agents of Moscow's two intelligence services per square kilometer of its territory. This island right under America's nose was used as an ideal bridgehead for electronic monitoring and as a base for sending agents into Latin American countries.

"Right up until the end of the eighties, Soviet agents in Cuba observed carefully as Castro's military and political intelligence services carried out terrorist acts on a wide scale from Argentina to Canada, not shrinking from attacks on banks and the kidnapping of major industrialists, and trained entire rebel armies on Cuban territory.

"With the start of the collapse of the U.S.S.R., Castro had to curtail these operations — the money stopped arriving from Moscow. However, a Russian radio-electronic center continues to operate on the island to this day."

According to a joint statement by the Russian defense and foreign ministries, the purpose of this radio-electronic center at Lourdes, a Havana suburb, is to track American missiles and maintain communications with Russian embassies in Latin America. Its most important task, however, is the overall monitoring of activities in the United States.

Izvestia reported that "the U.S. always regarded the Russian military presence on the island with great jealousy but does not object in principle to the continuing existence of the electronic center in Cuba, which Washington regards as a counterweight to an analogous American station in Turkey."

Russian policy is committed to preserving its presence in Cuba. With secret assistance from Western collaborators, Russia has succeeded not only in rebuilding the former Soviet Union's position in Cuba but also in dramatically improving it.

Despite the Russian Federation's financial collapse, Kremlin leaders are able annually to come up with hundreds of millions of dollars to help Cuba complete its nuclear power plant at Juragua, the construction of which was begun by the former U.S.S.R.

The ostensible reason for the Russian assistance is to help Cuba save about 4.9 million barrels of oil per year, to alleviate the country's energy crisis and to help Castro repay a $20 billion debt to the Russian Federation, as the Soviet Union's main successor.

In truth, however, the completion of this nuclear plant will give the Kremlin a permanent presence in the Western Hemisphere and allow it to blackmail the United States with the ever-present threat of a nuclear "accident" 180 miles south of the Florida Keys. Such an accident could be orchestrated at any time deemed advantageous to R.F. leaders.

The Juragua power plant allows Russia to establish a military beachhead in this highly geostrategic area, where it can easily station a wide array of military forces. This military presence will be directed not only against the United States but also against most, if not all, of the Atlantic allies.

Presently, Russia has only a limited military presence in Cuba, due to American policies in this area and to Russia's economic difficulties. Nevertheless, Russia and Cuba are now actively intensifying their cooperative efforts, while the Russian SIGINT (Signals Intelligence) station at Lourdes continues its usual activities.

These developments provide the foundation for a massive deployment of Russian forces to Cuba whenever the Kremlin-Castro axis feels it is to their benefit.

Controlled and operated by the Russian Military Strategic Intelligence Agency (GRU), the Lourdes station maintains a radio-intelligence field over the Atlantic Ocean and collects cyber-intelligence data in close cooperation with Russian military spy satellites and naval and air force reconnaissance.

The Lourdes station penetrates coded and ciphered radio-technical signals in the eastern part of the United States and tracks the patrol routes of U.S. nuclear subs around the Atlantic. But the station is providing the Russian military also with extremely important economic data about the United States and other Atlantic Rim countries.

The strategic importance of the Lourdes station has grown substantially since a secret order was issued by former President Boris Yeltsin on February 7, 1996, that requires Russian intelligence to intensify the theft of American and other Western trade and manufacturing secrets.

This military and domestic espionage presents a formidable threat to the United States. If there are still those who remain skeptical, "America's friend in the Kremlin" (to quote his own words) Yeltsin ordered his secret agents "to close the technology gap with the West and to make better use of industrial espionage."

The existence of the Lourdes SIGINT station is, nevertheless, well known to the West. But it is only one of a number of secret Russian military presences in Cuba. The others have still maintained a successful cover. Only a very limited number of intelligence specialists are aware that the Lourdes station is merely a part of the Russian intelligence operations in Cuba, which are under the general command of the main GRU center on the island.

This center, located near Havana, exists in addition to the GRU field office, which operates out of the R.F. Embassy. The operatives in the center, as well as those of the embassy, have as their chief assignment the recruitment of people from the Latin American countries. They train and send them to the United States, Canada and other areas of the world to spy against America and its allies. The Russian intelligence presence in Cuba comprises hundreds of highly trained professionals. In addition to GRU operations, the SVR (formerly the KGB) has its own separate field office, intelligence center and other intelligence stations. Hundreds of SVR intelligence officers in Cuba are doing the same job as the GRU agents, and their primary target is penetrating secrets of America as well as those of its allies. Thus, the Russian Federation is willing to pay any price to keep the Castro regime in power.

The new Russian elite considers Cuba an invaluable transshipment nexus for drug trafficking from the so-called Golden Triangle and Central Asia to the American continent. Moscow's *Komsolmolskaya Pravda* (July 1995) disclosed that Cuba is an essential linchpin in the drug operations of the most powerful Russian financial and industrial consortia, created in the 1990s by former KGB officers with former KGB and Communist Party money.

This organization is headed by a four-star general, who was the first-deputy KGB chief and boss of the Fifth KGB Main Directorate. He is known for persecuting Soviet dissidents. His former KGB officers took control of, and expanded, the drug route from Afghanistan to the United States and Western Europe via the Trans-Caucasus and Russia.

These former KGB officers, the Moscow paper noted, linked up with other former KGB men working in drug-producing areas of Laos, Burma, Cambodia and Korea and with the KGB stationed at Camran Bay, Vietnam. They then set up a shipment chain between Cuba and these regions and the drug lords in Italy, Romania and Colombia.

The Castro regime has not shed its totalitarian nature and it never will. In addition to Russian aid, it is being bolstered by support from other totalitarian and rogue states. These countries all have one major characteristic in common — they hate the United States and see Cuba as a springboard for their anti-American purposes. It isn't easy to assess the scope of these influences, but, in the words of the Russian newspaper *Segodny*, the Kremlin has proclaimed that "Russia needs the Freedom Island again."

With Moscow's ongoing rapprochement with Cuba, the prominent military analyst Pavel Felgengauer, well known for his high-level R.F.

military-defense contacts, stated in the same article, "If NATO seriously contemplates deploying its nuclear weapons in Poland, our nuclear missiles may reappear in Cuba."

Russia continues to play its game of giving with one hand and taking with the other. Despite the reduction in the size of its nuclear arsenal, it is not only using Western dollars to upgrade its nuclear missile and other military technology, but also is threatening to re-deploy its weaponry on the soil of our nearest Atlantic neighbor. Yet, many Americans would like to "normalize" relations with this neighbor.

In reality, so-called normalization boils down to the usual common denominator, "money." Normalization — i.e., accommodation of Castro despotism — means big bucks for profit-hungry businessmen in the short term, but would seriously weaken the United States in the long term. In the latter case, no one wins, for no one will prosper in the second-rate, subjugated America that will be the final result.

Let us hope we will not help fulfill Lenin's prophecy by selling communist dictators the "rope" with which to hang us.

Colonel Stanislav Lunev is the highest-ranking Soviet military spy ever to defect to the United States. He is a regular contributor to NewsMax.com and Vortex.

CHINA

China's Taiwan 'Obsession' Pushing Navy Buildup

NewsMax.com Vortex, June 2000 — Mainland China's growing obsession over the Taiwan issue is leading Beijing to vastly increase its naval power at the expense of all its other "regional security concerns."

That's the conclusion of Captain Richard Sharpe in his foreword to the authoritative world naval almanac, *Jane's Fighting Ships 2000-2001*.

"China's increasing obsession over Taiwan is casting a growing shadow over the whole of East Asia," Sharpe wrote, citing what he called the "harder edge" of Beijing's threats against Taiwan during the period before Taiwan's March presidential elections, "effectively threatening America with extreme long-range strikes should it seek to intervene to defend Taiwan."

Asserting that China has the power to mount an invasion of Taiwan or effectively blockade the island with its existing naval forces, Sharpe said, "Neither action would be possible in the event of the U.S. becoming militarily involved," but those who still question China's naval capability should take a hard look "at Beijing's four separate submarine-building programmes and the massive inventory of surface-to-surface and air-to-surface missiles of all types."

Sharpe said that Beijing now has the ability to transport 11,000 troops and 250 main battle tanks by sea and that this "is increasing each year and in the narrow Taiwan Strait the turnaround time for amphibious ships and craft would be very short."

He warned that "anti-submarine warfare would quickly become a priority for Taiwan."

The naval expert also raised the matter of China's activities in the disputed Spratly Islands in the South China Sea now claimed by Brunei, Malaysia, the Philippines, Taiwan and Vietnam.

"Further enforcement of Chinese claims seems inevitable in the future," he said. In the last armed conflict around the islands, China sank three Vietnamese vessels.

In response to the Beijing threat, Sharpe said, a regional security forum under the Association of Southeast Asian Nations that includes Brunei, Cambodia, Indonesia, Laos, Malaysia, Burma, the Philippines, Singapore, Thailand and Vietnam offers an opportunity for a mutual defense pact in the South China Sea area.

China's Air Power Shifts to Offensive

NewsMax.com Vortex, April 2000 — The Chinese air force is boosting its strike capacity and hi-tech capability, including the use of information technology, in line with the needs of the increasingly information-driven future, according to its commander.

Lt. General Liu Shunyao said China's air force "is shifting from national air defense towards defense plus offense."

"It is only with both offensive and defensive capabilities that we can effectively deter aggression and realize what Sun Tsu, a Chinese pioneer military strategist [3rd century B.C.], said: 'Achieve victory without fighting,' " Liu said.

He stressed that in the 21st century, the People's Liberation Army air force would be guided by the active defense policy as well as the aim of "winning local wars directed against China under hi-tech conditions on short notice."

The frontiers of war would stretch to outer space, and there would be "profound changes in air operational theory," he said.

—*South China Morning Post*

China Threatens Missile Strike Against U.S.

NewsMax.com Vortex, April 2000 — Missiles will fly toward the United States if it comes to the defense of Taiwan in an all-out war between the two Chinas, Beijing's official military organ has warned.

American intervention in any military conflict between Beijing and Taiwan would result in "serious damage" to U.S. interests in Asia, the newspaper warned, adding that China would use long-range missiles against the United States.

"China is neither Iraq nor Yugoslavia but a very special country," according to *Liberation Army Daily*, the official military newspaper.

"It is a country that has certain abilities of launching strategic counterattack and the capacity of launching a long-distance strike. The U.S. military will even be forced to [make] a complete withdrawal from the East Asian region, as they were forced to withdraw from southern Vietnam in those days."

The latest blast in the war of words over the Taiwan issue echoed a 1995 warning issued by Chinese Lt. General Xiong Guangkai, the army's top intelligence and foreign-policy official, who said the United States would avoid intervening in a war between the two Chinas if it cared more about Los Angeles than it cared about Taiwan.

Despite the ominous tone of Beijing's recent statements over the Taiwan issue, the Communist Chinese have left gaping loopholes in their official stance.

A senior official noted that in the section of a February 21 Chinese white paper threatening war, the official version of the document says that Beijing would use force only if Taiwan "indefinitely refuses to resolve the reunification issue by peaceful negotiations."

"Notice that there is no timetable in the document, so you shouldn't worry that we are about to invade," the official told the *Washington Post*'s John Pomfret. "We simply are tired of the Taiwanese avoiding the issues. We view Taiwan as ours. We think we have the right to affect events in that region."

In a revealing interview, the top Chinese official told Pomfret that Beijing's bellicose statements are merely meant to jump-start negotiations with Taiwan over the reunification issue.

"We want Taiwan to start negotiations. It's that simple," a senior Chinese government official told Pomfret, who said the white paper "was issued to get [Taiwan's] attention."

In that widely reported document Beijing threatened, again, to use force against Taiwan if it seeks formal independence. The paper warned that Beijing will use "all drastic measures possible, including the use of force."

"Any attempt to separate Taiwan from China through the so-called referendum would only lead the Taiwan people to disaster," the white paper said.

The latest threat is a clear attempt to undermine the American public's determination to defend Taiwan.

It came during a visit to Beijing by Admiral Dennis Blair, the commander of U.S. Pacific Forces, to discuss the issue of Taiwan with Chinese military officials.

It also coincided with planned U.S. fleet maneuvers in the area, which U.S. defense officials deny has any connection with current tensions.

Get Ready for War, Chinese Army Told

NewsMax.com Vortex, April 2000 — The Chinese People's Liberation Army has been asked to "prepare actively" for war with Taiwan, the army daily reported.

The call was made during a meeting of military delegates, the *Liberation Army Daily* said.

At the meeting, presided over by Defense Minister Chi Haotian, "12 delegates called for active and detailed preparations for a military conflict against Taiwan," it reported.

Central Military Commission member Fu Quanyou was quoted as saying: "We must strengthen the sense of the army's role and prepare with all-out efforts for the military conflict.

"If pro-independence forces seek to divide the country, we will have to take drastic measures."

—*South China Morning Post*

China Adds New Subs to Its Special Fleet

NewsMax.com Vortex, February 2000 — The China Ocean Shipping Company has contracted the building of two 18,000-ton submarines to form the Communist Chinese navy's Guangzhou "special purpose" fleet.

The Internet information site of COSCO, the government-owned ship-building company, reports this was the first order that mainland China's domestic shipyards have ever received for the building of such vessels.

It said the design for the subs, based on works of European companies, includes an advanced electronic propelling system. According to the Itar-Tass news agency in Russia, the Chinese government is also considering buying a third Project 636 submarine from Russia.

China Continues to Aid North Korea's Rockets

NewsMax.com Vortex, February 2000 — After promising to quit, China is still helping fellow-Communist North Korea develop the long-range missiles President Clinton hopes he can defend the United States against.

It is Clinton's proposed missile defense system that so infuriates Russia that Russia threatens to break the mutual-destruction Anti-Ballistic Missile Treaty, which kept the delicately balanced peace throughout the Cold War.

In turn, that is the rationale given by Russia for its increasingly aggressive anti-American military moves, including development of an advanced missile it says will be able to penetrate any shield the United States can create.

It was also the basis of then-President Boris Yeltsin's mission to Beijing, where he solidified even closer military, economic and political ties with the communist rulers of China.

In that package is a stepped-up investment of Chinese money into cash-poor Russia's expanding arms production.

Part of the material China has been sending to North Korea, in violation of its agreement with the United States and 28 other nations, is missile technology believed to have been obtained through Chinese spying in the United States and liberalized exports of U.S. high-tech equipment authorized by Clinton.

Congressional Republicans have asserted that the millions of dollars in illegal contributions China laundered into the 1996 re-election campaign of Clinton and Vice President Al Gore was a *quid pro quo* for administration approval of such shipments.

The latest piece to emerge in that mosaic of international intrigue was the discovery by the *Washington Times* of Pentagon knowledge of the heretofore secret shipment of Chinese long-range missile equipment to North Korea, which the State Department has branded a "rogue state." The *Times* reported that:

• The latest shipment was arranged by China through a Hong Kong company, according to an intelligence report passed to the White House in late December 1999 by the National Security Agency (NSA).

• "This is a deal for a direct shipment of Chinese missile technology," said a *Times* source who had read the report.

• The most recent missile dealing is further evidence China is reneging on promises President Jiang Zemin made in 1999, when he visited Clinton in Washington, that it would tighten exports of missile technology covered by the 29-nation Missile Technology Control Regime.

• In October 1999, U.S. intelligence agencies reported China had supplied fiber-optic gyroscopes to North Korea several months earlier.

• On March 8, 1999, the NSA reported China had sold specialty steel to North Korea for its missiles.

• Chinese and North Korean scientific institutes share space research that U.S. intelligence agencies believe masks missile technology.

• The Defense Intelligence Agency reported in June 1999 that China was supplying North Korea with high-tech machinery, including accelerometers and gyroscopes, needed by its missile manufacturers.

• A congressional national-security expert said links between China and North Korea on weapons technology are so close it is likely the Chinese have allowed North Korea access to its nuclear-warhead data.

• In October 1999, the Pentagon reported North Korea's long-range Taepo Dong missile, tested in August 1998, could be used in a missile crisis.

• A spokesman for the Chinese Embassy in Washington denied China has sold missile components to North Korea.

China Tightens Noose on Religious Freedom

NewsMax.com Vortex, February 2000 — A leading American rabbi says that repression of religious expression by China's communist government has increased alarmingly.

The warning was issued by Rabbi David Saperstein, chairman of the United States Commission on International Religious Freedom.

Writing in the official bulletin of the commission, Saperstein noted the sentencing of six Protestant Christian leaders in central China.

"The only crimes these Christians are guilty of is worshipping God according to the dictates of their consciences," he said.

"The exercise of state power in trying to quash religious expression — including arrests, imprisonment and the use of state-run media to slander people because of their religious practice, worship or teaching — is alarming to those who care about religious freedom."

The commission reported that repression of religion in China is not confined to any one faith but has worsened considerably for all.

This is backed up by recent reports in the *China Reform Monitor*, a publication of the American Foreign Policy Council:

• Chinese Communist authorities have blocked a religious dissident, Dr. Xu Yonghai, from attending a Christian gathering in Chicago to mark the new millennium.

The Associated Press reported that Beijing's Religious Affairs Bureau said it could not approve his trip because he was not a representative of an official church.

Xu is a practicing Protestant with connections to the underground church, and spent 2.5 years in prison for pro-democracy activities.

He recently wrote to the National People's Congress, complaining that government authorities were blocking religious exchanges with groups outside China.

• The communist government, which views religious freedom as a threat to the Chinese state, is using religious oppression to send a strong warning message to its own key party members.

Four top organizers of the banned Falun Gong religious movement who were sentenced recently to up to 18 years in prison were all prominent members of the ruling Communist Party.

• The *Washington Post* said President Jiang Zemin appears baffled by the strength of commitment to the Falun Gong meditation movement and lack of international support for China's crackdown.

It linked the severity of the sentences to the Communists' alarm at the tenacity and strength of beliefs of the Falun Gong practitioners.

• Frank Lu Siqing of the Hong Kong–based Information Center for Human Rights and Democratic Movement in China said the tough sentences were imposed deliberately on party members to warn of the consequences for those who refuse to break with the spiritual movement.

Many top Chinese officials — including members of the Communist Party's ruling Politburo, active and retired military officers and police officials — practice Falun Gong, he said.

Chinese Spy Manual Discloses Ruse Behind 'Research'

NewsMax.com Vortex, February 2000 — Communist China's handbook for spies discloses how the government abandoned its research efforts in favor of obtaining military technology by stealth from the United States.

The 361-page book, described as "shocking" by Western intelligence analysts, describes how China maintains a massive, thorough, multifaceted intelligence-gathering system abroad, with the United States as the prime target.

Titled *Sources and Methods of Obtaining National Defense Science and Technology Intelligence,* the manual has been detailed in the *Far Eastern Economic Review*, according to the *China Reform Monitor*.

The *Review* observes that the book negates Beijing's rebuttal of the Cox Commission Report, which accused Communist China of developing its military technology behind a facade of supposedly non-military research.

The *China Reform Monitor* reported:

• The book, published in 1991, is written by two of China's top military intelligence specialists, Huo Zhongwen and Wang Zongxiao, who have served in the China National Defense Science and Technology Information Center.

• Their book describes how the Center was setting up a database of "famous scientists" overseas, including details such as their home addresses and "whether they have ever visited China."

• It contends at least 80 percent of intelligence needed by the Chinese military is readily available through open sources including published materials, public events such as conferences or seminars and electronic information.

• The authors say classified materials can also be obtained through personal relationships, bribes or computer hacking.

• The manual devotes a special section to the United States as the source of critical technologies for China's military modernization.

• Detailed explanations are given of technical information sources in Congress, the Department of Defense, the Department of Energy and NASA.

• The manual notes that reports of research laboratories of the Energy Department "contain a lot of information on nuclear research that have both civilian and military application . . . they are a highly valuable intelligence."

• It shows that China made the decision in the early 1980s to switch from home-grown military research to foreign espionage.

Russia and China Get Jump on New Missile

NewsMax.com Vortex, February 2000 — Russia and Communist China have taken a giant step toward wresting tactical air supremacy from the West.

Using Russian technology backed by Chinese funding, the two new military partners in a coalition aimed against the United States have developed an air-to-air missile that can overtake and destroy any fighter plane in the world.

Attributing sources in British Aerospace, one of the aircraft companies competing to equip the new Eurofighter with missiles, the *London Telegraph* reports:

• The Russian-Chinese missile, already successfully tested, could be in production in early 2005, three years ahead of any similar missile being developed in Britain.

• Royal Air Force pilots would be "highly vulnerable if flying against an enemy" equipped with the Russian-Chinese system.

• This new "ram jet" propulsion, "the next great leap forward in missile design," gives the Russian-Chinese air-combat missile a thrust 10 times longer than the six seconds of traditional air-to-air rockets.

• It has a speed three times that of sound and a range of 50 miles after being launched from a plane.

• This enables the Russian-Chinese missile to outclass current and projected British and American designs.

• The Eurofighter will enter service in 2003, but equipped with an existing air-to-air missile known as AMRAAM, which Russian fighters already have the speed to outfly.

• To try to offset that disadvantage, British Aerospace has designed a ram jet called Meteor.

• Similarly, the American firm Raytheon will offer its modernized version of AMRAAM, which has a double-pulse rocket with improved range.

• The West long suspected that Russia possessed the technical know-how to build ram jets, but doubted since the collapse of the Soviet Union it had adequate funds to enter into full-scale production.

• Russia's new partnership with China has solved that financial problem and given the two countries the jump on the West in air-to-air combat missile capability.

Is China in Control of the Panama Canal?

NewsMax.com Vortex, May 2000 — A secret government report reveals that a Chinese company with close ties to the Beijing Communist government planned to take over operation of the Panama Canal.

And according to Admiral Thomas Moorer, with facilities at both ends of the canal and an agreement with the Panamanian government,

Hong Kong-based Hutchison Whampoa Ltd. has the ability to all but control the strategic waterway.

The company has long-term 25-year leases on the ports at each end of the Canal. They are run by the Panama Ports Company, a Hutchison Whampoa subsidiary.

President Clinton almost let the Chinese cat out of the bag back in November when he appeared to agree that the Chinese firm would be running the Canal but, after his staff realized the extent of what he revealed, he pulled back, saying that he "misstated this."

When asked by a reporter if he was worried about the Chinese controlling the Canal, Clinton replied: "I think the Chinese will, in fact, be bending over backwards to make sure that they run it in a competent and able and fair manner. . . . I would be very surprised if any adverse consequences flowed from the Chinese running the Canal."

The following day, *Los Angeles Times* staff writer Norman Kempster wrote that "Clinton administration officials were aghast at the president's use of the phrase "running the Canal," which confirmed what Admiral Moorer and his allies were charging. Subsequently, Clinton stated that his reference to China "running the Canal" was a "misstatement."

The release of the report is sure to give impetus to congressional efforts to nullify the treaty that handed the Canal over to Panama — a treaty which Representative Helen Chenoweth-Hage, R-Idaho, insists is not binding on the United States.

An Army intelligence report, declassified after a Freedom of Information request from Judicial Watch, a conservative public interest law firm, flatly contradicted Clinton's claim and those of the Panamanian government that the company would have no role in the operation of the Canal — a fact easily dismissed in the light of an agreement between Hutchison Whampoa and Panama that gives the company the right to choose the pilots who take the ships through the Canal.

"It's one more piece of evidence that the Clinton administration was lying about Communist Chinese intentions in Panama," Judicial Watch President Tom Fitton told the *Washington Times*.

According to the April 22, 1998, intelligence report, an article from the Defense Intelligence Agency headed "Panama: China Awaits U.S. Departure" stated "Li Ka-shing, the owner of Hutchison Whampoa

Ltd. (HW) and Cheung Kong International holdings Ltd. (CK), is planning to take control of Panama Canal operations when the U.S. transfers it to Panama in December '99.

"Li is directly connected to Beijing and is willing to use his business influence to further the aims of [the] Chinese government," the report states. An Army intelligence analyst is quoted in the report as noting that "Li's interest in the canal is not only strategic, but also a means for outside financial opportunities for the Chinese government."

Congressional efforts to throw the treaty out are spearheaded by Representative Chenoweth, who told *The New American* magazine:

"The Panama Canal issue is far from over. The 1977 treaties under which the transfer has taken place are still invalid, and the security problems presented by the Communist Chinese and the Colombian drug lords have not gone away. We cannot even begin to expect Panama to have near the capacity and ability to deal with these powerful entities and threats to the Western Hemisphere.

"We can either sit around and wait for something bad to happen and then react, or we can take pre-emptive measures now, restoring the security of the region and functioning under valid law.

"We must, as a Congress, declare that these treaties are already, in fact, null and void, and are now being officially terminated. In so doing, Congress will send a signal to Panama that we must re-establish the strength and authority of the United States for this critical area. That is what House Joint Resolution 77 accomplishes, and I intend to continue to strongly push this legislation in the upcoming year. In fact, as more and more members of Congress learn about the seriousness of this issue, the momentum of this bill will steadily increase — and I anticipate it being a major issue in the presidential and congressional campaigns this year."

The New American noted that Admiral Moorer has repeatedly pointed out that Panama Law No. 5, passed by the Panamanian legislature on January 16, 1997, did far more than grant Hutchison Whampoa port concessions.

According to Moorer, the law grants Hutchison Whampoa — and, therefore, China — exclusive concessions, including, among other things, "control of the port of Balboa on the Pacific end of the Canal and the port of Cristobal on the Atlantic end. In addition to these critical anchorages, Hutchison was granted a monopoly on the Pacific side with its takeover of Rodman Naval Base, a U.S.-built, deep-draft port facility capable of handling, supplying, refueling, and repairing just about any warship."

Moreover, Moorer observes, it grants Li Ka-shing's company responsibility for hiring new pilots. "Pilots have complete control of all ships passing through the Canal," says Moorer. "They determine which ships may go through and when."

As Representative Chenoweth said, the Panama Canal issue is far from over.

—UPI

Already in Control of Panama Canal:
China's New Base in Bahamas

By Christopher Ruddy and Stephan Archer

NewsMax.com Vortex, February 2000 — The same Chinese company that recently took operational control of the Panama Canal is currently completing construction here of the largest container port in the world, just 60 miles from Florida.

Several United States military experts say the activities of Hutchison Whampoa Limited, a Hong Kong–based conglomerate in both Panama and the Bahamas, pose a significant risk to U.S. national security.

Officials for Hutchison Whampoa have heatedly denied any links with the Red Chinese government, but several established connections — including new evidence uncovered by NewsMax.com — suggest the Chinese government has a keen interest in the company's activities.

Close to East Coast

One port facility that has captured the interest of the Chinese government is Hutchison Whampoa's sprawling port facility in this tourist destination on Grand Bahama Island.

According to the company's Web site, the port is at one of the most strategic spots in the world because "Freeport is the closest offshore port to the East Coast of the United States, at the crossroads of routes between Europe and the Americas and through the Panama Canal."

In 1995, Hutchison Whampoa entered into a 50-50 partnership with the Grand Bahama Development Company, a privately owned Bahamian company, to develop and expand the small Freeport facility that had catered to cruise ships.

Since then, Hutchison Whampoa has helped dredge and expand the port, making it capable of handling the largest container ships on the high seas.

According to Michael powers, Hutchison Whampoa's general manager for the Freeport development, the container port is simply a "dedicated deep-water transshipment hub."

Container Shipping 'Hub'

Large container ships coming from several directions can off-load their container boxes, which can be rerouted onto other large or small container ships for delivery. The port operates, he said, much like Miami's airport might serve as a "hub" for travelers going to destinations around the globe.

Already the port is doing a brisk business in container shipments, powers said, and has the capacity to become the world's largest container port. He said the company also plans to make the port the world's largest cruise-ship destination port. Disney cruise lines will soon make Freeport a port of call.

The company has ambitious plans to create the largest air-cargo facility, on land adjacent to the port. Hutchison Whampoa has a 50 percent stake in the Grand Bahama Airport Company, which owns one of the largest airport runways in the world — more than 11,000 feet long. According to powers, the runway is capable of handling the world's largest cargo and military aircraft.

On 800 acres of wooded land adjacent to the airport, Hutchison Whampoa plans to create the Grand Bahama Sea-Air Business Center that could potentially allow for 8 million square feet in warehouse space.

Communist Ties Cited

While Hutchison Whampoa has a sterling reputation as a commercial enterprise — and has not been linked to any illegal activities such as drug or gun smuggling — the firm's ties to Communist China have raised concerns.

Senate Majority Leader Trent Lott, R-Miss., and former Defense Secretary Caspar Weinberger have expressed concerns about Hutchison Whampoa's influence over the Panama Canal.

Lott has described the Hong Kong firm as "an arm of the People's Liberation Army."

Hutchison Whampoa's chairman, Li Ka-Shing, is also a board member of CITIC — the China International Trust and Investment Corporation. U.S. intelligence sources have described the firm as a front for China's State Council.

Representative Dana Rohrbacher, R-Calif., has stated that CITIC has been used as a front company by China's military to acquire technology for weapons development. A recently declassified report by the U.S. Southern Command's Joint Intelligence Center, prepared in October 1999, said that "Hutchison Whampoa's owner, Hong Kong tycoon Li Ka-Shing, has extensive business ties in Beijing and has compelling financial reasons to maintain a good relationship with China's leadership."

The military intelligence report also warns that "Hutchison containerized shipping facilities in the Panama Canal, as well as the Bahamas, could provide a conduit for illegal shipments of technology or prohibited items from the West to the PRC, or facilitate the movement of arms and other prohibited items into the Americas."

John Meredith, the group managing director for Hutchison Port Holdings, told NewsMax.com that comments made about Hutchison Whampoa have often been erroneous and "outrageous."

He said the firm's involvement at the port in the Bahamas is simply a transshipment service.

Just Cranes, That's All

"We have no pilots," he said. "We have no tugs. We have no boats. We have no ships. We have no containers. All we have is cranes."

Meredith angrily denied any connection between the firm and the Chinese government.

"We're a public company in Hong Kong. We're not an arm of anybody," said Meredith. He pointed out that fewer than 1 percent of all Hutchison investors are Chinese.

"I'm British for starters," he said. "I don't even speak the language. It would be very difficult for someone to instruct me as to what to do.

"We've had the most outrageous comments made about what we've got down [in Panama] — missile silos and all sorts of rubbish. Anybody can come and investigate."

No Chinese on Payroll

According to powers, Hutchison Whampoa employs about 500 Bahamians. Only five managers are not Bahamians, mostly British nationals. None is Chinese. Bahamian officials told NewsMax.com they have noticed no increase in Chinese nationals at the port or on the island.

Despite the strong claims made by Hutchison that China has no interest in their Bahamian port, evidence suggests otherwise.

A review of the visitor's log by NewsMax.com at the company's main office in Freeport shows that Chinese government officials have been frequent visitors to the port facility.

According to the log, China's ambassador to the Bahamas, Ma Shuxue, has visited the port facility at least half a dozen times in the past few years. He has also accompanied groups of Chinese government officials. On other occasions Chinese governmental or commercial representatives have also paid visits without the presence of Ambassador Shuxue.

Frequent-Visitor Record

The visitor logbook indicates Chinese officials have visited the port more often than officials from any other country, including the United States.

The logbook also shows that on June 2, 1999, the Cuban ambassador, Lazaro Cabeza, also paid a visit to the facility. Cuba is a strong ally of China.

"If they have no connection to Hutchison and the port, if they are not interested in this company, why is China sending its ambassador there?" asked retired Admiral Thomas Moorer. "Why are other Chinese officials showing up there? Why is Castro's ambassador going there?"

Moorer, former chairman of the Joint Chiefs of Staff, also served as former commander in chief of the Pacific and Atlantic fleets.

"Of course the Chinese military sees the benefit of having a base, a future base, so close to the United States," Moorer said. "What China is trying to do is get a kind of maritime position worldwide, and they need a home base, so to speak, in every ocean.

Even Wanted Long Beach

"Not only are the Chinese in the Bahamas, they're in Panama and the Spratly Islands right off the Philippines. They tried to get Long Beach.

"There's no question about the fact in my mind that the Chinese military forces are affiliated with Mr. Li, who in turn runs Hutchison Whampoa."

Moorer said that while the port facilities appear harmless today, they could be used as a staging ground by the Chinese at some future point if hostilities were to arise in the Korean Peninsula or over Taiwan.

The Bahamian government said it is pleased with Hutchison Whampoa's activities, however.

Bahamians Love It

Lindy Russell, the parliamentary secretary in the office of the prime minister for the Bahamas, said that Bahamians are excited about the economic development the port brings to the island nation.

Besides development of the port, Hutchison Whampoa has other investments on the island, including a 370-acre resort in Lucaya, Grand Bahama, which includes a 49-acre beachfront site.

Russell said that U.S. officials have expressed concerns to him regarding human cargo of Chinese labor possibly coming through the ports. They had no concerns about the actual operation of the port, Russell said.

Stephan Archer is a staff writer for NewsMax.com.

China's Cyberwar Plans Trouble: DIA Chief

NewsMax.com Vortex, December 1999 — A possible Chinese assault on the United States via the Internet worries America's new head of defense intelligence.

"We are clearly interested and concerned about this whole idea of information attack," Vice Admiral Thomas Wilson, the new director of the Defense Intelligence Agency, told the *Washington Times*.

The three-star admiral was referring to a recent article in China's official military newspaper that the People's Liberation Army is preparing for a war in cyberspace on a par with conventional ground, sea and air combat.

That Chinese army article, which was reported in the *Times*, forecasts an "all-conquering" computer assault to seize "the Internet command power."

"It's a big part of this asymmetric threat, and it's probably bigger than all of outdoors in terms of trying to get your arms around it," the admiral said in his interview with the *Times*.

Calling the U.S. economy and the Pentagon very "information dependent," Wilson said:

"We recognize that information dominance is going to be important to the future, and that has to do with acquiring better information about your adversary and protecting your own.

"So when the Chinese discuss [information warfare] in the PLA daily . . . we ought to take note, and we have.

"It's a little bit disturbing. And it could also be a little bit of psychology involved."

High-Performance American Computers Aiding China

NewsMax.com Vortex, December 1999 — The Clinton administration in the past three years has approved for export to China hundreds of high-performance computers capable of aiding that country's nuclear and other weapons programs.

And while U.S. law requires the government to check up on the machines to make sure they are not used to improve China's military might, the Commerce Department, which is supposed to perform the checks, has conducted only a handful.

China Plans World's Largest Exercise in Forced Human Resettlement

NewsMax.com Vortex, December 1999 — China is planning the world's largest exercise in forced human resettlement by moving 300 million peasants into 10,000 new towns in a period of only five years. The huge population shift is a risky operation. It threatens to spark violent protests by rural people evicted from their land, and will impact heavily on the environment.

The planned migration will be in the opposite direction from that ordered by Mao Tse-tung in the Cultural Revolution of the late sixties and early seventies, when tens of millions of urban residents were sent to the countryside to work on farms and "learn from the masses."

Red Chinese Takeover of Panama Canal Must Be Stopped

By Admiral Thomas Moorer

NewsMax.com Vortex, November 1999 — For the last two years I've been fighting an often lonely battle against Bill Clinton and what could well be the deadliest sellout of America in our history.

I feel today as I did on the eve of Pearl Harbor. America is in danger and we could face another Pearl Harbor — only this time it may be a nuclear Pearl Harbor.

I am referring to Bill Clinton's decision to OK the imminent take-over of the Panama Canal by Communist China. For over 80 years, keeping the Canal under the control of the U.S. was properly regarded as vital for the safety of all Americans.

The notion that a U.S. president could allow this Canal — built and defended by the U.S. at an incredible cost in treasure and blood — to fall under the control of our avowed enemies, the Red Chinese — without a shot being fired — is incredible. Yet we are just days away from that nightmare becoming reality.

Why is the Panama Canal so important?

Strategically, the Canal is a "choke point," one of four places in the world where a small area can block trade for an entire continent. The other three are the Suez Canal, the Straits of Gilbraltar and the Molucca Straits near the Spratly Islands. (In the past year the Clinton administration has allowed the Chinese to seize some of the Spratly Islands, and they are currently building naval facilities there.)

Built and maintained by the United States at a cost of American blood and treasure — over $32 billion — more than 13,000 commercial vessels transit the Panama Canal every year, carrying 190 million long tons of cargo. Every month, over 1,000 ships use the Canal to bring food and oil to millions of Americans.

The Canal is also vital for our national defense. In the past year, our naval vessels used the Canal countless times. This 51-mile waterway cuts 8,000 miles off the trip around the southern tip of South America, saving as much as two weeks of transport time. In warfare, time means lives and that much time can mean the difference between defeat and victory.

Imagine that there was a crisis over Taiwan, or North Korean troops were invading South Korea — massacring our men there — it would be critical to control the Canal and speedily move naval forces to the area.

Now Bill Clinton wants America to abandon the Panama Canal. Unless the American people raise a terrific outcry, on December 31 Communist China will take control of the Panama Canal and begin to occupy U.S. military facilities which are now being abandoned by our troops.

If you visit Panama today, you'll see ghost towns where just a few months ago there were 10,000 U.S. troops. They're gone and there is no Panamanian army to replace them.

The Clinton administration has been quick to dispatch American troops all over the world — to places like Kosovo, Haiti, and Timor — these are places not vital to American interests.

The Panama Canal is vital for us, yet the Clinton administration won't allow any American military presence.

That makes the Panama Canal incredibly vulnerable to attack by groups like the narco terrorists who are allied with Fidel Castro and hate the U.S. . . . communist guerrillas who are operating in the area . . . and to influence by foreign powers eager to move into the strategic vacuum left by the U.S. withdrawal.

Of greatest concern is the growing Chinese presence and domination of Panama and the Canal. Panama has signed a 50-year lease for two ports at each end of the Canal with a company called "Hutchison Whampoa" run by one Li Ka-Shing. Li is a member of China's ruling power elite and Hutchison Whampoa is connected to China's ruling council.

Panama's lease with Hutchison Whampoa gives China's Communist Party *de facto* control over the most strategic waterway in the West.

Under Panama's agreement, Hutchison Whampoa will control port facilities at both ends of the Canal . . . they'll control who is allowed to pilot ships through the Canal and can assign their own pilots . . . and they'll also be able to refuse access to the Canal by any ship for "business reasons."

Senate Majority Leader Trent Lott has stated that Hutchison Whampoa is "an arm of the People's Liberation Army" and that U.S. naval ships will now be "at the mercy" of Red Chinese.

China's takeover of the Canal is an immediate threat to all Americans

Control of the Canal will give China the ability to block vital food and oil shipments to the U.S. . . . . prevent deployment of our Navy in times of national emergency . . . and create an enemy beachhead within striking distance of our cities. Red Chinese J-11 attack jets — each of which can drop 13,000 pounds of bombs — launched from Panama can strike our cities.

When Taiwan conducts its national elections this spring, less than six months from now, China could make good on its threat of war against the U.S.

In 1996 Chinese officials told the *New York Times* they were quite prepared to use nuclear weapons against American cities like Los Angelos if we tried to stop their takeover of the democratic nation of Taiwan.

Just a few months ago, the official Chinese newspaper warned the U.S. that China was willing to use nuclear bombs against American aircraft carriers if they interfered in Chinese plans to invade Taiwan.

In fact, with our Navy blocked from moving through the Canal and Chinese missiles and jets poised to launch from Panama, China could intimidate the U.S. into surrendering Taiwan, Panama, and God knows what else without a shot being fired. If that didn't work, they could just lob a few missiles at our cities.

Make no mistake about it, Communist China is our enemy

This is the same regime that massacred thousands of students at Tiananmen Square and that supplies terrorist regimes in Iran, Syria, Libya and North Korea with missiles and weapons of mass destruction. This is the same regime that "harvests" the organs of political dissidents, burns churches and imprisons millions of its own citizens in concentration camps.

This is the same China that stole our most secret nuclear weapons, missile and satellite technology and tried to smuggle into California 100,000 automatic weapons and millions of rounds of ammunition. We still don't know for sure why China was smuggling these weapons into the United States. This is the same communist government that calls America "the No. 1 enemy" and threatened to attack Los Angeles with nuclear weapons if we interfere with its planned re-conquest of Taiwan.

Thanks to Bill Clinton and China's recent, wholesale acquisition of U.S. military technology, China is now building weapons of mass destruction at breakneck speed and rapidly becoming a global military power. Control of the Panama Canal will give Communist China a beachhead for expanded aggression in Latin America and direct assault on the U.S.

If that didn't work, they could just lob a few missiles at our cities. Panama is only 300 miles away from the United States — and China has plenty of short-range missiles capable of hitting Los Angelos, Houston, Miami and many other cities.

China's impending takeover of the Panama Canal is of utmost significance to the United States, but the Clinton administration and its media friends have turned a blind eye to this dangerous development.

In light of China's massive contributions to the Clinton-Gore campaign and the Democratic National Committee, and President's Clinton's subsequent radical changes of policy to benefit the People's Republic of China, one can only wonder if this is yet another *quid pro quo* for Chinese cash.

If we allow China to take control of the Panama Canal, we are setting ourselves up for inevitable conflict. We will be forced, as a matter of national survival, at some not too distant point in the future, to go to Panama and win back militarily what we have bought and built, and what is rightfully ours. When that happens, we will have to pay a high price in blood and treasure again, because the alternative will be far worse.

Stopping Clinton's giveaway of the Canal

Until recently, even Republican members of Congress seemed oblivious to the distressing implications of surrendering control of the Panama Canal to Communist China. Finally, however, at the 11th hour, a few in Congress are waking up.

Senate Majority Leader Trent Lott and Dana Rohrbacher of California have both protested the imminent communist takeover. Lott has also requested congressional hearings into the Canal giveaway. So we now have a small window of opportunity to rollback this disaster.

We must do everything we can to encourage them and stop the giveaway of the Panama Canal.

First, inform yourself. You need to understand what's at stake in the Canal giveaway and who is responsible for it. One way you can do that is by going to www.NewsMax.com and clicking on the "Panama Canal" link under Hot Topics.

Second, alert your friends, your neighbors, journalists, and local officials. Call local talk shows, write letters to the editor, get the word out to anyone who will listen.

Third, demand that your representatives in Washington take action to stop the Canal giveaway. Call your congressman and senator IMMEDIATELY at 202-225-3121. Tell them you agree with me, that the Panama Canal cannot, must not, be turned over to the Chinese, and that the U.S. must continue a military presence in Panama.

Admiral Thomas Moorer is former Chairman of the Joint Chiefs of Staff and former Commander in Chief of the Pacific and Atlantic fleets.

Jiang Orders Hi-Tech Arsenal

NewsMax.com Vortex, September 1999 — Chinese President Jiang Zemin has given his support for more spending on sophisticated weapons as a way to thwart Taiwan's independence and to counter the threat of what Beijing sees as an expansionist American foreign policy.

An army source has said that Jiang approved more military spending during leadership meetings at the seaside resort of Beidaihe earlier this month.

"We should devote more resources to modernization of weaponry," Jiang reportedly said.

"We should focus our limited funds on cutting-edge areas of military science and technology."

It is understood these included developing sophisticated weapons such as missiles and submarines as well as importing top-of-the-line hardware from countries such as Russia.

Defense analysts said an unusually large number of generals had attended the Beidaihe meetings, which were normally devoted to economic and political, not military, issues.

They said President Jiang's support for more spending was welcomed by the top brass, who had been complaining about the lack of funds for developing hi-tech hardware.

At Beidaihe, President Jiang and his foreign policy advisers cited the importance of boosting defense ties with Russia to counteract American "expansionism" and the possible extension of Theater Missile Defense technology to Taiwan.

—South China Morning Post

China Penetrated U.S. Bond Markets

NewsMax.com Vortex, July 1999 — One of the most potentially momentous, yet little-noted, conclusions of the report by the House select committee chaired by Representative Chris Cox, R-Calif., reads as follows: "Increasingly, the PRC is using U.S. capital markets both as a source of central government funding for military and commercial development and as a means of cloaking U.S. technological acquisition efforts by its front companies with a patina of regularity and respectability."

In fact, the latest data suggest that "wholly owned" Chinese entities have raised roughly $13.5 billion in dollar-denominated bonds worldwide since 1980, the bulk of it in the U.S. bond market. These undisciplined, "general purpose" funds can be easily diverted to finance activities inimical to U.S. security interests (e.g., proliferation, espionage, technology theft, nuclear force modernization, etc.) According to the Center's William J. Casey Chair, Roger W. Robinson Jr., of the 195 Chinese bonds issued since 1980, 24 have been offered by PLA-affiliated giant, China International Trust and Investment Company (CITIC), chaired by Beijing's most notorious arms dealer, Wang Jun. The total amount raised by CITIC alone on global markets is roughly $3.5 billion, some $800 million of which was offered in the U.S. Even China Resources (Holdings) Company Ltd. — a reported conduit for Chinese intelligence — is now in the bond market.

The grave implications for American national security of this multi-billion-dollar penetration of the U.S. capital markets by foreign bad actors will oblige congressional committees and executive branch agencies following up on the historic work of Representative Cox's panel to grapple with measures to remedy this situation. Wall Street would be well advised to consider ways in which it may be able to avoid some of the more draconian responses by voluntarily playing a constructive problem-solving role.

—Center for Security Policy

China Was Ready to Attack Taiwan In 1996

NewsMax.com Vortex, July 1999 — Reportedly, China would have invaded a Taiwan-controlled islet near the mainland during a 1995-96 crisis had the weather permitted.

Taiwan Defense Minister Tang Fei told legislators recently that People's Liberation Army (PLA) troops had marched from Hangzhou to Fuzhou on the mainland as part of a planned attack on the islet, which lies just off the Chinese coast. "But the weather was not favorable for them to act as scheduled. The PLA was later forced to alter the plans and conduct live fire drills on nearby Pingtan Island."

The Strait crisis did not end until the United States sent two battle carrier groups to waters near Taiwan.

—Agence France Presse

What Ron Brown Said About the Chinese

By Andy Thibault

NewsMax.com Vortex, November 1998 — President Wag-the-Dog can look forward to greater problems than Monicagate. Wounded, though not yet down for the count, Bill Clinton is vulnerable to more serious scandals. Foremost among these is the missiles-for-cash arrangement with Communist China.

Earlier this year, Jeff Gerth of the *New York Times* broke the story on how a cash-hungry president overruled the Pentagon and sold satellite technology to a front for Chinese military intelligence.

But the Gerth reports stopped short. They failed to look past the role of Commerce Secretary Ron Brown. The White House, bothered by objections from the Defense and State departments, had transferred decision making about such technology transfers to Brown's Commerce Department.

Still untouched by the major media are Democratic National Committee bagman John Huang and Huang's and Clinton's corporate masters, the Lippo Group. Still buried from public consciousness is the Chinese arms issue. With the recent reports that both North Korea and Communist China could strike us with nuclear missiles, public interest — indeed, public safety — demands that these issues come to the fore.

The missiles-for-cash deal manifested itself in the persona of Wang Jun. A notorious gunrunner and Chinese government agent, Jun came to the United States in 1996. He became a guest of President Clinton for a White House coffee fund raiser on February 6, 1996.

Before going to the White House, however, Jun met with Commerce Secretary Brown. Both meetings were set up by Charlie Trie, the former

Little Rock, Arkansas, restaurateur who dropped off a wad of cash to-taling $640,000 for Wag-the-Dog's legal expense fund.

Brown knew Jun was an arms dealer and that he represented the military. Brown's role was to give a signal to the Chinese Communist government.

That same day, President Clinton signed a lucrative waiver allow-ing the top contributor to the DNC, Loral Space and Communications Company, to use a Chinese rocket to launch one of its satellites into space. This was about the time China was also terrorizing Taiwan with missile tests.

Brown's business partner and confidante Nolanda Hill told me — in the course of dozens of interviews beginning in April 1996 — about the significance of the Wang Jun meetings.

"Ron said his role as a Cabinet official was to signal to the Chinese government that they were going to get more than just waivers," Hill said. "They were going to get a policy change on encryption. We dis cussed how this was all perilously close to sedition."

Brown shared his concerns with then–Secretary of State Warren Christopher, Clinton's boyhood pal Mac McLarty, and former Chief of Staff Leon Panetta, according to Hill.

"The waiver signature and the meeting with Ron happening the same day was significant — it was no coincidence," Hill said. "Ron assured Clinton he had taken care of Charlie Trie's people. That is the real story."

Encryption data is used by U.S. intelligence to keep government communications, such as instructions sent to satellites or nuclear missiles, undetectable. Such technology is among the nation's most guarded se-crets.

Also in early 1996, the U.S. Customs Service was conducting an undercover operation that targeted Wang Jun's Poly Technologies Ltd. — a wholly-owned subsidiary of the People's Liberation Army — for shipping 2,000 AK-47s and other automatic weapons into the U.S. Fourteen persons were arrested in April 1996 when the undercover op-erations was prematurely shut down.

Meanwhile, Congress and the FBI supposedly are investigating Loral CEO Bernard Schwartz — the Democratic Party's largest donor in 1997 — for passing sensitive data to China Aerospace. China Aerospace, also controlled by the People's Liberation Army, was cited by former

Democratic fund-raiser Johnny Chung as a source of illegal contributions to the DNC.

The money trail is there. Sex, lies and videotape speak to Wag-the-Dog's credibility. Forensic accountants, if turned loose on the China money trail, will likely produce similar results and safeguard the nation from more serious harm.

Andy Thibault, a Connecticut-based investigative journalist, covered the independent counsel investigation of Ron Brown for the Washington Times *and conducted the first full-length interview with Brown's business partner and confidante, Nolanda Hill. Thibault was cited in May by the Society of Professional Journalists for his exposé on the Woody Allen child abuse case, published in* Connecticut *magazine. He also serves as senior adviser for Judicial Watch, the Washington-based public interest law firm.*

Chinese Shown U.S. Air Vulnerabilities

NewsMax.com Vortex, January 1999 — *Aviation Week* quotes a report in the *China Reform Monitor* that "[a]n entire class of Chinese officers from the Chinese People's Liberation Army Air Force Air War College observed a series of U.S. Air Force Air Warfare exercises in Alaska, called *Cooperative Cape Thunder*."

"The exercises exposed U.S. air war vulnerabilities to enemy radar planes and computer warfare attacks," continued the report. "The U.S. planes suffered *huge casualties* and in some instances were completely blind in simulated combat to aggressor forces using Electronic Support Measures (ESM). Enemy info-warfare attacks on U.S. command-in-control systems caused the Alaska air command to be required to install a new set of fire walls against offensive computer attacks."

— www.afpc.org

Index